Rituals of Fertility and the Sacrifice of Desire

Chicago Studies in Ethnomusicology

A Series Edited by Philip V. Bohlman and Bruno Nettl

Rituals of Fertility and the Sacrifice of Desire

Nazarite Women's Performance in South Africa

Carol Ann Muller

The University of Chicago Press
Chicago and London

CAROL ANN MULLER is assistant professor in the music department at the University of Pennsylvania.

The University of Chicago Press, Chicago 60637
The University of Chicago Press, Ltd., London
© 1999 by The University of Chicago
All rights reserved. Published 1999
Printed in the United States of America
08 07 06 05 04 03 02 01 00 99   1 2 3 4 5

ISBN: 0-226-54819-8 (cloth)
ISBN: 0-226-54820-1 (paper)

Library of Congress Cataloging-in-Publication Data

Muller, Carol Ann.
    Rituals of fertility and the sacrifice of desire : Nazarite
women's performance in South Africa / Carol Ann Muller.
        p.   cm. — (Chicago studies in ethnomusicology)
    Includes bibliographical references and index.
    ISBN 0-226-54819-8 (cloth : alk. paper). — ISBN 0-226-54820-1 (pbk : alk. paper)
    1. Church of the Nazarites.   2. Zulu (African people) — Marriage
customs and rites.   3. Fertility cults — South Africa.   I. Title.   II. Series.
BX7068.7.Z5M85   1999
289.9′3 — dc21   99-17548
                                                                                        CIP

⊗ The paper used in this publication meets the minimum requirements of the American
 National Standard for Information Sciences — Permanence of Paper for Printed Library
Materials, ANSI Z39.48-1992.

For
My Parents
Avril Hermanson Muller and Douglas Muller

Contents

List of Musical Excerpts and Illustrations on
the Compact Disc   ix
Preface   xvii
Acknowledgments   xxiii
Map   xxv

1   Introduction   1
2   Isaiah Shembe and the Making of Religious Empire   23
3   Making and Exchanging Nazarite Sacred Forms   54
4   Nazarite Hymns: Indigenizing Sacred Song   88
5   Nazarite Hymns: Popularizing Sacred Song (1940–1997)   120
6   *AmaNtombazane* as the Mountains of Abstinence   159
7   Nazarite Marriage and the "Brides of Christ"   199
8   *AmaNkosikazi* as Maidens of Royal Blood   220

A Last Word   261
Glossary   267
Notes   271
References   293
Index   307

Photographs follow page 119

Musical Excerpts and Illustrations
on the Compact Disc

Musical Excerpts

1. Organ playing preceding the sabbath service at 1 P.M., *Ebuhleni,* July 27, 1991. Recorded by Carol Muller, used with permission.
2. Bell ringing to call Nazarites to prayer prior to the sabbath service, *Ebuhleni,* July 27, 1991 (see bell narrative, chap. 6). Recorded by Carol Muller, used with permission.
3. *Mvangeli* begins the sabbath liturgy, Ebuhleni, September 21, 1991. Recorded by Carol Muller, used with permission.
4. *Bonke u Jehova maNazaretha*, opening hymn for sabbath service with organ accompaniment, *Ebuhleni,* July 27, 1991. Recorded by Carol Muller, used with permission.
5. Extract from longer sabbath liturgy, July 27, 1991. Recorded by Carol Muller, used with permission.
6. *Umgido* with instrumental accompaniment at home of family in need of prayer, KwaMashu, September 21, 1991. Recorded by Carol Muller, used with permission.
7. End of sabbath service: Bongani Mthethwa plays the organ while monetary offerings are made to Shembe and he blesses and heals the Nazarites. Recorded by Carol Muller, used with permission.
8. Early recording of Nazarite hymn *Lalela Zulu* (Listen, O Zulu) composed by Isaiah Shembe. Recorded by Hugh Tracey, used with permission.
9. Opening excerpt of *Ngamemeza ubusuku nasemini* (Hymn 45) composed by Isaiah Shembe, performed by *ama14* at their meeting at *Vula Masango,* March 13–14, 1992. Recorded by Carol Muller, used with permission.
10. Instruments enter, other women clap hands to accompany the sacred

dance, singing *Ngamemeza ubusuku nasemini* (Hymn 45). *Vula Masango,* March 13–14, 1992. Recorded by Carol Muller, used with permission.

11. End of the stanza of text of *Ngamemeza ubusuku nasemini,* group voices and instruments drop out, and song leader starts the next stanza. *Vula Masango,* March 13–14, 1992. Recorded by Carol Muller, used with permission.

12–18. Excerpts from seven hymns recorded by Hugh Tracey and published in the *Sound of Africa* series, published in 1955, but recorded possibly as early as 1939. Used with permission.

12. Call to prayer and *Iqhude loKusa* (not in 1940 hymn book).

13. *Sidedele Singene* (Hymn 183).

14. *Waqala Izitha* (Hymn 210).

15. Hymn for the Morning Prayer (Shembe liturgy).

16. Hymn for the Evening Prayer (Shembe liturgy).

17. *Kula amakula kancane* (not in 1940 hymn book).

18. *Qubula Nkosi* (not in 1940 hymn book).

19. Excerpt from *Nkosi Yethu Simakade* (Hymn 242), sung by the Nazareth Temple Choir, KwaMashu, 1988, to Bongani Mthethwa's arrangement and keyboard accompaniment. Recorded by Bongani Mthethwa, used with permission.

20. Excerpt from *Thixo ulilanga* (Hymn 179), sung by the Nazareth Temple Choir, KwaMashu, 1988, to Bongani Mthethwa's arrangement and keyboard accompaniment. Recorded by Bongani Mthethwa, used with permission.

21–23. KwaMashu Youth for Shembe sing gospel-style songs at the blessing of *umshumayeli* in KwaMashu, June 1991. Recorded by Carol Muller, used with permission.

21. *We Are Together, We Are a Family* (applause, calls of *"ameni, oyincwele"*—"amen, he is holy").

22. *Sweet Shembe, What a Wonder You Are.*

23. *Shembe Is the Lord of My Life.*

24. KwaMashu Youth for Shembe sing *Oyinkosi amaKhosi* to the tune of "Joy to the World." Recorded by Carol Muller at Blue Lagoon beach, Durban, June 1991. Used with permission.

25. Rehearsing song using tonic solfa, sung by KwaMashu Youth for Shembe choir at a rehearsal in KwaMashu, November 23, 1991. They were rehearsing for the Shembe Choir Competition held November 30–December 1, 1991, at Madadeni, KwaZulu Natal. Recorded by Carol Muller, used with permission.

26. *Ukhona umfula* (There's a River), sung by KwaMashu Youth Choir, KwaMashu, June 23, 1991. Recorded by Carol Muller and used with permission.

27. *Nkosi Yethu* (Hymn 242), sung in the traditional Nazarite style without accompaniment at the funeral of Bongani Mthethwa, June 13–14, 1992. Recorded by Carol Muller and used with permission.

28. *Nkosi Yethu* (Hymn 242), sung by *ama14*, August 13, 1991, at *Ebuhleni*. Recorded by Carol Muller, used with permission.

29. *Nkosi Yethu* (Hymn 242), performed by Nathoya Mbatha on his *Ngivuse Nkosi* cassette. Recorded by Mbatha, used with permission from Nathoya Mbatha.

30. Excerpt from *ifortini* preaching at Isaiah Shembe's memorial service on May 1, 1991, at *Gibisile,* northern KwaZulu Natal. Recorded by Carol Muller, used with permission.

Illustrations

Photographs listed below may appear in several places on the compact disc.

RECORD-KEEPING AND VISUAL IMAGES

Visiting Nazarite girls watch video playback of themselves
Nazarite photographers and videographers record Amos Shembe's funeral
Image of Isaiah Shembe inside the Nazarite hymnal, 1940
Isaiah Shembe with white angels
Isaiah Shembe with white angels and African traditionalists
Isaiah Shembe speaks to Jesus the Shepherd
Amos Shembe in orange robe with shepherd's crook
Johannes Galilee Shembe wearing a Scottish kilt, rugby socks, military
    boots, and a pith helmet
Vimbeni Shembe in gown similar to Amos Shembe's
Amos Shembe enters his Ford Thunderbird
Amos Shembe in black-and-silver gown with his wife inside helicopter
Contemporary signs of power: Vimbeni Shembe's BMW
Necklace with images of four Shembe leaders (Amos, Galilee, Isaiah, and
    Vimbeni)
Poster of the holy mountain of *Nhlangakaze* showing all four Shembes
Nazarite member with new poster and "Shembe Is the Way" sticker
Mvangeli Magubane in front of the administrative office, which sells
    posters, hymnals, and Zulu Bibles

GENERAL RITUAL

Inkhonzo men sing in temple
Postpubescent girls wearing dance attire for *ukusina* (see also *Umgido* Sacred Dance Festivals)
AmaNtombazane signal the start of *umgido*
Women dance for Sunday's *umgido*
Boys' *umgido*
Woman healed by Shembe
Nazarite baptism in a lake
State President Nelson Mandela at Amos Shembe's funeral
Youth choir sings at Amos Shembe's funeral
Precious and her family celebrate her twenty-first birthday
Author's tent and cooking hut at *Gibisile*
Inside the *dokoda* of Makhosazane Nyadi and Cinikile Mazibuko
En route to a Nazarite site
Intombazane with flowers
Young women with laundry and reeds climb *Nhlangakaze*
Path leading up *Nhlangakaze*
The "Arc of the Covenant" being carried to the top of *Nhlangakaze*
Abavangeli holding traditional staffs
Intombazane wearing *inansook* shawl
Married woman wearing *inhloko*
"The Arc of the Covenant" leads the procession up *Nhlangakaze*
Imbongi on *Nhlangakaze*
Amos Shembe arrives on *Nhlangakaze*
Amos Shembe with *abavangeli*
Amadokoda on the side of *Nhlangakaze*
Youth choir keyboard players at a Shembe marriage
Nathoya Mbatha's independently produced cassette

INKHONZO (CONGREGATIONAL WORSHIP); HEALING

Nazarite men wait for the sabbath service
Abakhokheli wait between services
Married women wearing both types of attire for *umgido* and *inkhonzo*
Nazarite male member wearing *imiNazaretha* and necklace with three Shembes
Recently married woman and child walk into *Paradis*
Nazarite men sit quietly on their prayer mats in *Paradis*
Prayer mats left in place between sabbath services

Nazarite *phoyisa*

Abavangeli and *abashumayeli* kneel as they sing and recite the sabbath liturgy

Amos Shembe approaches *Paradis* as *amantombazane* kneel in his presence

Abavangeli consult with Amos Shembe

Ilayiti, Shembe's white pillow, is wrapped in a prayer mat and removed at the end of the service

Men bring offerings to Shembe

Vimbeni Shembe sits at table, accepting offerings and providing healing

Men cry out *"Ameni, oyincwele"*

Amos Shembe with two virgin members who make offerings

Samu and Thembi have water blessed

HEALING

Members and visitors wait in front of the office to see Shembe

Samu with water bottle and people waiting in line, all to be blessed by Amos Shembe

Woman healed by Amos Shembe

Woman healer outside her home in Durban; bottles of water to be blessed for healing

UMGIDO SACRED DANCE FESTIVALS

Men in sacred dance attire

Boys in *amaskotch*

Boys wearing helmets and green-and-white-and-black skirts

Young girls in dance attire (*see also* Ritual Practices of Virgin Girls)

Prepubescent girls wearing red skirts for sacred dance

Postpubescent girls wearing black skirts for sacred dance

Married women in dance attire

Nazarite boys from KwaMashu blow trumpets and beat the drum

Young girls lead the beginning of *umgido*

Nazarite men get into the *hlabelelo* groove

Women leaders perform exuberantly

Nazarite member photographs women's dance

BLESSING OF *UMSHUMAYELI*

Members are served tea and fresh scones

Tent erected for the blessing of *Umshumayeli*

KwaMashu male youth (and Eric, author's husband) perform *umgido*

KwaMashu youth choir enters the tent, singing
Nazarite member dances in celebration
Umshumayeli is given a blanket
Letters are read for the new *Umshumayeli*

FUNERALS

State President Nelson Mandela goes to view the body of Amos Shembe
Nazarite members throng the funeral of Amos Shembe
Nazarite members gather at burial ground
Young children with flowers and holy water to sprinkle on Nazarite graves

YOUTH CHOIRS

KwaMashu Temple Choir sing "We Are Together, We Are a Family"
KwaMashu Temple Choir bring gifts as they sing
KwaMashu Temple Choir after the Nazareth Baptist Youth for Shembe
    Choir Competition
Members of the KwaMashu Temple Choir
Young Nazarite men and boys respond exuberantly to song performance
Youth dance at choir competition

RITUAL PRACTICES OF VIRGIN GIRLS

Nazarite girls outside *Paradis* sell candles and Vaseline
Prepubescent girls prepare for *umgido*
Ntombazane and *Nkosikazi* in *imiNazaretha* on their way to *Paradis*
Nazarite young girl with *ujafeta,* shield, and umbrella stands in front of
    Isaiah Shembe's statue
Nazarite girls wear the traditional *ibhayi* on returning from *Nthanda*
Nazarite virgin in dance attire
AmaNtombazane wearing tartan skirts (*amaskotch*) parade
AmaNtombazane wearing veils
Ntombazane in black-and-white dance attire
MaSangweni fixes drum for *Ntombazane;* both in attire for *umgido*
Mpathi in her *dokoda,* with a sewing machine, bowls for washing, a radio,
    and food
Samu at the gate to girls' enclosure
Girls in *jafeta* with drums
AmaNtombazane play horns and trumpets

AmaNtombazane in *Paradis*

Samu and Nombuyiselo weave grass braids

AmaNtombazane help each other prepare for *umgonqo*

AmaNtombazane in *jafeta*, with bugle

AmaNtombazane in *jafeta*, with umbrellas and shields, in procession toward the temple

AmaNtombazane dry out drum skins at fire to improve sound

AmaNtombazane offer money to purchase gifts for Shembe

Virgins wait for Shembe in *Paradis*

Mpathi speaks with Amos Shembe in *Paradis*

Lines of *Ama25* dancers outside *Paradis*

Girls' procession around the fire, throwing in the grass braids; *Mkhokheli* stokes the fire

Shembe blesses members

AmaNtombazane and others kneel before Amos Shembe (seated in the chair)

AmaNtombazane prepare to leave *Ebuhleni*

Virgin girls form a circle

Virgin bodies form the walls for the house of Shembe

Shembe's house performed

AmaNtombazane enter the upper festival ground and form a circle with their sticks

Nazarite Marriage

Mothers of bridal couples kneel before the couples arrive

Young men dance at the marriage of Amos Shembe's daughter (see also *Umgido* Sacred Dance Festivals)

Mpathi negotiates marriage with young couple

Bride prepares for Nazarite marriage at home in KwaMashu

Bride's assistants gather up dowry of the daughter of Amos Shembe

Bride-to-be with head and shoulders covered in blue shawl

Bridal couples dance together before entering the temple

Group marriage vows in *Paradis*

Marriage vows authorized with hands placed on the Bible

Brides-to-be escorted to the area in front of the office by male kin

Leaving the office area, couples move into *Paradis* for the vows

Nazarite members gather at upper festival ground to watch bridal couples dance

The back of the bride and groom in full wedding attire

Intombazane with beadwork around her head
Daughter of Amos Shembe wears marital hat with handkerchief
Daughter of Amos Shembe prepares for marriage
Amos Shembe in leopard skins
Brides walk toward the temple
Nazarite bridal couple

AMAFORTINI PRAY, DANCE, AND PREACH

Abakhokheli meet at Ebuhleni
AmaFortini clap as they sing
AmaFortini await the installation of Vimbeni Shembe
AmaFortini sing at installation of Vimbeni Shembe
Mkhokheli leads the singing
Women dance at meeting of *amafortini*
Women dance at house of KwaMashu family in need
AmaFortini sing and clap
Women sing and beat drum
Women bring offerings to Shembe
Women dance as they come to Shembe
Women wash their hands before eating
AmaFortini prepare to preach and pray

Preface

On March 23, 1994 a white South African male police officer was visited by an angel who told him why the efforts at finding a peaceful settlement in South Africa were not effective. The angel stayed with Lieutenant Colonel Botha for about fifteen minutes, during which time he was able to ask him [the angel] many questions. In turn, the angel instructed Botha to tell South Africans they needed to spend one day on their knees in prayer to God. "Many churches are taking the colonel seriously and prayer services are to be held countrywide." [*Natal Witness*, April 5, 1994]

On the last Sunday in July 1993, masked gunmen entered the St. James Church in Kenilworth, Cape Town, South Africa, and opened fire on the congregation. There were several killed and others injured in the attack. The cold brutality of the murder of innocent victims shook many, both in South Africa and further afield as reports of the attack were relayed throughout the world. For white South Africans in particular, the "St. James Massacre" became a symbolic monument to their deepest fears of the rapid sociopolitical transformation that had taken place in that country since the State President's February 1990 speech to the nation in which he had unbanned the organizations of the liberation movement. These included the African National Congress and the South African Communist Party.

The response of some white South Africans was to arm themselves, to increase home security systems, or simply to sell all and leave the country for greener pastures. For many black South Africans, numbed by the ongoing daily violence in their own communities (the causes of which began to surface in testimonies of the Truth and Reconciliation Commission), there was a feeling of outrage. This outrage was rooted in the knowledge that if the massacre had taken place in a black residential area (of which there had been numerous), the world might never even have known that it had occurred. For those who were in the St. James Church that fateful

Sunday evening and survived, the close brush with death effected a transformation of the religious community itself. The shock, pain, and physical
disabilities inflicted on several of the congregation were used to creative
effect within the body of believers. People rallied around the victims in a
manner that radically changed the religious collectivity.

The St. James Massacre was, however, not simply an isolated instance
of violence targeting an individual community. Instead, it constituted a
microcosm of the far greater forces of destruction and violation that had
underpinned the structures of apartheid, enforced by the might of the
military. It is in this context that the moral outrage felt by both black and
white South Africans at the killing of St. James's members, and the mass
mediation of that event throughout the world, should be understood.
Both speak to the process of the "deterritorializing" of social space, discussed by Franco (1985). This process involves, among other things, the
loss of spaces of sanctuary and refuge that are traditionally associated with
the mother, the virgin, the nun, and the priest. Such spaces in the Western
world have conventionally been defined as sacred and feminine. In this
regard, the family, religious homes, and some musical repertories have
provided a place for "turning one's back on the world" (ibid., 415). In
apartheid South Africa, these "feminized" spaces were set up in opposition to the predominantly male centers of political, economic, and military control. They frequently created a locus of opposition to the intrusion
of the powers of the state into individual bodies and personal movement.

With this in mind, I return to the white police officer, Lieutenant
Colonel Botha, and his angel, and introduce you to the black South
African prophet, Isaiah Shembe (d. 1935), his followers (*ibandla lama-
Nazaretha*), and the Nazarite notion of the sacred as a feminine attribute.
This book examines the ritual practices and everyday experiences of the
female membership of this religious community, in large part to understand the construction of "the feminine" in an emergent industrial society.
Perhaps the most effective means of discovering this structure in a particular social order is to consider the way in which women and girls are constituted as social actors. In this regard, the location of the female body in
the center of Nazarite sacred space through ritual processes points to the
mechanisms employed for collective empowerment by the community as
a whole.

I argue that in the early twentieth century, Isaiah Shembe drew on two
discourses with which he shaped a religious empire in competition with
that established by the European and American mission in KwaZulu Natal. He appropriated aspects of Nguni custom and cosmology and West-

ern mission Christianity (with its stress on the market economy), and reinvented them as the building blocks of his religious empire. Mission Christianity and Nguni tradition had been competing ideologies of cultural empowerment in nineteenth-century KwaZulu Natal. With the emergence of the South African industrial economy at the end of the nineteenth century, they became increasingly devalued and marginalized by the industrial center and, from 1948 onward, the apartheid state. In this context, both discourses were effectively feminized and reconstituted as "other." The feminization of cultural and religious practices coincided with the destruction of the Nguni homestead economy, and the dispersal, not only of men (as southern African migrant studies have demonstrated), but increasingly of women as well. Black women, in particular, became the targets of male sexual desire—as domestic servants, prostitutes, or *shebeen* queens.

Deeply disturbed by these events, Isaiah Shembe established a place of spiritual and economic refuge for widows, orphans, and those women previously in polygamous marriages whose husbands had converted to mission Christianity, a belief system that insisted on monogamous alliances. Shembe created this hybrid religious community from the substance of archaic Nguni and biblical beliefs about women, virgin girls, and their bodies. In so doing, he reconstituted a sense of order, religious sanctuary, and ritual power by reinventing the feminized notion of cyclicity, a central principle of traditional performance, agricultural method, and cosmological understanding. He authorized these practices by overlaying them with literal readings of biblical narrative. The prophet Isaiah Shembe used his knowledge of the mission Bible and the mythical power of virgin girls to win his battles against the racist state. Political struggle assumed form as spiritual and moral warfare, with the virgin girls as the frontline warriors. The cost of this protection of female adherents, however, was the denial of sexual desire. In this context, sacrifice was reinvented in terms of an innovative combination of Old Testament and Nguni traditional practice, and located in the purity of young women's bodies.

Ibandla lamaNazaretha is one of the oldest religious communities in South Africa (Isaiah began preaching and healing in the region in about 1910). The membership continues to increase, and currently includes a good percentage of male followers. In this sense, the book also addresses strategies used by many black South African men and women between 1910 and 1994 to manage the intrusion of the state on their everyday lives. The brutality of the wider social order and its lack of sociopolitical and economic power for this group of South Africans was transformed, through the course of the twentieth century, by the intervention of the cosmology in the everyday lives of Nazarite members, both female and male. Such cosmological mediation was effected through the expressive forms of song, dance, and dreams. The social force of these media was located in the shared experience of individual and social loss, metaphorized in bodily pain, and articulated as structures of feeling and experience in hymns and sermons. Ritualized performances of these expressive media facilitated a return to wholeness, and the healing of the individual and social body through repetitive cycles of reenactment.

The visionary appearance of the angel to the white policeman in March 1994 (one month before the first fully democratic elections in South Africa) encapsulates a historical irony. While dreams and visions had played a critical role in the lives and experiences of many black South Africans, such media had not traditionally constituted the repertory of expressive forms for white South Africans, men in particular. As the Truth and Reconciliation Commission has revealed, until April 1994, in collusion with the South African Defence Force, elements of the South African Police (white and black men and women) frequently, and quite brutally, sought to subjugate such discourses and performances, and to annihilate the bodies of black South Africans. Located at the center of the political economy and acting in the name of national security, these military forces used weapons of war to carry out their mission. But it brought no peace. Violence continued to breed violence.

When Colonel Botha received his vision in late March 1994, the social order was undergoing momentous transformation from white minority control to black majority rule. There was a moment of reckoning for all those who had conspired with the state. The Day of Political Judgment was imminent. Many feared the law courts in South Africa would put those who had colluded with the state on trial. Each individual's name would then be sought in the Book of Life under *Apartheid*. The outcomes of this Judgment, and indeed of the whole process of political transformation, it was imagined, would result in the movement of such representatives and enforcers of state power from the center to the periphery. For some it would mean complete removal from society. Ironically, for those who suddenly found themselves in the margins or already on their way there, solutions to the moral crisis were increasingly being sought in the expressive and religious media located on the peripheries of the state. These were the feminized spaces of alterity—of dreams, visions, and the communicative structures of dance and song—so central to Isaiah Shembe's constitution of religious empire almost a century earlier.

Finally, it is too early to know just how the new democratic dispensation will affect *ibandla lamaNazaretha*. As the new South African democracy has begun to redefine its place in the global economy (1994–1997), there has been a marked commodification and sale of previously feminized and sacralized Nazarite expressive forms. In this "new South Africa," selected members of *ibandla lamaNazaretha* have been quick to co-opt the powers of the state—particularly the mass media—to Nazarite ends. Ostensibly, the motivation is to increase the strength of their empire, which is rapidly gaining new membership. There are also ambitious levels of Nazarite engagement with global capital and market exchange. To this end, the recently installed leader, Vimbeni Shembe, plans to visit the United States, the new Promised Land of commodities and capital. I often wonder, however, just how South Africa's rather tenuous relationships with the global economy will affect the lives of the ordinary women and men of *ibandla lamaNazaretha*, whose everyday survival is so intricately intertwined with the miracles invoked by the very locally fashioned spiritual powers of Shembe, the Nazarite provider.

Acknowledgments

This book is the result of many paths traveled and many rich conversations with a whole range of people, whose only point of convergence is perhaps in the way in which they have in some way shaped my thinking and encounters with *ibandla lamaNazaretha*. There are many people who have assisted me along these paths, including Pippin Oosthuizen, the late Bongani Mthethwa, Ntombemhlope Mthethwa, Khethiwe Mthethwa, Themba Mbhele, Richard Zondi, Cinikile Mazibuko, Makhosazane Nyadi, my most loyal field assistant, Samukelisiwe Ntini, the Rev. Amos Shembe, present leader Rev. Vimbeni Shembe, the late Petrus Dhlomo, and MaSangweni. To each of these I am truly indebted, for without them, this project would never have been possible.

The librarians and archivists at several institutions, both in South Africa and in the United States, have always proved to be willing and helpful. My colleagues at Natal University (South Africa) and the University of North Carolina have graciously inquired about my progress through this project, first as a dissertation and now as a book. While I was at the University of Natal in the mid-1990s, numerous colleagues in the History and Gender Studies seminars, including Keith Breckenridge, Duncan Brown, Cathy Burns, Michael Chapman, Margaret Daymond, Bill Freund, Jeff Guy, Michael Green, Lliane Loots, Ros Posel, and Yona Seleti, in some way stimulated my thinking.

All my teachers are also to be thanked: at the University of Natal in the early 1980s, Chris Ballantine, Veit Erlmann, Jim Kiernan, Beverly Parker, Eleanor Preston-Whyte, and Kevin Volans; at New York University, Stanley Boorman, Donna Buchanan, David Burrows, Allen Feldman, Faye Ginsburg, Julia Keydel, Edward Roesner, Bambi Schieffelin, Nadia Serematakis, Kay Shelemay, Elizabeth Tolbert, and, although she was not my teacher, the late Annette Weiner. All of these people consistently guided me along the academic path in a most gracious manner. I have valued their support, their questions, and their intellectual depth. While I have received assistance and advice from many quarters, I take full responsibility for the contents of this book. Any errors of judgment are my own.

There is a large community of people that have had a powerful impact on the way in which I have come to understand the Nazarite world and my own. These are the students that I have had contact with in a variety of places—the University of Natal, New York University, and the University of North Carolina at Chapel Hill. I think in particular of those at the University of Natal—Sazi Dlamini, Feya Faku, Vicky Godard, Thandiwe Magubane, Elliot Pewa, Ambigay Raidoo, Nishlyn Ramanna, Stacey van Schalkwyk, Toine Scholtz, Geoffrey Tracey, and Lee Watkins. These are the students I interacted with most, though there are numerous others who also helped me to understand the complexities of the society we all grew up in.

A special thanks must go to executive editor T. David Brent, who provided critical wisdom and editorial guidance at the University of Chicago Press. The readers of the manuscript provided both wonderful encouragement and acute insight into this text. Rob Allingham, the extremely knowledgeable archivist at Gallo Records (South Africa), and Andrew Tracey at the International Library of African Music were gracious with their time, knowledge, and recordings. My warmest appreciation to all of these people.

Finally, my immediate family and their spouses have provided enormous support for each of the research projects. Most of all, I thank my husband, Eric, who has seen me through some of the scarier moments of the field research, offered constant encouragement, and sometimes even ventured with me into places that certainly were for him, as a U.S. citizen, unfamiliar terrain.

My education has been financially supported by several institutions. I am deeply grateful to the Robert Niven Trust (South Africa) and the Department of Music at New York University. The research was funded by the Centre for Science Development (South Africa), the NERMIC Research Unit (South Africa), and the University of Natal Research Fund (South Africa). Finally, the Music Department at the University of Pennsylvania provided a research grant that assisted in the production of the CD that accompanies this book.

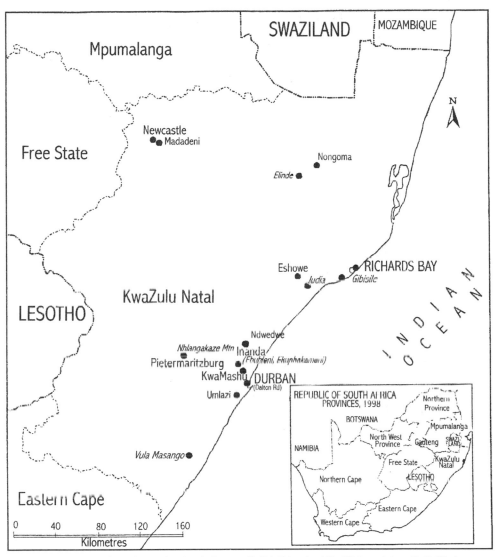

(Derived from Map by Cartographic Unit, University of Natal Pietermaritzburg, South Africa)

Selected Nazarite Ritual Spaces in KwaZulu Natal

ONE

Introduction

Nanti ilizwi elomemo	Here is the word of invitation,
Liya mema bonke abantu.	It invites all people.
Alikhethi noma munye	It does not discriminate against anyone;
Liya mema bonke abantu.	It invites all people.
AbaNsundu nabaMhlope	The Brown and the White,
Liba mema kwana njalo;	It invites them continually;
Alikhethi noma munye	It does not discriminate against anyone;
Liya mema bonke abantu.	It invites all people.
(Hlab. 153/1,2)	(Hymn 153/1,2)[1]

In this book, I examine the constitution of ritual and expressive culture as a feminized and sacred practice in one of South Africa's largest and oldest indigenous religious groups—*ibandla lamaNazaretha*[2] (the Church of the Nazarites, 1910–1997), more commonly known as the followers of Shembe. The performances I examine here include religious song and dance, dream and miracle narratives, and fertility rituals that focus specifically on the female members. The first part introduces the research into, and a historical analysis of, *ibandla lamaNazaretha*. The second part of the book is concerned with more generalized Nazarite ritual and expressive forms, with a particular focus on the composition and popularization of the Nazarite hymn repertory, both under apartheid and in the "new South Africa," the fledgling democracy that began to take shape in February 1990, when Nelson Mandela was released from prison. The third part highlights the ritual practices of young virgin girls and married women in *ibandla lamaNazaretha*. These are older individual Nguni fertility rituals for young girls that have been reinvented in *ibandla lamaNazaretha* as collective rituals celebrating the virginity and ritual purity of female bodies. A theme common to all three parts is the relationship between ritual and the sacrifice of desire.

Nazarite ritual practices and expressive forms are examined as one of the means through which to begin to understand the experiences of thousands of black South African women and young girls who have lived through the twentieth century on the margins of a continually changing South African political economy. Most of these women speak little English and are functionally illiterate. Some of the young girls have been educated at various levels in schools and colleges. Nevertheless, they all carry a rich store of cultural knowledge and experience that constitutes the essence of their treasure on earth.

Ibandla lamaNazaretha was founded in the early twentieth century in what is now the province of KwaZulu Natal[3] by a partially literate but highly astute individual named Isaiah Shembe. Initially an itinerant preacher and healer, Isaiah quickly gathered a faithful following consisting mostly of widows, orphans, and the victims of the state legislation that drove black South Africans[4] off the land, particularly from 1913 onward. Isaiah's first religious community, a place called *Ekuphakameni* (the elevated place), was established in what was then called the Native Reserve of Inanda, situated about twenty-five miles from the city of Durban on the eastern coastline of South Africa. (See map.)

Isaiah Shembe died in 1935, and was succeeded by his younger son Johannes Galilee, referred to in the text as Galilee. Galilee was murdered in 1977 by unknown assailants, at which point a battle over succession ensued between Galilee's elder brother, Amos, and his own son, Londa. This caused a split in the church, with the majority following Amos—with whom I worked—and a splinter group going with Londa, who was himself murdered in 1979. Amos's group moved away from *Ekuphakameni* to a new site called *Ebuhleni* (the place of splendor), while Londa's followers continue to meet on the original site. Amos died of old age on September 25, 1995. His son, Vimbeni, assumed leadership of the community.

The name *Shembe* has a multiple meaning in *ibandla lamaNazaretha.*[5] When used by members, it may refer to any of the above-mentioned leaders, past or present. What seems to be more important now is that the name *Shembe* also refers to the cosmological lineage. It does not always seem to matter which person is actually being referred to (though some members distinguish between individuals in dream and miracle narratives). In this regard, the name *Shembe,* like the name *Jesus* for Western Christians, is believed by Nazarite members to be imbued with power, and thus constitutes an important locus of group identity in terms of the wider political economy.

The size of the current following is extremely hard to gauge. A letter written by a white policeman in 1921 estimated Isaiah's following to be between 300 and 400. There was rapid growth in the 1920s, because Esther Roberts (1936, 74) writes that Galilee Shembe thought there were at least 40,000 members at the time of Isaiah's death in 1935. In the mid-1970s, estimates put the membership at about 250,000 (Becken in Kiernan 1992, 18), though Nazarite followers assured me in 1991 that there were closer to one million adherents. The newly published Nazarite Church Newsletter refers to the "multi-million members" of *ibandla lamaNazaretha* (Malimela 1997, 2). Numbers aside, it is important to realize that the six years (1991–1997) taken for most of my research and writing were monumental years in South African history. On the one hand, we saw the pillars of the apartheid regime slowly and often painfully dismantled, and a new nation born. On the other hand, the majority of South Africans witnessed and experienced first-hand the unleashing of endless waves of crime and violence in their communities.[6] The members of *ibandla lamaNazaretha* were not immune to this turbulence. More recently, many have been filled with an inordinate sense of both hope and disappointment in the possibilities presented by the larger historical moment.

Such epochal political transformation has meant that my study could not simply be located in an "ethnographic present." Instead, it has constantly been shaped and informed by both the daily sense of the urgency and rapid change that characterizes the historical moment, and the everyday uncertainties, shock, and disbelief at what have seemed to constitute ruthless killings, senseless theft, violation, and destruction. Much of my work has been situated in the context of a fragmented social order filled with fear and the continual threat of violence. This had become the way of life for many of the men and women who so warmly and willingly opened their lives and homes to me in the early 1990s.

For the majority of the Nazarite followers the new political dispensation has provided uneven levels of improvement in their standards of living, education, and employment. The right to vote has not necessarily created equal opportunity and widespread economic empowerment. (One notable exception is the Inanda Valley, where *Ebuhleni* is located. This was electrified between 1994 and 1996.) Nevertheless, Nazarites continue to hope, though their desires are channeled through their prophet/God Shembe and what he is believed to be able to do for them— if not in the present, then certainly in the future. This relationship with the Nazarite understanding of God is fostered through the expressive domains of song, dance, dreams, and miracles of healing. For most members, this continues to operate at a collective level. For a few enterprising individuals, the Nazarite repertory offers a particular set of possibilities as South Africa seeks to rejoin the world economy in the 1990s. Such is the politics of hope on the peripheries of the emergent South African democracy.

*   *   *   *

Although I had lived in the province of KwaZulu Natal for about fifteen years, like most other white South Africans at the time, I had never heard of *ibandla lamaNazaretha*. In search of a research site in early January 1990 (just one month before the momentous unbanning of the African National Congress and the South African Communist Party on February 2, and the subsequent release of Nelson Mandela on February 11), I was invited[7] to visit the mountain of *Nhlangakaze*. This is the Nazarite equivalent of the Old Testament holy mountain called Mount Sinai and the New Testament place of the "Sermon on the Mount."[8]

The drive from my parents' home to *Nhlangakaze* was about an hour long. While the distance was not far, the journey covered physical territory I had had no idea existed, and transferred me into previously unexplored intellectual, moral, and cultural terrain. February 2, 1990, would mark a major turning point in the wider history of the peoples of South Africa, but January 12, 1990, was the day I began to ask new questions about, and look for alternative narrations of, the cultural and religious history of the people of South Africa.

My mother came with me on that Saturday, perhaps a little concerned for my safety, but probably more curious about what we would find at the end of our journey, along roads neither of us had traveled. Since Saturday was the Nazarite sabbath, we were told to bring sandwiches and coffee— nobody was permitted to "light a fire" (i.e., boil water or cook) on this day of the week. In addition, since we would enter holy ground we would be required to remove our shoes on arrival at the mountain. We therefore took along a pair of socks to walk in. (Only white people whose feet had been made soft from wearing shoes were allowed this comfort!)

Once one turned off the national freeway running alongside the northern coastline of KwaZulu Natal, the road to *Nhlangakaze* was a long, bumpy dirt road, which winds, twists, and turns for about thirty miles. It passed through rolling green hills, frequently dry riverbeds, sometimes badly eroded terrain, and many, many African homesteads. There were no road signs—most people were unable to read. If you lost your way, you could drive enormous distances without having any clue in which direction you were headed. Consistent with the political geography of apartheid, areas such as that of the mountain of *Nhlangakaze* had not been marked out on official South African road maps, because white people, who predominantly owned motor vehicles and drew up the maps, rarely traveled on these roads. (New road maps and signs were one of the first changes made to the South African landscape beginning in May 1994.)

As we neared the mountain, we noticed a number of buses filled to capacity with Nazarite members arriving for the weekend. Standing alongside the road, young children held small bunches of flowers in their hands. Several members stopped to purchase these flowers, which would be carried to the top of the mountain. I would soon learn that such commodification and entrepreneurship were central characteristics of Nazarite spirituality. We managed to park our cars alongside the road leading to the mountain. Several other cars and buses were similarly parked. There was a signal to remove our shoes, gather our bags, and begin the ascent up the mountainside, for which there was some urgency, as the nine o'clock morning service was about to begin. Not sensing the same hurry as those with whom we had come, my mother and I took some time to absorb the totality of the spectacle around us.

What I witnessed on that day at the mountain filled me with a myriad of emotions. A single path led the way up the mountain.[9] On either side of this path were small makeshift huts, in which women and children were sitting and talking, and from which many displayed a variety of goods and religious paraphernalia available for sale. This included basic foodstuffs, such as dry beans, powdered milk, tea, coffee, sugar, candy, some meat, and the Zulu staple, cornmeal. The religious goods sold by the women included the white prayer gown, worn by all members and called *imi-Nazaretha;* photographs that bore witness to the heavenly and miraculous wonders of the first three Shembes—Isaiah the founder, Galilee the successor, and Amos the leader (who was succeeded by his son, Vimbeni, in 1995); some of the most beautiful beadwork I had ever seen; and dance attire for both young girls and married women.

In contrast to the goods sold by the women, there was a single tent at the beginning of the path in which senior male leaders were selling Bibles in Zulu, the Nazarite hymnal, the catechism, and bumper stickers with "Shembe Is the Way" printed in red and blue. This distinction between the domains of women and men embodied in the goods for sale—i.e., the printed word (Western forms), and attire for dance and worship (traditional forms)—would manifest itself in other domains. Ideally, Nazarite members come to the mountain on foot, walking about forty miles over a three-day period. The length of stay on the mountain varies from a day to about a month, depending on the larger political climate. Members return barefoot, once again, at the end of the time to *Ebuhleni*, the church headquarters. Many are unable to stay for the entire period, however, and so come in buses or minibus taxis for the weekend. On arrival at the mountain, each member is required to ascend the mountain immediately in order to give Shembe a gift.

It is quite difficult to judge the exact number of people on a Nazarite religious space (and there are many of these) at any one time. Since January is the pinnacle of Nazarite spirituality, however, there must have been several thousand who had gathered at *Nhlangakaze* that weekend. Despite the numbers, the entire religious space evoked a deep sense of peacefulness, of dignity, and of self-respect. No shouting or running was allowed on these spaces, and in the distance, one could hear the singing of the pilgrims as they climbed slowly up toward the summit of the mountain. Dressed in the white Nazarite prayer gowns, with the men carrying traditional shepherd's crooks, the young girls' heads covered with long white shawls, and the women proudly adorned in their beaded topknots, Nazarite members created an otherworldly experience for my mother and me on that first sabbath.

It took us more than an hour to climb the rough path to the top of the mountain. Each group of men, women, and young girls walked slowly, stopping along the way to pray at the painted white stones set at intervals along the side of the path, and to lay flowers on the ground at particular points. One of the male leaders, *Mvangeli* (evangelist), stood on a rock about halfway up. He had long hair, a beard, a flowing green robe, and a shepherd's crook, and was calling praises to Shembe in the style of the traditional Zulu *imbongi* (praise poet/singer). He reminded me of the New Testament illustrations that I had seen in storybooks as a child. As we neared the summit, large groups of young girls came scurrying down the path. A little curious, we realized that we must have missed the service. None of those climbing up with us seemed perturbed by the timing of events, suggesting that we were entering a concept of religious community and order very different from the one we were familiar with in the mainline Protestant tradition.

To our amazement, in the center of the plateau on top of the mountain was an organ[10] played by Bongani Mthethwa, an ethnomusicologist from the University of Natal in Durban (and a member of the church).[11] Two car batteries powered the organ, and large speakers were strategically positioned to spread its sound across the mountaintop. In front of it, Nazarite members were organized in groups of men and boys, married women, and then young girls in long lines. All were waiting on their knees, with small offerings in hand, which they put into baskets controlled by the male leaders seated in the center. While this was happening, members softly sang one of the hymns composed by the church founder, Isaiah.

Amos Shembe, then leader of *ibandla lamaNazaretha*, was not at the service that morning, though he was close at hand. In his late eighties, he was no longer able to climb the mountain himself. Instead, he was flown by helicopter every year to the top of *Nhlangakaze*, where a tent was set up for him, close to the peak. (The organ was brought up at the same time.) In addition, the women built him a traditional circular grass hut next to his tent for his prayer times. There were several photographs being sold down below that bore witness to the wonder of Shembe's arrival in the helicopter. (I discuss the significance of photographs as miraculous evidence in subsequent chapters.)

Several hours later we descended the mountain, and as we walked past the temporary shelters, or *dokoda*s, which had no running water or ablution facilities, I wondered if I would be able to undertake a research project requiring such enormous physical and emotional adjustment. Each shelter was situated close to the next one—there would be little possibility of privacy. At the time I spoke almost no Zulu, and I pondered how I could survive such obvious cultural differences. Hoping that I would be able to overcome this anxiety, I purchased the printed hymnal of *ibandla lamaNazaretha*.

I returned to South Africa from New York City in March 1991 in order to pursue my project with *ihandla lamaNazaretha*. This was at a moment in South African history when the first glimmerings of hope for the country's political transformation, as embodied in the release of Nelson Mandela and the unbanning of political organizations fourteen months before, had begun to fade. The fragmentation of the rather frail political hopefulness that had characterized the first few months after State President F. W. de Klerk's historic speech in 1990 was set in motion by a marked upsurge in violence against and within black communities.

In the years after Mandela's release from imprisonment, and prior to the democratic elections in April 1994, South Africa witnessed some of the worst violence in its history. Kane-Berman (1993, 13) writes, for example, that between 1983 and 1992 there were 118,000 murders in South

Africa, of which 15,000 were politically motivated, and of which almost two-thirds occurred after 1990. In the province of KwaZulu Natal, a Human Rights Commission report stated that during the thirteen-month period from January 1993 to February 1994, three thousand people died in politically motivated murders.[12] The majority of these killings took place in black residential areas, either rural or peri-urban.

These black residential areas were the spaces where I did my fieldwork. There was therefore a measure of risk in this project. I provide this information to acknowledge some of the constraints under which the research was undertaken, as well as to record the charged nature of the field in which ethnographers are increasingly finding themselves working.[13] The violent murder of American Fulbright scholar Amy Biehl in Guguletu, Cape Town, South Africa, on August 25, 1993, served to remind all scholars working in politically turbulent regions that nobody, regardless of political sympathies, is immune to random violence. In addition, the color of your skin continues to mark you as insider or outsider with respect to the camp of the powerful and the oppressor (in Amy Biehl's case, the surrogate settler).[14]

Swedenburg (1992, 70) put on the Palestinian headdress, *kufiya*, to ensure his safety on the West Bank. Similarly, I purchased a Nazarite bumper sticker that read "Shembe Is the Way" and stuck it on the rear window of my car, I wore the prayer gown while on Nazarite space, I almost always had other Nazarite members with me when I traveled, and I tried to drive only in daylight. There were, however, a few occasions when I came close to violence in the townships. Each time I was most wonderfully warned and protected by members of both the Nazarite community and the wider township, on whom I was totally dependent for help and direction.

I was also acutely aware at the time that the Nazarite community might not accept me into their midst to ask questions if I came armed with pen, paper, camera, and tape recorder, because in the history of the country these things had been part of the technology of repression and surveillance. Perhaps surprisingly, it was not so much in the camera, camcorder, or tape recorder that I used[15] as it was in the act of writing that I sensed the distancing effect of technology. Photographs were extremely popular among Nazarite members, and several church members had their own cameras, with which they took photographs and sold them to members for between two and three rand apiece. In October 1991, at one of the Nazarite spaces called *Judia*, all members who were university graduates had been called by radio to participate in a special commemoration of graduates. At that event, there were six or seven camcorders used by members for documentation.

While a few of the women I recorded on audiotape were nervous about speaking into the small microphone, it was writing that consistently blocked my communication with members. Abu-Lughod (1986, 24) solved the problem of recording information by making notes from memory at night. Because I shared my tent with Samu (a Nazarite member and my field assistant) quite regularly, writing at night became an alienating medium—because of its nonparticipatory nature. How could she and other Nazarites be sure that what I was writing reflected Nazarite thoughts, actions, and emotions? Conversely, audio and video technology could be played back and watched; it could even facilitate reenactment in exactly the way in which it had been performed. Further, there were not the same language and literacy issues inherent in the technology[16] as there were with writing. This in no way negates the power of the written word in the Nazarite community. Members who read want to know what I have written about them and are looking forward to the publication of this book.

In more conventional ethnography, the Malinowskian image of the ethnographer in his or her tent serves to mark the authentic ethnographic/ethnomusicological research experience. In my own research, it was the pitching of my tent that became the trope of my fieldwork experience (and frustrations), and the means through which I was incorporated into the Nazarite community. It was also the action that constantly reminded me that I was as "different" from the Nazarites as they were from me, and that my cultural ways were being observed by Nazarites as much as I was observing theirs.

I erected my tent for the first time about six weeks after I begun my research. Immediately thereafter, a stream of curious Nazarite members came by to say hello and to cast a curious glance into my tent. This curiosity confused and frustrated me, because I certainly was not the only person on the site with a Taiwanese-manufactured tent. I began to realize, however, that this tent symbolized my difference from the community principally due to its size—it really could comfortably accommodate only one person, or two at a squeeze. In this sense, it was intensely asocial, both in terms of numbers of people, and because as a young woman I should never stay alone. In addition, with the first winds and thunderstorm, I realized that the "magic" of my own material culture was perhaps not as wonderful as might have been thought. When the wind began to blow, I had to line the inner rim of the tent with heavy stones (instead of being secured by the number of people) so as not to be blown away. This was a poignant reminder that despite the global circulation of commodities, environmental and cultural differences shape the integration of these commodities into particular communities.

The tent further symbolized difference in its placement on Nazarite religious space. Each time I wished to erect the tent, I had to request permission from *umpathi* (the leader of the young girls), who would tell me where to go. Invariably it was strategically placed close to the temple area, in front of the girls' residential space, or somewhere where the maximum number of members and visitors would see it, and come and inquire what I was doing with the Nazarites. On the one hand, this was an honorable placement. On the other, it meant that everywhere I went, including to do my ablutions, I was observed and commented on by the maximum number of persons. (Inevitably, as I took an *igeja*—a small hoe—to dig the necessary hole, someone would come and ask me where I was going, and what I was going to do!)

Despite the tent, there were several factors that facilitated my entrance and acceptance into the religious community in the early 1990s. The late Bongani Mthethwa, the Nazarite church organist mentioned above, provided my initial point of entry. Married to one of Galilee's daughters, he was well known both to the church leader, Amos, and to the larger community because he played the organ for most of the sabbath services. He had previously taken several of his students to the Nazarite community. In that sense, my link with "the university" became a surrogate kinship link—one ascribed a positive value by many members. I was even asked on one occasion if I was Bongani's daughter.[17]

Bongani guided me in a number of ways, particularly in terms of finding the Nazarite temples scattered throughout KwaZulu Natal. As I mentioned earlier, these were often located in places that were not marked on maps or road signs. Many also required traveling through areas that most white South Africans had never been to, either because they did not know they existed, or because they were perceived from the outside to be dangerous and dirty. Bongani also facilitated the permission I required from Amos Shembe in order to work with his people. This was an experience I shall never forget.

In South Africa's complex history of racial and economic injustice and discrimination, the day I accompanied Bongani to acquire Amos Shembe's blessing was one characterized by the "puns and metaphors, jokes and irreverences . . . of everyday thought and action" that have been used by black South Africans to construct and "refashion in their own image"[18] the inequities of institutionalized racism. I became the object of these irreverences. If I was to see *Baba* (father) Shembe, I, along with everyone else there to see him, would have to remove my shoes, cover my head, and shuffle on my knees along the ground to the table where he was seated, attired in a 1950s gentleman's black hat and royal robe. Bongani accompanied me through the entire process, even paying the twenty-rand offering to Shembe. He later explained that this offering is always given to someone believed to "have a sixth sense."

After acquiring Shembe's permission, I returned to *Ebuhleni* the following Sunday for the festival of dance. This time, I came with my mother. For the Nazarites, it was important that I did not venture alone and without my parents' knowledge and approval. I met the young woman, Samu, who would act as both friend and guide while I worked among the Nazarites. Samu became invaluable to me in many ways, particularly in her support of me when cultural differences seemed insurmountable. She persuaded me to purchase and wear the white Nazarite prayer surplice, *imiNazaretha*. I wore this gown whenever I was on Nazarite religious space, an act that elicited many questions from Nazarite members: How did you hear about our church? Are you now a member? Did you have a dream? Are you telling your people about our church? These responses instilled in me the realization of the meaning and values ascribed to covering the body, and its relationship to personal experience and collective identity, and perhaps even to the significance of my being there with the Nazarites.

Finally, my entrance and acceptance in the research field was reinforced by two aspects of the religious community itself. The first was the hymn cited at the beginning of this chapter, which outlines Isaiah's attitude to the peoples of South Africa, and the second was my participation in the pilgrimage to the holy mountain of *Nhlangakaze* in January 1992. The hymn was repeated to me at several points when I was asked what I was doing with the Church of the Nazarites. My incorporation into the community was validated by the words of the founder, Isaiah, who invited all people to join, both brown[19] and white. I strongly suspect that with this hymn as with many others, popularity and acceptability varied with the fluctuations in the wider political economy. With the pervasive talk among South Africans, beginning in February 1990, of the "new South Africa," Hymn 153 was clearly enjoying renewed popularity.[20]

Although I had already spent eight months with the Nazarite community, the three-day walk to the holy mountain with hundreds of other Nazarite members in January 1992 was what finally accorded me a measure of legitimacy with the membership. Until that time, I had often sensed overwhelming cultural differences between myself and the people with whom I was working. I had always been able to "escape" the field, returning to the comforts of my home. On the pilgrimage it was different, because the way was long and difficult for everyone. The weather was hot and humid, the roads were rough, and no one really knew how far we would have to walk each day. This was the true test of one's spiritual and physical strength—the pinnacle of ritual purity and the positive assurance of entrance into heaven.

The pilgrimage was the closest I would come to identifying with the struggles, the hardship, and the pain of the women, as a way of knowing and accumulating understanding of the Other. This was a moment characterized by the empathetic insight described by Kirschner (1986). It was a moment in which the outsider almost "becomes the other" while remaining "inside one's own skin" (ibid., 218), usually through physical participation in the other's events, such as dance performance, and after an extended immersion in a community.[21] The emotional and epistemological bonds created among all those who participated in the pilgrimage were acknowledged by the Nazarite women themselves. For many weeks thereafter, I would meet Nazarite members who would introduce me to others as "the one who walked all the way up," and we would then compare the blisters on our feet.

In this research project "the field" was, therefore, both volatile and amorphous due to the nature of both the religious grouping itself and the political instability of the region. On the one hand, movement between religious spaces was intrinsic to a member's adherence to the ritual cycle. On the other hand, ritual events could be canceled, moved, or poorly attended because of sudden outbreaks of violence in the area. Unlike earlier researchers with this religious community, such as Esther Roberts (1936) and Absolom Vilakazi (1954), I have had to construct my own boundaries of "the field." At the time of Roberts's and Vilakazi's research, Isaiah Shembe's central religious community was a highly organized settlement focused on a single piece of land, and called *Ekuphakameni*. It was established as a means of creating a space of sanctuary for widows and orphans. After the split in the church in 1979, the majority of followers moved to a "temporary" place, called *Ebuhleni*, which is overcrowded and without the same sense of physical order and permanence as *Ekuphakameni*. In addition, *ibandla lamaNazaretha* is now a much larger religious collectivity, with temples[22] throughout southern Africa. Many of these temples are able to accommodate religious services only on the sabbath, because there is no fixed space owned by Shembe in the area. In other words, there is no residential grouping of the religious community on a single piece of land, such as Isaiah originally intended (see chap. 2). The members of these temples gather together once a week, at the very least, or may meet at each other's homes for daily services (see chap. 3). The field research in its broadest terms involved periods of intense immersion in the religious community, and then a retreat from the religious sites. This meant sharing my food, car, tent, and other resources with those around me—in particular, the young women from the township of KwaMashu, a peri-urban area located about twelve miles from the church headquarters. In addition, because church members lived both on religious sites and in surrounding townships and suburbs, I was able to visit many of them at their homes or local temples, and to talk with or more formally interview them then.

What really counted in the end was simply being there and "hanging out." Without this my project would have failed. This meant entering the townships at night, parking my car on the street (which meant that non-Nazarites knew I was around), feeling anxious and exposed, and thereby beginning to understand what Shembe means to these women. It also required staying awake all night to record women's meetings, or prayer meetings, choir performances, and funerals. Traveling long distances only to find an event canceled or a person unable to make an appointment, or being advised to stay away because of a sudden eruption of political violence, was not unusual. In a very real sense, the performance of fieldwork was accompanied by fear, isolation, and a lack of personal time and space. I also needed to be sensitive to the historical implications of discrimination and devaluation on the basis of race that my presence with the Nazarite community could easily evoke.

It is hard to say just how long I spent in the field. Because I am South African, the experiences that usually characterize the first few months of fieldwork, such as becoming familiar with a country's broader cultural ways—its banks, maps, transportation, foodstuffs, and so on—were already familiar to me. I had grown up in KwaZulu Natal and so I had a support network in place before I even entered the field. Nevertheless, the success of the apartheid structures was not just the creation of physical boundaries between its peoples, but also of emotional, cultural, and economic divisions. At this level, we all lived in separate worlds, and have been fearful of "crossing the borders" (Rosaldo 1993 [1989], chap. 9) between each other's spaces. Until July 1996, I continued to live within sixty miles of the church headquarters.

I have occasionally asked myself what motivated me to undertake this particular project in South Africa in the early 1990s. I was born in South Africa in the early 1960s, a time in the country's history when the state's policies of apartheid had been deeply entrenched in all aspects of South African society, and enforced through law and the military. Unlike those of most of my peers, my parents came to question the injustices of both racism and sexism as they were constituted in South Africa. As a Protestant minister, my father engaged in a discourse of reconciliation located in religious belief as his means of confronting apartheid. Like Isaiah Shembe, he believed that all people are called to love God and love their neighbor. My mother took the feminist line, perhaps best summed up in the slogan "the personal is political." At great personal cost, both of my brothers refused to undergo military service, which was compulsory for all white males once they left high school.[23] My younger sister and I seemed to address the societal conflict through the cultural or expressive domains of art and music, respectively. More recently, it is through academic endeavors that I have found the space to confront the horrors of apartheid, and to explore the implications of its manifestations for all the people of South Africa, particularly for the women.

This personal reflection resonates strongly with Foucault's statement that each of his works is part of his own biography, that at some point he had lived and felt the things he wrote about (Foucault 1988, 11). In a sense, the kinds of questions I have asked have arisen out of my own experience, although the data I have gathered have come from a community of people to whom I am an outsider at many levels. Foucault's claim therefore requires some qualification. This project has involved black women who live on the extreme margins of South African society. The political realities of this project are highly contested. They involve a white woman studying black women, the economically privileged working with the dispossessed, and the educated working with the uneducated.[24] There are therefore several ethical and political issues endemic to such a project that require evaluation and explanation.

In the apartheid years, the most common encounter between black and white women was in white households in a work relationship articulated as "maid and madam."[25] This relationship was characterized by a meager interaction between employer and employee, because of language barriers (South Africa now has eleven official and many other "unofficial" languages) as well as class, educational, and ideological differences. In addition, numerous laws were instituted in the era of apartheid that prohibited a black woman from having her family with her in urban areas. This meant that children lived far from both their mothers and their mothers' employers. In other words, any kind of social interaction between these two categories of women, even if it had been desired, was almost impossible to maintain.

Upholding the ideal of universal sisterhood by claiming that all women's experiences are the same was not one of the motivations behind this project. Instead, my intention has been to underscore the vast differences among the life experiences of women that emerge from the variables of race, class, education, and culture. The project is furthered by the exchange of accounts of those experiences. Many black women who have worked as maids in white homes have been privy to the secrets of a white family. Conversely, few white women know what constitutes the daily life of their employees outside of the workplace. My sense is that a minimum requirement for building a new nation is that we each have some understanding of how the past impinged upon the daily lives of fellow citizens, even if we can arrive at that understanding only by undertaking journeys of discovery that uncover the harsh, dirty, and violent forces of apartheid brutality.

Because apartheid's structures sought to "divide and rule," and to keep its peoples alienated from each other, the technique of participant observation essential to both ethnomusicology and anthropology has played a pivotal role in my being able to gather the kind of data I have. In this regard, it is precisely because I represented the powerful that my going to and staying with the community was significant for the women, particularly in terms of facilitating communication between us. While undertaking this research required considerable determination, I do not wish to construct myself as some kind of academic hero. Rather, I wish to stress the resourcefulness and courage demonstrated by these women (and so many other black women) in their daily struggles. It is important, however, to acknowledge the relationships of power and subordination that have existed historically in South Africa, and to examine the ramifications of these relationships within the context of field research. As a white South African I had had privileged access to educational institutions, which provided me with skills that enabled me to undertake this project. In this sense, I might be accused of social irresponsibility for *not* working with the disenfranchised. Certainly, it will be better for all when Nazarite women begin to write their own stories, and to represent themselves. Suffice it to say here, that in some sense, they *have* represented themselves, not in writing, but through the media privileged by their own community—narrative, dreams, and song—although the final transmission of the text here is my own.

Finally, in returning to the Nazarite material three years after writing it as a dissertation, I have realized more powerfully than before the extent to which my interpretation and understanding of the practices in *ibandla lamaNazaretha* are integrally entwined in my own personal history—growing up the daughter of a Protestant clergyman in KwaZulu Natal. In the mid-1980s, my father was accused by colleagues of being an "empire builder" because of the way in which he established religious communities in KwaZulu Natal, and did so with minimal financial resources. Isaiah Shembe was similarly accused by black and white state and mission officials. Both men, armed with their belief in the power of God and a burgeoning sense of racial injustice, purchased land and constituted religious communities. My own quest has been to begin to understand and critique the relationship between religious empire, male leadership, and female members in twentieth-century KwaZulu Natal. Could this be "White Skin, Black Masks," a reversal of Fanon (1986)?

Writing this book has been informed by much of the postcolonial writings on ethnography and texts, and then situated in the highly politicized context of doing ethnography in South Africa. I have consciously sought to move away from the descriptive ethnographic realism of so much South African ethnomusicological and anthropological literature. I have instead attempted to frame the data gathered in an interpretive mold that best facilitates cultural understanding between people, particularly, though not exclusively, those living in South Africa. Perhaps this book will help to open up a new category of ethnomusicology, one that begins to combine social reconciliation with cultural critique.

While I take full responsibility for the construction of the physical text, the shape of my fieldwork and the kinds of data gathered have been strongly influenced by what I have been told both by church members and by Zulu-language speakers and cultural insiders. For example, I was already five months into my work with *ibandla lamaNazaretha* when I made a most important, though almost accidental, discovery. This was to have a critical impact on the kinds of data I then began to gather, particularly in terms of the married women members. It was about eight o'clock in the evening, and I was sitting in my car with two married women, at *Ebuhleni*. We were waiting for the all-night meeting of the married women, or *ama14* (*amafortini*),[26] to be signaled by the beating of the drum. One of the women quite unexpectedly asked me if I would like her to tell me the stories of what Shembe had done for her. Would I like to record them on my Walkman tape recorder? I was delighted, and so she began:

> In the year of 1986, in my dream, I was sleeping at night. I was with my family then, at the bottom of the hill. I saw the sun, the moon . . . the light of the moon was lighting straight to me, and after that, I saw Shembe—Galilee. And I ran to that light. We were going down to the moon, and the *Baba* was flying after me. It was a long distance to this place—*Paradis* [the name of the open-air temple at *Ebuhleni*], to the temple of *Paradis*. [Mrs. Manqele, August 13, 1991.]

She continued on for about twenty minutes. As she spoke, I felt rather confused about what she was trying to say, but realized nevertheless that she had just opened a rich store of Nazarite narrative treasure, which I should begin to listen for more acutely. Mrs. Manqele was not merely spinning an imaginary world of fiction, but in some way, she was also articulating her own experiences in the metaphors and imagery of a culturally coded and intensely religious set of experiences.

Interwoven into my text, then, are some of the voices of my interlocutors, both those with whom I have spoken, and those cultural insiders who have written about or for the religious group. (I have whenever possible and appropriate inserted their names into the text.) There was, however, one group with whom I worked quite intensively, where ritual enactment superseded the spoken word. These were the young female virgins (discussed in chap. 6). In my analysis of these girls' experiences, I have resorted to fairly lengthy descriptions of ritual, with commentary on cultural meanings interpolated.

My text does not seek to represent a "cultural whole." Instead, I have examined *ibandla lamaNazaretha* from the particular viewpoint of female experience and expressive culture. In doing so I have consciously sought to insert female experience into the ethnographic and ethnomusicological record. Within this particular focus a subtext has emerged—one that enables a reconfiguration of some of those aspects of cultural history frequently dismissed (without further deconstruction or explication) as "traditional." Thus, for example, while African music is generally considered to be cyclical in form, in the context of *ibandla lamaNazaretha*, I ask what it means when cyclicity is linked to reproductive cycles embedded in the female body. What does this imply about gendered power over the flow and articulation of time, which in Nguni tradition is considered to be cyclical in nature?

In creating a text that seeks to convey the experiences of this group of black South African women, I have attempted to find a position that falls somewhere between total invisibility (such as is the case in contemporary Zulu politics); the tendency to portray them as victims of *apartheid* in the Griersonian documentary tradition;[27] and the images used by the male-dominated power structures of the liberation struggle. In this latter case, the leaders of the South African liberation struggle frequently constructed an image of women through the metaphor of the rock. This portrayal was created by women in their resistance campaigns in the 1950s, and embodied in the slogan "You have struck a rock."[28] While the slogan symbolized the determination of women at the time, it is easily distorted to force them to endure infinite suffering, because of their supposed ability to sustain themselves regardless of external circumstances.

In this book I strive to represent Nazarite members in terms of individual agency in a context of everyday struggle, violation, and violence. Their responses are typically highly poetic, structured out of a common stock of cultural symbols and meanings. The beauty of these representations, however, should not anesthetize the reader to the context of daily loss, grief, pain, and fear that characterized the lives of these women and men through the years of apartheid and before. The hope they express is a politically charged emotion. My use of the word *represent* should not be read as my claiming "representativeness." This text is the constellation of a multiplicity of voices, some of which are more articulate than others. The interpretive mode I have created will probably be one that not all church members agree upon. In this regard, data I have gathered in this large and disparate religious community have not always constituted a consensus. I have, however, sought to draw on the widest possible body of primary and secondary sources, if not to embody a single cultural truth, then at least to suggest the depth and breadth of what is a richly textured, polysemic, and often contested religious discourse.

Finally, Clifford (1988, chap. 2) makes a case for the shift in the claim to ethnographic authority as a textual strategy, moving from the experiential and interpretive frames to the dialogical and, ideally, polyphonic. Clifford suggests the goal is ultimately to accord "to collaborators not merely the status of independent enunciators but that of writers" (ibid., 51), to integrate those studied into the very process of writing. In South Africa this is difficult because more than half of the population is currently functionally illiterate. Even so, I suggest that the construction of ethnographic texts need not continue to be characterized by the ethnographic "voice-over," to borrow from the rhetoric of visual anthropology. Instead, we need to move beyond those whose focus is the written word, to find those modes of inscription, other than writing, in which others have encoded their own experiences prior to the advent of literacy. Perhaps the answer to a situation such as that in South Africa is not to be found in writing per se, but in the media of secondary orality—the audio and video recording equipment, which is more compatible with the imagistic inscriptions of experience through expressive forms such as dreams and song.[29]

Principal Themes

In the wake of the Bambatha Rebellion of 1906 (see chap. 2) and the Union of South Africa, Isaiah Shembe is reported to have arrived in southern KwaZulu Natal from Harrismith in the Free State province. Initially an itinerant healer and preacher, he sought to reconstitute a sense of community and collective identity among the African people in the region at a critical moment in its history. He emerged in the early 1900s, after a century of social transformation, domination, and fragmentation of the African people through intertribal warfare, colonization, European and American missionization, increased industrialization, and environmental factors of drought and disease.

While Isaiah Shembe did not initially intend to build a religious empire, his growing following of women, young girls, and orphans persuaded him to provide a space of sanctuary for them. He purchased the first piece of land in 1915 or 1916 using money given to him by those he had healed. On this site, called *Ekuphakameni,* Isaiah Shembe established what became the headquarters of a large and powerful religious community. Combining his deep knowledge of the mission Bible with his respect for Nguni traditional ways, and with some knowledge of commodity capitalism, he constituted a new and hybrid regime of religious truth (Foucault 1980 [1972]) in competition with the ideologies of the state and the Christian mission.

This regime of truth was articulated in a series of reinvented religious rituals that interfaced with three types of experience peculiar to the African people of KwaZulu Natal in the early twentieth century. The first was the rigidity embedded in the nascent industrial political economy and mission Christianity, as inscribed in the fixed, written liturgical ordering of congregational worship (*inkhonzo*) (see chap. 3). The second was the reinvention of traditional life-cycle rites to speak more specifically to contemporary African experience and epistemology. For example, traditional Nguni puberty rites for girls became the collective representation of historical moments in which, empowered by the elements of the precolonial Nguni cosmology, Isaiah triumphed over the state and colonial racism and injustice. Young virgin girls became the central actors in these historically situated rites. Whereas in precolonial times these rites celebrated the onset of puberty, and thus the fertility of a girl's body, in the Nazarite community the rites have been transformed into collective rituals that stress the ritually pure body of Nazarite maidens over the capacity to reproduce progeny (see chap. 6). The third type was the everyday personal experience of Nazarite members (see chap. 8), shared with others in a sacred structure that paralleled the secular and urban all-night Concert and Dance parties (Ballantine 1993). The sacred spaces were used for the performance of religious song and dance, and for the narration of sermons about the miraculous power of Shembe in individual members' lives. Constituted as religious truth, Nazarite discourses on the miraculous emerged in what had been culturally significant precolonial Nguni cultural forms—song, dream, dance, and narrative. They became the mechanisms for claiming cultural truth, because the state was increasingly rendering other domains—the political and economic—inaccessible to Shembe's followers.

In this context, song, dance, and dream narratives were commodified (Appadurai 1986) and constituted as "inalienable possessions" (Weiner 1992) for the purposes of ritualized exchange (see chap. 3). Such cultural treasures were always threatened by loss, but being stored in the body, they could be constantly reformulated through performance. They were frequently veiled in symbolism and euphemism as a means of retaining cultural traditions and memories in the multiple contexts of state surveillance and seizure (Abu-Lughod 1988 [1986]; Crain 1991; Comaroff 1985). In addition, if they were always shared with, and collectively reenacted by, the social body, they could be lost only to an individual, and then only through death.

Isaiah Shembe built a religious empire whose cultural truth facilitated a notion of power in opposition to the repressive and debilitating force of the state. For Isaiah's membership, power was induced as a creative force, enabling women and men to foster notions of hope and thereby to survive the devastation and violation of their communities. This destruction was instigated not only by economic, military, and political forces outside of their communities, but, particularly from the 1980s onward, also from within black communities themselves.

This book highlights three examples of the intersection of cultural power and the general politics of truth. Each illustrates the way in which Isaiah (and subsequent leaders) transformed the other's regime of truth in order to effect his own mechanisms of sociopolitical and cultural empowerment. In the first example, Isaiah manipulated the written and holy word of the mission Bible to authenticate his creation of ritual and liturgy (see chaps. 6 and 8). Throughout the published liturgy, the church catechism, and other ritual forms (see chaps. 3 and 6), the texts of the biblical narratives were interwoven with his own experiences—action that would cause conflict with other mission communities.

The second example concerns the constitution of a kind of feminized power. It was embodied in the Nazarite belief that the control of the fertility of young girls, and the maintenance of their virginity, secured the socioeconomic and political well-being of the religious community. This was a belief located in the traditional cosmological connection between the fertility of the agricultural yield and that of young girls, both of which secure the ability of the social collectivity to sustain and reproduce itself over time (Krige 1968). In Shembe's religious group, this belief was transferred into the sacred domain, where the young female virgins were considered the apex of ritual purity, and thus became the heroines of ritual performances that celebrated the power of Isaiah over the state in the acquisition of land. It was integrally associated with the conception of Nazarite expressive forms, and of sacred song specifically, because it was believed that the voices of female angels brought new songs to Isaiah Shembe in the early twentieth century.

The sacralization of the female virgin body was made at great cost. In obedience to the words of their prophet, these girls were expected to sacrifice sexual desire. The concept was well known to Zulu-speaking traditionalists, because the idea was associated with the military power of the mythical "king" Shaka. In Shaka's times, however, such sacrifice was required of young male warriors. They retained virility for times of real warfare. Shembe reinvented the practice by transforming the virgin girls into spiritual warriors (see chaps. 2 and 6). Similarly, participation in all-night sacred rituals required all married women, also known as *ama14*, to sacrifice sexual desire for their male companions on the fourteenth day of the month—symbolic of the most fertile day of the menstrual cycle—and to meet with other women to worship their God/Shembe instead (see chap. 8).

The third, more contemporary, example of the relationship between cultural power and the highly contested politics of truth is embodied in the rapid increase in the mass-mediation, commodification, and marketing of Nazarite sacred performances from the late 1980s. While limited engagement with the market economy has always been a central characteristic of Nazarite spirituality, as South Africa has moved toward full democracy and a redefined place in the global economy, commodification and commercialization of sacred objects are now taking place at a new and heightened level among Nazarite members. This has incited deep conflict within the community about the difference between a moral economy that stresses collective representation and communal good, and one that prizes individual artistic (and commercial) gain. Much of the conflict is located in the production of a new commercial cassette culture (see chap. 5).

TWO

Isaiah Shembe and the Making
of Religious Empire

Phakama Africa	Rise Africa.
Funa uMsindisi,	Seek the Savior;
Namhla siyizigqwashu	Today we are the doormats
Zokwesula izinyawo zezizwe	On which the nations wipe their feet.
(Hlab. 46/4)	(Hymn 46/4)

Namhla uyayakhla	Today he rebuilds
Imizi echithekileyo;	The ruined homesteads;
Namhla uvusa	Today he revives
Amanxiwa ezizukulwana.	The homesteads of the generations.
(Hlab. 95/5)	(Hymn 95/5)

After greeting the "children of Dinizulu,"[1] State President Nelson Mandela began the English section of his speech to *ibandla lama-Nazaretha* at the funeral of the third leader, Amos Khula Shembe, in October 1995.

> KwaZulu Natal has produced many outstanding personalities in our country's history, and the valley of Inanda has had more than its fair share of these heroes. We think of John Langalibalele Dube, . . . A. W. G. Champion, Mahatma Gandhi, and Prophet Isaiah Shembe. They walked the hard earth of Inanda on which their footsteps will forever be printed.
>
> Ohlange [High School], the Mahatma Gandhi settlement, *Ekuphakameni* House, the Shembe Memorial School, and, indeed, the African National Congress, were conceived in this valley. They are living monuments to the greatness of the leaders which this valley has given our nation.

At each mention of the name of Shembe, the large gathering responded *"Ameni, oyincwele, ameni"* ("Amen, [Shembe] is holy, amen"). Mandela continued:

> In conditions of extreme suffering, the human spirit reveals its inner strength. Only four years after the crushing of the Bambatha Rebellion [1906], the prophet Isaiah Shembe established the Nazareth Baptist Church in an act of defiance against those who hated everything African. . . . For prophet A. K. Shembe and other leaders of the church, spiritual healing alone was not sufficient. The creation of economic assets to better his people has always been central to the church's work. Critical to its activity has been the principle of self-reliance. This principle remains of central importance to our national task of building a better life for all.

For this auspicious gathering of about 200,000 Nazarite members and a large contingency of the new post- apartheid political leadership, State President Nelson Mandela skillfully located Zulu-speaking prophet Isaiah Shembe in the recently revised political history of KwaZulu Natal. The narrative is situated in the Inanda Valley, and includes Ohlange, the place in which Mandela cast his vote in the first democratic elections in South Africa in April 1994. Significantly, Isaiah, Galilee, and Amos Shembe were honored for the way in which they had combined the spiritual with the material needs of the peoples of KwaZulu Natal, through almost a century of brutal social, political, and economic oppression. Though his position in the region was more typically contested in his lifetime, Mandela's speech moved Isaiah Shembe into a place alongside the likes of political leaders John Dube (founder of the Ohlange School and the African National Congress), A. W. G. Champion (politician and trade unionist), and Indian pacifist Mahatma Gandhi (some of whose time in the Inanda Valley overlapped with Isaiah Shembe's).

In the early years of the twentieth century, church founder Isaiah Shembe was called in a series of visions[2] by what he named his "Voice." He traveled to the southern coastal region of KwaZulu Natal from Harrismith (Free State province) in about 1910, the year he was first recorded preaching in the region. That was also the year English and Afrikaans-speaking Europeans joined together to create the Union of South Africa in the hope of laying the ground for an all-white country and government. In 1911, Isaiah Shembe settled in the city of Durban. In his speech to the Nazarites, Mandela indicated that Isaiah's calling coincided with the period in which colonial forces had ruthlessly crushed the African people in what is now known as the "Bambatha Rebellion." Historian John Lambert (1989, 396–97) writes that 1906, the year of the Rebellion, marked a period of crisis in the history of KwaZulu Natal. He describes the situation:

> The "Bambatha Rebellion" is the last chapter in the saga which had seen, in the space of a mere quarter of a century, the undermining of the [Nguni] homestead economy. This was accompanied by the displacement of the traditional system of authority by one in which the chiefs became the puppets of the [British] colonial government, shorn of their traditional status, wealth and power. It was accompanied too, by the dislocation of African society itself, under the impact of the dominant settler culture and as more and more of its members were sucked into the white economy as wage-laborers. Significantly, the "rebellion" was followed by the deposition of [Chief] Dinizulu, the last remaining symbol of African independence, while the Natal government took the opportunity to confiscate firearms in the possession of the Africans.
>
> As a final blow, [1906] . . . also saw the outbreak of east coast fever, the tick-transmitted disease which by 1909 [had] decimated the cattle herds. . . . Few Africans now had the resources to maintain an independent existence.

Lambert's words poignantly portray the plight of the African peoples in the first decade of this century, and set the stage for the emergence of Isaiah Shembe, the prophet, healer, and evangelist to Nguni traditionalists.

Nazarite oral history suggests that Isaiah Shembe's father, Mayekisa, had had a dream in the early nineteenth century in which he had been told that he should move from KwaZulu Natal to the Free State province to avoid becoming a victim of Zulu king Shaka's ruthless killing. Mayekisa Shembe went to Harrismith with the knowledge that his then unborn son, Isaiah, would become a prophet in KwaZulu Natal (pers. comm., Patrick Ngubane, July 1997). Isaiah's mission was to preach the word of God, as he found it in the mission Bible, to the traditional peoples, whom Western missionaries had had little success in convincing. Shembe believed that these people could be converted to Christianity and still retain their own cultural ways, many of which were reflected in the narratives of the Old Testament (Roberts 1936). He sought to unite all African people, regardless of ethnic or linguistic differences (Patrick Ngubane, pers. comm., July 1997).

Oral accounts suggest that Isaiah Shembe did not originally intend to establish his own church in opposition to the European mission. Initially, he encouraged those he healed and converted to join established mission communities (pers. comm., Bongani Mthethwa, June 1991). Nevertheless, as a consequence of the 1910 Union, the effects of the iniquitous 1913 Natives Land Act, and the pleas of his followers, Isaiah Shembe used their offerings of money to purchase the first of numerous pieces of land. He established *Ekuphakameni* (the place of spiritual upliftment)[3] on thirty-eight acres of land in the Inanda Native and Mission Reserve.[4] *Ekuphakameni* became the headquarters of the Nazareth Baptist Church in about 1916. On this site, Isaiah's followers gradually built an entire village, including a school, a store, places of worship, gardens, and extensive dwellings for married and single women and men, as well as young girls and boys. By the time of his death in 1935, Isaiah Shembe had purchased more than twenty pieces of land in KwaZulu Natal.

I suggest, therefore, that while it may not have been his initial intention, Isaiah Shembe effectively created a spiritual and physical empire[5] in KwaZulu Natal in the early twentieth century that continues to increase in size and power in the region. The empire forged by this itinerant preacher and healer and his successors posed a direct challenge to the powers of European colonialism and mission Christianity. This empire was effective because Isaiah skillfully incorporated into his religious community[6] signs and practices of power from a variety of available sources: Nguni ritual and custom, capitalist commodification, the miraculous powers associated with the written word and other Western technologies, the might of colonial state security, and sacred images drawn from the European mission and the Salvation Army. Each was reinvented in Nazarite terms and overlaid with new interpretations and modes of authorization.

In this chapter, I use historical materials on precolonial and colonial KwaZulu Natal to situate Isaiah Shembe and his making of religious empire within a larger political history of the region. This is not a comprehensive historical account of the place or period. Instead, I have selected three separate themes in this narrative that are pertinent to understanding the Shembe empire. These are the transformation of the precolonial Nguni homestead economy from the late seventeenth century through the time of Isaiah Shembe; marriage as a political, economic, gendered, and spiritual alliance in these various formations; and, finally, the mechanisms by which Isaiah, Galilee, Amos, and Vimbeni Shembe authorized (and continue to legitimize) their spiritual leadership of the Nazarite community.

Nguni Precolonial Homestead Economy

Jeff Guy describes the African precolonial homestead economy and identifies the central role played by African women in its production and reproduction. He writes:

> The homestead was made up of a man, his cattle, and small stock, his wife or wives and their children, grouped in their different houses, each with its own arable land. Materially these homesteads were largely self sufficient, subsisting on the cereals produced by the agricultural labor of the women as well as the milk products of the homestead's herd. Animal husbandry was the domain of men, most of the labor time being expended by boys in herding. There was a clear sexual division of labor under the control of the husband/father, who allocated arable land for the use of various houses to which his wives belonged, on which they worked with their children for their own support and for that of the homestead. [Guy 1990, 34.]

The most important social institution in this economy was the marriage of a man and woman, which in effect served to establish the homestead, and with the death of the man, would signal the end of that particular unit, and the need for the creation of a new homestead unit by the sons born through that marriage. Marriage then enabled both the productive and reproductive units of the homestead, and facilitated the transfer of property from the household of the man's family to that of the woman's. This was usually in the form of cattle, through a system of exchange known in KwaZulu Natal as *lobola* or bridewealth.

Guy suggests that the institution of *lobola*, which scholars have frequently analyzed as important in transactions between kin groups,[7] has not been investigated as a social transaction involving two essentially male concerns—the control of women and the control of cattle—which were integrally connected in this region. Their connection is to be found in the notions of labor power and the creation of surplus value, which in precapitalist economies were based more on the accumulation of people than on material goods. While Guy concedes that the notion of labor power was used by Marx in the context of capitalism, he suggests that it is a useful analytical tool to understand polygamous marriage in precapitalist economies, and by extension, the concepts of production and reproduction as they pertain to women in these societies. He broadly defines labor power as realized "in productive activity and in the products of labor" (ibid., 38).

For African women, production took place within the domestic and agricultural spheres. Each woman lived in her own hut, and was responsible for her children and the cultivation of her own fields. There were also cattle apportioned to her that were inherited by her eldest son (Krige 1988 [1950], 47). Consistent with exogamous marriage practices, a woman's reproductive capacity was exchanged by her father for cattle from the husband's clan. It was, therefore, a woman's capacity to work that generated value in precapitalist economies, and in particularly fertile cases, surplus value. Similarly, cattle surpluses could generate additional exchanges for wives, thereby generating further overall surplus for a man's homestead. Guy concludes:

> The object of accumulation in southern Africa's precapitalist societies was indeed cattle, but cattle as the means by which men acquired and accumulated the labor power of women. [Ibid., 40.]

A man's wealth was, therefore, determined by his accumulation of women, their labor, and children. For this he required cattle, which in turn created surplus through reproduction of the species. Since marriage was the institution that legitimated the sexual relations of the man and woman, and thus the birth of children, the fertility of women was crucial to the productive and reproductive capacities of the structures of the precapitalist African homestead. It was "fertility that could create value, through its link with labor power, by means of cattle" (ibid., 41).

The central significance of female fertility in agricultural production was articulated in the Nguni myth of *Inkosazana yase zulweni,* or the Princess of the Sky, also known as *Nomkhubulwana.* Krige describes this mythological figure as a

> goddess of the corn . . . presiding over the growth of the grain, and from her it is said, the people learnt how to make beer. She it is, too, who has the power of bringing rain. . . . She is a maiden and made her visit to earth in the spring. [Krige 1988 (1950), 197–200.]

Her visit was thought to happen in the month of October (spring in the southern hemisphere), and it was celebrated through festivals and feasts. At that time, requests were made to *Nomkhubulwana* for relief from misfortune, such as drought, and protection from disease. In addition to the ceremony celebrating *Nomkhubulwana's* visit to the earth, a First Fruits Ceremony was usually held in December, when the first corn and vegetables became sufficiently ripe to consume. The latter ceremony was held as a means of strengthening those who would eat the crops, which were believed to be imbued with powerful medicines.

It was this stress on the control of fertility to retain ritual purity that Isaiah Shembe sought to reinstate in the life and ritual of his religious community, effectively situating the young unmarried female membership at the center of his following (as explained in chap. 6). In turn, the central importance of controlled fertility became a metaphor for purity, not only of an individual girl, but of the entire religious collectivity. This sanctity of Nazarite religious identity stood in stark opposition to the perception of the defilement incurred with the intrusion of the state on the everyday lives of Nazarite members. The cost, however, to girls and women for Shembe's provision and protection was the sacrifice of desire, either as lifelong adherents in a symbolic marriage to Shembe, or until physical marriage to a Nazarite male member (this is discussed in later chapters).

In the precolonial political economy, homesteads were not only economic and moral units, but constituted part of a larger grouping of homesteads into political units, called chiefdoms, that were controlled by local chiefs in residence. These chiefs were landlords who controlled access to land. When a man married, the chief was also expected to provide the necessary access to land. In return, the chief's subjects had to obey him, engage in military endeavors, pay tribute and taxes, and provide labor in his fields. Isaiah Shembe constructed a parallel social structure for his members on the land he purchased with the gifts they gave him. In these communities, Shembe acted as chief, and his followers were his subjects.[8] Roberts describes Isaiah's position:

> [T]he religious and political organizations of the Nazarites are closely interwoven . . . because Shembe and his counselors gained their positions from their religious functions. Shembe had all the powers of a Paramount Chief. He was an autocrat and had the sole control of the property and the revenue, which he could use as he chose. His position was as strong as that of a chief in the old Zulu society, because, like him, he was regarded as the Father of his people, the Chief priest of the group and a semi-divine being. [Roberts 1936, 71.]

In addition, like the chief in the precolonial homestead economy, Shembe provided land for his followers, and anyone else who wished to reside on the property.

> Shembe will allow any native, who makes application to him, to re-
> side on his land, irrespective of his sect or creed, and undertakes not
> to interfere with the religious persuasion of such natives nor to im-
> port natives from other districts without the approval of the au-
> thorities first had and obtained. [Excerpt from a letter from S. J.
> De Villiers to the Magistrate of Umzinto, June 20, 1929. State
> Archives, Pretoria, South Africa. JUS Vol. 334, Ref. 4/567/21.]

Shembe charged a two-pound rental for land outside of *Ekuphakameni*,
and ten shillings a week for lots in *Ekuphakameni*.[9] Widows and others
who were too poor to pay were exempted from the rentals (Roberts 1936,
76).

Finally, Duminy and Guest (1989, 430) remark that these precolonial
societies were relatively free of disease and had a high fertility rate. These
two factors are salient to the discussion of the mission of Isaiah Shembe.
By the early twentieth century, there is a noticeable decline in the fertility
of African women. At least some of this has been attributed to the transmission of venereal diseases in African men, who contracted the diseases
from prostitutes in the mining compounds in northern KwaZulu Natal
and Johannesburg.[10] As will become evident in subsequent chapters, the
healing of infertility and illness is central to Shembe's power as prophet
and religious leader, and explains the large proportion of women in his religious following.

Homestead Economy to Larger States

The discussion of the homestead economy so far is useful only in charac-
terizing the essential features of social organization predominant in
KwaZulu Natal through the late eighteenth century. In this period, the
size, specific shape, and characteristics of individual chiefdoms varied
considerably throughout the area. Furthermore, these chiefdoms began
to undergo significant structural changes in the late eighteenth and early
nineteenth centuries, becoming larger, more encompassing political entities called states (Wright and Hamilton, 1989) or "nations," as they are referred to in the Nazarite hymnal.

Centralization of homesteads was facilitated by tribal leaders through
increased militarization and political control of large groups over smaller
entities (a move primarily attributed to the growth in the international
ivory trade on the east coast of Africa) and by conflict over land and cattle
(from extensive raiding between chiefdoms), as well as by the drought and
disease that ravaged the region. Transformation also occurred in the inner

workings of socioeconomic infrastructures, changes that were to have a profound impact on the social position and status of African women through the course of the nineteenth century.

Wright and Hamilton (ibid., 62) and others suggest that one of the principal ways in which social organization was transformed in these large states was through the creation of *amabutho*. They were regiments of young men and women, perhaps initially used for initiation purposes, but ultimately employed by leaders like Shaka, head of the Zulu clan, in the centralization of his kingdom in the early nineteenth century. In this instance, these *amabutho* functioned to regulate the behavior of young men and women within the state. They ensured the extraction of tribute from the king's subordinates, and played a major military role in interclan warfare in the early to mid-nineteenth century.

The *amabutho* were instrumental in both the rise to power of the Zulu King Shaka in the early nineteenth century and the maintenance of the political power of the successive kingdoms of the Zulus through most of that century.[11] Essentially these regiments incorporated all young men and women, both those of the Zulu clan and those whose clans had been defeated by the Zulus, into highly disciplined military units. They lived in segregated royal homesteads (i.e., they were drawn away from the control of their father's homesteads, and as Wright and Hamilton [ibid., 69] remark, the Zulu state thereby subverted the labor power of young men and women from the homestead to serve the purposes of the Zulu state alone). Young Zulu men were socialized

> into identifying the Zulu king as their ritual leader and their source of welfare. Over time, as differences of social status began to emerge between the various *amabutho,* the system also served to locate individuals ever more firmly within an increasingly rigid social hierarchy. [Ibid.]

In this context, African women's productive and reproductive capacities assumed significant political value as they became increasingly subjected to Zulu state control. This control was enforced by the female *amabutho,* which controlled the timing of marriage and the choice of marriage partners for these women, and the king's *izigodlo,* the royal households of young women given to the king as tribute. They lived in secluded areas known as *amakhanda* and were called the sisters and daughters of the king. He in turn used them to create political alliances by marrying them to powerful men, who paid bridewealth to the king for them. Both kinds of organization continue in the Nazarite community. A select group of old and young virgin women also stay permanently with the Shembe leader. Although Roberts reports (1936, 129) that Isaiah allowed his daughter to marry Zulu King Solomon, the Nazarites do not appear to use exogamous marriage rules to create political alliances. Rather, in accordance with Isaiah's formulation of kinship as a spiritual rather than blood bond, there are rules about exogamy between temples—a spiritual kinship.

Hamilton (1985, 446–51) points out that these *amabutho* ushered in a new social order by creating a Zulu aristocracy in which a few select women were able to wield an enormous amount of political power. For the majority of women, however, social status declined through the militarization of society and an increased stress on male military power. In addition, the absence of men in the homestead economy transferred the burden of labor power to women.[12] Finally, state control over marriage meant that marriages tended to occur later in life, and that the rate of the creation of new homesteads decreased, enabling homestead heads to marry more wives. This correlated polygamy with the power of the state.[13]

By the mid-1820s the Zulu state under Shaka had achieved centralized power in the KwaZulu region (i.e., the area north of the Thukela or Tugela River; see map) through military force. Integral to this power was the newly created social hierarchy, with the king and the aristocracy (including chiefs) at the top, the *amabutho* men in the middle, and the majority of people at the bottom. These clear social cleavages were maintained not so much by military force as by the power of a three-pronged ideology. First, the rule of Zulu royalty was portrayed as an inherited position rather than one acquired through force. Second, ethnic or tribal rather than class divisions were emphasized; and third, the power of the aristocracy was condoned by reserving the right of the king to facilitate politically significant rites and ceremonies, such as those for rainmaking and fertility, and the maintenance of military might.

There are three important issues that emerge from this account. The first is the foreshadowing of massive social upheaval and transformation in the African homestead economy, brought about not just by the colonial encounter, but also through internal conflicts within African chiefdoms. The power of this newly formed Zulu kingdom did later become the target for colonial aggression and militarism, with the Zulu kingdom ultimately becoming subject to British and Union control in the late nineteenth century, culminating in the destruction of the Zulu kingdom (Guy 1994 [1979]).

Second, the Nazarite empire is fashioned somewhat according to the

Zulu image of kingdom. Shembe, who is mostly commonly called either *Baba* (Father) or *Nkosi* (which translates into "chief," "lord," or "king"),[14] is believed to be the unquestioned head, the leader of ritual enactment, the provider of material welfare, and he rules by an ideology of spiritual empowerment and religious calling. Directly below him, but with almost equivalent authority, are *abavangeli*, the evangelists; *abakhokheli*, the leaders of married women; and *abapathi*, the overall leaders of the girls and unmarried women. In the second tier are the leaders appointed by Shembe to be ministers and preachers, leaders of the women's groups, and the young girls who live permanently with him. On the lowest rung are the general membership, who live largely on the margins and peripheries of the religious economy.

Third, Isaiah and subsequent leaders have all maintained female *amabutho*, though not for military purposes. Instead, these *umabutho* are reinvented as symbolic warriors engaged in moral/spiritual warfare against injustice/sin. Their function is to protect the community from destruction by controlling their own fertility and reproductive capacity. They do this by abstaining from sexual intercourse prior to marriage.[15] For some of these women, this means a life of total sexual abstinence as a sign of commitment to their provider and prophet, Shembe.

The Zulu kingdom forged by Shaka remained fairly intact under subsequent leaders Dingane, Mpande, and Cetshwayo,[16] until the latter was deposed through the Anglo-Zulu War in 1879, and then through further battles with local chiefs in 1883. The end of the Zulu monarchy came in 1887, when Zululand was annexed by the British, though not without strong resistance to European domination.

Euro-African Homesteads

Ballard (1989, 116) reports that English immigrants Henry Fynn and Francis Farewell established the first permanent settlement of Europeans at Port Natal in 1824. Since they were beyond the jurisdiction of the British Colony in the Cape, and the British expressed no desire to assist the settlers with the indigenous population in Natal, Fynn and Farewell negotiated with Shaka over the occupation of the land around the port. While the initial contact between the Zulu state and European settlers was fairly agreeable, with the assassination of Shaka in 1828 by his halfbrother Dingane, relations between the two groups became less amicable.

The arrival of Europeans at Port Natal was quickly followed by a wave of African refugees fleeing the despotic rule of Zulu king Shaka (events that affected Isaiah's father, Mayekisa, as explained above). The original European settlement was patterned along the lines of the precolonial African homestead, using local materials and spatial configurations. It was not only in the layout of the land that the traders assimilated indigenous ways. These European men quickly became chiefs of the homesteads and husbands/lovers of the African women refugees. Ballard writes:

> The adoption of local African laws and customs were [sic] a significant feature of the settlement. Within six months of its establishment, northern Nguni[17] began to congregate around it. . . . These refugees were organized by the traders along African political lines, separated into villages acknowledging individual traders as their chiefs. The traders were too few in number and lacked the resources to impose a European-style, metropolitan system of government on them. Henry Fynn became chief of three homesteads. . . . John Cane and Henry Ogle also governed three homesteads each.[18]
>
> Another social characteristic of the settlement was the scarcity, if not total absence, of white women. The early settlers frequently took wives and concubines from the indigenous population. In consummating these relationships, they frequently adhered to local African marriage customs, situating the wives' huts around their residences, as was the custom among the Zulu. Serious efforts were also made by several white chiefs to legitimize their marriages by means of *lobola*, the payment of the bride price in cattle. [Ballard 1989, 118–19.]

Ballard's comments are provocative because they point to the otherwise unarticulated experiences of African women refugees at the European settlement. There are two pieces of iconography from the early settlement, one of which appears in *The Diary of Henry Francis Fynn* (1986 [1951]), and the other in Allen Gardiner's book *Journey to the Zooloo Country in South Africa in 1835 and 1836*.[19] Both of these illustrate the kind of settlement created at Port Natal. Each male trader had his own house constructed, sometimes in the shape of the African circular grass hut, with thatch roof, or in a more European-style linear building. The circular huts of the wives and concubines connected to the man's residence in a semicircle. Cattle owned by homestead members were kept in the center, and surrounded by the women's huts. Fields for the cultivation of agricultural products lay outside of the boundaries of each homestead. In light of the later history of the region, which was characterized by rigid social division in terms of race, class, and gender, this early evidence of European settlement, with its racial mixing between European men and African women, suggests a richly textured narrative on race and gender in colonial KwaZulu Natal.

This pattern of social interaction was quite typical of European colonies from the seventeenth through the twentieth centuries (Stoler 1989). Stoler discusses the colonial practice of European men having "non-European" concubines, defining concubinage as "the cohabitation outside of marriage between European men and [non-European] women." She adds that concubinage "glossed a wide range of arrangements which included sexual access to a non-European woman as well as demands on her labor and legal rights to the children she bore" (ibid., 637). It was a practice common in those colonies in which there were few European women, whose numbers were strictly controlled by colonial governments.[20] Furthermore, despite the "mixed-blood" progeny that concubinage produced, it was a practice tolerated and even encouraged by these colonial governments.

Concubinage was not, however, always extolled by European officials. The critical issue, says Stoler, was the maintenance and control of European prestige in the eyes of the local inhabitants. When concubinage threatened European superiority and prestige, the practice became a "political menace," and was quickly replaced by prostitution. Preferred marriages occurred between "pure," full-blooded Europeans. Stoler remarks that the most profound changes in the control and practices of colonial sexuality were ushered in with the entry of European-born women into the colonies. Finally, she provides a most convincing link between the demise of the practice of concubinage and the increased standardization of European administration (i.e., when white prestige came to be defined by specific class and conjugal identities). She writes:

> Critical to this restructuring was a new disdain for colonials too adapted to local custom, too removed from the local European community, and too encumbered with intimate native ties. [Ibid., 652.]

The control of sexual relations in terms of the settlement desired by colonial governments was closely connected to the type of economic activity required by such a settlement (ibid., 636).

In nineteenth-century Port Natal, there were three related factors in the development of the Euro-African homestead economy. These were a stress on women's agricultural production and men's hunting; the contin-

uation of African marriage practices alongside concubinage; and the political control of chiefs (albeit European chiefs). Each of these protected
the interests of settler and refugee against the whim and military power of
the Zulu kings. In addition, the reproduction of this mode of social organization in the European settlement shielded women and children who
had fled the dictates of Shaka, and, later, Dingane, in much the same way
as Isaiah's religious community was to provide protection a century later.

Central to this formation were the moral and commercial dilemmas
posed to the European traders by the arrival of the refugees, because those
Africans who fled to the Europeans were in fact officially subjects of
Shaka and then Dingane. But it was Shaka who had granted Fynn and his
party rights to the occupation of the land at the Port, in the southern part
of his kingdom. In addition, since Fynn and the other Europeans were essentially traders in ivory and brass, they were dependent on the goodwill
of the Zulu kings to supply them with their trade goods. Nevertheless,
Fynn's diary is replete with descriptions of the way in which the despotic
rule of the Zulu kings operated—with the rather random slaughter of his
subjects daily.

No doubt those who arrived at Fynn's settlement for assistance had
their own stories to tell of their fears of the horrors of Zulu rule.[21] The
"civilized" European must have felt some conflict between the demands of
business and those of morality, best resolved by the process of African
marriage and the re-creation of the traditional homestead. In return, the
African women refugees provided fresh produce for the settlers through
agricultural production, maintained the smooth running of the homestead while the men were away purchasing and selling goods, and in the
absence of European women, kept the traders sexually satisfied.

This informal social arrangement continued through 1833, when it
came under threat of attack from the power of Dingane's army. The settlers and refugees disbanded the colonial settlement in fear of Dingane's
retaliation for their having slaughtered about five hundred of his warriors.
They returned to the settlement again, and Lambert (1989, 373) remarks
that by 1834 there were about six thousand refugees living at the port.[22]
However, the tenor of colonial-refugee relations began to alter with the
accession to power of Dingane, who was less amenable to the settlers than
Shaka had been, and with the arrival of the Afrikaner *trekkers* in search of
large tracts of pastoral land in 1837.

Under the leadership of Piet Retief and Gerrit Maritz, the Afrikaner
trekkers had fled the yoke and control of British colonialism. This group
posed an enormous threat to the Zulu state, in that, unlike the British,

who were hunters and traders, the *trekkers* were pastoralists who required considerable land for grazing. In addition, they had fought frontier wars in the Cape Colony for almost three decades, proving adept in both defensive and offensive military action. The *trekkers* requested land from the Zulu king Dingane in 1838, and his response laid the ground for one of the major battles between Zulu and Boer—he killed their leader, Retief, and the members of Retief's party, and went on to attack Boer settlements. Dingane's forces managed to capture 35,000 head of cattle from the *trekkers* (Colenbrander 1989, 91).

The *trekkers* retaliated in late 1838 in a battle led by Andries Pretorius at the *Ncome* (Blood) River. About three thousand Zulus died in the battle, and Dingane lost the seized cattle, as well as large territories previously under Zulu control. (This is a particularly important landmark in Zulu oral history, about which a most moving account, from the Zulu perspective, is written in the Nazarite catechism.) The defeat signaled to Dingane's subjects the loss of his dominance in the region, and encouraged his subordinates to openly challenge his authority (Ballard 1989). To this end, Dingane's half-brother Mpande fled to the side of the *trekkers* in September 1839, and they destroyed Dingane's forces at the Battle of the Maqongqo Hills. Mpande became King of the Zulus. Many of those Africans (about sixty thousand in all) who had been subject to the rule of Dingane now returned to their previous land, much of which had been handed over to the *trekkers* through agreements they concluded with Mpande.

The British responded to the instability of the region by annexing Natal (the area south of the Tugela River) in 1844, and the British colonial administration took office in December 1845. In 1846, Theophilus Shepstone was appointed Diplomatic Agent to the Native Tribes. It was under Shepstone that the colony's land was divided into three kinds according to ownership—that held by the British Crown, that owned privately, and that specially demarcated Reserve land, on which Natal Africans and missionaries were to establish their residences (and of which Inanda was one of the largest pieces).

Shepstone's idea was that Africans living south of the Tugela River did so without any sense of the law operating among them (Etherington 1989a, 171). He felt that the only way to control this population was to provide these people with land on which to support their families. To this end, Shepstone oversaw the movement of about eighty thousand Africans into the Reserves between 1846 and 1847 (Ballard 1989, 125). They were then subject to governance by the unwritten "customary law,"[23] and not the codified Roman Dutch law under which the British were ruled. One might easily argue that the "Shepstone System," as his policies came to be known, sowed early seeds for the legalization of modern apartheid.

The tripartite arrangement of land ownership quickly facilitated British control over the entire population of Natal. It also allowed for colonial surveillance of the behavior of the African population and the colony's ability to tax residents of the reserves. Etherington remarks that taxing Africans

> produced an unexpected bonanza which paid for almost the whole government of Natal. The foundation of the system was the hut tax imposed on every black head of household. . . . Fines and fees for the registration of marriages was another source of funds which grew with the population. [Ibid., 174.]

While taxation of the African population was clearly advantageous to British rule, its implementation, which was concurrent with the birth of industrial capitalism through gold and diamond mining,[24] and the need for cheap (i.e., African male) labor, signaled the imminent death of the viability of the independent homestead economy and its associated social forms, particularly the institutions of polygamy and *lobola*.

The destruction of this precolonial socioeconomic form was particularly devastating for African women. As already discussed, women's agricultural production persisted despite colonial rule. Jeff Guy remarks, however, that

> [t]he ubiquitous hut tax, which colonial governments imposed on the various African chiefdoms during the latter half of the nineteenth century, which forced men into wage labor—and upon which the colonial state depended financially—was also a tax on the male productivity of his wives and their offspring—each wife being the occupant of one hut. . . . [T]he surplus created by wives and children was now appropriated not only by their husbands and fathers, but by the colonial state as well. [Guy 1990, 43.]

Where it continued, the homestead economy gradually became intricately entwined in industrial capitalist interests, which exploited both the male laborer, through low wages, and the women, who stayed at home to maintain the homestead economy. The placement of the reserves on poor land and the removal of young men from homestead production ultimately made the maintenance of this economic base impossible. Furthermore, colonial and Union legislation increasingly served to remove more and more land from the African populations, and to control their movements,[25] effectively keeping women on the increasingly barren land for as long as possible.

While several smaller skirmishes between the three groups—British settlers, *trekkers*, and Zulus—took place in the course of the century, the next important landmark was the Anglo-Zulu War of 1879, when the British invaded Zululand (i.e., northern KwaZulu Natal) with about seventeen thousand troops, half of whom, perhaps ironically, were drawn from the Natal Native Contingent. These were African soldiers drawn to the British colony after defecting from the Zulu state. They were then drafted into the colonial forces for the attack on Zululand (Laband and Thompson 1989, 193). This was a long-drawn-out series of battles in which both sides lost enormous numbers of troops, and King Cetshwayo was exiled to the Cape Colony. The power of the Zulu state was effectively destroyed when Zululand was annexed by the British in 1883.

The final monument of Zulu resistance to colonial pressure was the Bambatha Rebellion of 1906, mentioned in the Mandela and Lambert accounts above. While the details of this rebellion have been documented elsewhere,[26] it suffices to say here that the ostensible cause of the Zulu people's rebellion against British rule was the imposition of the poll tax, a tax levied in addition to the hut tax, both of which were intended to cut the cost to the Natal government of controlling the territory they had annexed in 1883. In 1905 a relatively minor chief called Bambatha refused to pay the tax, and threatened to kill a local magistrate if forced to do so. The final outcome of this refusal was the marshaling of British forces, who massacred over six hundred of Bambatha's people as well as Bambatha himself.

In all three instances of warfare between the Zulus and the colonists, it is the outcome of the events for the African peoples of KwaZulu Natal, rather than the details of the conflict, that is important here. Particularly in the case of the Bambatha Rebellion, some of these Zulu-speaking people were ultimately drawn to the preaching and healing ministry of Isaiah Shembe.

European Mission Model

Allen Gardiner was the first missionary to venture north of the Tugela River into the Zulu Kingdom in the hope of converting the Zulu nation en masse. As Etherington (1989b, 275) remarks, on a continent where disease and religious hostility were rife, the highly organized, healthy state of the Zulu kingdom, easily accessible through Port Natal, "seemed full of promise." He adds that in the light of these perceived advantages, KwaZulu Natal came to be one of the "most heavily-evangelized regions in the globe" (ibid.). The Zulu nation did not prove to be as easy to convert to European Christianity as Gardiner initially may have presumed. Despite their efforts to retain the goodwill of the Zulu monarchs—by writing letters for the kings, returning refugees to the Zulu state, bringing medicines, and so forth—by the mid-1870s, there was a total of four hundred and fifty converts in Zululand. Most of these converts had been "imported from Natal to serve as examples but were more conspicuous for their activities in trade than evangelism" (ibid., 280).

South of the Tugela River, American and European missionary success was more marked. One of the main reasons for this success was Shepstone's allocation to the missions of large pieces of land inside the Native Reserves. In addition, Sheila Meintjes notes that in Natal, missionaries

> mediated between the communal kinbound, patriarchal household of the indigenous people, which the state sought to manage and later recreate, and the rather different form of household developing on the stations. Missionary influence encouraged the formation of self-sufficient, petty commodity-producing units based in the nuclear household and on family labor. [S. Meintjes 1990, 132.]

Etherington suggests that there were three additional factors that lured Natal Africans to these mission stations. The missions offered an alternative economic base to Africans who had been driven off the land through the upheavals of the nineteenth century; they offered land for agricultural production; and missionaries warmly welcomed all those who had been ostracized or marginalized by their own communities. This was particularly important for women who wished to escape arranged marriages or to acquire land.

The ability of Africans to gain access to land for the cultivation of cash crops played an important role in the emergence of an African peasantry in the mid- to late nineteenth century. On this matter, Etherington (1989b, 287) writes that the *kholwa* (Christian believer) communities in KwaZulu Natal spearheaded the movement into the colonial marketplace by creating farms both on and outside of mission land. In the spirit of the capitalism encouraged by the missionaries, these African converts also became traders, landlords, and artisans. Coupled with economic successes, the missions in KwaZulu Natal were the only institutions that initially provided education for Africans, with all government aid being funneled through these institutions.[27] One of these was the Adams Mission, where Isaiah Shembe's eldest son, Johannes Galilee, taught until he was called to succeed his father. The second was the Inanda Seminary for Girls, located in the Inanda Reserve less than a mile from where Isaiah established his first community, which he called *Ekuphakameni*.[28]

For African women, conversion to Christianity offered a contradictory package. It created a dialectical tension between breaking free of precolonial traditions and courting the patriarchy and domesticity of colonial Christianity (Gaitskell 1990, 254). Sheila Meintjes (1990, 134–35) remarks that traditional duties were combined with new chores, all of which were linked to the European notion of "civilization" and of being "good wives." African women learned to sew clothes for the family, to wash and iron these clothes and household linen, and to care for the home, which, unlike the precolonial homestead, included several rooms and furniture.[29] Concurrently with the acquisition of new domestic skills, these women produced precolonial household products such as grass mats, baskets for portage and storage of food and goods, clay pots, wooden food platters, and mattresses and pillows.

In the transformation of African women's labor, the most contested issue between the demands of the mission and those of the precolonial homestead was women's involvement in agricultural production. The Victorian European missionary interpreted women's participation in such heavy labor as equivalent to the enslavement of women (along with the "sale of women" in marriage through *lobola*, and the institution of polygamous marriage) (S. Meintjes 1990, 135). To "liberate" these women from such arduous tasks, missionaries encouraged *kholwa* men to purchase and utilize the plow. Despite mission disapproval, many of these women continued to cultivate gardens and till fields.

Two additional social practices pertaining to marriage were profoundly undermined by the political upheavals of the period: polygamy and *lobola*. These were challenged by missionaries and state legislation. In the minds of many missionaries, *lobola* encouraged polygamy, forced young girls to marry old men, discouraged the older, more traditional men from converting to Christianity, and, finally, encouraged those young women who did not wish to marry to abscond to the surrounding towns, where they became sexually promiscuous and ritually polluted (S. Meintjes 1990, 141). The most frequent explanations for mission resistance to these practices center on these issues: the perceived lack of fit between the civilizing discourse of the missions, polygamy, and bridewealth;[30] the perception of bridewealth being the "sale" of women by men (ibid.); and the mission's failure to recognize in *lobola* the network of obligations the exchange created between kin groups, or the fact that within the old custom, a women felt it an honor to be married to a man who could afford many wives (Etherington 1989b, 282).

Klopper (1991, 162–63) explains that the increased codification of "customary law" into "Native Law" by the Natal government toward the end of the nineteenth century had severe ramifications for the customary practices of *lobola*. For example, Clause 177 of the Natal Native Code of Law (1891) stated, "All lobola cattle must be delivered on or before the marriage." While the legislation may have served to expedite litigation over *lobola*, it ultimately reduced the precolonial view of marriage as a long-term process involving extensive obligations between groups to a single transaction. As Klopper further remarks, this Clause 177 stressed the importance of cattle as symbolizing access to a woman's productive rather than reproductive capacity. By way of contrast, in customary practice, cattle signified rights to a woman's fertility: so a woman did not acquire the status of "wife" until she had given birth to her first child.

While the mission may have provided for those women who did not wish to remain within the gendered strictures of African tradition, their support of legislation for the standardization of *lobola* exchange ironically had the effect, in the opinion of some African converts, of reducing marriage from a long-term set of obligations to a simple sale. In 1869, for example, Law 1 was passed. It gave African women greater choice in selection of a partner and required all marriages to be registered for a fee of five pounds, while it restricted the number of cattle required for *lobola* payment. The final provisions were absolutely detrimental to the survival of women in marriage, for they prevented the woman's family from recovering cattle if the marriage was dissolved, and prohibited her father from protecting her interests once she was married (S. Meintjes 1990, 141).

It does seem that mission policy regarding these practices has not been sufficiently contextualized, for it was a policy probably based on one additional factor—that the knowledge of these two practices was derived primarily from the stories told by the women who fled from homestead communities to the mission stations. For the most part these were women who did not wish to marry, or who wanted to avoid the alienation of marriage associated with patrilocal residence, or who had absconded from bad marriages. One woman claimed that

> [i]n the mission stations [men] are consulting their women, and where they do not, misunderstandings always arise; I have noticed that there is a keen desire for independence and ownership arising

from the native women. . . . [T]here has been a change, a change has taken place, and the women at the mission stations are quite different from the women of 50 years ago. [Sibusisiwe Makanya, Native Economic Commission, Durban, April 4, 1931, State Archives, Pretoria K26/27/6313–14.]

It was clearly the socially marginalized who sought alternative living space and economic support through the Christian mission.

In structuring his community, Isaiah Shembe addressed the issues of polygamy and the payment of *lobola,* particularly as they pertained to his female following. The confrontation revealed Isaiah's deep personal conflict over the institution of marriage. Earlier discussion explained how marriage was closely intertwined with the political economies of KwaZulu Natal.[31] In contrast to Zulu and other Nguni traditional practices, for Isaiah Shembe, marriage was not necessarily essential to either the economic production or the social reproduction of his community. In the growing Nazarite empire, the majority of the members were women who were responsible for their own economic survival, a survival based on a highly diluted form of capitalist exchange (through buying and selling as opposed to barter). Social reproduction of these communities was not exclusively dependent on the creation of progeny through social marriage. It also included the spiritual union or "marriage" of these women with their God, effected through "conversion" experiences—brought on by song, prayer, dreams, visions, healing, and other "miraculous" experiences (discussed further in subsequent chapters). Therefore, if marriage was not critical to the survival of the community, neither were cattle, *lobola,* or polygamy as part of the marriage process. (The question of marriage as social, spiritual, economic, and political union in *ibandla lamaNazaretha* is discussed at length in chap. 7.)

The Religious Empire of Isaiah Shembe

The main economic principle in Shembe's villages was that of self-subsistence fostered through selected precolonial modes of production. The essential features of this economy stressed by Isaiah were agricultural production and the development of women's traditional material production. The initial reason behind Isaiah's focus on women's production is evident in the accounts written by Union officials about Isaiah's following and settlement. They reveal that the majority of his earliest adherents were young girls and women, and that the young girls in particular joined Shembe's following to the chagrin of both their fathers and tribal chiefs

(Gunner 1988). In addition, Roberts (1936, 70) observes that in Shembe's settlement

> there are several independent unmarried Native women who keep themselves with their earnings. These women are the product of the break-down of tribalism and their lot is a particularly hard one, and Shembe's movement has provided a refuge for many women of this type, who, otherwise, would lead very lonely lives in towns, or else end up as prostitutes.

This body of data suggests that Isaiah's community offered an economic and moral alternative for women and girls who (1) did not want to stay within the confines of precolonial traditional life, (2) did not want to go to the European/American missions, (3) did not migrate to the urban areas, where opportunities for young women were extremely limited in any case, (4) were divorced or widowed, and (5) did not come from the family of a *kholwa* (Christian believer)—the only Africans able to send their daughters to boarding schools in the Cape Colony, or, later, to the Inanda Seminary for Girls (Hughes 1990).

The numerical predominance of female followers is further reiterated and explained by a Union official in the following excerpt:

> I have the honor to inform you [Secretary of the South African Police, Pretoria] that the native Isiah [*sic*] Shembe continues to hold meetings, his followers number about 400 of which 95% are women and girls. . . .
>
> There is no danger to be feared as far as the Europeans are concerned for the reason that there are few males in the congregation[,] [t]he chief evil being the attraction of so many females from their *kraal*[32] allegiance, and the conduct that is alleged . . . goes on at the prayer meetings. This is much resented by the *kraal* heads[,] but they appear to be powerless to prevent their women from going.
>
> Shembe's success in attracting females is the dress and spectacular shows which he arranges. All dress in white, wear a band around the head and carry palm leaves, they then go in procession to the places where the so[-]called religious rites take place accompanied by dancing. [State Archives, Pretoria, South Africa. JUS Vol. 334 Ref. 4/567/21.]

The predominance of women and girls in the early days of Isaiah's following probably explains Isaiah's aversion to cattle herding, despite the socioeconomic value attributed to the ownership of cattle (Krige 1988

[1950], 185–89). It also explains the central role the women and young girls, in particular, played and continue to play in Isaiah's creation of religious ritual, with the control of fertility as the quintessential feature.

All Nazarite economic production was underpinned by a Protestant work ethic/ideology of hard work as honorable and indolence as sinful. This was formalized by Galilee and published in the liturgy for the morning service at the front of the Nazarite hymnal in paragraphs 19–21, 24, and 33 of the morning service. It reads as follows:

> Give us diligence, Lord Jehovah, in those duties we perform in order to sustain our lives. May the sleep of indolence not shroud us. Lord Jehovah, give us a spirit of diligence that we may plow, weed, and watch over that which we have cultivated.
>
> Bless also the work of our hands, Lord Jehovah. We entreat you, accept our pleading, not through our word alone, but through your word, our Lord, our God.
>
> Never be idle. It is a sin to be lazy. A lazy person is like a dog which survives by begging food from human beings. At the end of this prayer, take your hoe and till, that is how you will live, and refrain from begging.
>
> Even where there is drought, plow, because you do not know the time when God will bring the rain. Even if it rains, plow, weed, and watch; so that what you have cultivated may not be spoiled. Hopefully you understand: never despise these words.
>
> For it is said that a human being shall eat of the product of the sweat of his hands, thus said the God of Adam. Deuteronomy 17:12.[33]

Roberts reports that the agricultural production at *Ekuphakameni* in the 1930s included maize, millet, sorghum, beans, calabashes, ground nuts, sweet potatoes, potatoes, watermelons, pineapples, tomatoes, peas, and sugar cane. Individual families cultivated their own gardens, using plows and other implements that Shembe purchased and lent to the community. Both men and women were involved in harvesting crops.

Women's traditional cultural production included basketry, pottery, beadwork, and making grass mats. The skills acquired by women on the Christian mission, such as sewing clothes (and ultimately church uniforms) and mattress- and pillow-making, were also encouraged. Some of these products were utilized in running the homestead, or they were sold to those living on Shembe's land. He therefore admonished his followers to support each others' trade, and not to purchase goods from outsiders. In the early days, Nazarite women were encouraged to sell their products through the tourist trade in the city of Durban.[34] In this way, they remained protected from exploitative engagement with the larger political economy.

The location of women's production at the center of the village spiritual economy has provided Shembe's female followers with a critical mechanism of economic empowerment. This empowerment has been consolidated with the gradual institutionalization of church uniforms and other religious paraphernalia, most of which is produced by women members. In the early days of Shembe's movement, only men wore the white prayer surplice, called *imiNazaretha*. The women were required to cover their heads with a long shawl made from a white cotton fabric and called *inansook*. (It is now only the young girls who cover their heads in this manner.) In 1942, under the leadership of Galilee, and as the Nazarite empire increased its presence in the region, the white prayer gown began to be formally required of all members.[35] In addition, church myth has it that Shembe had a dream about the blood that would be shed in South Africa through political violence. He suggested that protection would be afforded to all members who wore the white prayer gown. To this end he instructed each of his followers to acquire seven prayer gowns.[36] Woven grass prayer mats and specific dance attire (all produced by women) have also become indispensable elements of Nazarite religious ritual.

This has placed women's production at a high premium in the Shembe community. Nazarite women are always busy—weaving prayer mats, creating dance attire, and furiously sewing prayer gowns. Despite a membership running into hundreds of thousands of people, there is no assembly-line production of religious paraphernalia. Thus while women generally occupy few positions of religious authority in the public forms of worship, the legitimation of the authority of men in those spaces is constituted from their religious attire—which is dependent on women's productive capacities. I discussed earlier how women in precapitalist Nguni societies played a central role in the creation of surplus value in terms of agricultural production and social reproduction. I propose that Shembe has accorded Nazarite women a similar position in the production and reproduction of his religious communities—though the primary goal of accumulation is in the symbolic rather than the material domains. In this critical space, Nazarite women hold the reins of cosmological power for the entire community. Without white prayer gowns, there can be no ascription of ritual practice, of ritual and bodily power to any Nazarite member. In this manner, symbolic capital is accumulated only at the expense of material capital (Bourdieu 1979, 180). Furthermore, this accumulation of symbolic capital involves the investment of time (ibid.). Thus, while the sale of these gowns is transacted through monetary exchange, the real value lies in the power of Nazarite members to transcend the immediate space and moment by covering the body with a gown.

Mandela proposed in his speech to the Nazarites (cited earlier) that Shembe's political economy was structured on a policy of self-government, self-sufficiency, and non-engagement in work outside the religious community. It sought to reinstate precolonial/traditional modes of production and subsistence that were marginally modified by the introduction of money into economic transactions in the community. The bulk of the economy was formulated around older and simpler modes of female production. Social organization was constructed from a combination of the more traditional Nguni principles of reciprocal exchange with limited market exchange, and a protocol of respect that was variously applied according to age, gender, and political status. The wider religious community was required to support the local industry and agricultural yield, creating what Appadurai calls an "enclave market" (Appadurai 1986). This is a market that engages with a bounded community, where the goods exchanged are targeted at community requirements.

Authorizing Leadership

I began this chapter proposing that Isaiah Shembe created a spiritual empire because he paid attention to both the spiritual and the material in his community. So, for example, as the state pushed Africans off their own lands, Isaiah Shembe provided economic stability for the destitute through land purchase. In addition, as the colonial and later apartheid government restricted opportunity for black South Africans, the Nazareth Baptist Church constituted itself as a site of bureaucratic power in competition with the state. Even though successive governments would not officially recognize the church, Nazarite leaders began to issue certificates of birth, baptism, marriage, and death, and cards that granted permission for members to move freely between religious sites and their homes. They were signed by whichever Shembe was the current head of the church. Thus far, the emphasis has been largely upon the economic and material aspects of the Nazareth Baptist Church. The remainder of the chapter will focus on the personal leadership styles of Isaiah and his three successors, Galilee, Amos, and Vimbeni.

While little is known of Isaiah Shembe's early life, and his followers claim he had minimal contact with the European mission, Isaiah definitely worshiped with the African Baptists and the Wesleyans, by whom he was baptized. Though illiterate in his early life, he learned to read and write in order to both read the Bible and write down his visions, particularly as they pertained to song composition (see chap. 4). The mission Bible became a critical source of power for Isaiah in the building of empire. He was reported to have been able to cite biblical references by chapter and verse, outwitting most European missionaries (Roberts 1936). In addition, Isaiah's power as spiritual leader was evaluated by the way in which he was able to not just imitate, but indeed, to outdo the miracles of healing and provision reported in the Old and New Testaments (see chaps. 6 and 8). He engaged with the same kinds of battles with the state as the Israelites had done, and he and his community were victimized in a manner parallel to Christian persecution outlined in the New Testament. Shembe used his beliefs, drawn from Nguni traditions and biblical narrative, to overcome racism and injustice in twentieth-century South Africa (see chap. 6). Furthermore, much of the religious attire worn by Nazarite members bears remarkable resemblance to the visual imagery of early-twentieth-century biblical pictures. Through a literal reading of both written and visual texts, Isaiah Shembe's community "proved" that in many ways, they were more faithful followers of the Word of God as contained in the Holy Bible than white Christians were.

Although Isaiah Shembe had little mission education, he clearly understood the power of the written word, Western courts of law, and modern technology. In the early 1930s, he called on a young man, Petrus Dhlomo, to act as church secretary and to record all the testimonies of those who had been healed by the powers of Shembe. Mr. Dhlomo continued to act as secretary for the church until his death in August 1993. The early Nazarite community had its own courts of law to deal with transgressions, and each of the Shembe leaders has had regular contact with the larger South African legal systems, particularly in disputes over land acquisition and succession to leadership.

Isaiah's attention to land purchase was mentioned earlier, though these efforts to buy land were consistently contested by the magistrate under whose jurisdiction the land in question fell. Shembe solicited the assistance of lawyers in many of these instances. One of the pieces of correspondence between Isaiah and his lawyer reflects the near impossibility of African land purchase—even if the land lay within the boundaries of the Native Reserves, and the financial resources were available. J. De Villiers, Isaiah's lawyer, writes:

It will be seen by (Monday's) reply that unless the question of the Governor-General's consent is settled in the near future, my client stands the risk of losing the opportunity of acquiring land. There are not many such opportunities for Natives to acquire land at a reasonable price these days and I would respectfully ask for an early consideration of my client's application for permission to buy this land. [Letter dated July 29, 1929. State Archives, Pretoria. JUS/ 334/4/567/21.]

As his following increased, Isaiah continued to purchase large tracts of land in the Eastern Cape and through the full extent of KwaZulu Natal. (In this context, Isaiah's idea of empire extended beyond the boundaries of what had been the Zulu Kingdom under Shaka.) Esther Roberts (1936, 40–41) tells a story about land that Shembe and several other African people had purchased, which was situated outside of the area allocated for African ownership. When the local European magistrate tried to persuade Shembe and the others to exchange their farms for plots in the allotted areas, all the Africans agreed except Isaiah. He insisted on keeping his piece, and eventually the sale was sanctioned. Evidence from the State and Provincial Archives suggests that Galilee also purchased land for his followers, and endured considerable conflict with government officials over these purchases. Much of the conflict is framed in a discourse of disease, unruliness, sectarianism, and trouble on the part of the state officials toward Galilee and the members of his following.[37]

As Nelson Mandela suggested, the construction of the *Ekuphakameni* village in the Inanda reserve was a politically astute move on the part of Isaiah Shembe because it was located in a nexus of political power in the Inanda Valley. *Ekuphakameni* lies less than a mile from the Ohlange School, established by John Dube, who also founded the African National Congress. Dube's school educated many of South Africa's black political leaders, and was attended by Isaiah's two sons, Johannes Galilee (Isaiah's successor) and Amos Khula. Isaiah and Dube clearly were well acquainted, as evidenced by Dube's biography of Isaiah Shembe, which was published the year after Shembe's death in 1936.[38]

Ekuphakameni was also positioned about five miles from the Phoenix settlement established by Mahatma Gandhi in 1904. While I have not explored the full extent of the possible links between the two men as yet, suffice to say at this stage that there were remarkable parallels in the two men's philosophies of nonviolent, passive resistance as the preferred response to the political violation of the rights of their respective peoples—

the Nguni peoples of KwaZulu Natal and the eastern Cape in Shembe's case, and the Indian immigrants and indentured laborers in that of Gandhi. In addition, both men "communicated . . . dignity [despite] poverty, the dignity of labor, the equality of all [Indians/Africans], and the greatness of [Indian/African] civilization, as well as [their] own saintliness" (Bean 1991, 368). Both Gandhi and Shembe preached a message of national self-sufficiency and self-government through the development of national industries, located specifically in women's production.[39] In Gandhi's case this was the spinning industry; for Isaiah Shembe, self-sufficiency lay in the (re)development of traditional cultural products such as basketry, pottery, and beadwork.

The third significant landmark (not mentioned by Mandela even though almost all black women currently in parliament from KwaZulu Natal were educated here) was the Inanda Seminary for Girls. The seminary was founded in 1869 by the American Board missionaries and located less than a mile from *Ekuphakameni*. A unique establishment in terms of its concern for the education and socialization of African girls in the region, it was ultimately transformed into an institution for the training of elite young women in the cultural ways of Western civilization.[40] In this regard, the seminary rules reflected a disdain for African practices of polygamy and *lobola,* and forbade traditional African pastimes, particularly dance (Hughes 1990, 205). Nevertheless, both Isaiah's settlement and that of the seminary were viewed as proper places for the safety and protection of young African girls once they had reached puberty (ibid., 206).

Modern technology has been incorporated into the Nazarite community in the form of photography, printing, and motor vehicles. All three have been used to great effect in commodifying and articulating the spiritual power of each Shembe leader. For example, the photographic image of Isaiah Shembe that is contained inside the Nazarite hymnal published by the church is believed to have the power to heal followers. One of the photographs frequently sold in Nazarite markets is a picture of the head and shoulders of Isaiah Shembe. Flanking his head are two blurred images of black African men in traditional Nguni dance attire—that is, animal skins and shields. White female angels fly above his head. Another photograph has a Victorian image of Jesus the Shepherd with his lamb and crook, and kneeling before him is an equally Victorian image of Isaiah, with an inscription in Zulu, which translated reads, "Speak, Lord, for your servant is listening." These images can be read in numerous ways. At the very least, they speak to memories of Zulu herdboys, and open up to black South Africans a spiritual domain previously available only to white Europeans.

The parade of images continues with each leader, with similarities between leaders and their successors occurring closest to the time of change in leadership. Galilee Shembe, for example, is shown in one photograph wearing a Scottish kilt, rugby socks, military boots, and a pith helmet, attire that resembles an earlier picture of Isaiah on his horse. Similarly, Amos and Vimbeni (father and son) have been photographed wearing the same "Harlem"/"Small Heaven"/"Convertible"-style gentleman's hat and thick black-rimmed eyeglasses to suggest the continuity of spiritual power to the larger Nazarite community.

The power of money was not lost on Isaiah, his successors, and their followers. One example of this is found in the Shembe modes of transportation. In response to his calling on the holy mountain of *Nhlangakaze* (see chap. 4), Isaiah Shembe traversed KwaZulu Natal on foot and on horseback, preaching and healing. His skill in handling horses and his use of them earned him the title *Bombela*, likening his movement to that of a train. Though his followers wished to give him a car, Isaiah refused the gift. His successors did not. In 1980, Amos was given a Ford Thunderbird at a cost of R 25,000 to the community (about $25,000 at the time). In the late 1980s, the married women members paid cash for a new Mercedes-Benz, which they presented to Amos. As he became too ill to ride in a car, the membership was asked to subsidize his travels by helicopter. When the present leader, Vimbeni, became leader in 1995, he was given a Mercedes-Benz. Not satisfied, the male hostel dwellers from KwaMashu township in Durban purchased a new 3 Series BMW at a cost of R 120,000 and gave it to Vimbeni Shembe in July 1996. Clearly, the followers of Shembe well understand the relationship between commodities and spiritual power.

The photographic image of Isaiah the servant with Jesus the shepherd provides material evidence to Nazarite believers that their founder and his successors mediate between the living and the dead. They are able to intervene on the part of their followers, to plead with the ancestors on behalf of those remaining on the earth. It is in this sense that Shembe occupies a critical position as the omnipresent and omnipotent *Baba* (Father) of a community of people for whom patriarchal power continues to be a resonant cultural memory.

The power of Shembe to draw new followers is perhaps most evident in his capacity to heal those who come to him sick and in emotional and physical pain. In addition to hearing the voice of God through the media of dreams and visions, Isaiah was endowed, according to early reports on his ministry, with a remarkable power to heal. Vilakazi et al. (1986, 24–26) suggest that his personality and troubled early life, which included a severe illness in his youth, point to patterns similar to those of the calling of a traditional healer, or *isangoma*.[41] An integral element in this system of health care is the reintegration of relationships between the living and the dead through the expressive forms of dreams, visions, religious song, and dance. The spiritual force of the cosmology in the lives of Nazarite followers is evidenced in the power of Shembe to work the miraculous in their lives. The work of miracles has become a central part of Nazarite ritual practice. Isaiah chose, however, to use these powers as a vehicle of religious evangelization rather than for traditional purposes. From the earliest days of his labor for God there are reports of his capacity to rid black South Africans of illness and disease.[42] These powers are passed on to successive leaders.

Conclusion

Despite Isaiah Shembe's stress on material self-sufficiency acquired through hard work, simple industry, and agricultural production, the majority of the current Nazarite membership is still extremely poor. The system of economic independence that Isaiah encouraged his initial membership to create has largely broken down. This is best explained by the shortage of land relative to the large number of people who have flocked to Shembe for healing and protection in the wake of increased violence and rural impoverishment, particularly in the past decade.

The negligible engagement of Nazarite members in the systems of formal economic exchange is characterized by the sale of labor in predominantly low-paying, physically demanding employment found in the urban areas. In other words, for the most part, engagement in the wider political economy provides neither access to the creation of surplus value in material goods, nor participation in the systems of exchange that guarantee some form of social obligation or reciprocity.[43] Some Nazarite members benefit from the sale of Nazarite-related goods in enclave markets (Appadurai 1986) on the sites of *ibandla lamaNazaretha*. These markets sell goods necessary for effective participation in Nazarite ritual. Most followers also believe that Shembe will meet personal welfare requirements (if not immediately, then sometime in the future). Perhaps more significantly, it seems that what Shembe now provides for his followers is not so much economic prosperity as a dynamic system of socioreligious organization in which surplus is created through the accumulation of cultural capital that derives its value as a cultural "treasure" through its links with the cosmology. The value of this cultural capital increases through cycles of ritualized exchange, which are systems of what Weiner (1992) calls the "keeping-while-giving" of "inalienable possessions." A discussion of these forms the substance of chapter 3.

THREE

Making and Exchanging Nazarite
Sacred Forms

Ngiyakuthandaza	I shall pray
Ngamasuku onke;	Every day;
Khona ekuseni	Even in the morning,
Nase kulaleni.	And before I go to sleep.
Ngimbonge uThixo	I shall give thanks to God
Ngenhliziyo yami.	With all my heart.
Izinyawo zami,	My feet,
Nenhliziyo yami,	And my heart,
Nawo amehlo ami,	And even these eyes of mine,
Nezindlebe zami,	And my ears,
Ziyakusebenza	They shall do the work
Okuthandwa nguwe.	That you desire them to do.
(Hlab. 224/3,5)	(Hymn 224/3,5)

On October 13, 1991, Nazarite member Mr. Hlatswayo from Kwa-Mashu, Durban, told this story to *ama14*, one of the Nazarite groups of married women.

> When I was standing here behind this house, looking there, up in the sky, I saw the heavens open like a TV. I stood there silently and looked at it, amazed. I asked myself, "What is it that is being turned on like a TV?" Then I saw another land. When I saw this land, *Bombela*[1] appeared. He appeared riding a horse, his horse that you know.[2] He appeared in three dimensions. He came down, down with the horse, and when he turned to go to the house, he was now in single [two] dimension. When he arrived at the house he was going to, he got off the horse. He tied it up outside and he went inside. . . . Then I saw a LARGE house far away, very far, very far from the house. I was amazed. I looked at this house that had so

many other houses surrounding it. That house was supposed to be hidden—it was a hidden place. . . .

After I saw the house, I was shown something else. I was shown white kings, I was shown kings, but I didn't see African kings at that time. I only saw whites. The kings that I saw had their badges on. I just watched in my dream, and I was quiet. Then I said, "What is God trying to show me?" Then I turned around, and as I did so, I saw a dark maiden. She was wearing a net on her head. I looked at her very carefully. And I said, "What is God trying to show me?" *Hauw!*

After seeing all these things, I saw something like a school. Then I saw my child who had died a long time before. *Eheh*. . . I saw this child of mine coming out of the school and playing with other children. Then I said, "Here is this child." Then I said, "Here is this child, but this child is dead." I was silent. . . .

Then in my dream I was shown something else. It was like I was taken by the wind.[3] I was going very high, up to the heavens. Taken by the wind (3x). Then I said, "Where am I going to? Where am I being taken to?". . . Then I turned and saw mist[4] in front of me. . . . As I turned, I saw it was God, the creator of the heavens and the earth. Do you hear? I saw him with my own two eyes. . . . God didn't know who this person [Shembe] was who was standing in front of him. The king [Shembe] was just quiet. I stood there and just looked. . . .

When I woke up, I lit a candle.[5] I was alone that night. . . . I was just amazed. "What is being shown to me?" *Haia!* I didn't sleep until dawn. In the morning, I was still asking myself, "What is it that is being shown to me?" At the time, my heart was beating really fast. *Titititi.* When I touched myself over here, I could feel my heart was just beating fast. *Tititi. Eheh! Hauw!* It was amazing. "What is it that was being shown to me?" Such an important thing. I was being shown God. Not a picture, but God. The real God we are going to, the God of *Ekuphakameni.*

It would perhaps be fairest to commit an entire chapter to the analysis and explication of Mr. Hlatswayo's narrative. His story is typical of the "sermons" Nazarite members preach to each other in ritual contexts: congregational worship, all-night meetings, and less formal moments when Nazarites sit quietly witnessing to others about the power of Shembe in their lives. Following the lead of Isaiah, the founder, members weave together a range of materials to create these miraculous accounts. Mr.

Hlatswayo, for example, correlates the power of Western technology with heavenly revelation; he reimagines colonial narratives about a white heaven (Sundkler 1948) by inserting a black maiden (with the hairnet that identifies Nazarite maidens) and Shembe himself alongside white kings with badges; he sees his deceased daughter in a school in heaven. To Mr. Hlatswayo, this dream represents the extraordinary. It suggests that amazing things—the true God of *Ekuphakameni*—can be revealed to ordinary men and women. This was truly a rare and sacred moment.

For the purposes of this chapter, I wish to use the text to draw attention to the quite remarkable ways in which Shembe and followers like Mr. Hlatswayo have reconfigured the central tenets of mission Christianity and Nguni epistemologies to create an innovative and peculiar set of religious rites and contexts for their performance. Some of these practices resonate with precolonial times, and some are more easily recognized as emanating from the Euro-American mission. These hybrid forms have frequently transgressed and undermined the powers of mission Christianity, race-based colonial ideology, and the power ascribed to traditional Nguni ways. Nazarite ritual practices have, therefore, always occupied a contentious place in the religious history of KwaZulu Natal.

For example, Isaiah Shembe redefined expressive culture as sacred and inalienable in the early twentieth century because African people in KwaZulu Natal were forbidden by European and American missionaries "to perform the dances and dance songs that had been indispensable to organized social interaction in the traditional community." So, "mission Africans channelled their desire for musical socialization into Christian congregational singing" (Coplan 1985, 29). Isaiah Shembe took this one step further in the 1920s, when he combined congregational singing with religious dance, because, as Roberts (1936, 43) explains, he

> thought it was possible to teach Christianity to the old, uncivilized natives and to improve their ways of life without civilizing them and breaking down tribalism. He said, "My people should not be ashamed of their past because there is much of which they should be proud."

In *ibandla lamaNazaretha*, sacred dance and dreaming are tied to the realm of the ancestors, who intervene in the lives of the living and watch over them. While dreams and visions occur on almost every page of the Bible, black South Africans have not simply accepted the appearances of a white God for white people (Brandel-Syrier 1961, 159). Instead, as Mr. Hlatswayo's account demonstrates, they have actively accumulated their own sets of visions and revelatory dreams from their God, their own bases for religious authority. Nazarite religious culture has reclaimed the integral role of dreams and visions as communication from and with the cosmological realm in the everyday lives of Nazarite members.

To reach an understanding of these sacred forms and ritual enactments it is pertinent to ask which particular elements were selected by Isaiah and his successors in the constitution of Nazarite ritual, and how they have continued to speak to black South African experience through the course of the twentieth century, because not all expressive culture is considered sacred. What defines the sacred—what imbues individuals with authority—is located in the religious imagination and given form in reports of the intervention of cosmological figures in individual lives, primarily through having dreams, seeing visions, or hearing voices. In this sense, both song performance and dream experience mediate between the living and the dead—both forms have the potential to create connections with the cosmology. Nazarites have ascribed sacred power and value to traditional forms through the force of personal emotion and the encounters that members have with God, who for many is Shembe himself.[6]

These miraculous experiences have been institutionalized through ritualized exchange. Each member becomes a witness to the powers of Shembe by giving her or his story to other members in specific ritual contexts. These people in turn share their own encounters. The contents of these domains have been collated into a collective archive of inalienable cultural treasure from which all Nazarite members draw and then exchange as proof of the powers of their God/Shembe. The accumulation of such experience is equivalent to the creation of surplus value in a material economy. But in the context of *ibandla lamaNazaretha,* it is symbolic rather than material exchange that creates a morally rather than materially based economy.

Through the course of the century, these religious experiences have been coupled with colonial power conveyed in the Western technologies of writing and photography to construct a more permanent regime of cultural truth. The most obvious ritual manifestation of this is the creation of a fixed liturgical order for congregational worship. In addition, as I suggested in chapter 2, photographs sold in the community have simulated images of both Jesus and Shembe. These icons manifest an equality of power between the two religious leaders, and are congruent with the way in which personal dreams have traditionally provided evidence of ancestral intervention and empowerment. Just as songs are stored in the memory of an individual and externalized by means of performance, so the

words of Shembe are inscribed in the written text and enacted only in ritual performance.

   In this chapter, I examine these Nazarite ritual forms and sacred practices as they memorialize the historical moment (described in chap. 2), and
the embedded contest between the signs and practices of precolonial
Nguni ways and those of the emergent industrial economy and mission
Christianity. In the first part, I discuss the concept of "inalienable possessions" (Weiner 1992) as it pertains to Nazarite ritual practices. The second
part details the formation and structure of Nazarite ritual spaces both on
the land purchased by Isaiah and elsewhere. The bulk of the chapter focuses on ritual practices peculiar to *ibandla lamaNazaretha*, many of which
articulate a direct response to Isaiah's sense of resistance to Nazarite participation in the wider South African industrial economy. The chapter concludes with a brief discussion of ritual attire and the protection it is believed
to afford Nazarite members. This attire imbues the body of a member with
power, to protect her or him from violence and violation, and to ensure the
safe passage of Nazarite members to the ancestral domain after death.

Reconstitution of Nazarite Community through Ritual Exchange

Inalienable possessions in *ibandla lamaNazaretha* are artifacts of emotion
and experience given form through expressive culture, and circulated
among members in systems of ritualized exchange. In such exchange
structures there are two types of possessions and two modes of giving.
Weiner differentiates these in the following way:

> [W]hereas other alienable properties are exchanged against each
> other, inalienable possessions are symbolic repositories of genealo-
> gies and historical events, their unique, subjective identity gives
> them absolute value placing them above the exchangeability of one
> thing for another. [1992, 33.]

   In the Nazarite community, alienable possessions are those objects for
which people exchange money—such as clothing, baskets, pottery, and
agricultural products—which are not inscribed with cosmological value.
The inalienable possessions are those precolonial artifacts that Isaiah reclaimed for his community in the face of their complete devaluation and
dismissal by the Christian mission. These are the "transcendent treasures"
of religious dance accompanied by drumming, precolonial song performance practice and aesthetics, and dreaming. They have been reinte-

grated into the Nazarite community as the media of cosmological exchange for the creation and renewal of spiritual alliances, both among the living and between the living and the dead.

There are two locations for the exchange of inalienable possessions by Nazarite members—that with other members, and that between members and the ancestors believed to inhabit the Nazarite cosmos, as effected through the person of Shembe. The nature of reciprocal gift exchange between the living and the ancestors is one in which the living give monetary gifts to Shembe, who, as the personification of the ancestors, acts as intercessor for the living. In return, the ancestors provide protection from misfortune that comes in the form of violence, theft, illness, infertility, and unemployment. Should misfortune occur, which it does quite frequently, the ancestors speak through Shembe to explain the causes and prescribe remedies. These remedies usually involve slaughtering animals, consuming holy water (Comaroff 1985, 200–202), and the rubbing on the body or ingesting of Vaseline petroleum jelly if one has been injured.[7]

The gifts exchanged between the living take the form of personalized artifacts of emotion and religious experience embodied in the expressive modes of religious song, dance, and dream narratives. The construction of personal or religious experience through these domains constitutes what Serematakis (1991) calls "historicizing discourses." I suggest that through an analysis of the form and content of these discourses we might begin to extract larger patterns of social reality, and thus to understand social experience on the margins of what was the apartheid state.

In these two domains of exchange, money (as the objectification of capitalist exchange in a fully commodified society) has been interwoven into the transactions between Nazarite members and the ancestors (as the objectification of social interaction in precapitalist exchange). Mary Douglas (1966, 69) uses the metaphor of money as a means of explaining ritual efficacy. She writes:

> Money mediates transactions; ritual mediates experience, including social experience. Money provides a standard for measuring worth; ritual standardizes situations and so helps evaluate them. Money makes a link between the present and the future, so does ritual. Money is only an extreme and specialised type of ritual. . . . Money can only perform its role of intensifying economic interaction if the public has faith in it. So too, with ritual, its symbols can only have effect so long as they command confidence.

An analogous equation of social value with both ritual and money is made in the Nazarite system of moral exchange. In this system money becomes the mechanism for the transfer of value between the living and the ancestors, and socioreligious experience the medium of exchange among the living. There is therefore a reversal of exchange objects and ascription of value in the two systems. This suggests that while money is used in everyday economic transactions between Nazarite members, in all the transactions Nazarite members have with Shembe himself, money has been ascribed a value in the exchange of inalienable rather than alienable possessions.[8] As Jean Comaroff remarks for the Zionists,

> Rather than being a medium of self-estrangement, then, money becomes a vehicle, in the ritual context, for regaining control over the self in the gift, a personalized contribution to the fund of the power of the collectivity. [1985, 236.]

There are three aspects of Weiner's exchange theory that are pertinent to understanding the ritualized transfer of inalienable possessions among Nazarite members. First, the modes of discourse that convey the subjectivities of personal experience and emotion have been elevated to the domain of the sacred through techniques of truth claiming (Serematakis 1991; Foucault 1988) that resonate with those of the European mission and are vested in the authority of the "Word of God." Already denied the right to perform traditional music and dance by the colonial mission, Shembe and his followers located absolute value in those domains that are stored in the human body, and hidden from state surveillance and seizure. Through sacred authentication, Nazarite members sought to prevent the loss of those forms that carried the remaining vestiges of their history, mythology, and collective identity. As Weiner (1992, 42) remarks,

> What gives these possessions their fame and power is their authentication through an authority perceived to be outside the present. Connections to ancestors, gods, sacred sites, the legitimating force of divine rulers or ideologies such as the reciprocal freedom of the marketplace authenticate the authority that an inalienable possession attains.

Second, my classification of Nazarite expressive discourses as "inalienable possessions" requires some qualification in terms of Weiner's application of the theory to various cultural objects. While she remarks that these inalienable possessions may be contained in orally transmitted traditions such as "myths, genealogies, ancestral names, songs and the knowledge of dances intrinsic to a group's identity" (ibid., 37), a potential contradiction emerges between the fixity of cultural objects and the fluidity of oral performance. Weiner acknowledges the contradiction by remarking that "ideally objects and words remain unchanging" (ibid.).

I suggested in the introduction that while initially all expressive culture was fairly fluid, over time songs, dreams, and even narratives became fixed through the media of dominant technology—such as the printed word and the photograph. In this sense, one might be tempted to assume that inalienable possessions have become permanently objectified, and have lost their spontaneity. Nevertheless, I wish to stress here that the permanent representation of expressive forms assumed a continuity with more traditional modes of experience. For example, the extraordinary imagery of dream and other miraculous experiences has been objectified through the telling of dream experiences in narrative form. These experiences gradually became encoded in the magic and power of Western technology—the still photograph. Both the dream and the still photograph essentially represented noncontinuous images or snapshots inserted into the flow of everyday life.[9]

In the permanent codification of expressive culture in the Nazarite body of inalienable possessions, of religious song, dance, and dream narratives, inalienability is constituted at two levels. On the one hand, fixity of form and content is contained in both the hymn texts written down by Isaiah and Galilee Shembe and the dance movements believed to replicate the patterns created by the ancestors (Mthethwa n.d.). On the other hand, the principle of "keeping-while-giving" is most fittingly applied to the exchange of artifacts of emotion and the power of religious experience between members. In this process the giver of the possession is able to give without ever completely giving away the gift. The content and form of religious experience as articulated through the juxtaposition of song and narrative is stored in the memory and body of the giver. In turn, it is received by another member, stored, and later given and received through endless cycles of performance and exchange. In this context, it is not the immutability of song or narrative structure that matters so much as it is the power of religious experience, manifested through the intervention of Shembe/God in the lives of individuals. This will be discussed in considerable detail in chapter 8.

Third, it is the acquisition of religious experience and the ability or obligation[10] to exchange this with others through the modes of song and narrative that serve to create alliances between nonblood kin. In this way Shembe has developed mechanisms for the formation of kinship bonds based on transcendent experience, rather than on blood ties alone. In chapters 7 and 8 I argue that, for the women followers, this involves a spiritual union or "marriage" with Shembe. In other words, the social reproduction of his communities is effected by privileging spiritual over blood ties or alliances. The formation of the Nazarite community and its continuity over time is therefore not solely dependent upon progeny created through marriage.

In the context then of overall material need, the Nazarite community has transferred the acquisition of surplus value from the uncertain domain of material acquisition and accumulation, with its constant threat of loss and deprivation, to the cosmological arena. This realm is believed to fulfill obligations and embody principles of social reciprocity. Thus Nazarite treasure is retained in the minds and bodies of its membership, vigilantly guarded, but also exchanged. Each transaction serves to incorporate more and more people into the collective wealth of the religious community. In turn, as more people become members, additional value is added to the store of cosmological treasure because it signals a greater accumulation of cultural truth and power.

Having explained the Nazarite moral economy in terms of the exchange of experience and emotion through the reinsertion of reciprocity as a social principle between Nazarite members, there is another face of the coin of material need that requires discussion. While Isaiah and his followers have created a space that reinstates precapitalist ethics pertaining to social relationships, Isaiah clearly felt enormous moral anguish over the poverty and destitution of his people, a situation that seems to have deteriorated through this century. Isaiah's explanation to himself and his followers of their impoverished material condition emerges in the texts of his hymnal and liturgy, and requires some discussion here, if we are to fully understand the structuring of Nazarite ritual time, space, and the body.

Thus we find that Isaiah's reading of the Old Testament, and of the book of Deuteronomy in particular, addresses the significance of impoverishment. In biblical exegesis, economic prosperity is a metaphor for the blessing of God and a result of the obedience of the Israelites (Douglas 1960, 50). The destruction of communities caused by drought, disease, and defeat in warfare is the outcome of disobedience and the curse of God. The parallels in the explanation of societal disintegration and the historical experience of African communities in the nineteenth century are quite obvious.

Isaiah contextualized the African experiences as the punishment of God for the sins of their forefathers: Dingane, Senzangakhona, Mpande, Shaka, Cetshwayo, and Dinizulu. Hymn 67 (stanza 2) reflects this belief.

Usikhumbule Nkosi Jehova	Be mindful of us, Lord Jehovah
Ekusishayeni kwakho	When you punish us,
Ngenxa yezono zebaba bethu:	For the sins of our fathers:
Zawo Dingane no Senzangakhona.	Dingane and Senzangakhona.

Stanzas 4 and 6 follow the same format, with the fourth lines naming four other Zulu kings.

Isaiah suggested to his people that this curse could be removed through ritual purification and obedience. He therefore formulated Nazarite ritual by harnessing principles of social order into the opposing notions of purity/holiness and pollution/sinfulness. (In this manner the enormous moral debt incurred by the ancestors is repaid through generations of suffering.) These notions were extended to construct boundaries between the Nazarite senses of self and other.

Ritual Order in *Ibandla lamaNazaretha*

In contesting mission and colonial hegemonies, Isaiah Shembe did not seek to engage his followers in any kind of armed struggle.[11] Rather, the battle over salient signs and symbols was contested in the very structures of religious music and ritual (Comaroff 1985; Shepherd 1991, chap. 1). In the face of domination and subsequent loss, Isaiah created new ritual forms in which the encounter between opposing cultures was memorialized. This was effected through a process of bricolage (Hebdige 1979; Comaroff 1985) in which opposing cultural ways were made to coexist in dialectical tension with each other, or were amalgamated and ascribed new meanings.

The memorialization of the demise and destruction of African society was effected through three mechanisms. First, Isaiah constructed the boundaries of his community through the formulation of clear, ritualized distinctions between the Nazarite senses of self and other. These distinctions came to be embodied in the Nazarite reconfiguration of the oppositional notions of purity and pollution. This occurred at a number of levels. In its broadest terms, pollution was equated with any outside action that contravened the moral bounds of African society.[12] This eventually included all Nazarite encounters with the wider South African political economy through forms of labor that induced servitude and the loss of self-respect, such as migrant labor in the gold and diamond mines, domestic service, illicit beer-brewing, and prostitution. Loss of life through warfare and other forms of dying in alienation from the community were similarly defined as polluting.[13]

More specifically, Nazarite members could incur defilement/sinfulness by breaking any of a number of rules and taboos—such as eating pork, engaging in sexual intercourse during a holy month, lighting fires on the sabbath, and wearing footgear on Nazarite religious space. Perhaps the most dangerous form of pollution to the Nazarite community as a whole was that brought on by the loss of control of the fertility of young female virgins, a theme explored in great detail in chapter 6. In addition, as will become evident in the subsequent discussion, these states of purity and defilement were not simply emblematic of the sinfulness of the inner soul as in European Christianity (Douglas 1960, 11), but assumed a physical manifestation in the Nazarite organization of time and space.

The second mechanism of memorialization was the reinsertion of the traditional cultural trope of cyclicity into the articulation of ritual space and time (De Pina-Cabral 1984).[14] Isaiah's insistence on this trope[15] most powerfully reflected the symbolic contest between colonized and colonizer, whose organization of time and space was symbolized in the principle of linearity. In this context cyclicity referred to recurrence and reproduction in the form of seasonal, menstrual, and agricultural cycles. It carried with it possibilities of continuous repetition and renewal. Linearity was goal-directed, rationalized, and pointed to notions of development, and the equal division of time into periods with clearly defined endings.

Third, Isaiah encoded historical experience into ritual experience. This was mediated through the body in a number of ways and given expression in the Nazarite construction of gender. Cyclicity was connected to female menstrual cycles and fertility. Linearity was associated with the rationalization of time, particularly in the workplace of industrial labor (Thompson 1967), which was a predominantly male domain. This parallels the gendered ascription of deities related to nonrenewable (mineral) and reproductive (agricultural) resources by Bolivian tin miners (Taussig 1980; Marcus and Fischer 1986, 89). Finally, it is the covering of the body through Nazarite uniforms that most powerfully communicates the concepts of both purity and pollution, cyclicity and linearity, and ultimately of the difference between the Nazarite self and other.

Creation of Nazarite Ritual Spaces

The Native Reserve System that became the cornerstone of legalized apartheid was introduced through the Shepstone System in the 1870s in Natal. It had become well entrenched by the time Isaiah began to purchase land in the early part of this century. As I explained in chapter 2, Isaiah's first settlement, *Ekuphakameni*, was established in the Inanda Reserve in about 1915. This was one of the land areas designated for African purchase and missionary settlement, and was situated just north of the city of Durban. I suggested in chapter 2 that Isaiah's intention in acquiring this land was to create spaces of sanctuary for those women and children widowed and orphaned by the devastation of drought, disease, warfare, oppressive legislation, unfair taxation, and the migration of men from the rural areas to the emergent industrial centers in Durban, and Gauteng in particular. In so doing, Isaiah sought to create alternative means of production and self-subsistence to prevent women from migrating to the urban areas.

In this chapter I suggest that Isaiah's persistence in land acquisition[16] is to be understood as a part of a larger set of rituals of resistance[17] to increased state control over the ability of African people to purchase land and retain freedom of movement[18] and the right to assemble. These controls culminated during the apartheid era in the infamous "influx control" legislation.[19] Isaiah's insistence on the rights of his people was reinforced every time he purchased a new piece of land, for he did not seek to limit the boundaries of his religious following through consolidation in the Inanda Reserve. Instead he spread his power along the length and breadth of KwaZulu Natal.[20] He then created a ritual cycle in which each site was sacralized and celebrated, at a specific moment in the cycle. Thus the freedom to move between sacred sites was claimed from the state and authenticated by the Nazarite religious epistemology, and, indeed, became a requirement for entry into heaven after death. In this regard, the narratives of Shembe's women followers (discussed in chap. 8) explain that every member is required to visit each site at least once, in order to "write her name in the Book of Life," so that the "angel" of every sacred site will recognize the woman when she gets to the gates of heaven.

The physical layout of each Nazarite sacred space embodies and historicizes the cultural conflict between the colonizer and the colonized. This is manifest in the dialectical tension between (a) pollution and purity and (b) linearity and cyclicity, and further overlaid within the religious space by (c) divisions of gender.

PURITY AND POLLUTION

All sacred sites are considered pure and holy ground, in opposition to all areas outside the space. The latter are thought to be polluting. Each piece of land constitutes a site for Nazarite worship. Temples are demarcated through the ritualized performance of song and prayer, animal slaughter, and painted white stones. The latter are arranged in a circular form[21] by the local members and anyone else who is able to attend the event.

In addition to the main sites owned by Shembe,[22] the Nazarite community continues to claim the right to public assembly even in some of the most defiling areas of urban space. In a few places services are also held on Saturdays after work on temporarily sacralized land. One example of this is the sabbath service held in the backyard of the Dalton Road Beer Hall in Durban (see map), where members don the prayer gown and remove their shoes to demarcate the space as temporarily holy. The juxtaposition of the most pure and the most defiling is not a contradiction in terms, but in fact is one of the permutations of the notions of purity and pollution that one finds even within the boundaries of Shembe's own spaces. Religious dance, for example, may take place on a festival ground situated next to a rubbish dump. Similarly, Nazarite sacred spaces are situated in the center of squatter communities in the squalor of black South African townships. In other words, purity and pollution are notions that are set up both in opposition to each other and as a means of establishing boundaries between self and other (Turner 1967).[23]

This opposition between purity and pollution manifests itself at several levels through various permutations of the name *Ekuphakameni* (the elevated place). This refers to a kind of heaven.[24] It is the name given to Isaiah's initial site for the widowed and orphaned, the landless, and the dispossessed. First, it refers to the specific site, in Inanda, where the first Nazarite settlement was initially established. Second, it is used interchangeably with *Ebuhleni,* the current headquarters, to indicate the place where Shembe may now be found. As a corollary, *Ebuhleni* is often referred to as *Paradis,* or Paradise. Third, *Ekuphakameni* is associated with heaven itself.

These three interpretations of the word seem to suggest that there is no clear distinction between "heaven," "heaven-on-earth," and the physical space where many Nazarites live and worship. Instead, I argue that the notion of "heaven" constitutes a Nazarite formulation of alterity—of Otherness—through the demarcation of ritual purity in terms of space, a daily attitude of "holiness" embodied in the traditional ethic of *hlonipha* or "respect,"[25] and the enactment of particular ritualized performances.

Nazarites construct this alterity by setting up boundaries between these "heavenly" spaces and the defilement characteristic of the wider South African state. These boundaries cannot be crossed other than through the figurative "gate" at which the symbolic angel watches those who enter. This angel stands guard, checking that everyone who comes to this space is ritually clean. This may be effected at a number of levels[26]—through adherence to dietary and sexual taboos, baptism as a rite of purification, the removal of shoes, and covering the body with the pure white surplice, the prayer gown called *imiNazaretha* (the latter two are discussed at the end of this chapter).[27]

Having passed through this "gate" the followers of Shembe enter into a restructured and highly disciplined social order, one built on communal values of respect for those older and more senior in status. The ideal is that the most senior will reciprocate by conferring respect on even the most lowly. It is a social order that provides sanctuary—a space relatively free from the daily toils and defilement of political violence and violation that have ravaged black communities over the past century, but particularly in the last decade.

The aura of order and cleanliness extends to the maintenance of the ritual spaces, in which the dusty ground is swept and cleared of litter daily. Ideally, gardens are tended and houses immaculately maintained, despite extremely limited resources. Nobody may run or talk loudly; children are strictly disciplined if they argue or fight. Ritual purity extends to outlawing sexual intercourse between parties staying on the site, regardless of marital status, and the prohibitions against eating certain foods, such as pork and leavened bread.

LINEARITY AND CYCLICITY

The contest between linear and cyclical spatial configurations manifests itself on most Nazarite spaces and, as I shall explain in chapter 6, is integrally linked to the centrality of young girls and the maintenance of ritual purity in the Nazarite community. In the center of each site is situated the circular open-air temple, demarcated by painted white stones and usually shaded with trees. Church members enter this area through different entrances according to gender and marital status, and each group sits together in rows. These create a semicircle around the place where Shembe is seated. The area demarcated for Shembe is usually rectangular in shape.

Behind the temple lie Shembe's own houses. These are usually more European and linear in construction, and to the left are situated the traditional circular huts in which the wives and daughters of Shembe reside. Next to these buildings is the festival ground where religious dance takes place. This may be rectangular or circular in shape. To the right of Shembe's houses is the circular enclosure in which the virgin girls reside. The outer areas of this site consist of shelters and informal markets, usually rectangular in shape, in which the married women and their children live, with the men and older boys on the opposite side of the temple. At the extremities of the site, before the gate, one finds the dumping ground for waste disposal, ablution facilities in linear formation, and the water pumps, which are typically circular in shape.

GENDER DIVISION

All Nazarite space is divided according to gender and marital status, and beliefs about ritual purity and authority. For example, when there is a linear arrangement of members, as in ritual processions, the men are in front, with the young girls next, and the married women at the end. In circular arrangements, such as in the temple or in the residential patterns at *Ebuhleni,* the girls are always closest to Shembe on the right, with the men on his left. The married women are located directly across from Shembe.

Gender hierarchy is most evident in ritual leadership, and embodied in the seating patterns of each group. Overall religious leadership is vested in *ibandla lamaNazaretha* in the figure of Shembe, who sits in a shelter specially constructed for him, or at a table under an umbrella. Despite the predominance of women in Isaiah's early following, *ibandla lamaNazaretha* currently adheres to the precolonial (Guy 1990) and mission (S. Meintjes 1990) structures of political leadership by vesting authority in its male membership.[28] Shembe is the leader and beneath him is a hierarchy of religious authority appointed by him.[29] The network of leaders includes both those who reside permanently with Shembe and those responsible at local temples. New leaders are usually announced and blessed by Shembe during the final sabbath service in July.

Those directly below Shembe the prophet are the evangelists (pl. *abavangeli;* s. *umvangeli*), distinguished in the church by the flowing green or blue robes they wear over their white prayer surplices. They are seated in rows in the front of all the men. Located behind the evangelists, and below them in the hierarchy of authority, are the teachers (pl. *abafundisi;* s. *umfundisi*), and then the preachers (pl. *abashumayeli;* s. *umshumayeli*), both of whom might be identified by special white gowns. There are specific ritual roles assigned to each of these layers. These include reading the liturgy, leading the singing, and preaching.

There are two kinds of leadership roles ascribed to women—*abapathi* (s. *umpathi*), who are the leaders of the young girls (pl. *amantombazane;* s. *intombazane*), and *abakhokheli* (s. *umkhokheli*), the leaders of the women (*amankhosikazi;* s. *inkhosikazi*) at local temples. There is no distinctive marking on the attire of an *umpathi*, though she sits in front of the girls, close to Shembe. All *abakhokheli* wear black semicircular bibs over their white prayer surplices, and, like the evangelists, are seated in rows in front of all the women. These women leaders do not participate in corporate services by reading the liturgy, leading prayers, or preaching sermons. Bongani Mthethwa told me that during Isaiah's time, the women used to preach in these services. During Galilee's reign, however, the practice was stopped by him.[30] Nevertheless, all women preach to each other in the monthly meetings.

Nazarite Ritual Cycle

There are three levels at which religious ritual is enacted in *ibandla lamaNazaretha:* that of the large, collective gatherings of members who assemble from all parts of southern Africa at specific times in places scattered throughout KwaZulu Natal; that of the individual congregations, called "temples," which consist of the equivalent of kinship groups, who live and worship in a particular geographical area; and those in the private homes of members, who conduct daily services at 6 A.M., 6 P.M., and midnight.[31] The religious cycle under discussion pertains only to the large congregational gatherings.

The corporate annual gatherings of Nazarite members are spread along the length and breadth of the province of KwaZulu Natal. (See map.) Each of these sites (with the exception of the Holy Mountain of *Nhlangakaze*) hosts both a local temple membership throughout the year, and the corporate gathering of people at specific moments in the Nazarite ritual calendar. The two most important months in the ritual cycle are January and July,[32] both of which are considered to be holy, and therefore require adherence to a number of food and sexual taboos.

Early in January, a large group of Nazarite followers sets out on a forty-mile, three-day pilgrimage to the holy mountain of *Nhlangakaze*, where members gather for the entire month. July is the festival month at the church headquarters called *Ebuhleni*. It is a particularly busy month in the ritual cycle, for it includes the opening on July 1, the girls' camp July 7–8, the girls' dance festival in the week following the camp, large sabbath services, corporate dance festivals, the girls' conference July 24–26, and the annual visit to the Nazarite graveyard to commemorate the dead, as well as weddings, marriage proposals, and baptisms.

The girls' conference that opens at the end of July is concluded with the girls' meeting from the evening of September 24 to the morning of September 26. This conference, along with the girls' camp in July, reinforces for the community at large the significance of ritual purity in the face of the pollution of the state. In addition, during the September conference, the girls reenact a particular moment in the life of Isaiah and *ibandla lamaNazaretha* as ritualized performances. This conference culminates with the memorialization of the third leader, Amos, who died on September 25, 1995.

The church's birth is celebrated throughout the month of March, but particularly on March 10, at a site on the KwaZulu Natal south coast called *Vula Masango* (Open the Gate).[33] The death of Isaiah is commemorated at a place on the KwaZulu Natal north coast called *Gibisile* (To Conquer Misfortune) on May 2 and for the remainder of the month. June is spent at *Elinda* (To Wait), located far to the north in a remote part of KwaZulu Natal, near to the town of Nongoma. *Judia* is the site for the month of October. In December local chiefs' days and Dingane's Day are celebrated on December 16, also at *Judia*.[34]

Each of these sites has its own story in terms of Isaiah's association with the place—particular events in his life, or in the life of the church itself. One of these was told by an elderly *ifortini* (*i14*), a married Nazarite woman, in the women's meeting at *Vula Masango* on March 13, 1992. She recalled:

> One day, *Ilanga* said that this March conference, of all the others that come after it, this is the leader. Because the conference, it's the memorial of the birth of this church. When this March conference was done for the first time, there was a star that was seen. Everyone all over saw it. It is said that it was big. And had silver wings.
>
> This star, they said, was moving slowly between other stars when the night falls. I won't forget the word that was spoken by *Ilanga*. He said that even if you don't come for the whole month of March, you must try to be here on the tenth of March. He said that this star will come out every night and move slowly between other stars. When the night falls, children will wait for it to come out and look there.
>
> But on the tenth of that month, the star disappeared. Then Shembe asked if anyone knew about this star. But no one answered. And he said, "This disappearance of the star has been worrying me a lot because I don't know what it has been all about."
>
> Then Shembe told the people that this star was a sign or signal of the birth of the heaven's child.[35] He said, "I saw earth looking very far. . . . Then I saw fire coming. The soil was burned to ash.

When I was still afraid of what I was seeing, I saw bread falling. Then the ash was being lifted upward, as though there was a moon. From this ash a child came out, a boy.[36] When I was still looking at this and some big boy, I heard a voice calling from above saying, 'Today the King of Nazareth is born.'" I am talking about what we are here for today. And when he heard the voice, he was filled with joy.

As she closed, she exhorted the women to go home and read the Old Testament, Daniel 6:9. The biblical narrative parallels the structure and content of the woman's story, as well as the heavenly communication in the form of a "voice from heaven."

While this woman detailed the history of the site, she also alluded to the numerous ways in which an essentially preliterate community, one surviving on the margins not only of the South African political economy, but also of centralized religious discourse, has created monuments of historical experience and cultural truth. As I shall discuss in greater detail in chapter 8, Nazarite ritual is not simply hymn-singing, prayer, and dancing. It is also a religious discourse deeply embedded in an array of expressive culture—of narrative, myth, dream experience, of cosmological interaction, rich in symbolic gesture, and all authenticated through parallel evidence found in the missionary's Bible.

Running alongside the larger structure of corporate religious ritual is the ongoing ritual cycle of the smaller, regionally based Nazarite groups. This occurs on a weekly and monthly basis in congregations called temples. The temples function as kinship groups based on spiritual alliances created through religious experiences with, or conversions[37] to belief in, Shembe/God. These experiences are communicated in the form of song, dance, and dream and miracle narratives to other members. In this sense the temple constitutes a spiritual "family." It adheres to incest taboos and practices exogamous marriage. (A Nazarite from one temple may therefore only find a marriage partner at another temple.)

At the temples the seven-day week includes a five-day work period from Monday through Friday, with the Old Testament sabbath occurring on the Saturday, and Sunday as the day for religious dance, baptism, and marriages. These weekly *Sabatha* services are held at 9 A.M. and 1 P.M. each Saturday. They are led by the resident male authorities—*Mvangeli* (evangelist), *umshumayeli* (preacher), or *umfundisi* (teacher)—with the service following the main *inkhonzo* (congregational) format as presented in the front of the hymnal. Shortened versions of these services are held in all Nazarite households on a daily basis. They are led by the father, eldest son, or mother. In this case the service follows the liturgy for the Morning or Evening Service, again as contained in the hymnal.

Local temples are also responsible for holding other rituals and ceremonies as they pertain to the life of local membership. Between 1991 and 1993, I went to three such gatherings with the KwaMashu temple, each of which followed a far less formal ritual structure than those of religious services. These included the blessing of a newly appointed *umshumayeli;* the call for a night of prayer, singing, and dancing to assist a family in dire economic need; and finally, the *ukubuyisa* ceremony, which welcomes the spirit of the deceased a year after his/her death. A cow or goat is slaughtered on this occasion. Services are also held at the homes of members to bless the house and to paint white stones that surround the property, indicating to outsiders that the home belongs to a follower of Shembe. I suspect the blessing is also believed to afford protection from home invasion, from fire, and from theft.

Monthly meetings organized according to age and gender divisions are held both among local temple members and at the larger corporate ritual spaces. These take place at different times in the month—for young, unmarried girls (*amantombazane*), the meetings start on the evening of the 24th day of the month and end on the morning of the 26th. This age group and their meetings are known collectively as *ama25.* Married women (*amankhosikazi*), known as *ama14,* meet on the evening of the 13th through the morning of the 15th of the month. All boys and men, whether married or not, are known as *ama23,* and meet over the period of the 22d through the morning of the 24th.

Two contrasting forms of religious worship exist in *ibandla lama-Nazaretha—inkhonzo,* based on Western Christian services, and *ukusina,* or religious dance.[38] This duality represents the cultural accommodation Isaiah sought in what were quite clearly the conflicting demands of mission Christianity and traditional culture. It is important to note here that while these two forms embody a total system of religious ritual, the traditional form of dance and the European style of congregational worship are clearly disparate and never performed in the same religious space. In this context it is, however, time more than space that is constituted as the "carrier of significance" (Fabian in de Pina-Cabral 1984, 716).

Inkhonzo is the form of worship followed on *Sabatha.*[39] It is also utilized in the morning and evening services held daily. The structure of these services has been formalized into a set liturgy[40] that is printed in the front of the hymnal and strictly adhered to at all times. There are special liturgies for *Isiqalo Somthandazo Wokuvuka* (the Commencement of the Morning Prayer—literally for when you wake up); *Isiqalo Somthandazo Wokulala* (the Commencement of the Evening Prayer—literally for going to sleep); and *Umthandazo we Sabatha* (the Sabbath Prayer). (CD tracks 1–5.)

Just as the form of ritual has been commodified, so too has its timing been fixed.[41] Nazarite services thus occur at set clock times.[42] Sabbath services always commence at 9 A.M. and 1 P.M. (or 2 P.M. if that is what has been agreed upon by the local temple, to accommodate those who work on Saturday mornings). Communal daily services are held at 9 A.M., 6 P.M., and 12 midnight. All services, including the children's service (held at 6 A.M.), are announced by ringing a bell[43] about twenty minutes prior to the start of the service. This calls for silence, kneeling, and prayer throughout the sacred space, and then members move toward the temple for the service. The midnight service, however, is signaled either by the call of a praise singer (*imbongi*), or simply by singing a hymn.

This rigid organization of time is adhered to even if a member is not at a local temple. The head of a household is expected to lead the family in prayer and worship at home at these times, or as close to them as possible. (My field assistant's father was a highly disciplined man and strict father who would wake the entire family for prayer and the service at his home at 4 A.M., because he had to leave for work at about 5:30 each morning.)

The liturgy is a combination of text read by an appointed minister or evangelist with short responses from the congregation, ranging from a simple "Amen" to some slightly longer passages. A hymn is sung near the beginning of the liturgy. Its first two lines are always new, but the second two function as a chorus. The same tune with different opening lines is used for single verses scattered throughout the text, and similarly for the full hymn at the end. The set liturgical part of the service invariably lasts about forty-five minutes. At this time a senior evangelist prays and calls for communal prayer, and a male preacher begins his sermon.[44] In the 1 P.M. sabbath service, held wherever Shembe is staying, this usually lasts fifteen to twenty minutes, until a young *intombazane* is seen coming out of Shembe's house, leading him toward the temple area.

At this moment, everyone kneels and there is a general call from the congregation of "*Oyincwele, oyincwele*" (he is holy, he is holy). One by one people rise up and call a line of praise—"God bless *Ekuphakameni*." The congregation responds with "*Ameni*." After several people have made their calls, Shembe arrives inside the temple and is seated at the table. One of the male leaders intones a hymn. With the congregation kneeling in respect for Shembe, the hymn is sung through, usually accompanied by the organ. Shembe then prays with the congregation, and the service is considered complete. Before anyone is allowed to leave, however, one of the more important leaders usually stands up to make general announcements, which regularly include an appeal for one of the groups to make monetary contributions to the church for a particular purpose.

Thereafter people scramble to form lines to be blessed by Shembe. The young girls living in the compound arrive with their bottles of Vaseline and sit on the boundaries of the temple, selling the petroleum jelly always recommended by Shembe as a healing agent. Women, men, and children wait in long lines with bottles of water and this Vaseline to be blessed. Some come with the physically disabled and invalids to be healed by Shembe. Whatever the need, each encounter with him requires the giving of a monetary gift, the exchange of which is explained above in terms of the Nazarite cosmology.[45] In a manner that mimics the monitoring of movement by the state and represents the guardianship of the angels, all walking by members in and around the temple area is strictly controlled by appointed guards or *phoyisa* (police). The only sounds permitted in the temple at this stage are the organ, hymn-singing, and perhaps quiet talking between individuals. There are no drums, trumpets, or wood clappers, as used for *ukusina*.

The second kind of ritual performance in *ibandla lamaNazaretha* is sacred dance (*ukusina* or *umgido*), and it takes place in *umgido*—what Nazarites translate into English as a festival.[46] (CD track 6.) In strong contrast to the fastidious adherence to clock time and the signaling of this time through the mission/school icon—the ringing of a large brass bell—*ukusina* allows for much greater flexibility in the articulation of time. Similarly, the fixity of the written text is completely transformed in the performance of sacred dance.

While it usually takes place on Sundays, Tuesdays, or Thursdays, the performance of *ukusina* is totally dependent upon the whim of Shembe. Its start is signaled by the beating of the double-sided *ughubu* drum, a highly traditional mechanism of community communication in Africa (Chernoff 1979). *Amantombazane* (young girls) initiate the start of the festival of dance. In contrast to this leading role in *ukusina*, these girls are the least visible in the congregational worship. Both the shawl draped over the head and the head bowed in an attitude of *hlonipha* (respect) serve to veil the girls' faces, and thereby hide the communicative centers—the mouth and the eyes.

Esther Roberts commented on Nazarite dance attire in 1936. She wrote:

> At the Festivals many of the uncivilised members wear typical Zulu dress, consisting of *umuthsha* (loin cloths made of skin or fiber), skins, bead ornaments and the women wear blankets.
>
> The more sophisticated adherents have special ceremonial dresses which were designed for them by Shembe. They show that he imitated various European fashions without any knowledge of their true significance.
>
> The unmarried girls, between the ages of twelve and twenty-five, wear short scarlet or black skirts decorated with bells and jangling ornaments. They are naked from above the waist except for necklets, armlets and girdles of beads. . . . [Roberts 1936, 92.]

The excerpt suggests that in the 1930s, there was some conflict felt in the definition of "civilized" and "uncivilized" articulated through "sophisticated" and "unsophisticated" dress in *ibandla lamaNazaretha*. Linked to the first conflict was the naked bodies of young girls. What is clear is that Shembe used dance attire to convey his own responses to this contest of signs and meanings. Nazarite uniforms embodied the historical encounter in the 1930s between European and African, between colonizer and colonized, between (from the European perspective) civilized and uncivilized. Drawing on visual models encoded in and authenticated by cosmological communication in dreams and visions, Isaiah designed religious attire that he believed would be imbued with the material power of the European colonizer on the one hand, and the moral power of Nguni tradition on the other. This historical consciousness was most effectively communicated in the series of uniforms he introduced for the young female virgins (discussed in chap. 6).

The instrumentation used in *ukusina* presents an alternative mode of time-reckoning to the linearity of clock time. The even duple pulse of the drumbeats forms the base of Nazarite temporality. Overlaid with the drum is a complex interweaving of large indigenous alpine horn–like instruments that are blown in cross-rhythm to the drum. The final layer is the military bugle, sounding out intervallic progressions of thirds, fourths, and fifths. The timing of these instruments is controlled by the rhythm suggested by the feet of the dance leaders, who in turn interact with the rhythmic motives created by the singers.

The Nazarite concept of time reckoning as articulated musically through rhythm is a concept fairly evenly spread throughout the continent of Africa (Chernoff 1979). It embodies notions of rhythmic counterpoint between instruments, of cyclicity and repetition, all of which effectively disrupt the rationalization and linear flow, the sense of progression and development, intrinsic to the Western musical fabric (as experienced by Isaiah primarily through Western [Wesleyan] hymnody [Tshabalala 1983]). In Nazarite dance performance even the melodic parameters that create the sense of line in Western music and of "voice" in the Baroque harmonization style of European hymnody are subverted to become aspects of a texture that I call rhythmic heterophony.

The restructured temporality is not limited to the techniques of transformation in musical form and texture. In contrast to the fixed schedule of the liturgical service, *ukusina* can last five or six hours, with a break in the middle of the afternoon taken rather randomly (when the girls decide they are ready for food). This larger structure of ritual enactment is created in the performance of religious dance, through the accumulation of endless repetitions of small melodic and rhythmic units. Such repetition of the smaller units, the layering of one cycle of dance upon another, allows Nazarite *ukusina* to stretch ritual time to far greater limits than is possible with *inkhonzo*. In this manner repetition becomes the mechanism for the reconstitution of the Nazarite social body through corporate and ritualized dance performance.

An important distinction is made between these two ritual forms in terms of the leadership: according to biblical accounts, it is men who are the ordained leaders of religious ritual. According to members I have spoken with, in *ibandla lamaNazaretha* it is the men who lead *inkhonzo*. I suggest, however, that there is an additional reason for their leadership in this domain. It is linked to the differing approaches to temporality in both *inkhonzo* and *ukusina*, which is started by the young girls.

I have already argued that *inkhonzo* is characterized by its adherence to the fixity and rationalization of Western industrial time. In Shembe's following men have historically been engaged in migrant labor. They have therefore been the ones most exposed to capitalist time-discipline (Thompson 1967). It makes sense that the men would lead the more linear and directional religious ritual. By way of contrast, *ukusina* performances are largely dependent on the young girls. They signal the time of its beginnings and endings. I propose that the reason for this lies in the articulation of music and dance time through mechanisms of repetition and cyclicity, which are metaphors of larger patterns of reenactment. These are embodied in those domains in which young Nazarite women are believed to play a central role—the natural and biological cycles of production and reproduction.

In the Nazarite religious epistemology, all ritual time and space are considered holy, contrasting starkly to the ordering of time and space on the outside, which is defined as "matter out of place" (Douglas 1966), in terms of the traditional structures. As de Pina-Cabral writes in connection with rural Portuguese, "the destruction of community autarky is interpreted in terms of irreversible (linear) time, whilst its maintenance is dependent upon repetitive (cyclical) time." The disorder of the outside is viewed as fragmenting to the inside. It requires a reformulation to create a new sense of wholeness. This process is facilitated in *ibandla lamaNazaretha* through rituals of purification and sanctification. This transition from the outside to the inside is, however, a potential source of danger that can threaten the order of the inside if the rules of holiness are not adhered to by all those who enter. These rituals of transition and purification are thus performed in order to guarantee the safe passage of the individual, to provide the way into a restructured social order, and thereby to reincorporate that person into the holy community (Van Gennep 1960, 36–37).

In the early history of *ibandla lamaNazaretha,* these rites of purification were initially aimed at those people who did not live permanently with Shembe, but entered his religious spaces on weekends or at the end of labor contracts (which usually lasted either three or six months). For the most part these were the young men. Eventually this also included the older men who were engaged as migrant workers on the mines on the Witwatersrand, or at the harbor in Durban. The men's engagement in these labor contracts was defined as polluting because of the structural ambiguity in which it placed them as men, both in terms of the African community, and of the South African political economy. It was the men, therefore, who required the symbols of purification. This is borne out by Esther Roberts's (1936) comment that in the early days of *ibandla lamaNazaretha,* only the men were required to wear the white prayer surplice—the emblem of ritual purity.

Ibandla lamaNazaretha believe that they are more faithful to the requirements of the Bible than white Christians are because they adhere to the concept of sabbath worship. Vilakazi et al. (1986) write that Isaiah began secretly observing Saturday as the sabbath some time before it became an institutional practice in *ibandla lamaNazaretha* in the 1920s. This adherence to Saturday as the day set aside for congregational religious ritual has consistently been used by Nazarite members as proof to me that they are more biblically correct in their religious rites and practices than European Christians. They have explained, "It is written in the Bible. . . ." I suggest however, that there is an additional explanation for the change from Sunday to Saturday for sabbath worship. It pertains to the purity-pollution trope and the memorialization of the historical encounter between colonized and colonizer in the workplace.

While Isaiah clearly stressed a noninvolvement in the processes of industrial capitalism for women and girls, young men were usually the first to engage in wage labor in order to pay taxes, acquire agricultural implements, and earn sufficient income to cover the payment of *lobola* (Walker 1990, 177). Nowadays both men and women participate in the wider political economy to some degree, even though it is still strongly discouraged by religious authorities. These workers are cleansed from the defilement incurred in the workplace by participating in the sabbath rituals that encompass the three stages outlined by van Gennep (1960)—separation, purification, and reintegration.

In this regard, the rite of separation begins with the sabbath—at dusk on Friday evening (once a man or woman returns home from the workplace)—at which time a number of taboos and practices are adhered to. The central prohibition is against the lighting of fires. This rule has enormous ramifications for Nazarite members, who, for the most part, live without electricity. It means bathing in cold water, eating cold food, and drinking only cold water and beverages until dusk on Saturday.

The rite of purification and reintegration is embodied in the Nazarite liturgy and ritual performed on the sabbath, which in its participatory mode of song performance in particular (discussed in chaps. 4 and 5), serves to reconstitute the collectivity. In addition, this is the time that Shembe makes himself available for healing the afflicted. Having participated in two congregational services by dusk on the sabbath, a Nazarite member is completely cleansed of outside impurities and reintegrated into a collectivity whose cultural practices resonate with the ways of the ancestors. Now fully integrated into the religious community, the Nazarite member is free to participate in those rites and practices that symbolize complete sanctification and the highest form of religious ritual—*ukusina*, marriage, and baptism.

In chapter 1, I described my first experience of the pilgrimage to the Nazarite holy mountain called *Nhlangakaze*. At one level, the annual pilgrimage to the mountain in January must be seen as a rite of purification, particularly in terms of the requirement to climb to the top of the mountain as soon as one arrives at the site. This applies to both those who have walked for three days, and those who come to the mountain either on foot or by public transport. All those members who have not walked the forty miles put on the white prayer surplice and proceed to the top. As they go they sing stanza 3 of Hymn 173, laying flowers at fixed points on the way. This is the hymn that members perform for the duration of the pilgrimage. The text is as follows: *"Livuliwe ngubani/ lelisango/ We Mkhululi weziboshwa"* (Who opened it,/ This gate?/ Oh, Liberator of the prisoners!). This is a highly emotive hymn, sung in several other contexts of Nazarite ritual performance. A number of people told me that the hymn symbolized Isaiah's victory over the missionaries, who would not allow Nguni people to incorporate the ancestors into their religious worship.

It is the hardship of the three-day walk to the top of the mountain—the physical and spiritual apex—that cleanses members from the ritual impurity of the workplace and the residential spaces filled with violence in the form of rape, robbery, and death. When they reach the summit, Nazarite members join lines created according to divisions of age and gender, in order to give the gift of twenty cents to Shembe.[47] While some members remain on the top of the mountain in an attitude of prayer for several hours, most descend to the foot of the mountain to find their goods, brought by public or private transport.

Those who stay on the mountain for the whole month construct temporary shelters called *amadokoda*[48] on the mountainside. These are arranged in fixed residential spaces according to gender and marital status. Shembe lives closest to the top, near a cave; the men are situated a little further down, with the young girls next; finally, the married women and their young children are located toward the bottom of the hill. This month is also defined as a time of prayer, and so everyone is required to wear the white *imiNazaretha* for the duration of their sojourn on the mountain. These are washed and ironed frequently, as the pure whiteness reflects the ritual purity of the individual. Daily services are usually held on the mountainside, while sabbath services and religious dance take place at the summit.

Having walked to the mountain in January 1992, I was assured that I would be able to enter heaven when I died, along with all my family, because when I reached the heavenly gates, God would see the mountain imprinted on the soles of my feet. In fact, each time I was introduced to a Nazarite member after January 1992, it was always explained that I had walked all the way up. Thereafter, women would ask after my feet. Certainly, in early February, we went through a week or two when we all compared blisters caused from the heat and stones on the roads. This figurative imprint of the mountain on one's feet is a central trope in Nazarite belief, particularly in the structuring of women's expressive domains (see Muller 1997).

Similarly, the pilgrimage to the mountain, a journey of hardship, pain, and struggle, is iconic of the difficulty incurred in the "journey" of everyday life, a theme that resurfaces in the discussion of the Nazarite hymnal and aesthetic of song performance. In addition, I believe that this pilgrimage, which is so costly to the self, and particularly to the physical body, is emblematic of precolonial forms of body scarification and ear piercing. As Paul Bohannan (1956, 121, quoted in Keil 1979, 223) remarks for the Tiv, "scarification, one of the finest of decorations, is paid for in pain." In this sense pain might be understood as a precapitalist notion of personal cost—of expense vested in the human body rather than in monetary terms.

Finally, because this walk extends through various areas under the control of different tribal chiefs, it is important historically, as it insists on the freedom of movement of Isaiah's people.[49] Correspondence written from Isaiah and Galilee to government officials requesting permission to undertake the pilgrimage indicates that this pilgrimage was highly contested for a variety of reasons. In this regard, several mechanisms of control, particularly through bureaucratic rigmarole, were set in place to discourage the event. First, the walk requires passage through land under the jurisdiction of several different chiefs, which, in the opinion of the officials, would only create problems. Second, in the time of Galilee all Nazarite members were required by the state to be vaccinated against smallpox. This created enormous conflict with members for whom Western medicine is considered defiling. Third, the state insisted that the South African Railways had to be notified about the influx of members into the area. (This is no longer an issue, as most people arrive by minibus taxi or bus from KwaZulu, whose government is extremely sympathetic to *ibandla lamaNazaretha*.) Ultimately the pass laws[50] in the apartheid era were to set the final seal on state surveillance over African peoples' travel.

The next element of Nazarite ritual is the performance of rites of healing (CD track 7). In chapter 2 I suggested that Isaiah Shembe's renown in KwaZulu Natal from the early years of this century was established through his ability to heal his people. They in turn were converted to some form of Christian belief. I also argued that he emerged in the region at a critical historical juncture—the moment that epitomized the destruction of what had been the foundation of African society for at least two centuries—the precolonial homestead economy. In other words, there was a remarkable correspondence between bodily disorder or illness and social rupture in the construction of Isaiah's religious community, *ibandla lamaNazaretha*.

Jean Comaroff remarks for the Zionists, a parallel South African indigenous religious group, that

> the metaphors of social contradiction deployed by these cults are often rooted in the notion of the body at war with itself, or with its immediate social and material context; and desired transformations focus upon "healing" as a mode of repairing the tormented body and, through it, the oppressive social order itself. [Comaroff 1985, 9.]

This "body at war with itself" is a body that, according to the Nazarites (and Zionists), is "sick." Nevertheless, Shembe is believed to be the one person who is able to heal their afflictions. In this lies his inordinate cosmological power.

In the discussion of illness and healing in *ibandla lamaNazaretha* "sickness" is not to be viewed as an absolute empirical reality, curable only by Western medication. Instead, illness experiences and healing processes are also to be understood as socioculturally constituted (Roseman 1991, 13). In this context, Roseman creates a paradigm in which she distinguishes between "disease," the malfunctioning of the biological system, and "illness," which is defined by social and psychological criteria. Roseman's distinction between two types of bodily affliction and two kinds of healing is a useful one. Her use of terminology is less helpful. For example, the way in which she draws on the "psychological" requires some refinement as it pertains to Shembe and his followers.

In Nazarite epistemology the "psychological" as a mode of explanation for thought, emotion, human behavior, and consequent bodily disorders would be located in the realm of the cosmological, rather than in the individual subconscious as in Western exegesis.[51] This distinction between ways of knowing is important for the way in which illness and healing are interpreted, as well as in the later discussions of song, dance, and dreaming in the Nazarite membership.

In Turner's terms, illness is defined as social affliction, and healing as a "ritual of affliction" (1967, 9) that involves community rites enacted on behalf of the afflicted to supplicate the ancestors, who reside in cosmological time and space. These ancestors are also the guardians and safekeepers of Nazarite morality (the proverbial angels or holy messengers), and thus are an indispensable aspect of the creation and control of the moral boundaries of the Nazarite community. Relationships between the living and the ancestors are established and sustained through the expressive modes of song, dance, and dreams. Social relationships between Nazarite members are created and nurtured in turn through the exchange of these artifacts of emotion and religious experience.

Turner (1967, 9–16) explains that for the Ndembu of northwestern Zambia, misfortune in hunting, infertility among women, and various forms of illness are all attributed to the work of the ancestors. In the Nazarite context, I suggest that illness is not only caused by the afflicting actions of the ancestors, but extends to the totality of the South African political economy and the state itself. Illness or bodily disorder is caused by "unharnessed pollution," which is a social condition manifest in the individual body (Ong 1988).

In the South African context, pollution is unleashed in all processes of social rupture, dislocation, and subsequent alienation. Pollution, defilement, disorder, and sinfulness are all metaphors for those processes that violate and transgress the moral boundaries of African societies. Historically, these processes have been integrally linked with colonization and the marginalization of the African peoples through the formation of the modern industrial capitalist state. More recently, bodily disorder has been integrally linked to daily violence, theft, and bodily violation, particularly of the female membership of *ibandla lamaNazaretha*.

Healing and religious conversion are the mechanisms of transformation and empowerment for Nazarite members. These processes have caused a "psychomoral reorganization, new social alignments and altered relationships within the spirit world" (Cucchiari 1988). Sanctification as the goal of *ibandla lamaNazaretha* enables members to reconstitute the moral bounds of their fragmented social world.

One further mechanism of ritual purification is that of baptism by immersion. While the ritual strongly resembles the form of baptism in the Christian mission, the Nazarite meanings ascribed to it diverge from that of the Christian church. This is best illustrated by a story I was told by Mrs. Manqele from KwaMashu. She explained to me (August 1991) that everything she did happened first to her in a dream. In other words, Shembe appeared to her and instructed her, and she acted upon these instructions. Baptism was no exception.

> Since that day, I follow him. And when it's the time of baptism, I must go to the water. And he came again to me. "Now you must go to the baptism."

I asked her, "Does he come to you in a dream? What was the dream like? How did he look?"

> First, I was in the *kombi*, with people from Durban, from my work. And when you passed Springfield area, then the bird, the brown big bird, was on the end. And we came out [of] the *kombi*, and bow our knees down. And he said to me—the bird, not him—it was halfway. And he said to me, "You know all these people, those who died. They killed them or [they died] by accident. It's not easy [for them] to go to heaven, to see God. Because first their family must do everything to ask for, and excuse for to clean their ways."
> And he explained [to] me about the rivers. He said, "You see the rivers when they go to the sea, it's not easy, but they must be clean." So, even us, when they shoot us, or they kill us or do anything to us, it's not easy. To see God, they must do something. And even the people in heaven, they must do something that side. . . . And after that he said, "You are going to go to the, you must be ready to go to the river, to get the baptize. They must baptize you. You are the full member of the Nazareth now."[52]

Mrs. Manqele's account establishes a complex discourse on the intersection of religious ritual and belief in the everyday experiences of vulnerability, violation, and even death for a woman in KwaZulu Natal. From her account, I suggest that at its most obvious level, baptism effects the cleansing of the body through immersion in water. Such cleansing ensures the safe passage of a body to heaven in the event of sudden death. Entry into heaven is also facilitated by Mrs. Manqele's full membership in the earthly community of *ibandla lamaNazaretha*. In the context detailed by the dream narrative, baptism also empowers the weak and vulnerable human body against the unpredictable forces of violation and death. Baptism effectively armors the body against the forces of daily violence over which this woman has no control, and the absolute anxiety and fear that encompasses her body in the face of imminent death. The fear of death is located in the *kombi*—a minibus taxi. While these taxis have mobilized black South Africans in an extraordinary manner through the 1980s, they have also been the sites for thousands of deaths—through road accidents and being held at gunpoint. Clearly in a moment of anxiety while riding in the taxi Mrs. Manqele had this vision—of Shembe appearing as a large brown bird, to warn her about the need for baptism.

There is a remarkable blurring of boundaries in this account. This happens between waking and dream reality, between heaven and earth (with the bird mediating between the two domains—"halfway"), and even in the act of kneeling. In the latter instance, this act of loyalty to a king or chief, where the leader traditionally provided protection to his subjects, is confused with kneeling to the imaginary person who was perhaps brandishing the power of life and death in the form of a gun—holding up the taxi driver. In other words, there is confusion over the feelings evoked in the body posture, first that of loyalty, which in Mrs. Manqele's case is replaced with fear of death. Thus a single body posture elicits opposite consequences—respect or violation. Baptism signals full membership in the community of *ibandla lamaNazaretha*—a membership that affords a cleansing from moral impurity and the protection of the body from its own frailty in a context where the fear of death and violence constantly haunts ordinary women such as Mrs. Manqele.

The final element of ritual practice involves the sermons preached by individual Nazarite members. As Mr. Hlatswayo's account suggests, in the Nazarite religious epistemology, personal dream narratives frequently form the substance of a member's "sermon." These are preached by the male followers in the context of *inkhonzo*, or by the men and women at the meetings of *ama23* and *ama14*, their respective monthly meetings. In this context, dream narratives, like hymn texts, constitute what Foucault (1980) calls a mechanism of truth claiming. Nazarites clearly view the experiences encoded in dreams and visions as holding equivalent weight to waking reality, and as embodying some notion of Nazarite cultural reality and truth.

Dreams and visions are held to be both true and powerful because they transgress the boundaries of social order at several levels (Douglas 1966). They create disjuncture in the circumscription of space—connecting the ordinary with the extraordinary. They cause rupture in the flow of time—connecting the past with the present by juxtaposing the living and the dead, and halting the normal passage of everyday time. Dreams occur when an individual is asleep—when the body is in its most antisocial state. Their occurrence cannot be predicted; therefore, they cannot be harnessed or controlled. The lack of order in their appearance is considered both dangerous and powerful. In this regard, communities such as the Nazarites create ritualized spaces in which the "out-of-placeness" of dream matter can be given form and domesticated. Thus the dream, which originates in the body, is stored in the memory of the individual, and given external form through its construction as a "sermon"—the quintessential format for the telling of religious truth.

The Nazarite dream template includes a range of ways in which dreams function in the lives of individuals and the community as a whole. These parallel research done with other cultural groups.[53] Dreams are interwoven into the history of *ibandla lamaNazaretha* and have intervened in the life of Isaiah as a means of religious calling (Reynolds 1992 for Zezuru), instructions about succession to religious office (Ray 1992 for the Igbo), patterns for religious symbols, such as uniforms, to communicate with the ancestors (Shaw 1992 for Temne), and guidelines for creative process, such as song and dance composition (Dilley 1992 on Tukulor weavers). Among the Nazarite membership, dreams are instructive and used in a modified form of divination (Shaw 1992; Jedrej 1992).[54] In other words, Nazarite dreaming is best explained as containing messages,

> but these are not communications from different localities within the architecture of the dreamer's personality [as is the case with post-Freudian psychoanalysis] but communications from components of a cosmology in which the dreamer is situated. [Jedrej 1992, 111.]

Like Jedrej's description of dreaming among the Ingessana of Sudan, the Nazarite situation suggests that these dreams are not simply the characteristic precolonial communication with the ancestral realm, and linked to individual action within Nazarite religious life. Instead, dreams frequently make explicit reference to relationships of power and subordination embedded in both the history and everyday experiences of Nazarite members with the wider South African political economy (see chap. 8).

Ritual Attire

Paul Connerton (1989, 10) discusses the transformation of styles of clothing during the revolutionary period in France (ca. 1789), suggesting that the changes reflected a temporary liberation from the practices of the established social order. In doing so, the French attempted to mark a new set of "typical" bodily practices. Similarly, the infusion of uniforms into Nazarite ritual life and religious worship has carried with it a new vision of social order and bodily practice. These uniforms are ascribed enormous value in the Nazarite community in a number of ways: as symbols of purification and resistance to outside defilement, as metaphors of civilization, as protective wraps in the face of ongoing township violence, and as markers of identity.

As with the two types of religious worship, there are two separate uniforms that are central to the construction of Nazarite identity: the white prayer gown, called *imiNazaretha,* which is worn by all members while they are on Nazarite space and not dancing; and the attire for *ukusina,* which reflects a hybrid composite of more traditional African styles. Both of the uniforms indicate differences of age and gender, although in the first instance it is only in headgear that these categories are distinguishable, while in the second, it is the entire covering of the body that varies. Both uniforms also indicate the purified body. In the case of *ukusina,* a member may not participate unless she or he has adhered to rules of fasting, sexual abstinence, and so forth. Isaiah introduced similar regulations pertaining to *imiNazaretha.* The difference between the uniform for *inkhonzo* and that for *ukusina* lies in the inclusiveness of the uniform. By requiring the removal of shoes at the gate, Shembe eliminated personal displays of social differentiation. In the use of white, which traditionally signified purity, Shembe also effectively neutralized the physical body from its references to the dirt, defilement, and ritual impurity associated with all matter outside of Nazarite space. The only members who do not wear white prayer gowns are the male leaders—*abavangeli*—who are closest to Shembe. They wear either blue or green gowns.

Clothing and uniforms and what they signify, however, have not gone uncontested in the history of the church. Esther Roberts (1936) describes how Shembe allowed the older generations in the early 1930s to wear traditional attire, but expected the younger generation would prefer Western clothing. It would seem that initially, he even encouraged his followers to wear Western dress, for surely this kind of clothing reflected "civilized" society. But there are incidental references to changes in the preferred attire of Nazarite members. These coincide with variations in wider ideological positioning, and the consequent renegotiation and shaping of Nazarite identity. At one point this transformation involved the rejection of Western dress as the embodiment of civilization. We find in the catechism that in 1942, en route to the mountain of *Nhlangakaze,* members were instructed that no sandals, shirts, or trousers were to be worn in Nazarite ritual any longer. All members were to wear the white prayer gown.

In a similar narrative to that told by the woman who wanted to be baptized, one woman described in a meeting of *ama14* at *Vula Masango* how wearing her *ifortini,* the white fabric band usually wrapped around the topknot to indicate membership, afforded protection for both herself and fellow passengers. She said:

> Last year, when we were traveling in a van from here at *Vula Masango* to *Ebuhleni,* I had taken off my *inhloko*[55] and my *14* for the head

after church. And when we were in the van, a thought came to me. "Why did I take off my *14?*" Eh, I just took it but I didn't put back *inhloko*. I just put back the *14*. When I just finish, it was hardly a minute, when I finished putting it back on my head. A speeding car came straight to the side of our van and he smashed it. The two cars were badly smashed. People thought that everyone was supposed to come out [dead] from the car. But, instead of corpses coming out, we came out with not even a single minor injury. But the car was all smashed up. We were supposed to have died, but because of Shembe we didn't.

As I was leaving Dube Temple in Soweto in April 1992, I was advised by the members there to keep the *imiNazaretha* on my body until my father and I were safely out of Soweto, where Dube Temple is located. It was understood that this would keep us safe in a climate of extreme violence.

I was also told, however, that wearing the women's topknot or *inhloko* in public put women in danger, as this traditional item of clothing was felt to represent "Zuluness" associated with membership in the Zulu cultural organization and the Zulu nationalist Inkatha Freedom Party. In the townships around the city of Johannesburg, as well as in the province of KwaZulu Natal, membership in one political group, or the wearing of apparel that even suggests links to a party, can provide reason for an opposition group to kill.

Conclusion

In this chapter I have discussed the parameters of the sacred space and practice in which Isaiah Shembe reconstituted a sense of community among Nguni traditionalists in KwaZulu Natal. In concluding this chapter I suggest there are several reasons for Isaiah's formulation of his community through a discourse of the sacred, rather than through a more explicitly political or revolutionary manifesto. When Isaiah was faced with uncontrollable social rupture and the fragmentation of his people in the region, the sacred domain enabled him to protect from loss some of those cultural forms that had traditionally constituted cultural power and collective identity. The sacred created the sense of wholeness through holiness (Douglas 1966, 51), of "permanence in change" (Weiner 1992, 103). The sacred also circumscribed places of shelter and sanctuary. It subdued violence both within and between communities (Girard 1972). This community became a home for the socially displaced—a place of warmth, nurturance, surrogate kinship, and protection.

FOUR

Nazarite Hymns: Indigenizing Sacred Song

Kwafika izazi	There came the wise ones
Ziphuma empumalanga	Coming from the east
Zathi uphi lawo	They said, "Where is the one
Oyi Nkosi yaba Juda?	Who is the King of the Jews?"
	Chorus
Kunjaloke namhlanje	It is like that today
Emagqumeni as'Ohlange.	On the hills of Ohlange.
Bafika bathi, yebo	They came and said, "Yes,
Kulotshiwe kanjalo	It is written like that,
Nawe Kuphakama	'Even you, Kuphakama,
Masquma as'Ohlange;	Hills of Ohlange;
Awusiye omnciyane	You are not the smallest
Kunababusi bakwa Juda	Of the rulers of Juda;
Kuyakuvela kuwe	From you shall emerge
AbaProfithi	The Prophets
Abaya kusindisa	Who will redeem
Umuzi was'Ohlange.	The village of Ohlange.'"
(Hlab. 34/1,4,5)	(Hymn 34/1,4,5)

Nazarite myth contends that when Isaiah Shembe was called by God in a dream to minister to the Nguni traditionalists of KwaZulu Natal, he recognized the people in his dream by the style of their singing and bodily attire. One version of this narrative was recounted to me by Nazarite member Cinikile Mazibuko in January 1992. We were on the mountain of *Nhlangakaze*, inside Cinikile's *dokoda*, when she explained:

> First he used to see nice things, there were those wonderful things that say, "Here is God, you must follow him." And he say[s], "No, that is not God." Till [in] the end, he just felt there is something, a nice smell of something, smelling like flowers. Whatever it was [it] was smelling like that. And he said, "Here is God." . . . Then he

heard voices singing, you know, the friends. Then he just heard some people were just singing so softly, and they were singing Zulu songs. But songs that have got no notes, you see. Different hymns, you know. Different styles. He was listening, you see. And he just feel there was something smelling very nice. Then there came, then he saw old men dressed in skins. It was after . . . he saw those old men coming dressed in skins [that] he heard a voice saying, "Those are the people to go and preach the word of God to . . . *Ja*, it was somewhere in Zululand. [Cinikile Mazibuko, pers. comm., January 1992.]

Cinikile Mazibuko's poetic account correlates the emergent moment of Shembe's ministry with a particular style of song performance—the songs of friends that were different and without notes (not written down or perhaps without fixed pitch or fixed melody)[1]—and bodily cover—the skins worn by old Nguni men. These songs were not religious songs in the style of the Christian mission as Isaiah may have learned them from the Wesleyans and African Baptists, but were more closely aligned with the performance practices of Nguni oral tradition. Isaiah's mission was clearly to preach to and heal the people of KwaZulu Natal, by drawing on expressive forms considered sacred and inalienable to that community. As the hymn text cited above suggests, and Mthethwa (in Vilakazi et al. 1986, chap. 9) argues, these expressive forms were selectively interwoven with the hymns and biblical texts of the Protestant mission to create a style of song and dance performance peculiar to *ibandlu lamaNazaretha*. In KwaZulu Natal, these hymns are popularly known as *izihlabelelo kwa-kwaShembe* (the hymns of the place of Shembe).

Isaiah Shembe was not the first black South African who desired to articulate Christianity within his own cultural frame. In 1816, Xhosa-speaking Ntsikana Gaba (died 1821), the first "Bantu Prophet," was converted to Christianity, and while he gave up traditional dance and body decoration, his conversion "reflected the need to fuse Xhosa belief with Christianity in order to construct a world view that could accommodate military defeat and colonization by Europeans" (Coplan 1985, 33). Ntsikana left four hymns that were transcribed into solfege and published by John Knox Bokwe in 1884. These continue to be transmitted orally as both religious and wedding songs in contemporary Xhosa-speaking communities (Dargie 1982).

Several other church leaders are remembered for the hymns they wrote. The first ordained Presbyterian African minister, Tiyo Soga (1829–71),[2] and his successor Gqoba (Coplan 1985, 29–30) composed hymns for their more European-fashioned congregations. John Knox Bokwe (also Presbyterian), the Xhosa minister and composer, wrote the biography of Ntsikana that contains Ntsikana's hymns. Bokwe also composed his own hymns, many of which were published by the Lovedale Press (Dargie 1982). Nehemiah Tile, founder of the Ethiopian church in 1884, composed hymns for his followers (Chirenje 1987, 23). Finally, John Dube, a contemporary of Isaiah Shembe, was a composer, though he is better known for his secular compositions.[3]

By the latter decades of the nineteenth century, the small mission-educated black elite in South Africa had begun to realize the need to construct a self-image that was not exclusively based on European/Western models (Coplan 1985, 30). Coinciding with rapid urbanization, the indigenization of mission Christianity, and the emergence of Zionist and Ethiopianist religious movements,[4] many black South Africans began to look elsewhere for more appropriate "African- derived" guidelines. In this historical context, a strong relationship was established between African-American performance and the Ethiopianist movement in South Africa. (*Ibandla lamaNazaretha* is categorized as Ethiopianist.) Erlmann (1991) details the historical complexities of the links between African-Americans and Ethiopianism in South Africa. He argues that the jubilee songs and spirituals performed by the Virginia Jubilee Singers (an African-American group led by Orpheus McAdoo that visited South Africa several times between 1890 and 1898) were enthusiastically promoted by senior Ethiopian church officials in South Africa. Some of these Ethiopianists formed their own African Jubilee Singers ensemble. As a result,

> church leaders soon also set out to reshape the Afro-American idiom and to mold it into a new African church hymnody that was relatively free of European influences. Sinamela [choir leader] composed a series of hymns including "Kgoshi Sekukuni," a hymn which blended Afro-American material with traditional Sepedi praise poetry. . . . Eventually some black students . . . among them Jacobus Xaba and J. Z. Tantsi, translated American jubilee hymns into the vernacular. [Erlmann 1991, 49.]

Isaiah Shembe was therefore one of a number of religious leaders who engaged in the cultural translation of transatlantic form and style[5] into a more clearly identifiable genre of South African religious hymnody.[6]

Isaiah Shembe seems, however, to have been the first black South

African to create a large corpus of his own religious poetry and songs in the Zulu language. His hymn repertory has been examined and commented upon by a number of scholars in a variety of ways. Sundkler (1961 [1948]; 1976) draws on hymn texts as a means of uncovering the central tenets of Isaiah's indigenized belief system. Similarly, Oosthuizen's controversial work (1967) considers the hymnal as the lens through which to view Nazarite theology.[7] Vilakazi et al. (1986) respond to Oosthuizen's phenomenological interpretation of these hymns in a single chapter on Isaiah's hymns, by providing some of the indigenous cultural data lacking in Oosthuizen's work.

Similarly, Tshabalala (1983) reconsiders Isaiah's hymns in the light of Oosthuizen's work, and his own view of the Wesleyan influence on the hymnal and other aspects of Nazarite ritual. Mthethwa (in Muller 1999b, forthcoming) draws on the work of Oosthuizen and Tshabalala as well as his own understanding of the hymns. His knowledge is derived from membership in the community, and the transcriptions of the hymns he made in the early 1980s to provide organ accompaniment for Nazarite congregational singing. The strength of Mthethwa's work, in my opinion, is his accounting for the re-Africanization of the European and American mission hymnody into a repertory of song consistent in its stylistic principles with that of Nguni tradition.

In contrast to Mthethwa's insider knowledge of hymn practices, Brown (1995) draws together the secondary writings of other scholars on Shembe's hymns. His concern is "to direct attention to the hymns of Isaiah Shembe as literary texts" (ibid., 71). Like Oosthuizen's (1967), Brown's material is limited in its usefulness because it lacks a Nazarite perspective on the poetics of the texts and the circulation of meanings attached to these hymns. Despite Brown's physical proximity to the Nazarites, like so many literary critics, he fails to create a dialogue with the community by gathering something of the wide litany of meanings attributed to such texts. This kind of move would have provided a more richly textured reading of Shembe's hymns as popular forms, a central element in Brown's project.

In this chapter, I examine the early history of the sacred repertory of Nazarite song. In the first part, I discuss Nazarite beliefs about the composition of these songs by Isaiah and Galilee Shembe and the close ties to female cosmological beings; how Isaiah integrated local cultural memory with the powers vested in mission hymn repertories; and the process by which these new songs were constituted as sacred and inalienable to *ibandla lamaNazaretha*. In the second part I focus on the poetics of *izihla-*

belelo zamaNazaretha; in the third I explain how the hymn compositions were fixed as a repertory through the making and printing of an official Nazarite book of hymns and liturgy. Last, I examine this repertory as it is performed in the context of married women's religious dance or *ukusina/ umgido.* I suggest that the considerable disjuncture between the forms of the written and performed words of Nazarite hymns that characterizes this repertory might provide a contemporary example of what Gates (1988, chap. 4) terms the trope of the "talking book." In the Nazarite context, we might extend the trope to the hymnal by referring to it as the "singing and dancing book."

Composing *IziHlabelelo zamaNazaretha* (The Hymns of the Nazaretha)

It is not known exactly how many hymns church founder Isaiah Shembe composed for his community in his lifetime. Throughout his life, much of the new religious song repertory was transmitted through oral means only. On occasion, individual followers either hand-wrote or typed selections of Shembe's hymns, prayers, and sermons. A glimpse of the early history of the Nazarite hymn repertory is outlined by Galilee Shembe in the preface to the hymnal. He writes that the opening hymn was sung by children journeying with Isaiah in 1910, the year when he first came to KwaZulu Natal. The second came to him in 1913 when he climbed the mountain of *Nhlangakaze.* Between 1914 and 1919 no hymns were composed, but in 1920, Isaiah began to create hymns and prayers prolifically. Mthethwa (in Vilakazi et al. 1986) cautions that the numerical order of hymns in the hymnal cannot be used to indicate chronological compositional sequence. For example, older church members have told Mthethwa that they remembered Isaiah singing Hymn 173 (*Sidedele Singene*) to musical bow accompaniment as early as 1916. Its delayed position in the hymnal might suggest a later date of composition. Clues to individual dates of composition are found written above a few hymns in the published hymnal; other hymns are referred to in personal recollections and sermons, sometimes with specific dates.

Galilee adds in the preface that "[t]he majority of these hymns came with messengers of heaven. In most cases [Isaiah] was awake and not asleep" (G. Shembe 1940, v). Dreams and visions in which heavenly messengers appeared were clearly the media through which both Isaiah and Galilee Shembe received the words, melodies, and rhythms of what was eventually collated into a book called *IziHlabelelo zamaNazaretha,* the official hymns of the Nazarites. Many of these dream narratives have become central to Nazarite sacred lore. They certainly contributed to the credentials of the Shembe lineage as spiritual leaders of the community (Vilakazi et al. 1986, 130).

Virgin girls played a critical role in this process of transformation and reinvention of the past through dreams, visions, and song composition. Sundkler describes the compositional process, as it was explained to him by Galilee Shembe. He writes that

> [Isaiah] would hear a woman's voice, often a girl's voice, singing new and unexpected words. He could not see her, but as he woke up from a dream or walked along the path in Zululand, meditating, he heard that small voice, that clear voice, which gave him a new hymn. He had to write down the new words, while humming and singing the tune which was born *with* the words. [Sundkler 1976, 186, my emphasis.]

There are two additional elements in the production of this repertory of song discussed by Sundkler (ibid., 186–90). The first is the path, and the second is the stress on rhythm as constituting the most important and memorable musical parameter in the creation of the songs. Mthethwa (1990) comments that in Zulu thinking, the melody of a Zulu song is likened to a path. In other words, walking along a physical path becomes iconic of both the dream that facilitates a pathway to the cosmology and results in the birth of song, and the melody of religious song, which enables cosmological communication.[8]

In terms of rhythm, Sundkler writes about Isaiah's conception of a hymn:

> With Is[aiah] Shembe it was the rhythm that moved in him even while he was sleeping; it was the rhythm that first came to the surface and had to be caught and written down. This rhythm expressed itself in two or three words to be sung to the accompaniment of the beat of drums, and the feet of the dancing faithful. Here he found the chorus, and he built the hymn on this foundation. . . . Waking up from his sleep, he still carried within him the rhythm of what he had heard in the dream-dimension of life. [Ibid., 187.]

In contrast to the quite mythical image-centered space of Isaiah's song compositions, Galilee, the son educated at the College of Fort Hare and a schoolteacher by profession until he succeeded his father as church leader, recalled that his visions of song composition came in the form of a chalkboard on which the words of the songs were written. While both men immediately translated the imagistic experiences into written form, Isaiah focused on the sonic dimension as he recalled the rhythmic motive of words and created a larger text from the rhythmic core, while Galilee remembered the visual image of the entire written text, and simply wrote it down.

This distinction between the two modes of conception—the one as auditory and the other as visual—may well account for the differences in the style of the two composers as embodied in the hymn texts. In this regard, Sundkler (ibid., 189) remarks on the differences in poetic sensitivity in Hymn 103 (by Isaiah) and Hymn 243 (published after Isaiah's death). He writes that

> one cannot but notice that Isaiah Shembe had much too delicate and sophisticated a sense of the Zulu language to allow such a combination of sounds. . . . It reminds one too forcibly of European hymn-carpentry in Zulu churches![9] [Ibid.]

Similarly, Bongani Mthethwa frequently commented to me about the simplicity of Galilee's poetic texts compared with those of Isaiah. He attributed the complexity to Isaiah's use of vocables for rhythmic rather than semantic purposes in hymn performance; the mix of Xhosa and Zulu languages in the text, which paralleled the language mix used by missionaries when they translated the Bible; and Isaiah's common incorporation of "deep" Zulu words. Ultimately, as I demonstrate in the discussion of singing for women's religious dance, it is Isaiah's stress on rhythmic play and complexity that supersedes textual precision in Nazarite performance practice.

The compositional process may have been fairly consistent for the Nazarite hymn repertory. Mthethwa (in Vilakazi et al. 1986, chap. 9) explains that there are three distinct kinds of melodies used in the composition of this repertory: those that drew on the Western mission repertory (one or two are marked in the hymnal as being songs of the Wesleyans),[10] those that modify older Zulu *amahubo* and *isigekle* repertory, and those that Mthethwa describes as the more syncretic "Shembe-style" melody. Most of the hymns were composed using the Western mission and Shembe-style melodies; only a small number articulate the older historical tunes. These are the hymns that are used for the most sacred of Nazarite rituals—religious dance, called *ukusina* or *umgido* and introduced to *ibandla lamaNazaretha* in the 1920s.

There is a small twist in the early history of Nazarite song composition.

While all hymns are believed to have been given to Isaiah and Galilee Shembe through the medium of heavenly messengers, there are three hymns that generated controversy in the early years of *ibandla lama-Nazaretha*. These are the songs rumored to have been composed by Isaiah Shembe after he "rose from the dead." Sundkler (1948) dismisses the rumors, explaining that these three hymns were in fact given by Isaiah Shembe to three women followers of Shembe, again through the media of dreams and visions soon after his death in 1935. Rising from the dead in the New Testament sense occurs within the frame of a dreamlike reality in the Nazarite epistemology. Isaiah has thus been transformed from earthly conduit of heavenly female voices, to heavenly messenger for earthly female conduits, an intriguing play with gender reversal.

Because the production of song for ritual performance is believed by Nguni traditionalists to be given by the ancestors, in the form of sonic and visual images through the media of dreams and visions, its performance is considered holy and should never be altered. Each enactment is expected, therefore, to replicate the original patterns given by the ancestors. In this regard, Vilakazi et al. (1986, 140) write that

> Isaiah Shembe did not see himself as a composer but rather pointed out that each hymn was brought to him by different heavenly messengers. A strong belief within the Nazareth Church, is that whenever a hymn is sung, the original unseen heavenly messenger who delivered the hymn, becomes pleased. He[11] listens rather intently to the singing, and becomes offended if the singers do not sing all the stanzas, or if they do not sing the hymn correctly. We think this belief has gone a long way to preserving [*sic*] these hymns.

This immutability of the Nazarite repertory is coterminous with its sacralization by the Nazarite community, and its value as an inalienable cultural possession. There are, therefore, at least two aspects of the hymn repertory created by Isaiah and Galilee Shembe and its performance practice that protect it from adulteration: the Nazarite belief that it is the embodiment of the word of the ancestors, or, in the Christian mission terms, the word of God, and the distinguishing element of "rhythm" in its rendition. In this regard, one woman told me that rhythm was what she liked most about Shembe's hymns. To learn the rhythm, however, took a long time. When I asked the woman if she would perform one of the hymns for me, she said she could not because she had been a member for only a short time (three or four years)! In direct opposition to the musical aesthetic of mission hymnody, which prized melody and harmony above all else, rhythm is reclaimed in *ibandla lamaNazaretha* as the most sacred, and certainly the most "African," performative element in *izihlabelelo zamaNazaretha.*

Officially, there is, therefore, no new composition of *izihlabelelo zamaNazaretha* in *ibandla lamaNazaretha.* Instead, individual members conventionally construct provinces of meaning through the performance of Shembe's songs, which become intertwined in the interpretive fabric of everyday existence for each member. In this regard, the ancestral sounds of such traditional performance practice are thought to imbue the faithful with spiritual power—they become an "affecting presence" (Armstrong 1977) for every member. The words of the texts too, as the holy utterances of the Nazarite God, are vessels of ancestral force, which in their repetition by Nazarite members become empowering and enabling media. In the larger politics of race and gender, what is significant about song composition in this community is that the mediation between, and communication with, the earth and the cosmology is effected through the voices of angelic female figures.

Standardizing the Repertory into Book Form

> [W]hat is important here is . . . [that] what is in effect obtained through the purchase of . . . books is the magic of the printed word as print has acquired this power in the exercise of colonial domination with its fetishization of print, as in the Bible and the law. . . . The book of the Church, nature as the book of the Lord, the books of law, writing, paper atop official paper—these leak magic into the hands of the people they dominate. The symbol of all that is civilized, Christian, and the state itself, writing and books create their counterpoint in the magic books sold in the marketplaces by wandering Indian herbalists. . . . [Taussig 1986, 262–64.]

A powerful subtext runs through the entire fabric of Nazarite religious life and ritual, and indeed through Isaiah's creation of this community. It is located in the clash and accommodation between domains of literacy and orality as they pertain to the formation and sustenance of Nazarite ritual and performance. As it is for the Indians in Taussig's work, this clash embodies the historical contest between the power of the colonizer and the resistance of the colonized in South Africa. To this end, Jeff Guy (1991, 398) remarks that the issue of imperial conquest is synonymous with the advent of the written word in that country.

Although semiliterate for most of his life, Isaiah Shembe clearly understood the authority and power vested in the written word, particularly in his interactions with the South African state in its various forms through his life. He acquired permission for his annual pilgrimage to *Nhlangakaze* through letters; legal documents were written to Isaiah and by his own lawyers to secure land purchases; and the written word of God as contained in the mission Bible carried with it the authority to both validate religious experience and invalidate other forms of ritual performance previously modeled on traditional cultural principles located in the body.

Ritual, religious experience, and performance were therefore quickly formalized into written texts, transforming the transience of performance sounds into the fixity and permanence of the transcribed word (Guy 1991, 411). Isaiah employed a scribe or archivist, Mr. Petrus Dhlomo, whose job it was to record the religious experiences of men and women who had been healed by Isaiah. (Petrus told me that he was himself initially only partially literate, but was instructed by Isaiah to learn to read and write by reading both the Bible and the newspaper.)[12] Isaiah also had a follower write down his dream experiences, a process that facilitated his own sermons, prayers, and song composition (Sundkler 1976). Galilee Shembe had the hymns and liturgical cycles formalized and printed into a hymnal as early as 1940. Prior to this, each member was provided with an individually inscribed collection of hymn and miracle narratives that are no longer in use (Gunner 1987).[13]

There are two official printed documents currently utilized in *ibandla lumaNazaretha* that function as literary monuments to the historical experiences of the followers of Shembe. These are the hymnal called *Izihlabelelo zamaNazaretha* (Nazarite Hymns), and the church catechism, entitled *Nazareth Baptist Church Umngcwabo* (NBC Burial/Interment). Though the latter functions and has been translated as *Catechism*, this word does not really reflect the translation of the term *umngcwabo*, which literally means funeral or interment. Perhaps it is no coincidence that the document opens with funeral rites. While these are the rites used for burying the dead, they may also signify the symbolic passage by Nazarite members from death, or the outside, into *Ekuphakameni*, or the "heaven" created by Isaiah, both on the earth and in life after death. In the next section I demonstrate that the hymns are certainly to be understood as laments over the loss of land and the death of African communities in this century in South Africa.

It is the hymnal, however, that contains the best-known and loved words of the Nazarite prophet. This small black book is either carefully wrapped in a towel or prayer mat or placed in a man's briefcase. In both instances, the encased hymnal is faithfully carried to religious services by all Nazarite members—regardless of whether they are able to read or not. The printed hymnal of *ibandla lamaNazaretha* contains 242 hymns, with music and text composed predominantly by Isaiah—the last 22 were written by Galilee between 1938 and 1948. The hymnal was initially published by W. H. Shepherd in Durban in 1940, in a shorter (220-hymn) version. The most commonly used edition (still dated 1940) contains a title page, a note from Galilee, a photograph of Isaiah (taken by Esther Roberts in 1936), an index of hymns, the liturgies for morning, evening, and sabbath services, and the full corpus of 242 hymn texts. (At one stage there were 243 hymns. There are also several hymns believed to have been composed by Isaiah that have not been included in the official hymnal.)

As a printed visual image, the 1940 version of the Nazarite hymnal *Iz-iHlabelelo ZamaNazaretha* strongly resembles the textual layout of a European or American Christian hymnal. There are 242 hymns in the most recent publication of the book, all of which are organized into a verse-refrain or verse-only structure. The refrains are occasionally incorporated into the verse-only format, either at the beginning or the end of the stanza. Refrains are also indicated as the "chorus" between stanzas. Thereafter, the hymnal diverges from its Euro-American model.[14] Significantly, the music was not transcribed in the hymnal at all. Publishing texts without musical notation was quite common among Euro-American missions in South Africa. Even though the missions used the tonic solfa system for teaching choral groups Western "classical" music, to my knowledge, most of the hymnals contained written texts only. One exception is the recent edition of the Catholic Book of Prayers and Hymns (*Incwadi Yemikhuleko namaCulo* [Mngoma 1991]), which has tunes written in tonic solfa. This contrasts with the common use of tune books among mission communities in Hawaii, for example (Stillman 1996). The first transcriptions of the Nazarite hymn repertory were made by church organist Bongani Mthethwa in preparation for introducing organ accompaniment into *inkhonzo* worship in the late 1980s.

For the most part, however, the Nazarite song repertory is passed on through oral performance only, for a number of reasons. First, the hymn performance practice is extremely complex, requiring sophisticated improvisational skills and a deep understanding of African rhythm. It is therefore not easily transcribed. Second, it is a performance practice that, in its reliance upon the participation of all members to create the total sense of rhythm and musical fabric, reconstitutes a sense of community. In this dependence on the total participation of all people is embodied its treasure for the community, and its value as an "inalienable possession." A written transcription could never fully represent the rhythm, timbre, and density of its musical texture. Furthermore, as I suggested above, the inalienability of the hymn repertory—its value as a sacred artifact—is partly embedded in the amount of time it takes a member to learn how to sing it in the Nazarite style.

Hymn Texts and Poetics

I have previously suggested that Isaiah Shembe (and his successors) established his religious community by constructing a regime of cultural truth in opposition to the hegemonic rule of the South African state in its various guises through the twentieth century. Shembe fashioned a specific identity for *ibandla lamaNazaretha* by reimagining religious discourses as "structures of feeling" (Williams in Rosaldo 1993 [1989], 106). These became formal vehicles for individual and collective articulation of a historical and political consciousness shaped by contemporary South African history and politics.

Perhaps the most important of these poetic structures is his repertory of sacred song, which, following Bongani Mthethwa (pers. comm., May 1991), I have equated with the English word *hymn*. This is not an entirely accurate translation. The noun *isihlabelelo* (pl. *izihlabelelo*) has two meanings in the Zulu language. It refers to the Psalms of David found in the Old Testament of the Bible, and it is the word for songs from childhood composed by mothers for their children. These are sung in infancy, at the time of the first menstruation, and at the marriage of the child. The verb *hlabelela* refers to singing both of birds and of people in chorus, or reciting. The words for hymn specifically are *iculo* (hymn, chant, or song) and *ihubo* (ceremonial, tribal, or regimental song or hymn). (I have drawn all these definitions from the *English–Zulu, Zulu–English Dictionary,* Doke et al. 1990). Isaiah and Galilee Shembe exploited each of these ideas pertaining to song performance and integrated them quite freely into their new repertory of sacred song.

As a religious and cosmologically connected discourse, Isaiah's hymns in printed form look like hymns but are in content more closely aligned with the biblical Psalms. In the spirit of the Psalms, Isaiah's texts are both individual monologues to God and exhortations to the people of the earth to worship God. The contents of these Psalm texts range from personal

lamentations focused on the poverty and struggle of the soul to outpourings of joy and thanksgiving. In addition to this, reference is made to the
poor, the destitute, the oppressed, and the enemies of the believers. In a
quite remarkable manner, these texts embody experiences and utterances
that strongly parallel those of Isaiah. I suggest, therefore, that the Psalms
provided him with a model for his own more indigenized poetry. Galilee's
hymns are similar in content, though far easier to understand.

While the biblical Psalms were one model of religious poetry, the poetic
techniques employed by Isaiah in structuring his texts resemble those of
the traditional Zulu praise-poets/singers rather than those of Western
hymn writers. Thus, for example, rhyming line endings, so common in
translations of European hymns in South African vernaculars, are seldom used. For example, the Zulu translation (Hymn 156 in the United
Church of Christ hymnal) reads as follows: "Baba wethu bavu*mele*/ Laba
abaphambi kw*akho*/ Ubavume uba*mkele*/ Bona bab'abantu b*akho*." This
kind of crude rhyming line ending is seldom found in *izihlabelelo zamaNazaretha*. Instead, poetic coherence and aesthetic value are created
through a variety of techniques, such as repetition, lexical and semantic
parallelism, textual elision, and allusion (Okpewho 1992, 70–104). These
techniques are more consistent with the constitution of the Zulu language,
which is structured to a large extent around the creation of corresponding
sounds between prefixes of words, and groups of words, in a more comprehensive manner than the rhyming line endings in Western poetry. In the
Zulu language, prefixes for verbs vary according to that of the corresponding noun: "*u*muntu *u*khona" (a person is here); or "*a*bantu *ba*khona" (the
people are here). In addition, as the Zulu language is both characteristically
ideophonic and tonal in a much greater degree than is the case with English, for example, it requires the poetic sensibility of a cultural insider to
pay attention to the finer details of poetic structure, tonal fluctuation,
rhythm, and semantics. In terms of content, Shembe used rhetorical techniques like euphemism, allusion, and metaphor, and incorporated a wide
repertory of praise names and phrases addressed to God, the ancestors, and
cultural heroes. Shembe thereby marked important places and historical
processes.[15] I shall discuss below how hymn performance practice in
ibandla lamaNazaretha diverges from that of the Euro-American mission
church, particularly in terms of the printed versus performed structure.

Why did Isaiah select song to inscribe his people's experiences? In their
discussion of song and poetry in southern Africa, Vail and White (1991,
40–42) suggest three characteristics of song form, content, and perfor-

mance that are pertinent to Isaiah's choice. These are the ability to *(a)* capture the historical moment, *(b)* transcend the historical moment, and *(c)* criticize structures of power controlling the political economy without recrimination precisely because it is "just a song" in the eyes of those in power. They write (ibid.) that the song's "ultimate importance is that it transcends [the] moment, turning a timely, bald, intervention in history into a symbolic statement" about the politics of race, class, and colonization in twentieth-century KwaZulu Natal.

Though we might translate *izihlabelelo* as "hymns," Isaiah's texts reflect what Vail and White (1991) suggest is a central aesthetic principle of southern African verbal performance generally—that of "poetic license." In this regard they write that "there is no doubt that in the . . . apartheid state the belief in the right of the black poet to comment without redress [was] fundamental to the creation of both oral and written poetry" (ibid., 75). Blacking (1980) similarly discussed the political meaning of Zionist hymns, which was articulated not so much in the words of the songs as in the way in which these "hymns" were re-Africanized in performance. It was in the manner of performance that Zionist hymns articulated a political freedom for the Zionist community.

SONG POETICS

The poetics of song generally involves "the making and imagining" of the "material worlds, of things and persons made and unmade" (Serematakis 1991, 1) and a particular form of historical consciousness that "may be created and conveyed, with great subtlety and no less 'truth' in a variety of genres" (Comaroff and Comaroff 1991, 35). Nazarite spiritual song laments the passing of one world, conveyed in intense emotions of loss, grief, and pain, on the one hand, and imagines the possibility of renewal through expressions of hope and desire on the other hand. This is what Serematakis (1991, 99) calls the fusion of "categories of performance with the categories of feeling." Central to this poetics of song performance is the desire for the reconstitution of a sense of community through the collective enactment and sharing of these songs as structures of feeling. Serematakis (ibid., 216) calls this embodiment of feeling "shared substance." She remarks that

> [s]hared substance is not merely the sharing of objects but rather the exchange of artifacts of emotions [song, in this instance]. . . .

The shared artifact historicizes exchanges of feeling. It is a treasure kept and revered and acquires a sacred quality. [Ibid.]

The desire for community extends Nazarite song poetics beyond the earthly community to the cosmology. In Roseman's words (1991, 181), patterned sound sets the "cosmos in motion." It is thought to thereby mediate between disjunctures not only on the earth, but also between the earth and the cosmological or ancestral realm (Robertson 1979). In this manner, the ancestors intercede in the everyday lives of Nazarite members. They do so through a variety of media, which include the presence of animals and bird life. The following story told to me by a Nazarite member provides a poignant illustration. She recalled:

[M]y father was always working in the hospital. He says he used to get up every morning at about three o'clock. Go to the stone under the trees. There by himself. And he used to go and pray. "Shembe, you've promised me that my children won't die anymore. I'm praying you please to be with me and my children." That was before he got, uh, my younger sister—that comes after me.

So my father says when he was praying under those trees, he used to hear the watucal, the snake. Not the snake. Now, the bird.[16] It was singing. When my father prays, the bird says "Twiree, twiree, twiree." When my father stops praying, the bird stops—every day when my father prays.

Now my mother was pregnant. When my mother went to hospital, my father went to pray again under the tree, calling Shembe. "Now my wife is in hospital. She's going to have the baby. I pray you please to be with my wife. That she must deliver that child, give birth in the right way. I don't want the child to die anymore." Then the bird was singing there with my father. After my mother got the baby, when my father went to pray, the bird was no more there.

It was finished now because now it means that Shembe is send[ing] the bird there to be with my father. When my father prays, the bird is singing. When my father prays, the bird is singing. When everything is finished, the baby was born. The bird was gone. Can you believe that? [C. Mazibuko, pers. comm., January 1992.]

In addition to the inclusion of birds into the Nazarite imagination, the hymn texts are filled with images of the natural environment, all of which are constituted as beings who worship the same God as the Nazarites. Mention is made of the sun, moon, stars, rivers, springs, hills, mountains, dawn and dusk; of hens, eagles, and monkeys. The sacralization of the natural environment[17] in the hymnal is reminiscent of Isaiah's sanctification of traditional expressive forms—his rendering of them as inalienable—in the context of imminent loss. For black South Africans the loss of access to land was instituted by the state from the late nineteenth century through taxation, migrant labor, and the series of Land Acts instituted by the state through the course of this century.[18] The inscription of natural icons into the hymnal locates desire for, and the collective memory of, a past that is gone forever. It also connects Nazarite members with the cosmology, because black South Africans traditionally believed the land to be owned by the ancestors, and only temporarily given to the living.

The poetry of the songs is also filled with bodily metaphors of disorder, destruction, vulnerability, and loss on the earth for the Zulu people. These include hunger, material poverty, tears, thirst, homelessness, disease, grief, infertility, and silence. In contrast, there is another image of *Ekuphakameni*, or heaven, which is metaphorized as a space of joy, glory, light, warmth, love, healing, justice, splendor, mercy, no weeping, nourishment, and fellowship.

In this frame, Isaiah's texts diverge from conventional hymnody because they embody a multitextured discourse of emotion that reflects on the collective experiences of millions of black South Africans through much of the twentieth century. Shembe's texts have thus retained an unusual capacity to articulate emotions associated by his followers with suffering, pain, and death. The texts are popular in large part because, while they may have originated in a particular historical moment, they are also able to speak to parallel moments in the life of the Nazarite community. These are two brief examples of such texts:

Ngamemeza ebusuku nemini	I cried out night and day,
Awu ngizwanga ngani.	Why did you not hear me?
(Hlab. 45/1)	(Hymn 45/1)

Izinyembezi ziwukudla kimi	Tears are the food
Okudliwa yimi;	Which feed me;
Kepha ngimi phambi kwakho	As I stand before you
Ngamkele ungigeze.	Welcome me and cleanse me.
(Hlab. 8/5)	(Hymn 8/5)

In content these texts allude to the peculiarities of black South African experience and those of the Old Testament Psalmist. In this context, some of Shembe's *izihlabelelo* are perhaps better categorized as "historicizing discourses" of emotion (Serematakis 1991) over the loss of community of the African people of South Africa. They are not simply the poetic outpourings of two individuals, but structures of a collective consciousness that encompasses a wide spectrum of the African people.

Pain is deeply embedded in Nazarite religious epistemology as a metaphor for the totality of African experience in twentieth-century South Africa. This metaphor is frequently located in illness and disorder as signs of body parts out of order. These include the eyes, through tears; the voice, in weeping; and the tongue, through forced silence. One such example is in Hymn 15, which reads:

Khanyisela abadabukileyo	Give light to the despondent,
Abanhliziyo zino sizi.	Whose hearts are sorrowful.
Zibheke Baba izinyembezi zabo	Father take care of their tears,
Nolimi lwabo selushwabene	And also their tongues which have shrunk.
Sebejiyelwe na ukuthandaza	Despite their prayers, they are in a dilemma.
Samkele Baba isililo sabo.	Father, take heed of their laments.

Hymn 22 similarly uses body metaphors to articulate social disruption in African society. Isaiah writes:

Baningi ababe njengawe	There are many who were like you,
Babephila bengenalutho	They were well and healthy.
Namhla sebehlezi osizini	Today they dwell in sorrow
Emehlweni abaningi	In the presence of many.
Nababe bona ngokuthanda	Even those who had good sight
Namhla abasaboni;	Are unable to see today;
Ngokuba ukuma kwalelizwe	Because the matters of this world
Kuya dlula ngokushesha.	Are rapidly deteriorating.

The central emotion of pain will emerge once again in my analysis of women's narratives as they are used to evoke their relationship with Shembe. Many women preach about Shembe's capacity to remove their pain.

Nazarite Song Performance Practice: Women's *UkuSina*

Isaiah Shembe was a supreme bricoleur. In song performance he combined the hegemonies of both Nguni tradition and European Christianity to create his own repertory. These hymns in their written form reflected the powerful medium of mission Christianity, and, in practice, that of Nguni tradition. He then juxtaposed song performance with sacred dance, accompanied by an indigenized trumpet and bass drum[19] (which may also have been copied from the model of the Salvation Army marching bands).[20] Isaiah thereby constituted a music and dance style that articulated the tensions between the powerful signs and symbols of mission Christianity and those of his own religious tradition.

Isaiah instilled in his repertory of song and its accompanying dance performance practice the privileges and untouchability of hegemonic practice. He inscribed Nazarite song and dance into the domain of the sacred—where it is (theoretically) immutable, and always capable of reenactment, wherever there is a collective gathering of Nazarite believers. The earliest recorded evidence of the emergence of Nazarite style is found on a recording made by Hugh Tracey[21] and issued by Gallotone (South Africa) in 1948. It contains one of Isaiah Shembe's best-known hymns, number 183,[22] entitled *Lalela Zulu* (Listen, O Zulu). (CD track 8.) Percival Kirby comments on the recording. He writes:

> There is no doubt that in Shembe's hymn "*Lalela Zulu*" we have authentic Zulu choral music,[23] such as the early pioneers in Natal must have heard. This hymn is of great interest, for its music dates back at least to the days of Chief Mpande (1840–72).
>
> The main melody is pentatonic, as might be expected,[24] and it is executed by baritone voices. But at times, deeper voices, which normally sing in parallel with the others, double the melody in the lower octave. The "embroideries" sung by the women are of a comparatively free nature. [Kirby 1971, 249–50]

Both Kirby's remarks and Tracey's rather early recording are particularly salient for the analysis of Nazarite performance practice and style, specifically as they pertain to women's participation.

Kirby comments on the free nature of the women's sung "embroideries," pointing to the seemingly ornamental (and implicitly peripheral) function of women's voices in the sound image. This is perhaps a result of Hugh Tracey's recording technique, because the women are placed so far from the recording equipment that they can hardly be heard. It was obviously the "main" melody, as sung by the mostly male voices singing in parallel (among which there may have been the voices of young girls), that was deemed the most important musical parameter by these two men.

Based on my own field recordings of women's song performances, I suggest that it is rather the "free nature" of the women's voices that constituted the emergent sense of Nazarite style. This is what sets it apart from other mission-derived African hymn performance in the late 1930s, the time when the recording was apparently made. While Tracey and Kirby may have been correct in attributing different musical functions to men's and women's voices, they were wrong in privileging the function of a main melody over the freedom of the women's voices. I propose that this "freedom" forms the substance of the Nazarite melodic and rhythmic texture. It is indeed this "free nature" and complex rhythmic texture articulated in song and dance performance (along with the indigenous poetic texts) that has defined Nazarite performance style in the region. I argue, therefore, that the definitive element of Nazarite performance style is embodied in the Nazarite notion of rhythm, particularly as it is articulated in the women's performances at the meetings of *ama14*.[25] This conceptualization of style emerges most powerfully in the contexts in which song is integrally related to religious dance (*ukusina*). It is this style that encapsulates the most sacred form of Nazarite ritual, and also represents the strongest break with Western hymn performance practice, thereby encapsulating the "objections to the ruling ideology" (Hebdige 1979).

In order to understand Nazarite rhythm, I shall briefly elaborate on the intersection of rhythm, text, and melody in the formulation of Nazarite style. In the critique by African and European scholars of the European missionary's translation of hymns into indigenous African languages, the problems involved in setting translated texts to preexisting melodies have been condemned in no uncertain terms (Axelsson 1981; Mthethwa n.d.; Sundkler 1961). What fewer scholars have commented on in this kind of analysis, however, is the intersection of rhythm and text. For Isaiah Shembe this text-rhythm connection constituted one of the core elements of the nascent Nazarite style, and enabled the reformulation of the flow of time from linearity into a more repetitive and cyclical construct (Mthethwa n.d.). This was effected at several levels.

First, in religious dance and song performance, a song leader may start anywhere in the written text, and the women respond with text that either echoes that of the leader or comes from some other place in the structure of the printed hymn. In other words, rhythmic interaction between textual phrases is privileged over linguistic and semantic form and continuity. Second, printed hymn texts are continually elaborated through the addition of vocables, which serve a strictly rhythmic as opposed to semantic purpose. Third, by not starting at the "beginning" of the printed text, there is ultimately no sense of beginning or ending inherent in the musical structure. Instead, all beginnings and endings are determined by the leader, who creates musical form according to the moment at which she feels that everyone is in harmony, or unity. This is clearly determined by an emotional and spiritual sensibility rather than purely aesthetic principles. Furthermore, because there is no fixed point of entry or conclusion, or definitive sense of the "piece" of music, the leader is at liberty to repeat rhythmic and textual phrases at whim. In this sense, *ukusina* performance is truly a "structure of [and by] feeling."

There is, nevertheless, an apparent contradiction in the Nazarite aesthetic sensibility. On the one hand, all songs are supposed to be sung correctly, and from start to finish. On the other hand, in the enactment of *ukusina*, singers may fragment words at will, add to them, and delete them. I suggest that the contradiction is resolved if we understand the historical accommodation Isaiah created in *ukusina*—this most holy of performance styles. This is best explained by juxtaposing two notions of the sacred (truth)—the first is the Christian idea of the primacy of the (written) Word of God,[26] and the second is the traditional Zulu idea about the sanctity of rhythm as ultimately ensconced in religious dance (Muller 1999b). In Foucault's sense, both ideas embody cultural truth, in a historical context of the battle over the forms and meanings of a specifically religious discourse.

In the creative minds of Isaiah Shembe and his followers, these two discourses are not necessarily incommensurate. Indeed, in the performance of sacred song and dance, the Western and Nazarite discourses are reconstructed as a single body of truth. In this regard, the Word of the Nazarite God—the hymn text—is transformed into the sacred temporal order or rhythm of God—religious dance. The word is the rhythm, and the rhythm is the word. That is why texts can be fragmented, reordered, extended, and reduced, without violating the sanctity of the text in the context of *ukusina* performance.

Nazarites perceive a close connection between the performance of dance and the singing of hymns as expressive forms. This is revealed in a number of domains. I have been told on several occasions that Isaiah Shembe taught new hymns to his followers by first teaching them the rhythms of the dance movements that corresponded to the hymn. In chapter 3, I suggested a close relationship existed between *ukusina* (sacred dance) as the quintessential ritual performance of the body, young female virgins as the embodiment of ritual purity, and the reformulation of the passage of sacred time from a linear movement to a more repetitious and cyclical one.[27] The relationship between the virgins' bodies, dance, and cyclicity was informed by traditional Zulu correlations between female and agricultural fertility and reproductive cycles.

In chapter 8, I argue that one of the most powerful messages communicated through *ukusina* is that of the reuniting of the social body through Shembe's healing of the individual physical bodies of married women,

particularly in terms of infertility. This healing is reflected in the reproduction of the religious community at two levels, through the physical
birth of children and in the reconstitution of the community created
through dance. The corollary to this is that since each dance performance
lasts five to six hours, *ukusina* requires that a woman's body be strong and
healthy if she is to complete the dance session. In this section, I briefly
consider *ukusina* as it has been inscribed into the hymn texts by Isaiah and
Galilee, before turning to an in-depth analysis of the song-dance performance itself. Many of the features that emerge in the hymn text are reconsidered in this latter analysis.

There are two hymn texts that together locate the sacred song-dance
complex. These are Hymn 124/2,3, written by Isaiah, which reads:

Ngohlabelela ngentokozo	I shall sing with joy
Emzini oyincwele;	In the holy place;
Bajubule abahlangabezi bani	My heavenly escorts will be jubilant
Ngokungena kwami.	With my entrance.
*Ngiyahamba weGuqabadele	*I am traveling, O Lord
Ngaloluhambo lwakho:	On this journey of yours:
Yelula isandla sakho	Stretch out your hand
Ulubusise uhambo lwami.	And bless my progress.
Ngomsinela obongekayo	I shall dance for him who is praiseworthy
Nginasena nhloni.	Without being shy anymore.
Phakamani masango	Lift up the gates,
Phakamani singene.	Lift up that we may enter.
*Ngiyahamba . . .	*I am traveling . . .

and Hymn 158/1,3:

Bhekuzulu	Behold, the Zulus are
Esinela uSimakade	Dancing for the Eternal One.
Ak'uthi thuthul	Just wait a little while—
Uyeza uJehova.	Jehovah is coming.
Silibonile lelo lizwi	We saw that word
Livela emafini	As it came out from the clouds.
Lizwakele xilongo	The trumpet was heard—
Lomkhosi wezulu.	[It was] the call of heaven.

These hymns project several characteristics of Nazarite music and dance,
such as singing as a holy activity, the stress on traveling on paths, the dance
as an act of praise and as the entry into heaven it enables, the link between
dance and waiting, and finally, the predominance of the trumpet as the instrument of heaven. Other than in the sabbath hymn, what is remarkably

absent from the printed collection, however, is mention of the drum or its associated rhythm.

While I have no insider's explanation for this absence in hymn texts, it points to several issues. First, the absence is reminiscent of the powerful mission ideology, which prohibited the use of the drum for ritual enactment. Second, it suggests that the drum, like *ukusina* itself, was introduced into the church quite late in the initial history of the religious group, and conversely explains the invention of indigenous trumpets for Nazarite worship. Third, as an icon of cosmological power, it is superseded in the hymn texts by the Christian imagery of the trumpet of heaven,[28] and the prevalence of the appearance of the "word" (rather than the creation of rhythm) from the clouds/heaven itself. This reinforces my argument above regarding the metaphorical equivalence between the "word" and "rhythm" as the icons of the sacred in song performance. Finally, it indicates an eschatological problem—the apparent blurring of cosmological boundaries between the ancestral (and by extension the drum/sacred dance) domains, which Sundkler (1961 [1948], 21) writes is in "some subterranean mode" or underground, and that of the Lord of the Sky (heaven/trumpet). This drum-trumpet ambiguity (in terms of the hymn texts) elucidates the battle between mission and Nguni epistemologies over the valency of signs, particularly in the lifetime of Isaiah Shembe.

Married Women's *UkuSina* Performance

For the purposes of analysis, I have focused on a single kind of Nazarite song. This is the genre that accompanies religious dance. The specific performance includes two stanzas of Nazarite Hymn 45, *Ngamemeza ebusuku nemini* (I cried out night and day), which I recorded at a meeting of *ama14* at *Vula Masango* on March 13, 1992. At the meetings of *ama14*, women's dance[29] usually takes place in the first half of the meeting. This particular performance of the two stanzas lasted about forty-five minutes (see CD tracks 9–11).

The overall structuring of a Nazarite hymn for dance performance was explained to me by Bongani Mthethwa's daughter Khethiwe. Although her explanation is lengthy, I cite it in full because it embodies the central principles of Nazarite form and aesthetics of performance. (The numbers inserted in the text are my own, for ease of reference in explanation.)

> [1] The leader starts to sing—and everyone follows the leader of the song. [2] After about a minute, she [and others] form a line and

start to dance—very slowly, until all are in unison. And they dance
following the song. [3] The others—those who aren't dancing—
start to clap, taking the rhythm of those who are dancing. When
they have the good rhythm for that song, when the drum beater
feels that those who are dancing and those who are clapping are in
full unison, [4] [s]he will take the cue and start to beat the drum,
and have to pick up the right rhythm.

After a very long time, maybe about ten minutes or so, again, the
one who is blowing *izimbomvu* [alpine horn–like indigenous instru-
ments], should [5] blow it in a key that will be in harmony with the
whole key used in the song.

The people who are in control of the rhythm are the dancers, because those who are clapping look at their [the dancers'] feet. And
according to the way they are dancing, then they clap. The drum
beater too, will look at the way they dance, and beat according to the
way they dance. If there is a foot that is stronger, maybe the right foot
is stronger than the left, that should be heard in the drum. So the
strong beat is heard in the drum, so the drum beater should be in
unity with the dancers. Everything is in rhythm.

When the one who had started the song feels they've warmed up
enough—the warm-up is the repetition of the first two lines (that
may be about thirty minutes of the song)—she'll [6] change to the
third and fourth lines of the song, which is faster and with more variations. When she changes, [7] everything will be quiet. Everything
breaks and they all listen to the changing.

[8] Everyone will sing from the starter. Then those clapping
come in according to the right rhythm, and the drum beater follows, and the blower comes in, and everything is in unity again. But
faster this time. When the dance is at its climax, there may be a
trumpet blower coming in, blowing according to the rhythm. [K.
Mthethwa, pers. comm., December 1992.]

Drawing on the performance frame created by Khethiwe in this text, I
shall fill in the specific details of the recorded performance (as numbered),
in order to articulate a theory of the aesthetics of Nazarite song.

1. THE LEADER STARTS TO SING

Treitler (1989, 3) writes that the medieval practice of troping "was a way
of making ancient matter available for active engagement by members of
the community." In a similar manner, the leader of women's song in

ibandla lamaNazaretha opens the performance by singing, unaccompanied, through the first two lines of hymn text. In so doing, she presents the textual content to a predominantly illiterate community, and sets the musical landscape within which the song should be articulated. She then repeats the first line of text, which in Hymn 45 reads "*Ngamemeza ebusuku nemini.*" (CD track 9.) At the end of this line, a small chorus responds by singing "*Ngamemeza,*" which creates a strong rhythmic pattern through the *m* alliteration, and a sonic symmetry with the *a* sounds at the beginning and ending of the textual unit. It is in fact this unit that functions as the rhythmic pattern for the two lines of text. Much of the subsequent rhythmic improvisation undertaken by the women derives from this unit.

For the duration of several textual repetitions and responses by the women, the group explores the pitch, textual, and rhythmic materials outlined by the leader. This "tuning in" process resembles the opening musical materials of the Zulu neotraditional guitarists known as *maskanda.*[30] It starts with a few women singing, but gradually includes all present, as they begin to sense the rhythm of the song. Slowly the voices begin to form smaller units within the larger performance structure. Each of these units sings in parallel thirds and fourths, creating a sense of harmony within each unit, which in turn functions as part of a multilayered texture of rhythmic tension and interaction between units.

Since Zulu is a tonal language, the concept of melody in Zulu song is integrally linked to the tonal fluctuations of the spoken word.[31] In this regard, melody translates as *indlela yegama,* or the path of the words, and it is this path that is laid out by the song leader, and subsequently followed by the rest of the women. Once these women have "tuned in" sufficiently, the leader then outlines a more specific melodic contour or path. It is a path that does not, however, simply follow the spatial/melodic variations of pitch typical of a tonal language, but in this *14*'s performance, incorporates a large proportion of vocables that seem to instill a strong rhythmic motion in the song performance.

The leader's path in the recorded performance begins on a pitch roughly equivalent to g below middle c, ascends a fourth to c, then a third to e, and moves between e and f a second above, rhythmically playing with the word *memeza,* and then descends. She then picks up the next phrase, *ebusuku nemini,* rises, reaches a plateau, and descends. This pattern is repeated by the leader through several repetitions of textual and musical phrases, until there is a final sense of descent, at which point she outlines the intervallic pattern—fourth, third, second, utilizing the *Ngamemeza* textual unit.

The increased involvement of women in the singing results in the embellishment at the top of the melodic contour becoming an extremely dense, multiple layering of rhythmic and textual improvisation, lasting about seven or eight seconds. The layering comprises both individual and small groups of women's voices, moving in and out of each other's phrases. All of this is framed by the ascent and descent of the melodic line at the beginning and end of the overall musical phrase, as sung by the leader. There is an additional layer sometimes created between two song leaders, perhaps two *bakhokheli,* who weave together an antiphonic and overlapping texture of melodic and rhythmic phrases in dialogue with each other. This conversation is often heard over and above the more general fabric of pitch, rhythm, and text improvised by the larger ensemble of women.

2. She and others form a line and start to dance

The song leader is the first to stand up and move to the space for dancing. She is soon followed by other women, who move into the line one by one. The dance movements involve a slow left-right foot movement in duple rhythm, with the torso bent slightly forward. The arms provide the sense of flow. Bent at the elbows, they swing back and forth. They eventually extend outward and upward at the climactic moment of the performance. Consistent with the traditional *isigekle* dance patterns, women's *ukusina* is characteristically slow and extremely fluid in its movement. There is absolutely no display of sexuality through bodily performance.

Musically speaking, the start of the dance adds several layers to the initial melodic frame created by the leader. First, the regular pacing of the feet in right-left or right-left-left-right patterns externalizes what Nketia (in Merriam 1981, 128) calls the "time line." He describes this as a subjective metronomic sense kept by the African dancer in a context of cross-rhythmic interplay. Unlike the inner metronomic sense of Nketia's time line, in Nazarite performance the time line is objectified and sounded out by the dancer's feet, hand-clapping, and the drum. Second, the smoothly curved back-and-forth movements of the dancers' arms replicate the fluidity of the melodic lines of the singers, whose vocal contours characteristically slide between pitch points and do not adhere to a predetermined definition of absolute pitch. The arms are "the limbs in their muscular strength," from which "melody derives" (Keil 1979, 197). The overall melodic range is defined by the song leader and is quintessentially relational, requiring each woman to listen to what the others are singing before responding. (There is, however, no unison singing, other than the collective humming of the hymn tune at the end of the song performance.)

3. THE OTHERS START TO CLAP, TAKING THE
RHYTHM FROM THE DANCE

While some of the women replicate the patterns of the ancestors in dance movement, the others sound the rhythm of the dancers (and by extension, the ancestors) through clapping. In this context, the social body is unified through the uniform movements of the physical bodies —not only of those dancing with their feet, but also of those keeping the rhythm in their hands. Nevertheless, there is still some sense of difference between those who are dancing and those who are clapping. Khethiwe explained that the dance leader uses a phrase, *washiwa* (you are being left out), which is said to those not dancing, but serves to encourage the dancers. This is both a moral and a musical exhortation, because musically, it signals an increased tempo of performance, and morally, if they do not dance properly, their places will be taken by those not dancing. Furthermore, the letter from Isaiah, cited in chapter 6, suggests that "fooling about" while dancing constitutes a violation against *Ekupahakameni* and the ancestors.

This stress on dancing correctly is a moral force, for it reiterates the process of sacralization of traditional forms such as dance into inalienable treasure. Thus, a woman engages in dance as a means to increasing personal capital on earth. Sacred dance is considered hard work. One woman told me that to dance was "heavy." This "heaviness" is what instills moral value into dance. Such moral worth is metaphorized as "good works," which are "written in the Book of Life" and ensure a woman's safe passage to heaven after death. In this manner, physical strength is inextricably linked to spiritual maturity. Furthermore, by clapping the dance rhythms, the women who are standing by create a panel of jurists who judge the performance of the dancers. In this sense the nondancers become the bearers on earth of the judgment of the ancestors as to the value of the accumulation of spiritual worth by each individual dancer—which in this instance takes the form of sacred dance. As both dancers and nondancers, all members thereby "move in an expanded social universe" (Roseman 1991, 181).

4. THE DRUMMER TAKES THE RHYTHMIC CUE
AND STARTS TO DRUM

The Nazarite drum, *isigubhu,*[32] is a large, indigenous version of the military band bass drum, struck with two beaters, one in each hand. With each beater it gives sonic form to the left-right duple foot stamp of the dancers, and in turn to the traditional patterns of the ancestors. In this regard, the rhythm of the drum connects with the beating of the earth (where the ancestors reside) by the dancing feet. It thereby mediates between the ancestral and earthly domains. Furthermore, this duple rhythm, now articulated at three levels—by the feet, the hands, and the drum—also establishes an iconicity with the travel/walking involved in the journey of the Nazarite pilgrim on the earth (see Hymn 124 above). Finally, Jean Comaroff (1985, 230) comments that for the Zionists (a parallel indigenous religious movement in South Africa),

> [t]he pounding drum not only declares the onset of the special "work" of ritual time and space; it also dramatizes the gulf between the children of Zion and the followers of Wesley. The drum is *the* signal of Zionist identity.

Comaroff's analysis may as easily apply to *ibandla lamaNazaretha*.

5. THE TRUMPET TAKES THE KEY FROM THE SONG AND STARTS TO BLOW (CD TRACK 10)

The trumpet (*imbomvu*) is the last layer of the extremely dense and contrapuntal musical texture created in *ukusina*. There are no finger holes or valves, so, as with the Swiss alpine horn, pitch content is created and adjusted by lip movement and breath control. Like the song leader, the trumpet outlines the intervals of a third, a fourth, or its opposite, the fifth. The specific pitch at which these intervals are located is determined by the singers.

The trumpet parallels the voice in *ukusina* performance, in its combination of strong rhythmic patterns with a fairly limited pitch content. (This perhaps explains its connection with the cosmology—as the human voice connects earthly members with the cosmology.) Both pitch and rhythmic content are intensified by the trumpet, with the addition of a second and sometimes third trumpet, which play(s) a rhythmic and intervallic counterpoint to that of the first trumpet. This is an important point in terms of situating the Nazarite musical texture within the broader context of the fabric of African music. Although the trumpets play their patterns fairly slowly, I suggest that they function to some extent like the lead drummer in West African drumming, as explained in Chernoff's work (1979) on African rhythm.

Like the drummer (ibid., 75–82), the trumpet player creates both pitch and rhythmic content and variation with her instrument. In both contexts, pitch selection is related to the tonal flow of linguistic contours, which are articulated through a minimum of two pitches. These two pitches, a fourth or fifth apart, frame the melodic range of the singers. Both trumpet players and drummers improvise on rhythmic patterns, which are repeated for as long as they need to be in order to be heard and understood. Then they are changed, as smoothly and fluidly as possible. In both musical textures, the rhythms created by one instrument (or the resultant pattern created by interlocking two phrases) are always contrasted and in tension with the rhythms of the rest of the musical fabric. In drumming ensembles this cross-rhythmic tension is usually created on other drums, while in Nazarite song performance it is heard in its rhythmic and timbral complexity—in the hand-clapping, drum beats, foot stamping, and the "embroideries" of the women's voices that continually weave together rhythmic and melodic counterpoints (see figure on p. 117).

6. AFTER THIRTY MINUTES THE LEADER CHANGES
TO THE THIRD AND FOURTH LINES OF THE SONG,
BUT FASTER AND WITH MORE VARIATION (CD TRACK 11)

One of the most powerful aesthetic preferences, not only in song performance but indeed, in the religious community as a whole, is to do things slowly, never to hurry, and always to take time. Similarly, the singing of a single stanza of a hymn can take as much as an hour to complete. The momentum of performance, however, is maintained through a gradual intensification of all musical parameters over an extended period of time. In this regard, the song starts at about 60 quarter notes per minute, and speeds up to about 90 quarter notes per minute before it suddenly drops off; the "key" of the performance rises gradually (in this recorded performance, it moved up a fourth from ca. C major to ca. F major); the improvisation becomes more intricate, and a greater number of musical layers appears as more women sing different parts, and all the drummers and trumpeters enter.

The increased musical intensity is paralleled by an augmentation of emotional excitement, of bodily movement, and of the sense of social unity. This is the feeling of community wholeness articulated by Feld (1988) as "getting into the groove," or finding "the beat." Such collective unity, however, is not created by everybody singing or playing the same pitches or harmonies, as happens in Western hymn-singing. Instead, the ideal Nazarite performative texture is one in which every voice is individually heard in the context of a densely articulated texture—in relationship to the multiplicity of other voices. The melodic lines in particular facilitate the weaving in and out of the fixed beat of the dancing, drumming, and handclapping. More than any other. "voice" in the fabric, the singers create what Feld defines as the "in-sync" but "out-of-phase" sensation of musical performance. This sense of style is crystallized by Keil's (1987) concept of "participatory discrepancy"—those who are "out of time," and "out of tune." The most spiritually mature, and certainly the most proficient song performers, are those who always just "miss the beat." This is clearly evident in recorded performances of women's meetings in which there were a large number of spiritual leaders performing.[33]

The skill of the song leader is to know at what point the level of musical, emotional, and bodily intensification is at its peak. This is the moment at which the maximum number of discrepancies is heard—because of the optimum participation by Nazarite members—and at which the greatest sense of sociability is created. It is at this juncture that the song leader once again enters the musical fabric—in order to be heard. She sings the last words of the end of the couplet of text, utilizing a descending melodic contour—the intervals of a second, third, and fourth. The descent signals a cadential moment when the entire performance thins out to the single beats of the drum. Those who were dancing move away, and a new line of women begins to form, slowly at first, but picking up speed quite quickly this time. The new group builds a sense of solidarity. It starts with the rhythm of the first dancer, with the others either joining the dance line or standing on the side to judge the performance of those dancing.

7. They all listen to the changing

"Getting into the groove" and "feeling the beat" emerge from the music but are components of an inherently social process. Each singer and dancer must actively "tune in" to what is happening musically (and emotionally) around her in the context of *ukusina* performance, and respond accordingly. This participation requires sonic reciprocity—what one person sings or calls is answered by another. But this answer is never an exact repetition of what was heard. It creates its own sonic space and identity through slight rhythmic or pitch discrepancies. The answer always overlaps to some extent with the end of the call—it takes on something of the musical identity of the caller—to create a sense of continuity, and to avoid rupture and silence. It then fabricates its own sound and rhythm. In turn, this answer becomes someone else's call, which is then answered in a slightly discrepant tone and form.

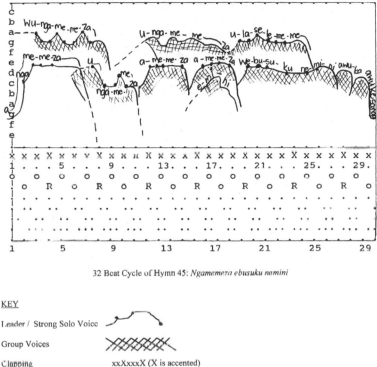

32 Beat Cycle of Hymn 45: *Ngamemeza ebusuku nemini*

KEY

Leader / Strong Solo Voice

Group Voices

Clapping   xxXxxxX (X is accented)

Drums   O O O O   R Right Foot in Dance
                              R O R O R   (Coincides with drum beat)

Trumpets . . . . . .
            . .   . .} m. 3rd
            . . .   . .} p. 4th

HYMN 45 TEXT: *Ngamemeza ebusuku nemini*   I cried out night and day

8. Everyone sings from the starter

The song leader is usually *Mkhokheli* (the leader of *ama14*), or one of the more spiritually mature and older women. As a spiritual leader she should guide the women members along the path of life, to reach the greatest heights of ritual purity and thus spirituality. As she teaches by the example of her own life, so she is expected to lead women singers along the melodic paths that are sonic metaphors of the paths these women travel in the journey of life. Both life and melody are, however, difficult paths to follow. The way is heavy, requiring experience, endurance, skill, and especially the support and interaction of others in the surrounding community.

In this sense, the musical fabric, started by the song and spiritual leader, becomes a metaphor of the social fabric. The complexity and difficulties of life are articulated in the density and textured nature of the song performance. It is not a texture that is simply a solo call, with a chorus of response, followed by a solo call and choral response. Instead, it has multiple occurrences—a call, and two or three staggered responses, or a solo call answered by another solo call, in the context of a choral response. As in the journey of life, some women are stronger than others, and are thus able to sing their own parts individually, while others are less able, and thus join the vocal group of those closest to them.

Nevertheless, everyone "sings from the starter." The starter does not initiate melody only once, but continually creates new paths for further explorations of texture and tone color, for new ways of articulating rhythm and melody. In this manner, the starter transforms two single lines of text, which in the printed form are linearly directed, through endless repetitions and variations into an essentially cyclical structure, which is listened to, echoed, and repeated, over and over. Through her endless melodic/rhythmic calls, the song leader facilitates the integration of women into the Nazarite community. She does more than this, for in the reshaping of the linearity of the hymn text into a highly repetitive and cyclical form, she reclaims for song performance a temporal sensibility that is inextricably traditional and gendered. As the words and rhythms of the song are continuously repeated, they establish an iconicity with performance cycles of precolonial culture, which were in sync with those of the natural environment, and indeed with the bodies of women.

Conclusion

In this chapter, I have discussed the creation of a new song repertory by Isaiah and Galilee Shembe in the early decades of the twentieth century. I suggested that this repertory was authenticated as sacred and immutable by the Nazarite community because it is believed to have been given by the ancestors through the medium of female-voiced heavenly messengers, and because it encompasses the peculiarities of a collective African experience in the face of Euro-American colonization and missionization in KwaZulu Natal.

Isaiah and Galilee Shembe were cognizant of the power of the written word and ensured that written documentation was made of the song texts. As Gates explains about the literary production of Anglo-African slaves in the United States (1770–1815), writing "became the visible sign, the commodity of exchange, the text and technology of reason" (Gates 1988, 132). And literacy was also the West's measure of African humanity, an integral dimension of the black African self that began to emerge in late-nineteenth- and early-twentieth-century South Africa. For both the eighteenth-century African in America and Isaiah and Galilee Shembe, one of the core problems was to fashion a means to "make the white written texts speak with a black voice" (ibid., 131). Gates argues that this process is exemplified in the trope of the "Talking Book" in Anglo-African slave narratives. In the move from a primarily oral to written culture, the book is viewed by these slave writers as an expressive form that quite literally lacks a capacity to talk to its (African) bearer. It is a European cultural form without a black voice; it fails to articulate black experience. In its written mode, Isaiah and Galilee Shembe's hymn repertory attempts to speak to African history and experience. To authenticate the voice for the mission-educated, it is assembled into a material form (a book) that parallels the Western mission hymnal. To give it a cultural coherence for the traditionalists they sought to minister to, the poetic strategies combine the rhetoric of the Nguni praise poet and that of the Old Testament Psalmist.

There was, and still is, however, a tension in *ibandla lamaNazaretha* between the written and performed forms of these sacred texts. I have suggested that it is not so much in its written version that the Nazarite hymn repertory is held to be sacred and inalienable, as it is in the way in which these words are articulated in song and dance performance. While Nazarite women believe that their ritual performances enable them to individually "write" their names in the "Book of Life," it is the "re-Africanized" style of performance that is held to be inalienable. This style is believed to reconstitute a sense of community through a particular notion of rhythm, an all-encompassing term for the cultural harnessing and domestication of the passage of time; the icons of the path (as spiritual and melodic) and the mountain (the site of Nazarite origins and identity); and the formal pattern of cyclicity, which functions as the quintessential element of Nazarite sociomoral purity, female empowerment, and the expression of Nazarite ritual and musical time.

Isaiah Shembe with white angels and Nguni traditionalists (photographer unknown).

Image of Isaiah Shembe, from inside the Nazarite hymnal, 1940 (photographer unknown).

Johannes Galilee Shembe in *iskotch*, with pith helmet and traditional Nguni shield juxtaposed with colonial image of Scotsman. These come from "C to C" (Cape to Cairo) cigarette boxes sold in South Africa (photographer unknown; images compiled by Carol Muller).

KHULUMA NKOSI INCEKU YAKHO IYEZWA

A popular photograph sold in *ibandla lamaNazaretha* with Jesus the Shepherd and Isaiah the prophet kneeling before him. The words translate from Zulu to "Speak, Lord, for your servant is listening" (photographer unknown).

A visually suggestive parallel image of Amos Shembe with his long orange cloak, beard, and shepherd's crook (photographer unknown).

Married Nazarite women singing in a service to bless the new church leader, Rev. Vimbeni Shembe, in October 1995 (photograph by Carol Muller).

Abakhokheli, the leaders of the married women, share stories about the wonders of Shembe after sabbath worship, *Gibisile*, May 1991 (photograph by Carol Muller).

Two virgin girls, Samu and Thembi, with water to be blessed by Amos Shembe, *Gibisile*, May 1991 (photograph by Carol Muller).

Virgin girls return from *Nthanda* at *Nkatheni* on July 8, 1991, with their long sticks. They are mimetically constructing a house for Shembe (photograph by Carol Muller).

Zulu Bibles, Nazarite hymn books, and posters of the holy mountain are for sale at "the office" every sabbath. Standing in front is Mvangeli Magubane (photograph by Carol Muller).

Nazarite woman faith healer Njengobane Manqele, at her home in KwaMashu, poses for the photograph with the sticker of Amos Shembe stuck to the front of her hymnal, February 1993 (photograph by Carol Muller).

Nazarite group marriages are solemnized in the temple at *Ebuhleni* in July 1991. Men and women lay their hands on the open Bibles as the marriage vows are read (photograph by Carol Muller).

FIVE

Nazarite Hymns: Popularizing Sacred Song
(1940–1997)

Uyinkosi amakhosi,	King of kings,
Mawuphakaniswe;	He must be praised;
Izizwe zonke zonhlaba	Nations of the world
Zibongubukhosi bakhosi.	Praise you king of kings.
Zishozithi hanana, (2x)	We say "Hallelujah," (2x)
Zishi halalala Shembe wethu.	We say "Hallelujah" to our Shembe.
	(Sung to the Tune "Joy to the World.")[1]

In September 1996, while visiting *Ebuhleni* with my field assistant Samu, I was struck by the development of a new product on the Nazarite market: commercially produced audiocassettes of Nazarite hymns. On that day, several dozen cassettes of church member Nathoya Mbatha's performances were displayed by a young man in his makeshift store at the entrance to the religious site. As we walked away from the gate and up toward the temple area, one or two small boomboxes broadcast recordings of earlier live and mass-mediated Nazarite preaching, religious singing and dancing, and *inkhonzo* worship performances. These were all on sale for the Nazarite community.

The title of Mbatha's cassette *Ngivuse Nkosi* (Awaken Me, Lord) is the name of Hymn 63 in the Nazarite hymnal, *iziHlabelelo zamaNazaretha.* Typical of the rather limited market of Nazarite religious music, Mr. Mbatha's cassette contains a selection of Nazarite hymns. When Samu and I arrived at *Ebuhleni,* only one of these cassettes was in the original commercial format with a printed cover inserted in the box. All the others available for sale were pirated copies without the covers. The young entrepreneur could not be persuaded to sell us the one original version, so we went away. A couple of hours later, we returned to the cassette store, only to find that all the pirated cassettes had been replaced with the original commercial copies and were being sold for the same price as the home-made versions.

Back in South Africa in July 1997, I returned to *Ebuhleni* to see if any other cassettes had been produced and whether I could find Mr. Mbatha. I was not disappointed. There were several new Nazarite recordings available for purchase. With the exception of Mr. Mbatha's solo production, all the others for sale were group performances of Shembe hymns. They included a range of both commercially produced, officially sanctioned models of Nazarite worship and homemade recordings of Nazarite hymns and gospel-style items, as well as pirated copies of Nazarite services recorded from other professionally produced recordings. Even though each of these kinds of recordings demonstrates a commodification of sacred performance that I suggested in chapter 1 was central to Nazarite spirituality, none of these cassettes has generated as much controversy within the Nazarite community as has that of young Nathoya Mbatha. Later on, as Mr. Mbatha and I talked together, I realized that pirated copying of his cassette was not the only contested issue in the making and marketing of his gospel-style renditions of the hymns of *ibandla lamaNazaretha*.

Nazarite identity and sense of difference as a religious collectivity in KwaZulu Natal is powerfully articulated in their belief in the inalienability of the words and performance practice of *izihlabelelo zamaNazaretha*, i.e., the hymns of the place of Shembe, because this style is set apart from all other religious song in South Africa. This includes groups like the African Wesleyans, the Apostolic Faith Mission, and the Zion Christian Church, all of which have produced similar cassettes and compact discs of their sacred repertories for the popular market since the mid-1980s. The problem is that Nathoya Mbatha's commodified musical style threatens to dissolve the particularity of Nazarite hymn performance practice as much by the changes in performance practice as by its potential to penetrate a large and unknown set of markets outside of the direct control of the Nazarite religious regime. Even though the cassette was independently produced and officially sanctioned by Amos Shembe, the connection with BMG Records troubled the church elders. There was an unnerving sense that it signified the beginning of a significant loss of control over the maintenance of the boundaries of what was held to be sacred and inalienable in *ibandla lamaNazaretha*.

Mbatha's cassette also appeared at a critical historical moment—as *ibandla lamaNazaretha* stood poised to take a powerful and possibly central position in the religious life and history of KwaZulu Natal. The presence (admittedly contested) of State President Nelson Mandela at the funeral of Amos Shembe in October 1995 provides one example of the means by which the church began to reunite the realms of the religious with the political (a precolonial Nguni unity). As State President Mandela reminded *ibandla lamaNazaretha* at their leader's funeral, qualities of "Africanness" were, once again, coming to the fore in the public spheres of the "new South Africa." To gain a position of religious power in the terrain of a fragile, emergent post-apartheid political economy in South Africa, the Nazarites would have to remind the region of their founder Isaiah Shembe's unflagging commitment to things "African." There is little doubt that Nazarite sacred song and dance repertory has long been recognized for retaining such signs of "Africanness" and "Zuluness" through the harsh years of colonial domination.

Negotiating a place in the contemporary religious and political topography is, nonetheless, fraught with conflicting demands from within the religious collectivity. On the one hand, if *ibandla lamaNazaretha* is to retain its claim to almost a century-long commitment to African ways in religious worship, it is imperative that, now more than ever, the authenticity of Nazarite religious rituals and performances be maintained. On the other hand, there is considerable pressure from within the community both to seek new converts and to allow for selected changes to religious ritual practices, to modernize "Africanness" (in song performance specifically) in order to attract and keep the interest of township youth in the religious group.

To add pressure to the already contested practices within the community, South Africa's new political dispensation brings with it a range of possibilities for economic empowerment, locally and globally. The shift is articulated in a song text of the Thulisa Brothers, an *isicathamiya* (now marketed as "Zulu Gospel") group. The song, *Akesiyibongeni Leyondoda*, is about State President Nelson Mandela. The text is translated and summarized as follows:

> Let us thank the man [Mandela] who said that South Africa should return to the international arena. We were called to cast our votes, not realizing that this was the way of bringing South Africa back. South Africa re-entered the international scene when a pen was put to paper for democracy. Black and white people jointly brought South Africa back to the people. [*The Spirit of African Gospel*, 1996/1.]

While it may be surprising to some that economically marginalized peoples from the edges of the global market imagine themselves as members of the world economy, the Thulisa Brothers comment in another song that it is precisely through participation in song performance that the world is coming to know about them. "We talked to Mshengu [Joseph Shabalala, leader of Ladysmith Black Mambazo, of *Graceland* fame] . . . who told the world about us. We are now invited to London, but it's very far" (*The Spirit of African Gospel*, 1996/12). As for the Thulisa Brothers, there is no doubt that individuals like Mbatha, who have embarked on similar recording projects, hope to use the commodified and "different" sounds of Nazarite religious belief and practice to send their message out beyond the physical confines of the local community. Unlike the Thulisa Brothers, who sing the more secularized *isicathamiya* genre[2] and have been rewarded for their achievements, Mbatha and other Nazarite youth are encountering unexpected resistance from segments of the religious community because of the way in which they are using the sacred repertory for commercial and individual gain. Nathoya Mbatha's *Ngivuse Nkosi* cassette is situated in the nexus of these conflicts.

In this chapter I draw on the example of Nathoya Mbatha's *Ngivuse Nkosi* cassette production to examine how the Nazarite community is facing the contemporary challenges of appealing to new followers through its song and dance performance (as it did in the 1920s) while holding true to the authentic performance practices of *izihlabelelo kwakwaShembe* (the hymns of the place of Shembe). I suggest that it is not in the commodification and mediation of the repertory per se that the conflict arises. As I demonstrate in the first part of the chapter, the history of the repertory is synonymous with a limited form of commodification in book form and sound recordings. Rather, the debate ensues over two specific issues: Mbatha's new arrangements of the sacred *izihlabelelo* repertory, and the attempts to popularize the repertory beyond the bounds of the religious community through more mainstream gospel music channels. However, Mbatha is in many ways only following in the footsteps of official changes to the Nazarite repertory instigated in the late 1980s by Amos Shembe and Bongani Mthethwa. The second part of the chapter narrates this transformation. In the third part, I focus more specifically on Mbatha's cassette production. The chapter concludes by probing whether it is really possible to popularize the sacred. I revisit my earlier discussion of the distinction between inalienable objects and practices that are held to be sacred and inviolable by a community, and alienable objects that are freely exchanged as commodities. The contest between sacrifice and desire resurfaces again, this time as a moral choice of individual profit, the way of the music industry, over the collective good, the way of the religious collectivity.

Early Sound Recordings and Radio Broadcasts

Chapter 4 provides a fairly detailed discussion of the composition and early transmission of the hymns of Isaiah and Galilee Shembe. In that chapter I suggest that there is a selective commodification of the song repertory in *ibandla lamaNazaretha*. In precolonial times, a religious song repertory would have remained an orally transmitted performance practice. In the early twentieth century, both men had the texts of these sacred songs transcribed into written form: Isaiah had them written down by others, and Galilee appears to have made his own record of his visions of song performance. Galilee took the text production one step further and standardized the repertory and published it in book form. The initial version appeared in 1940, and set a new path for the commodification and circulation of paraphernalia sacred to the Nazarite community. These books began to be sold by designated church leaders for a cost closely aligned with production costs (about R 15 in 1997) on Nazarite sacred sites. The tunes, however, were not transcribed into any form of notation or made available for congregational use, but continued to be transmitted orally.

In the same period, the first sound recordings of Nazarite religious song and dance performance were made by South African musicologist Hugh Tracey. As with the chronology of the songs, the actual dates of these early recordings are contested, because it is not clear what the time lapse was between recording and publication. In the 1920s, Hugh Tracey was given a grant by the Carnegie Foundation to undertake one year of full-time music research in southern Africa. With little training and crude recording equipment, Tracey cut discs "ploughed onto aluminum" (Andersson 1981, 19). At that time, there was no record plant in South Africa. Between 1928 and the late 1940s, musicians who were to be recorded were sent to studios in London, or aural transcriptions were made with mobile recording units in the South African countryside (Coplan 1985). Tracey may well have recorded one or two pieces of the Nazarite repertory during this period.

Tracey then went to work as director of the Natal Studios in the state-controlled South African Broadcast Corporation (the SABC) from 1936 to 1947. During this term of office, he recorded numerous African performers, including "Shembe's choir," i.e., a group of men and women selected for recording purposes. (There was no official church choir until the late 1980s, when Amos Shembe had Bongani Mthethwa introduce organ accompaniment for congregational worship. This is discussed below.) At least four recordings of Shembe's hymns were made at the SABC under Tracey's direction: Hymn 183 (*Lalela Zulu*), Hymn 126 (*Kuphakama sabela wena*), Hymn 173 (*Sidedele Singene*) and Hymn 223 [226] (*Yini Gebeleweni*). All of these hymns were broadcast by the Natal Studios in the 1940s. Tracey commented in 1948 that "not only are the hymns well sung but the choirs appear to retain the Zulu harmonic structure as well as their own melodies. The African radio audience has often expressed its satisfaction with Shembe's hymns, both in their manner and matter" (Tracey 1948, ix). Furthermore, he remarked that these hymns were part of a large corpus of Zulu-language material aired by the SABC in the 1940s that "had already been recorded commercially and were available for broadcasting, together with a number of others specially recorded by us for the Zulu programmes while I was still in charge of the studios and Masinga was my head Zulu announcer" (Tracey 1948, v). This is one of the first declarations on the "authenticity" of Nazarite performance as a truly "Zulu" sound savored by the "African" radio audience. (It resurfaces in the early 1990s with the proliferation of cassettes in the Nazarite community, and new nationalist discourse that privileges "Africanness" over "Westernness.")

After leaving the SABC in 1947, Tracey worked in close association with Eric Gallo, the founder of South Africa's largest commercial record company. Gallo provided the headquarters and financial support for what became Hugh Tracey's *Sound of Africa* series. The series was issued by the International Library of African Music, which Tracey established in the early 1950s. The association between Tracey and Gallo resulted in the recording of the 78 RPM disc of two of the most popular Nazarite hymns, numbers 183 (*Lalela Zulu*, discussed in chap. 4) and 210 (*Waqala Izitha*). They were issued in 1948 on the Gallotone label. Rob Allingham, the archivist currently working at Gallo Records, has suggested that even though these two recordings were not released until 1948, because they sound like wire recordings these songs may have been recorded as early as 1939 (Allingham, pers. comm., August 1993). Tracey made a second recording of both hymns, later issued in the *Sound of Africa* series in 1955. (CD tracks 12–18.)

The *Sound of Africa* series has eleven tracks of Shembe material recorded by Hugh Tracey. This includes the two previously released items, a call to prayer, the "Morning and Evening Hymns" (contained in the liturgy), and three other hymns that are not in the contemporary hymnal.

Iqhude loKusa (The Cock Crows at Dawn) and *Qubula Nkosi* (Hold Us, Lord) were recorded but do not seem to have been included in any of the published versions of the hymnal, while *Kula [a]maKula ka[n]cani* (Grow up, You Who Grow Slowly) is listed in the catalog as Hymn 175, though it does not appear in the most recent version of the hymnal. Each of these hymns is used for religious dance. Tracey suggests that many of the recordings he made in central and southern Africa were sold commercially in the country where the music originated. For the most part, however, the *Sound of Africa* series was placed in academic libraries and archives around the world, keeping this sacred repertory out of general circulation and away from popular consumption.

Nazarite religious performance continued to be aired on local (Kwa-Zulu Natal) Zulu-language radio at least through the early 1960s. Charles Hamm lists the discs of Shembe's Church Choir as some of the "hundreds of commercial recordings" readily available to Bantu Radio broadcasters in the early 1960s (1991, 162). Hamm's comment alludes to what had become a triangular connection between state broadcasting, early ethnomusicological pursuits, and commercial interests in South Africa, at least until the early 1960s.[3] At some point in the late 1960s or early 1970s, the SABC policy toward the programming of music and preaching by indigenous church groups like the Zionists and *ibandla lamaNazaretha* shifted. The Nazarite church occupied an ambiguous position in apartheid policymaking. On the one hand, its performance practice sounded "Zulu" (see Hamm 1991, 160); on the other, its theology (as embodied in the hymn texts) would have been deemed a threat to society, inciting members to rebel against the regime.

The official line for religious broadcasting on Radio Zulu, the main format for Zulu-language programming in South Africa, was that it had to have a (narrowly defined) Christian content. (The only preachers allowed on Radio Zulu were those who had four years of seminary education—in South Africa this eliminated almost every Zulu-speaking religious leader.) In 1994, with the change of national government and the accompanying transformation of the state media and the promotion of religious tolerance, Radio Zulu divided its religious programming to more broadly reflect listener religious diversity. From representing Christianity exclusively, it moved to 75 percent Christian programming, 5 percent Muslim, and 5 percent indigenous or traditional, with the remaining 15 percent committed to other religious interests in KwaZulu Natal.[4]

Other changes started to be made in the early 1990s to the rather limited format for religious broadcasting on Radio Zulu. In 1992, a small group of Nazarite male leaders (none of whom had had any formal theo-logical training) approached Reverend Mbatha, then radio station man-ager, about broadcasting Shembe services. He agreed to give them a short program because of the large proportion of Nazarite members in the Ra-dio Zulu audience. The church was offered a fifteen-minute slot at 8:30 A.M. on Saturday mornings (the Nazarite sabbath). These programs cur-rently include one or two stanzas of a Nazarite hymn, a prayer, and a short sermon preached by *Mvangeli* Mthethwa (a Nazarite evangelist from the township of Umlazi, just south of the city of Durban). The Nazarites re-cently changed their 8:30 A.M. slot to an earlier one, so as not to interfere with the sabbath morning service, which conventionally begins at 9 A.M.

With the new government, public broadcasting has come under pres-sure to become economically viable. The present manager of religious programs for Ukhozi Radio (the new name for Radio Zulu), Rev. Prince Zulu, commented that as a commercial radio station, they are now having some difficulty with the Nazarite radio slot because of a drop in radio au-dience during their broadcast. The evidence for the decrease is borne out in the market research surveys undertaken for the SABC by a market re-search company in Johannesburg. Rev. Zulu attributed the reduced lis-tener interest to several factors: the repetitive nature of the content of the program; the interpretations of biblical texts that the more mainstream Christian audience found offensive; and the reluctance of the Nazarite representatives to include more hymn-singing in the fifteen-minute pro-gram. Overall, he suggested that the difficulties pertained to a lack of for-mal education on the part of those who conducted the radio broadcast. He thought these problems might be solved if he conducted a workshop for the Nazarite representatives on how to present their service for a radio au-dience (Rev. Zulu, pers. comm., July 11, 1997)

From the outset, the Nazarite representatives clearly sought to use Ra-dio Zulu/Ukhozi Radio (which claims an audience of at least five million listeners, one of the largest radio constituencies in South Africa) to gain new converts to *ibandla lamaNazaretha*. Under the leadership of the third Shembe, Amos Khula, in the late 1980s and early 1990s, members were encouraged to preach on public buses and trains, and to gain whatever ac-cess they could to the mass media (Bongani Mthethwa, pers. comm., June 28, 1991). But these new media for preaching, prayer, and Nazarite sacred song required marked changes to the conventional congregational wor-ship, as outlined by the liturgy in the front of the hymnal. What is typically a 90- to 120-minute sabbath service was compressed into a mere 15 min-utes on the radio in 1992. The possibility of gaining new converts overrode the compromises made to standard liturgical and hymn performance practices.

In 1997, there is a new pressure to change the Nazarite religious format. The demands of commercial viability, market surveys, and audience numbers threaten to shape the new structure, this time digressing even further from the desires of the Nazarite committee that negotiates with Ukhozi Radio. Rev. Zulu explained that Saturday morning is prime radio time, because there is no competing interest from television (whose prime viewing occurs in the evenings). If the Nazarites want to keep their radio time, they will have to compromise on the format—by preaching less and adding more singing.

> You know if listenership goes down, we'll be having fewer adverts and less money for the station. . . . Our adverts are expensive because of the listenership we command. So in fact, if the listenership goes down, the program will be taken away. [Rev. Zulu, pers. comm., July 11, 1997.]

Rev. Zulu had also encouraged the Nazarite committee to allow one of the youth gospel groups to come into the recording studio to lay down the tracks for a Nazarite hymn (number 242) to be used as a signature tune for the program. When I spoke with him, he had still not succeeded in persuading the committee to make the change, which Rev. Zulu insists is inevitable. As a final comment, the Nazarite committee did try to negotiate television time for their community. It was unable to do so. It seems unlikely that this will ever happen, because as of September 1, 1997, the SABC cut its religious programming budget by 75 percent.

An Organ, a Church Choir, and the Nazareth Baptist Youth for Shembe (1987–1990s)

In the late 1970s, church member and music educator Bongani Mthethwa undertook to transcribe the melodies, rhythms, and harmonies of the Shembe hymns. In 1982, while teaching at the University of Zululand in South Africa, Mthethwa was approached by then church leader Amos Shembe about these transcriptions. Mthethwa played a selection of his keyboard arrangements of the hymns for Shembe, who encouraged Mthethwa to continue, and to test the accuracy of his work by forming a small choir. As he left the university, Shembe reminded Mthethwa that these transcriptions did not belong to Mthethwa but would become the property of *ibandla lamaNazaretha*. (I return to the question of ownership and intellectual property in *ibandla lamaNazaretha* later in the chapter.)

In this community, religious and political leadership are believed to be reinforced through musical leadership. Amos Shembe (who died in September 1995) is warmly remembered by *ibandla lamaNazaretha* as having been a schoolteacher and classically trained violinist before he became church leader. Though Amos was not a composer of hymns as his father and brother had been, he sought to leave his mark on the music of *ibandla lamaNazaretha* by introducing the organ as the instrument of church worship to accompany congregational (*inkhonzo*) singing on the sabbath. The organ would help to distinguish between the two types of worship in the community: *inkhonzo* (the congregational style, with hymns and an organ) and *umgido/ukusina* (religious dance with horns, trumpets, and drums).

If Amos was to leave the mark he desired, however, he required a set of notated scores of the hymn performance practice. In October 1987, after several years of work on the transcriptions, Bongani Mthethwa introduced organ accompaniment into what had been a largely improvised, relative-pitch hymn performance practice that relied on the techniques of leader calls and congregational responses. Mthethwa wrote about the difficulties he encountered in making transcriptions that would adequately convey the peculiarities of the melodic, harmonic, and rhythmic elements in the performance of *izihlabelelo zamaNazaretha* (Mthethwa 1990). Briefly, these included the problem of fixing a single melodic line when melody is usually shared between voices; allowing for a cyclical structure with a nondirectional harmonic (tonic-supertonic chord) movement; and continuing a call-and-response form. Perhaps his greatest challenge came when he played in the service. Despite the presence of the organ, which one might expect to fix the pitch, the old tradition continued of the caller starting randomly on a pitch that suited his voice. It was, therefore, up to the organist to find the key once the song leader had intoned his opening line. (See CD track 3.) Mthethwa solved the problem with an electronic gadget that he could slide up and down at the beginning (and frequently through the course) of each hymn to find the correct pitch.

The organ clearly set in motion a whole new set of possibilities in Nazarite song performance practice. Its introduction was sorely contested by the older church members, some of whom had recalled the way in which the church founder, Isaiah, had sung the hymns. They did not wish to modernize (Eric Nthuli, pers. comm., October 1991). At the most basic level, most Nazarite religious sites were not electrified, so the organ was powered with two large car batteries and amplified for the very large gatherings of the festival months (January and July in particular). Then Nazarite members had to learn to sing with a kind of instrumental accompaniment that provided more than the rhythmic counterpoint of the instruments for religious dance (see discussion of *ama14* sacred dance in chap. 4). To facilitate this process, Mthethwa formed a youth choir in KwaMashu, one of the townships in the Durban metropolitan area. This choir learned to sing four-part-harmony arrangements of the Nazarite hymn repertory. They began with the hymns that had the most clearly identifiable and singable melodies in the Western sense, i.e., those drawn specifically from the Wesleyan hymnody (see chap. 4). For a period of time from October 1987, this choir would sit around the organ, where Mthethwa was playing, in order to teach *ibandla lamaNazaretha* how to sing with a strong melodic and harmonic, fixed-pitch instrumental accompaniment.

Mthethwa made his own amateur cassette recording of the KwaMashu choir singing the most popular Nazarite hymns in SATB parts with piano accompaniment. (CD tracks 19, 20.) A limited number of copies were made of the cassette and sold at Nazarite festivals. Mthethwa explained to me that he hoped that new and old members would purchase the cassette so that they could learn how to sing *izihlabelelo* with keyboard (piano in this case) accompaniment. I have selected one of the more popular Nazarite hymns for cursory analysis of the changes in performance practice incurred by the addition of keyboard accompaniment. This is the last hymn in the hymnal, number 242, *Nkosi Yethu Simakade*, which was composed by Galilee Shembe. (CD track 20.)

Hymn 242 is one of the most popular hymns in the church, and is certainly one of the most frequently recorded. In the late 1980s recording, this *hlabelelo* has been arranged in the SATB texture that was particularly common with black school choirs in KwaZulu Natal in the 1980s. The recording starts off with an introduction played by Bongani Mthethwa on the piano. This arrangement is in 3/4 time, with a clearly identifiable melody, suggesting it is more in the style of what Mthethwa calls the "Western hymn" category of the Shembe hymns. Unlike the performance practice I discussed in chapter 4, in this context, the hymn is sung syllabically, with no repetition or fragmentation of the text to create the small rhythmic units of *ukusina* song performance. The piano tends to standardize pitch articulation, though the choir grapples with its fixity on this recording. Mthethwa has attempted to retain something of the parallel

Slow ♩ = 96

Full Choir

Nko-si ye - thu.   Si-ma-ka-de - Si- mi pha-mbi kwa-kho

Si-ya ce - la   u-be-kho-na - Na-we kha-nye na -

thi - Na-we kha-nye   na - thi.

Bongani Mthethwa's Choral Version of Hymn 242

harmonic intervals typical of earlier Nguni vocal practices. In this particular song, there is no distinction between lead and chorus voices; all sing together to create a homophonic texture. (This is not the case with all of the songs Mthethwa transcribed. Hymn 90, for example, is sung in a call-and-response, overlapping-phrases, and fairly cyclical manner, hardly articulating the stanza format of the text in the hymnal.) This version will be compared with two others later in the chapter.

Youth Choirs

One of the outcomes of the introduction of the organ and the formation of a choir to accompany the singing was an unprecedented interest on the part of Nazarite youth in forming similar choirs, now collectively called the choirs of the Nazareth Baptist Youth for Shembe. My first exposure to these choirs was in June 1991, when I was invited by Samu, my assistant, to attend the blessing of a new preacher (*umshumayeli*) in KwaMashu. She told me that her choir would be performing. Only two months into my research at that point, I had assumed that they would sing youthful versions of *izihlabelelo*. This was not the case. Instead, a group of about fifteen young men and women entered the tent where the service was held, singing an upbeat a cappella gospel tune in English called "We Are To-gether, We Are a Family." (CD tracks 21–23.)

The innovations extended beyond the text, language, and musical style to encompass the way in which this performance was integrated into the service and how the members (all were Nazarite members and many were parents of the singers) responded to it. At the start of the service we were all given a printed schedule of events, with times assigned to each item. The youth choir was scheduled for the hour between 10 and 11 A.M., coming after the 9 A.M. morning prayers. When the prayers were over, everyone was given tea and cookies, and at about ten o'clock, the youth choir arrived and lined up at the opening of the tent. They were singing "We are together." The choir sang two items lasting about ten minutes in total, and left. The group returned periodically through the hour to sing additional songs.

Each item was performed with exuberant body movements. The members responded with obvious enthusiasm, applauding after each song. By the end, when the service was almost over, several men and women were articulating their support of the choir with energetic gestures—clapping, dancing, and ululating. The response contrasted markedly with the seriousness and discipline required for *izihlabelelo* performance. Mthethwa explains that "during the Sabbath worship, the congregation sings the hymns. Clapping, dancing, or any other 'undisciplined' behavior is strictly prohibited" (1990, 2). These differences pertain to a distinction in the minds of Nazarite members between genres of performance—gospel versus *izihlabelelo*—but also suggests that song performance takes on a more strongly commodified, "concert" format, with a written program, separate song items, an audience, and applause at the end of each song to signal appreciation.

The youth choir that sang that morning in KwaMashu had numerous counterparts in *ibandla lamaNazaretha*. All of these groups came under the umbrella organization of Nazarite youth, which was formally constituted in 1990. Despite the gospel style's divergence from the sacred repertory of *izihlabelelo*'s strictly controlled performance practice and the clear demarcation of gospel as a marginal repertory in *ibandla lamaNazaretha*, I was surprised to discover that the youth choirs were strongly supported by Amos Shembe, then church leader. There were several reasons for this. Many people underscored the fact that the youth choirs had formed with the introduction of the organ into Nazarite worship. As was so often the case in this community, they argued that the precedent for this innovation had been set by church founder Isaiah Shembe. He is remembered as having been a musician, composer, and consummate poet, whose vision was to have brass band accompaniment for sacred dance (perhaps modeled on the Salvation Army brass bands that were so pervasive in the region). Amos had created a counterpart to his father's vision by introducing the organ into sabbath performance. A powerful image in the Nazarite collective memory is of Isaiah's passion for the children and young people who followed him. It is said that he used to ride a horse all over KwaZulu Natal, and as he moved around, would teach his hymns and dance steps to children before passing them on to the adult followers. Furthermore, one of the KwaMashu choir members commented that "in his time, Isaiah was preaching to people . . . who all went to different churches. . . . He was not forcing [anyone]" (pers. comm., Ndodo Mkhwanazi, June 28, 1991). Isaiah was remembered for his tolerance and acceptance of difference within his following, suggesting he would not have a problem with the new styles sung by the youth.

In the late 1980s, Amos Shembe, the ex-schoolteacher, also felt concerned about the youth and their lack of desire to attend *ibandla lamaNazaretha*. Advised by leaders like Bongani Mthethwa, *Mvangeli* Mthethwa, and Eric Nthuli (the Assistant Secretary General for Youth), Amos Shembe encouraged the official formation of the youth choirs even though they articulated their commitment to Shembe in a new musical style. The incentive for youth choirs was drawn from outside of the religious community. One report states that in the township of KwaMashu, gospel choirs were the most popular leisure activity in the late 1980s and early 1990s (Moller 1991). In addition, many of the children of older Nazarite members belonged to school choirs, which sang both gospel-style songs and pieces of "classic" or *makwaya* music.[5] The problem with these school groups was that they tended to rehearse and perform on Saturdays, the Nazarite sabbath. If Shembe wished to attract the young people to sabbath worship, he would have to give support to the plethora of gospel groups that emerged with the formation of Bongani Mthethwa's youth choir.

There was at least one other reason why Amos accepted the gospel style of the youth choirs. It seems that when youth choirs first flourished, many began to alter the sacred words and melodies of *izihlabelelo* (which take considerable time to learn) by putting new tunes to the texts (what Nathoya Mbatha is doing on his cassette). As I explained in chapter 4, these *izihlabelelo* are believed to be sacred to the community, because they were given by ancestral voices to Isaiah and Galilee through dreams and visions. In this sense, the words and tunes are considered inviolable. The youth were then advised by senior members of *ibandla lamaNazaretha* that while they could not change the repertory of the founder and his successor, they would be permitted to write new songs about the power of Shembe. Eric Nthuli commented, "Our leader [Amos] Shembe is very dynamic. We see that he likes these modern things" (Nthuli, pers. comm., October 1991). Not all the older members, even among the senior leaders, were content with this innovation. For a complex set of reasons, discussed later in the chapter, some members strongly opposed the changes.

Official sanction for the gospel choirs was, nonetheless, articulated in the organization of an annual Nazareth Baptist Youth for Shembe choir competition, the first of which was held in 1990. I attended the second competition, which took place November 30–December 1, 1991, in the township of Madadeni, located close to Newcastle in northern KwaZulu Natal. This was a weekend-long event, because the choirs gathered late on Friday evening in their home communities before starting the long drive to the competition. Choirs came from all parts of KwaZulu Natal and the city of Johannesburg. Most organized a minibus taxi to transport their group to the event. We traveled through the night on Friday, arriving at the community hall in Madadeni at about 6 A.M. The actual competition began only in the early part of Saturday evening. There were about fifty choirs competing that weekend for the trophies. The organization of the competition paralleled the practices of the pervasive secular choir competitions in South Africa, whose history goes back to the *eisteddfodhau* described by Coplan (1985, 116–17). In 1992, there were four separate regions, each with a minimum of ten choirs represented: Durban, Pietermaritzburg, the mid-coastal region (between the Tugela and Mkhuzi rivers) and the Newcastle-Johannesburg region. Each choir was required to sing one set piece and one of its own choice. The set piece for 1991 was *Oyinkhosi Amakhosi, Wena Shembe Wethu*—King of Kings, You Are Ours, Shembe) which was sung to the tune of the well-known Christmas carol "Joy to the World." (CD track 24.) Eric Nthuli, who wrote the text, borrowed the popular melody, but arranged it in the all too familiar Baroque SATB choral texture. Presumably this is why the choirs classify it as a song in the "classic" genre. (The second stanza of the Nazarite version is cited at the beginning of the chapter.)

One of the residual anomalies of South Africa's colonial past is the vast number of choirs that exist, and that, for many, are the lifeblood of their communities. Without its being the focus of their scholarship, Cockrell (1987), Coplan (1985), and Erlmann (1991) have all discussed the historical antecedents of the phenomenon known as *makwaya* (a Zuluized version of the English word *choirs*). For the most part, these black choirs sing SATB arrangements (written in solfege) of a wide range of songs that were popular in nineteenth-century England, Europe, and the United States. These range from the "Hallelujah Chorus" of Handel's *Messiah* to Stephen Foster songs of love and courtship to spirituals sung by African-American jubilee singers who visited South Africa in the 1890s (see chap. 4). Lumped together into a single category called "classic" music, this style of performance is regularly featured on regional and national radio and television.[6] Several large corporations in South Africa have sponsored national and regional choir competitions through the course of the century. Perhaps the most popular one today is held annually in Johannesburg and sponsored by the Old Mutual Insurance Company.

In about 1990, however, there was a significant national shift in the repertory, the style of dress worn by choirs, and the manner of perfor mance toward a more strongly "African" performance aesthetic. For ex-ample, at the December 1994 Old Mutual National Choir Festival in Johannesburg, the tension between the old, more "Western" mode of per-forming choral music and the new, more "traditional" modes was keenly felt.

> Besides choirs dressing up in traditional dress for their "own choice" items, body movement, which was traditionally part of African mu-sic, accompanied the singing [of] a number of choirs. Music crit-ics felt that the adjudicators, who condemned such spectacle and referred to it as "absurd," missed the significance of the reassertion of African performance aesthetics. [Pewa 1995, 9–10, citing com-ments from the *Weekly Mail and Guardian* 10/49 (1994): 34.]

For many school choirs in KwaZulu Natal that historically sang the *mak-waya* style (without body movement and wearing more "Western" attire, like school uniforms), there has also been a desire to sing more gospel-style songs. Gospel is believed to give choirs more expressive freedom— in vocal inflection, the opportunity for good voices to take solos, and the ability to dance in performance. I have frequently heard it said that gospel is an "African" performance, and *makwaya* is "Western."[7] These national trends were not lost on Nazarite youth, for whom the set piece at their an-nual choir competition in 1990 was the "classic" piece, i.e., the SATB ver-sion of "Joy to the World" with Nazarite text; while in 1991, the texts and music were both newly composed by one of the Nazarite members.

A Nazarite gospel group typically formed at the initiative of one indi-vidual. Thereafter, the leader of a group would be voted for in a democratic manner. Without the strict gender divisions characteristic of Nazarite religious sites and gatherings, the choirs included both young men and women. Regular rehearsals were organized on the sabbath, particularly in the months preceding the choir competition. At the rehearsals of the KwaMashu choir there seemed to be considerable latitude in who would take a solo and who would conduct the choir through particular items, several of which were written in a solfege form of four-part harmony. (CD track 25.) Typically, membership of the group required some form of monetary contribution, though this seemed to have lapsed with the Kwa-Mashu group when I interviewed them in 1991. (When I asked Samu about the choir in July 1997, she told me the group had disbanded because the original members were working or living elsewhere.)

The goal of these choirs was to deliver the message of *ibandla lamaNazaretha*, a message about the power of Shembe in the lives of his followers. In the past, individuals would have joined more mainstream Christian groups in their schools and communities. While these Nazarite youth desired to sing about Shembe exclusively, they sought to do it through a musical medium that young people outside of the church could understand and respond to (Eric Nthuli, pers. comm., October 1991). This is perhaps the most compelling explanation for using English in much of this repertory. With eleven official languages in South Africa, English frequently becomes the lingua franca for intergroup communication (both Inkatha Freedom Party leader Mongosutho Buthelezi and African National Congress leaders typically switch between English and Zulu, for example). In the early 1990s, English came to be considered a sign (albeit contested) of political, economic, and social progress. Using English for gospel singing enabled Nazarites to create ties with their school peers, to sound the same as the others, and to feel part of the wider community (Bongani Mthethwa, pers. comm., June 28, 1991).

The ideal format for youth choir performance was a conductor, the choir, an electronic keyboard player (preferably with a rhythm section included), and some form of sound amplification. In addition to the organ–church choir combination and secular school choirs, Nazarite youth looked to at least one other set of models in shaping their groups: those emerging from the mass media, and from radio in particular. There were three or four significant developments in the South African gospel scene at the time. The first was a group called the Holy Spirits, whose producer, J. Dumako, created the successful formula for black South African gospel music in the late 1980s—drum machine, keyboard, and small choir (pers. comm., Rob Allingham, July 1997). Their sound combined punchy religious lyrics with contemporary township popular music. The music of this Sotho-speaking group was played in both sacred and secular contexts like taxis, discotheques, and township *shebeens* (speakeasies). Second, wealthy South African musician Chicco[8] began to produce large batches of Zionist choral music on his own label in cassette format.[9] The Zionists are thought to have a membership of about four million people. Chicco easily generated fifty thousand copies of a single cassette, and claimed to have made considerable profits from the sales (Rob Allingham, pers. comm., July 1997). The third important personality in the South African gospel scene was the number one South African gospel performer, Rebecca Malope, who established a definite market for local gospel in a variety of South African languages. She was also the first black South African woman to be invited to perform at the State Theater in Pretoria, the old bastion of apartheid high culture (on September 21, 1995). Her musical style creates a hybrid sound gleaned from African-American gospel music and local South African religious performance. Fourth, the SABC's national television channel began to broadcast American gospel performances in combination with a wide variety of local gospel events. This was particularly important in the early 1990s with, among others, the Sunday morning television show, *Gospel Gold.*

The KwaMashu choir cited the radio as their main source of new songs for the group. Conventionally, the choir would record a gospel song from Radio Zulu on cassette. They would then attempt to transcribe the words from repeated listening to the tape. Although they acknowledged that, as followers of Shembe, they should be singing *izihlabelelo,* they found the rules pertaining to the sacred repertory too restrictive. Accompanying *izihlabelelo* on the keyboard was particularly difficult. Most keyboard players had minimal access to keyboards and were self-taught. They simply borrowed or rented a keyboard for a performance. Christian songs taken from the radio, however, were relatively easy to learn, and because they came from an outside repertory, individuals and groups sensed a greater freedom to experiment with solo sections and vocal inflections. While the melodies were quite straightforward, transcribing the words from the radio was more complex.

For the most part, these songs used English or Zulu or a mix of the two in a single song. Occasionally, the transcribers (all first-language Zulu-speakers) would struggle over one or two of the English words, which they either could not identify or simply did not understand. Unable to solve the problem, they would simply sing the song, making the words in question sound as much like the English equivalent as they could, even if the words did not all make sense. Once the text had been satisfactorily transcribed, the group would transform it in various ways to coalesce with Nazarite theology and evangelism. The most basic conversion of the texts was to replace the name "Jesus Christ" with "Shembe." For example, the revised version of the popular song "There are many rivers to cross" reads:

> There are many rivers to cross,
> There are more mountains to climb,
> There are many waters to swim,
> But Shembe, he's the savior.
> He's above all, (2x)
> He's the master,
> Shembe, savior of my soul.

Odd theological discrepancies emerged in these translations between Nazarite religious history and Western Christian understandings. For example, gospel songs that referred to Christ dying on the cross could not simply be used verbatim—either in English or in Zulu (Ndodo Mkwanazi, pers. comm., June 28, 1991). In this situation, the choir either discarded the song completely, or, more frequently, would simply alter some of the words to suit the Nazarite experience. Another possibility was to translate the English texts into Zulu. One example of this is the English song "There's a River," whose text was revised and translated and is now sung in both Zulu and English. (CD track 26.) The Zulu version is a rather rough translation of the English. The complete song reads:

> Ukhona umfula
> Umfula omkhula (2x)
> Igama lawo umfula iJudia.
>
> Uma ufuna ukusindiswa
> Masiye kuwo uzosindiswa.
>
> There's a river flowing down there,
> And the name [of] this river
> Is the river of *Jordan.*
>
> If you wanna be saved,
> Why don't you join us?
> We are going to the river,
> Where we're gonna be saved.

(The next stanza is not translated, but modified.)

> We are going on a highway, highway.
> Shembe, Shembe,
> Heaven, Heaven,
> Saved.

Considerable latitude is taken in the translation of the English song text, amounting to more than a simple word-for-word equivalence. There is a certain amount of cultural translation in the process. This is embodied in the idea of the river. The choir has taken the name of the river Jordan and replaced it with the word *Judia*. Judia is one of the Nazarite sacred sites north of the Tugela River. Judia is also a significant site in this book because it is the place where I first discovered cassette productions of Nazarite gospel performance, the place where the youth were called to come and celebrate their educational achievements, and also the location in which Nathoya Mbatha was given permission to make his cassette of Nazarite songs.

While Western Christians might read the word *river* metaphorically, in *ibandla lamaNazaretha*, rivers generally play a central role in religious epistemology (baptism in particular), and indeed, in the ritual cleansing and renewal of virgin girls (see chaps. 3 and 6). In Nguni tradition, rivers are the place where young girls gather together daily. While this song is typically sung by a youth choir of men and women, the solo is most commonly sung by a female voice. It is perhaps noteworthy, too, that several of the texts of gospel songs sung by the KwaMashu choir (and many others) refer to the faith of young women, underscoring the special place they hold in the ritual life of the Nazarite community in a manner unparalleled for young male members. The final stanza might easily refer to the religious pilgrimage to the holy mountain (discussed in chap. 3), which requires one to walk without any foot-covering on gravel roads for three days. That walk is believed to help individuals gain entrance into heaven.

Nazarite Cassette Production and the Problem of Nathoya Mbatha's Recording

Much of the contemporary worldbeat/world music literature centers on a critical reading of the politics of worldbeat and world music collaborations and appropriations, with the West as the perpetrator, colonizer, and miner of "other" musics for Western consumption.[10] While a fair proportion of the contents of worldbeat is sounds from repertories held sacred by these "other" communities, scholarly debate has tended to ignore the hotly contested distinction between sacred and secular genres in many music cultures. For example, the debate about the demarcation of the sacred and the secular is timeworn in American gospel music communities (Burnim 1980). When Tommy Dorsey and Clara Ward moved their spiritual singing from the church into secular spaces, like bars and clubs, the reaction from religious leaders was swift and sometimes severe. A parallel controversy has simmered for decades in contemporary Christian music over the legitimacy of religious music as entertainment versus ministry (Baker 1979, chap. 19). The argument resurfaced recently over *Nu Nation* hip hop artist Kirk Franklin's collaboration with West Coast gospel choir God's Property and female rapper Cheryl "Salt" James, of Salt 'n Peppa fame.[11]

Though ethnomusicologists and cultural studies scholars have been slow to examine these tensions as they unfold in the category of world-beat/world music, there are some passing references to the distinction in the literature. Tim Taylor addresses the ties between worldbeat and the commodification of spirituality in his discussion of discourses of authenticity and performance as they pertain to this category of recorded sound (Taylor 1997, 23–24). Steve Feld makes a rare mention of commodified spirituality almost incidentally as he lists some of the world music genres recorded on Peter Gabriel's album *Passion Sources* (Feld 1995, 109). George Lipsitz makes a fleeting reference to the "fusions of politics and popular culture, of nationalism and internationalism, of religion and revolution" in the music of Haitian popular artists Boukman Eksperyans (Lipsitz 1993, 11). I am hoping that the Nazarite controversy over particular kinds of commodification of ritual practices will open up a new avenue for reconstituting scholarly ideas about the sacred-secular binary as it is pitched against the increasing global commodification and circulation of song and dance repertories held sacred by so many musical cultures, like *ibandla lamaNazaretha*—i.e., are there limits to popularizing the sacred?

In October 1991, Radio Zulu made an announcement that all Nazarite youth were to gather at *Judia* (the Nazarite site referred to in the previous section). They were gathering to give their leader, Amos Shembe, a series of gifts. While I was at *Judia* that weekend, I purchased the first commercially produced cassette of Nazarite hymns that I had seen at *ibandla lamaNazaretha*.[12] Shembe follower and musician Robert Ndima approached me with the cassette he had made. One year later, at the same place, Nathoya Mbatha was instructed by Amos Shembe to record a cassette of Nazarite hymns instead of doing a disco album (pers. comm., Nathoya Mbatha, July 5, 1997). From 1993 to 1997, apparently in response to Mbatha's cassette,[13] several commercial and home-produced cassettes were made and marketed on Nazarite religious sites. With the exception of Mbatha's *Ngivuse Nkosi* cassette, the commercial formats produced on mainstream music industry labels (like Gallo and BMG

Records) represented "official" versions of Nazarite hymn and liturgical performance, while the home-produced, more amateur tapes included a mix of Nazarite hymns and newly composed pieces in gospel and popular township musical styles. These amateur groups began to make their own demo cassettes in the hopes of getting a break in the local record industry, or at least having their music aired on radio. Mbatha's cassette is situated between these two trends.

I have suggested in previous chapters that Shembe religious epistemology has consistently urged for a selective engagement with the wider political economy. Nazarite members have recently interpreted such activity in two quite different ways. This has resulted in two kinds of cassettes being produced in the community—one for the community itself, and the other directed at the wider world. There are also two kinds of markets. the enclave (Appadurai 1986), or what I have termed a "captured" market—one contained within the boundaries of the community—and the freer global market. There are also two kinds of performers, those who are primarily church members, and remain nameless on the cassettes, and those who desire greater recognition as popular artists, and perhaps even dream of music industry stardom. Their coexistence in *ibandla lamaNazaretha* does not mean that the church leadership is content with the division. Rather, as this chapter will reveal, the emergence of the free market artists performing the Nazarite sacred repertory has incited considerable consternation among church elders and ordinary members alike. At the very least, this kind of appropriation of Western technology and the commodification of sacred songs through individual agency "creates new economies of prestige and undermines traditional hierarchies" of religious power and authority (Lipsitz 1993, 32).

Nathoya Mbatha's *Ngivuse Nkosi* cassette brings to light many of these conflicts. His cassette production highlights the tensions endemic to the commodification and popularization of Nazarite sacred performance by individuals and groups who have harnessed the local mass media: radio, television, independent recording studios, and the ubiquitous audiocassette in post-apartheid South Africa. With the development of the audio microcassette in the 1970s, individual and independent production of regional popular performance has become commonplace in the contemporary global political economy (Manuel 1993). Aside from the well-known problems of access to equipment and the potential for economic exploitation, these independently produced popular and mediated forms of a broadly defined gospel performance have typically remained relatively uncontested in South Africa. Rather, because of the relative lack of access to modern technology and the mass media, the sheer fact of their existence has been viewed as somewhat miraculous.

On the one hand, such independent cassette production has demonstrated how, in the words of Appadurai (1997 [1996], 4, 5, 7), "ordinary people . . . deploy their imaginations in the practice of their everyday lives"; the imagination becomes "the staging ground for action"; and "electronic media provide resources for self-imagining as an everyday social project." In this vein, Peter Manuel's work on cassette cultures in India suggests that cassette technology has been used as an agent of democratization (Manuel 1993). It has reinforced, rather than diminished and secularized, traditional religious practices. On the other, it also begins to articulate a web of complexities endemic to individuals commodifying the communal nature of religious repertories. These include questions about authenticity and individual versus collective performance rights, as well as ideas pertaining to the relationships between religion, performance, and intellectual property.

Nathoya Mbatha's Recording

Nathoya Mbatha is a self-taught musician who, from a young age, has played a variety of popular genres including jazz, disco, and gospel. In several respects, his story typifies the ways in which many Nazarite members construct the narratives of their own lives and religious ideals. He became a member of *ibandla lamaNazaretha* in 1990. In 1992, when he was confronted with the challenge of producing his own recording of disco dance music, he went to Shembe to ask his permission and blessing so that the project would succeed. As this brief account will reveal, Mbatha's cassette is the product of remarkable individual ingenuity and tenacity, because the odds have typically weighed against most individuals wishing to record their own music. For someone with no regular income or political connections, it is practically impossible to fulfill the dream.

Denied access to the advantages of the industrial economy when he was growing up, like so many others, Mbatha constructed himself as a "self-made" man.[14] The only force outside of himself that he believed would assist him in his musical endeavor was the power of Shembe. In October 1992, he went to see Shembe at Judia. He explained that when he arrived to get the authorization and receive the blessing, he was first told that he should not come on a Sunday, when there were many people to see Shembe, but should return to perform for him the following day. "I had to sing and play in front of him until he was satisfied" (Mbatha, pers. comm.,

July 5, 1997). It seems the elderly man was so impressed with Mbatha's performance that he stood up and danced to it himself, the ultimate sign of Nazarite religious authorization.

Shembe gave the permission, but changed Mbatha's musical direction from disco to Nazarite music. Mbatha said he was "informed [by Shembe that he should] go and sing the music of Shembe. I was the first guy to be sent to do something like that" (Mbatha, pers. comm., July 5, 1997). He commented that he was authorized to do the recording in the presence of senior Nazarite leaders—preachers and evangelists. Ironically, however, both the change in musical direction and the matter of authorization would become thorny issues once his recording was ready to sell. Mbatha went ahead with his Shembe hymn project because he was also encouraged to do so by Shembe, his producer, and friends in other gospel groups.

Mbatha started his project with an independent recording studio called Natal Studios/C and G Records, an outfit that had a distribution agreement with BMG Records, the transnational music corporation. Under pressure from the church leadership, however, BMG Records advised Mbatha that it was not allowed to sell his music. So Mbatha had to change his plans and find another studio. Unlike the majority of aspiring gospel performers in South Africa, Mbatha was able to access a studio owned by a cousin of *Sarafina!* producer Mbongeni Ngema. Mbatha was unemployed at the time, so was fortunate to be able to record all the tracks of the hymns himself at no cost. He then overlaid these individual tracks onto a master tape. The artwork was done by a professional designer at a cost of R 1500.[15] Revolver Records (a small outfit in Empangeni, a town on the northern coastline of KwaZulu Natal) made five hundred copies of the cassette.

What sets Mbatha's cassette apart from some of the other cassettes produced by Nazarite members of their own gospel-style renditions of Shembe's hymns, which are home-produced, is its professional packaging. Mbatha's final product lends itself to marketing and potentially to worldwide distribution by the major labels, signaling a first step in the alienation of this sacred music from its home community. The front cover of the cassette insert has a photograph of Mbatha kneeling on a turquoise carpet. He is wearing the Nazarite prayer gown. In front of him, there is an open Nazarite hymnal and a closed Bible. The backdrop is a photograph of palm trees, a river, and a bridge. The image is quite typically Nazarite. There are several Nazarite photographers who set up informal "studios" at Nazarite festivals and take pictures of members in their sacred attire. Mbatha establishes authentic church membership (and authority to produce the cassette) with this set of images. Unlike all the other commercially produced cassettes of Nazarite ritual performance that label themselves collectively as *ibandla lamaNazaretha* on the covers, Nathoya Mbatha's name is written in large letters above the photograph. Underneath, and in smaller type, is the title of the cassette, *Ngivuse Nkosi*, the Nazarite hymn. This is a second sign of the ambiguity of Nathoya's position in terms of church membership and aspiring gospel music stardom.

Typical of many Christian gospel music cassette and compact disc liner notes, on the inside of the cover, Mbatha addresses select individuals and the larger community with a few personal words: He thanks his mother, Mr. Mathe of Revolver Records, Mr. Hlola, and a Rev. Dlamini. The next section reads: "Most prominent thankful [*sic*] is to my 'Father,'[16] the King of Nazareth Baptist Church, our 'Father,' Mr. M. V. Shembe." My guess is that it would have been safer for Mbatha if he had simply ended his acknowledgments with Shembe. Instead he writes: "Also to all my fans within and outside the Church of Nazareth. I LOVE YOU ALL." It is in this sentence that the religious community is commodified and redefined as a potential market.

At first glance, the cassette cover seems to be patterned after the practices of the transnational music industry. It indicates the contents of the cassette, which includes ten tracks. A closer examination, however, suggests that, as with the discrepancy between the written and performed words of the hymns discussed in chapter 4, the contents reflect Mbatha's tenuous position between Western literacy and those less bound to the printed word. To some extent, the cover resonates with the tension articulated in women's performance between the written and performed Nazarite hymns. Nine of the songs are identifiable as Nazarite hymns. These are hymn numbers 151, 142, 160, 114, 63, 179, 88, 106, and 233. I have had difficulty in identifying the tenth, because the song title written on the cassette liner diverges from the titles in the hymnal itself. Track A/ 2 is written as *Mangethwase Nkosi* (which may be a reference to Hymn 61, *Mangingozeli Nkosi*). The other hymn titles have some differences between the hymns as written in the hymnal, though none diverge to the extent of this title. What conventionally would be considered indicators of the length of an item in minutes and seconds simply makes no sense on Mbatha's cover. These numbers may refer to the counter numbers on a cassette recorder, rather than minutes and seconds. For example, track A/ 4 has the numbers 1.60 next to the title. If this indicated minutes and seconds, it would have been 2.00. The piece runs for several minutes. The performing rights simply say "South Africa," limiting their jurisdiction to

South Africa. The copyright is held in the name of TNS Production, either the production company of Mbatha, or a subsidiary of Revolver Records.

When the cassettes were ready, Revolver Record company personnel instructed Mbatha to distribute one hundred copies wherever he thought he would reach potential consumers. Seeing *ibandla lamaNazaretha* as a sure, or what I call "captured," market, he took the cassettes directly to *Ebuhleni* (where I purchased my own copy). He sold them for R 25 apiece, of which R 15 had to be returned to Revolver Records, and R 10 he kept himself. This was when his troubles began. Despite the instructions from church leader Amos Shembe that Mbatha should record the hymns of the Nazarites, its presence incited considerable consternation in the religious community. As with the introduction of the organ and formation of youth choirs, any change to Nazarite ritual or performance practice frequently elicits strong opposition from sectors of the community. The question of authorization is a particularly difficult one in *ibandla lamaNazaretha* because there are several ways in which members acquire permission. Individuals have dreams and visions in which Shembe appears to them, instructing them to undertake various missions. As Mbatha did, a member may also have face-to-face conversations with the living Shembe, where he advises them on particular matters. These are usually quietly spoken, brief, and fairly infrequent encounters. The wider community is seldom party to such authorization, and Shembe rarely intervenes in, or makes public statements about, these agreements when controversies over authorization occur. Finally, members can request permission for certain activities from the leaders of their home temples.

Mbatha confronted two other problems: the proliferation of pirated copies of his cassette that are sold in the Nazarite community (described at the beginning of the chapter), and the control of the senior members of *ibandla lamaNazaretha*. He told me that no one in the church had informed him directly that he should not have produced the cassette, but BMG Records had been instructed by Nazarite elders to discontinue selling Mbatha's music. Despite the censure, the cassette is still for sale at *Ebuhleni*. The few people that I spoke with in the community about the cassette were fully aware of, and some quite annoyed with, Mbatha's controversial interpretation and commercialization of the sacred repertory of *ibandla lamaNazaretha*.

There are many explanations for Nazarite displeasure over the Mbatha cassette. It is possible that he was being accused of using the sacred song repertory of this large and old religious community for personal commercial gain; some may feel that the repertory should never move outside of its context of live, face-to-face performance within the community. In addition, I propose that the Nazarite disquiet rests on three critical issues. First, Mbatha is accused of singing the hymns in the wrong way—"the words, melody, rhythm, everything," one woman told me (Nazarite member, July 5, 1997). Second, this cassette has come at a critical moment in the political history of KwaZulu Natal and the new South African nation. I argue therefore that the Nazarites are unhappy with Mbatha's cassette because it is pivoted at the threshold of the very core of Nazarite collective identity and power in the region. Third, the controversy over Mbatha's appropriation (albeit authorized) of the Nazarite repertory for personal gain alludes to a far larger set of questions about the ownership of commodified versions of sacred repertories; about the individual and collective rights to perform and profit from sacred rituals and practices, particularly as the potential increases for the global circulation of the sounds through the alienated media of commercially produced cassettes.

Without a doubt, Nathoya Mbatha's *Ngivuse Nkosi* cassette occupies a position in the "dangerous crossroads" of popular culture. Lipsitz describes this place as

> an intersection between the undeniable saturation of commercial culture in every area of human endeavor and the emergence of a new public sphere that uses the circuits of commodity production and circulation to envision and activate new social relations. [Lipsitz 1993, 12.]

In the same vein, it is unlikely that the other cassettes produced for the Nazarite community specifically will ever really reach that dangerous place, because there are clearly two kinds of cassette production taking place in *ibandla lamaNazaretha*. The first is intended for the collective good of the Nazarite community, and the second, while perhaps aimed at the younger members, who are more interested in the gospel than the older style of hymn performance, also looks to the larger national and global community.

The model for the first kind of cassette was Bongani Mthethwa's amateur copies of the hymns as sung to keyboard accompaniment with a formally constituted and trained Nazarite choir. Mthethwa's model has been taken up by several Nazarite groups, all of which have used the conventional channels of authorization in making their music. These include a compact disc and cassette of the Rockville Temple Choir in Soweto, entitled *Ama-Nazaretha, Ngiyalithanda Ngokulizwa*, which was recorded at the Downtown Studios in Johannesburg and published by Gallo Music Productions in 1995, and two more cassettes by two separate temple choirs: one is titled *AmaNazaretha, Isikhumbuzo* and was published by Gallo Music (1997); the other, called *Shembe: Abadumisi base-Kuphakameni, iBandla lamaNazaretha,* was published in 1995 by a small label named Khula Music, marketed by the popular group Soul Brothers, and distributed by Tusk Music (a subsidiary of Gallo). This ensemble of cassettes is intended for Nazarite community consumption, with the possibility of the compact disc being broadcast on regional radio stations. Both Bongani Mthethwa and *Mvangeli* Mthembeni Mpanza assured me that their cassettes had been authorized by the leadership and were intended to help new members learn the Nazarite song and dance repertory, in addition to teaching the older members how to sing with keyboard accompaniment. This set of cassettes thus serves to reinforce the almost century-long traditions and status quo of *ibandla lamaNazaretha*. It retains the structures of power and religious hierarchy. In this frame, the cassettes have a specific educational purpose, and thereafter have no real value for the community. This is what Appadurai classifies as the "brief commodity mode of sacred relics," which serve a very specific purpose and then are decommodified (Appadurai 1986, 24).

The model for the second kind of Nazarite cassette is Nathoya Mbatha's. There are several others, but they are amateur productions; i.e., they are not packaged in terms of music industry conventions. These cassettes have two kinds of material: the new style of singing Shembe hymns and the singers' own compositions (frequently with texts that directly address their spiritual relationship with Shembe). Some of these songs are sung in Zulu only, some in English, and others in a mix of English and Zulu (or one or two other local languages). The target audience appears to be those who operate within and outside of the Nazarite community and lifestyle. The standard format of the ensemble parallels the Shembe youth choirs—electronic keyboard (with accompanying sound and rhythm effects), perhaps a drummer and bass player, and a mixed-voice choir. These groups tend to draw freely on the more diffuse sounds of mainstream Christian gospel, township popular music, *isicathamiya,* and township music theater (such as Mbongeni Ngema's *Sarafina, Township Fever,* and *Magic at 5* A.M., and his recent exploration of gospel performance in KwaZulu Natal).

Both kinds of cassettes have versions of Hymn 242, *Nkosi Yethu Simakade.* For purposes of comparison, I have selected Mbatha's version on *Ngivuse Nkosi* (n.d.) (CD track 29) and one from the cassette *Shembe:*

Abadumisi base-Kuphakameni, iBandla lamaNazaretha (1995). (CD track 27 has a version of the "traditional" unaccompanied style of hymn-singing.) The latter version was led by *Mvangeli* Mthembeni Mpanza, in association with then Radio Zulu producer Mthunzi Namba (who worked with some of the top gospel performers when he was living in the United States and has produced several of his own gospel recordings, though he is currently working for Sony in Johannesburg). The first represents the "unauthorized" and the second the "official" version of this hymn. I examine both versions as a means of illustrating, through the ruptures with the older style that Mbatha's performance creates, just why his music is deemed to be so troubling to the community.

Mvangeli Mpanza was involved in two separate recording projects connected with *ibandla lamaNazaretha*. These were initiated by two recording interests, Mthunzi Namba, who was producing for the Radio Zulu Studios at the time, and BMG Records, the transnational record company that entered the South African market in the early 1990s after economic sanctions against South Africa were lifted. The Nazarite senior leadership agreed to the projects in light of the production of cassettes like Mbatha's. They hoped to use these recordings to remind the religious community of the correct and authentic sounds of Nazarite *izihlabelelo* performance (pers. comm., M. Mpanza, July 5, 1997). The recording interests clearly saw huge commercial possibilities in this captured market—a large religious group like *ibandla lamaNazaretha*. Because of the substantial constituencies of religious groups like *ibandla lamaNazaretha* and the Zion Christian Church (Zionists), and the lack of attention to religious music as popular culture by Gallo Records (the mainstay of South African commercial music) through the apartheid era, this music obviously held potential for huge industry profits.

The BMG project with *ibandla lamaNazaretha*, however, did not go as planned. *Mvangeli* Mpanza recalled that after the cassette had been recorded and packaged,

> [t]he BMG people brought the cassette to the church. They showed it to various people. These people sold it, but they did not bring the money back. Some did not sell it. Then apparently the person who was promoting this [project] at BMG, the person s/he was working there, I don't know what happened to her/him. So, it would appear that BMG realized there was no profit. Thereafter they did not do anything. They promised us to do a lot of things, but then they continued selling the cassettes and they are gaining a

lot of money. Since they did not give us anything, we lost interest. I find now that people are copying the cassettes. [Pers. comm., July 5, 1997.]

While I have no specific data on the profitability of the BMG/Nazarite recording collaboration, Mpanza's assessment of the breakdown in these kinds of projects between large communities and the music industry in South Africa was reiterated by Gallo archivist Rob Allingham. He explained that what frequently happens with recording projects in South Africa is that the industry will agree to record a musician or group, and give the artist(s) a monetary advance to prepare the music. (Mpanza recalled vaguely that BMG had given the church a television monitor and that other promises were made, but he could not remember the details.) Once the recording is complete, the artists get a copy of the master, mass-produce it, and sell it out of the trunks of their vehicles, thereby undercutting the industry's margin of profitability. The corollary to this problem is the piracy issue. One year before I purchased a cassette of the BMG/ Nazarite collaboration, I had heard what I thought was a recorded radio broadcast of Nazarite performance being played on a boombox at *Ebuhleni*. I purchased a copy of the cassette and labeled it "Radio Zulu?" In July 1997, I found someone selling the BMG/Nazarite cassette, but had to buy a copy of the cassette with the original copy of the cassette insert. On closer examination, I realized it was simply a version of the original BMG recording that was being sold in homemade copies. Nathoya Mbatha has encountered similar difficulties with his *Ngivuse Nkosi* cassette, and like the industry, he has no idea how to counter the obvious pirating of his cassette.

Although the official Nazarite repertory as a whole has three separate sources of inspiration for its melodic material and compositional style— precolonial Nguni song, Western mission song, and Isaiah Shembe's eclectic musical style—there are several musical elements that characterize *izihlabelelo zamaNazaretha* as a genre of hymn-singing distinct from conventional Euro-American performance practices. These include:

> *(a)* call-and-response structure that lends itself to a cyclical rather than linear structure;
>
> *(b)* overlapping phrases between hymn leader and members, and between members each singing his or her own rhythmic segment of text;
>
> *(c)* a single tempo, usually slow and steady;

(d) syllabic treatment of text;

(e) melodic interest in lower voices;

(f) prominent cross-rhythmic tension;

(g) pentatonic and hexatonic modes, no minor tonality, modulation, or chromaticism;

(h) melodies tend to descend (start high and end low);

(i) melodic lines correspond to tonal contours of the Zulu language;

(j) the hymns are characterized by what Mthethwa calls "delayed harmonization." "The leader sings and you delay for so many pulses and then you attack and harmonize what he has sung. At some point you separate and at some point you come together with him" (Mthethwa, pers. comm., June 29, 1991); and

(k) the result is a texture that is much more dense than the conventional four-part harmony of the mission hymn.

These elements are clearly evident in the "official" version of Nkosi Yethu, as led by Mvangeli Mpanza, and the version on track 27 of the CD. Hymn 242 was composed by Galilee Shembe in the most "Westernized" of the three compositional styles—the mission melodies. The text of Hymn 242 is as follows:

Nkosi yethu simakade	Lord, our Eternal One
Simi phambi kwakho;	We stand before you;
Siyacela ubekhona	We request your presence,
Nawe kanye nathi	You, together with us.
Nawe kanye nathi	You, together with us.
Yehla Moya oyiNgcwele,	Descend, Holy Spirit,
Ngena wena kithi.	Enter into us.
Usebenze kubo bonke	And work within everybody
Loko okuthandwa nguwe.	In the manner you desire.
Loko okuthandwa nguwe.	In the manner you desire.
Zonke izono maziphele.	May our sins be wiped away,
Nazo zonke izifo.	And all diseases.
Ubumhlophe nobumnandi	Let purity and sweetness
Mabuhlale nathi.	Dwell with us.
Mabuhlale nathi.	Dwell with us.

Mbatha's version of Hymn 242 reflects many of the musical elements found in the songs sung by the Nazareth Baptist Youth for Shembe. These include:

Mvangeli Mpanza's "Perfect" Version of Hymn 242

(a) call-and-response has been transformed into soloist (verse) and chorus (refrain), with some overlap in melodic lines;

(b) overlap in melodic phrases is used in an "echo" effect rather than an extension of the call;

Slow waltz ♩ = ca. 84

Nko-si ye - thu.   Si - ma - ka - de - Si-mi pha-mbi kwa - kho

Si-ya ce - la [o-wu] u-be-kho na   [mm] Na-we kha-nye na - thi -

Na-we kha-nye   na - thi.

Nathoya Mbatha's Gospel Version of Hymn 242

(c) melodic interest lies in the higher voicing and extensive liberty with rhythmic articulation of text;

(d) moves toward more homophonic, block chordal texture, rather than the interweaving of voices one hears in *ukusina* singing;

(e) some songs have a single line and cyclical form, most use a verse-refrain structure with a clear start and finish, musically and textually;

(f) a tendency to use major scales spanning the octave, some use of chromatic inflection;

(g) melodic contours are more in the Western classical arch form;

(h) English texts with little attention paid to tone-tune relationship; and

(i) harmonization in four parts and with the chord sequence I–IV–ii–V–I, common to much South African (and other) popular music.

In addition, in Mbatha's recording there is a definite shift in aesthetic sensibility in terms of the role of the voice vis-à-vis the instrumental accompaniment. When I discussed the introduction of the organ into *inkhonzo* performance, I suggested that despite the fixed pitch of the keyboard, the human voice continued to be privileged over the organ. In Mbatha's recording, the keyboard and other sounds have taken on a far stronger role as harmonic and rhythmic foundation, allowing the voice to freely elaborate on the melodic path that is shaped by the tonal contours of the words. Contiguously with the larger popular versions of South African gospel, Mbatha takes enormous liberties with rhythmic articulation and the use of falsetto vocal timbre, and he frequently clips the ends of syllables. This contrasts markedly with the smooth, continuous wall of sound created by the older style of Nazarite hymn-singing.

Mbatha evokes a powerful sense of his own individual voice and presence in this performance, a presence typically aligned with popular performance styles outside of *ibandla lamaNazaretha*. At the end of the hymn text, he continues playing the rhythmic and melodic foundation while he talks (in Zulu) over the music. As he did on his cassette cover, and modeling his performance on those of other gospel singers, Mbatha addresses Shembe, praying aloud to him, as if he is articulating the collective wishes of his imagined audience or community. Roughly translated and summarized, his prayer asks that all sins be wiped away, and that the Lord of the Nazarites and the Holy Spirit stay with them; he prays for peace on the earth, and says that it is time for the Lord to come, they are praising him at all times. The public articulation of collective prayer in *ibandla lamaNazaretha* seldom takes place, except when it is led by the few Nazarite elders who hold officially sanctioned positions in the church. In this kind of prayer, Mbatha is once again transgressing the hierarchies of Nazarite power and religious authority, though his style is consistent with mainstream South African gospel performance.

Mbatha remains undaunted. He hopes that with his new song recording projects he will be able to combine the religious vision of the late Amos Shembe, who encouraged members to go out and preach to the South African nation, with the pervasive political discourses of nation-building and community reconstruction and development. To this end, he hopes to get his music broadcast to the larger Zulu-language community on Ukhozi Radio. Before he can do so there is yet another hurdle to jump. Mbatha will have to get his music onto compact disc. Rev. Zulu assured me that queuing cassettes was simply too difficult for radio deejays. While both Radio Zulu and cassette technology have provided channels for ordinary communities to air their music in the past, this is no longer the case at Ukhozi Radio.

Perhaps because of the controversy generated by his first cassette, Mbatha now clearly identifies himself not so much as a performer (of

Shembe hymns), but as a composer. His narrative about the process by which he composes new songs is provocative, particularly in light of the significant shifts in the ways in which Isaiah and Galilee Shembe received hymns from holy messengers: Isaiah by hearing a female voice, and Galilee by seeing the words written on a chalkboard (see chap. 4). He explained:

> When I am dreaming, or when I am just sleeping, it happens that I see myself in front of people, singing and all that. . . . When I wake up, I wake up and go to a keyboard or an organ or a tape if it's necessary, and tape what I have seen. . . . In the dream, it happens that I am with the choir, or I'm alone, sometimes in the forest or bush, seeing myself singing and a lot of people who are seated down. . . . They are just an audience. [Pers. comm., Nathoya Mbatha, July 5, 1997.]

This excerpt from my interview with Nathoya Mbatha invokes the sense of flux and possibility that political and economic change in the 1990s, and music's place in that transformation, promised to black South Africans generally. In Mbatha's understanding, the compositional trope was no longer either Isaiah's path in Zululand or Galilee's chalkboard in the school setting. It was not even confined to Amos's insistence on the organ as a mainstream cultural medium. Rather, it encompassed an imagined and inclusive space of commodified gospel performance, with a stage, a singer or choir, and an audience on the one hand, but which also enabled Mbatha to liken himself to Isaiah alone "in the forest or bush" on the other. This resonates with the older, more traditional and feminized space for Isaiah Shembe's visions of musical sounds. It also corresponds to, and expands upon, Amos Shembe's more modernist desires for keyboards and youth choirs in church ritual.

The dialectical tension that Mbatha speaks of between the forest or bush and the concert stage and audience reflects larger Nazarite conflicts over the terms of social, musical, and gendered transformation and how this impacts upon their own community. In contemporary South Africa, the forest and bush suggest past forms of creative force and resources, long defined by the political center as feminized, while the stage and its audience embody more centralized, masculine signs of power. Nathoya Mbatha, like his Shembe ancestors before him, plays with these tensions. He claims his authority to arrange the hymns in a contemporary gospel style, and to compose new songs of his own, by describing the more traditional and sacred authority vested in his dream experiences, which are co-incidentally filled with modernist imagery and empowerment.

The tension between the forest and the stage speaks to a conflict about the terms of Nazarite engagement with the wider political economy, now not simply a regional concern, but one integrally connected to the world at large. Nathoya Mbatha is at the forefront of the conflict. Like Amos Shembe and the younger members of the community, he is committed to promoting songs about Shembe beyond the community through the channels of the local music industry and mass media. As other Nazarite members do, Mbatha believes he was authorized to act by Shembe himself. His beliefs are consistent with the entrepreneurial spirit that has characterized *ibandla lamaNazaretha* from its early history. One might ask quite legitimately how this kind of appropriation of Western material culture and transformation of it to Nazarite ends differs from the production and sale of hymn books and prayer gowns by other church members. Like Mbatha, these individuals profit financially from the sale of their goods.

The only viable means of dealing with the local music industry is as an individual composer and arranger. The trouble is that this brings Nathoya Mbatha's goals and desires into direct conflict with Nazarite beliefs about the power of their music to articulate the very core of collective identity in the region. These tensions also evoke anxiety in the local music industry over questions of authorship, intellectual property, and the politics of performer's, arranger's, and "composer's" rights when dealing with religious repertories.[17] These problems arise in communities like *ibandla lamaNazaretha* that believe that sacred songs were not composed by human beings, but were rather the result of heavenly mediation. In *ibandla lamaNazaretha* heavenly messengers gave the songs to Isaiah, to the three women after Isaiah's death, and to Galilee Shembe.

It seems to me that the problem begins when a sacred song is ascribed a market value. In metaphorical terms, this articulates a conflict between what I have termed the feminized and sacred hymn repertory of the Nazarites (collectively owned, performed, and protected from violation) and the more masculinized concerns of the political center (over the arrangements of this repertory by individuals for individual gain) that Mbatha's *Ngivuse Nkosi* cassette alludes to. Historically, the performance of Nazarite song and dance has been an intrinsically social process. To become a full member of *ibandla lamaNazaretha*, and indeed, to gain entrance into heaven after death, all followers are required to participate in its performance. In other words, all Nazarites have a stake in collective access to the words and tunes of their founder, Isaiah Shembe. Individual ownership of a communal repertory would constitute a violation of the very core of individual and collective religious identity.

So, why do the Nazarite leaders not ban Mbatha's cassette outright? The "problem" with Mbatha's cassette is that it testifies to the spiritual power of Shembe, and hence, it has a collective value for Mbatha individually, and the Nazarite community as a whole. The sheer fact that an individual like Mbatha is able to produce a cassette at the level of professionalism he has attained is a mark of the miraculous force of Shembe in the contemporary world. Unlike with the live performance of Shembe's hymns, in the commodified version, there are at least two levels of skill and creative input required in the production of a cassette like *Ngivuse Nkosi:* the compositional and performance skills and the entrepreneurial and technological knowledge to get the music commodified and sold.

While Mbatha may have drawn on the power associated with the Nazarite song repertory, he has also moved it outside of the confines of the enclaved market and into the dangerous, but potentially exciting, "crossroads" of popular culture. Both *ibandla lamaNazaretha* and Mbatha might stand to profit from such visibility, the community with increased membership through conversion, and Mbatha through enhanced sales of his music. There remain many gray areas pertaining to questions of intellectual property, and performance and composer's rights in *ibandla lamaNazaretha*. On some occasions this ambiguity works against the community as a whole. There are some who think that this is the case with the commercial cassette production of Nazarite hymns like that of Nathoya Mbatha. At other times, individual initiatives pertaining to the sacred repertory work for the community. One example is found in the individual transcriptions of *izihlabelelo zamaNazaretha* that were so carefully created by church organist Bongani Mthethwa before he died. These were later claimed by Amos Shembe, as the singular property, not of Bongani Mthethwa, but indeed of the religious collectivity as a whole.

Conclusion

In chapter 4, I examined the way in which a new repertory of Shembe song was constituted as sacred and inalienable within the Nazarite religious community and feminized by the wider political context. In the early twentieth century, a historical period of rapid sociopolitical transformation and crisis, Isaiah and Galilee Shembe's songs were regarded as sacred by the Nazarite community because in word and performance practice, they enshrined elements of precolonial cultural practice and collective identity necessary to move African people in KwaZulu Natal into South Africa's emergent industrial economy. It was feminized heavenly messengers, the female voices of the African ancestors, who facilitated the transition by inscribing African experience into the historical record, as it is now contained in Nazarite hymns. These hymns were integrated into the Nazarite moral economy. Their performance practice, which relied on the call of a spiritual leader, and the collective though staggered responses of individuals, facilitated the constitution of a new, albeit marginal, sense of community for many African people in KwaZulu Natal.

In the late 1980s, the sacred path of the song repertory began to diverge and to seek a place closer to the political and religious center. Within the community, Amos Shembe, with the help of Bongani Mthethwa and the KwaMashu Youth Choir, introduced organ accompaniment to *izihlabelelo* performance. Nationally, Christian gospel performance, with its use of vernacular languages, keyboards, and a freer singing style, was introduced to the South African market. In addition, in the early 1990s, South Africa witnessed momentous economic and political change as a nation and as a reintegrated member of the continent of Africa, and of the global political economy. The democratization of technology (cassettes and inexpensive home recording equipment), the success of individual Zulu- (and Sotho-) language groups (like Ladysmith Black Mambazo, Mahlathini and the Mahotella Queens, and the Thulisa Brothers) in the international market, the appearance of Zionists at the Smithsonian Folklife Festival in Washington, D.C., in 1997, and a small Shembe group at the Music Village in London in 1996, as well as the rapid growth in the South African gospel music market, have combined to force the Nazarite community to address and perhaps reconsider the place of its very "African" sacred repertory in the contemporary world.

The tensions in the religious community over the cassette commodification arise out of a shifting and contested sense of the changing boundaries of the religious community, the market, and its means of exchange. Is the commodity for Nazarites only or for the world at large? On the one hand, internally, *ibandla lamaNazaretha* wishes to abide by the old principle of sacrificing desire (in this case, the desire for individual stardom and commercial profit) for the larger common good. On the other hand, it seems that at the end of the twentieth century, if the community is to redefine its place beyond the confines of the religious community, the hymns of Shembe may have to be subject to a limited commodification.

Can the Nazarite repertory retain its sacred quality in the "dangerous crossroads" of popular culture and nation building? There are no simple solutions to the dilemma. If the Nazarite community is to retain its sense of collective power and identity in South Africa in the twenty-first century, the leaders of *ibandla lamaNazaretha* will have to meet the challenge of what Annette Weiner terms "keeping-while-giving." In order to hold on to its sacred power and value, the hymn repertory cannot simply be thrown to the whims and fluctuations of the transnational music market in the hope of gaining new converts. Instead, Nazarite engagement with the popular music market through mass-mediazation and commodification of its hymn repertory will have to be thought of as a kind of "temporary loan" to the world (Appadurai 1986). It will never be fully given, because its worth as a sacred commodity in *ibandla lamaNazaretha* rises above monetary value. Nazarites will have to work out how to give something of the social force of religious song and dance performance through the mass media while still keeping something of its human value and ritual power out of circulation. As Isaiah Shembe so skillfully managed in the early twentieth century, they will have to learn to market Nazarite ritual forms without reducing them to alienable commodities, separated from their source of female-guided spiritual empowerment. In this lies the real challenge and value of *izihlabelelo zamaNazaretha* in the twenty-first century.

SIX

AmaNtombazane as the
Mountains of Abstinence

We ntombi yaseNazaretha	O Nazarite maiden
Mawu kahle umpompoze	May you weep like a waterfall
Ngehlazo elikwehleleyo	Over the shame that has befallen you
Ezweni lakini.	In your own land.
Zizwe lalani uzulu ezwakale	The nations are sleeping so that the Zulus
Phambi ko Msindisi	Can be heard before the Savior.
(Hlab. 45/3)	(Hymn 45/3)

There is a story told in *ibandla lamaNazaretha* about a white girl from England who had a dream in which Shembe appeared. In this dream, Shembe had told the young girl that she would be healed from her inability to menstruate.

> Her parents then consulted world experts, sages, and seers, and they all agreed that they didn't know if the man in the girl's dreams was like Elijah, Moses, or Jesus, but they knew he was somewhere in Africa. . . . And so they traveled to South Africa. On their arrival in Cape Town, they inquired about this prophet and they were told that there were many prophets in Africa. They were shown pictures of African prophets, and when she saw his picture, the child identified the Prophet [Shembe]. . . . So they traveled to Durban and soon they were on their way to where Shembe was known to live.

They arrived at *Ekuphakameni* in the month of July, when the virgin girls have their dance festivals, and Shembe instructed the young white girl to join the virgin dance.

> She danced for a while. Shembe said, "*Hauw!* Have you ever seen a white person dance? Bring her back here." And so the Lord

Shembe said to the parents, "Take her away, she is healed." And so they took the girl to Durban and booked a place in one of the hotels. They wanted to see the truth of what God's prophet had said without even praying for, or laying hands on, the girl.

After three months, the girl started to menstruate, and the family returned to *Ekuphakameni* to thank Shembe.

> They asked how much they could pay Shembe. The man of God said, "God's gift is not to be bought by man." He suggested that they should go back to their land and preach, and tell the people that the savior had arrived and that he was at *Ekuphakameni*. So they went back, and when they returned to their country, they bought and sent to *Ekuphakameni*, a flag, a square clock, and a bell. The bell is used to summon the people for the beginning of the church service. . . . They wrote a letter to accompany the thing they had bought. It read, "Remember us always when the bell rings, the clock will tell the time for the beginning of the service. May the Lord remember us when he calls the people into church. With the flag I am saying that Africa has triumphed. . . . The nations of the world have been waiting for the Lord. Now they have heard that he is at *Ekuphakameni*." [Story told by *Mkhokheli* Ntuli, Lamontville Durban, to church secretary Mr. Petrus Dhlomo.][1]

A provocative narrative, Mrs. Nthuli's telling of this Nazarite cultural treasure powerfully links together Isaiah Shembe's ability to heal with the ritual purity of the dancing bodies of virgin girls. He did not even lay hands on her. All she had to do was participate in the sacred dance of virgin girls, and wait for her body to heal. The outcome, a young girl's body made whole, had both local and transnational ramifications. Ultimately, it would force a recognition from the English, the dominant colonial force in KwaZulu Natal, that spiritual efficacy was now to be found in Africa. The narrative also signifies a hybrid spiritual economy in which the Nazarites fuse elements of British cultural and ritual practice (flags, clocks, and bells) with more local signs of ritual power (a prophet, virgin bodies, and sacred dance).

In the first part of this book, I discussed the formation of the Nazarite religious community and ritual cycle by Isaiah Shembe in KwaZulu Natal. While life events of young girls and women were woven into the text, the focus of those chapters has been the Nazarite community as a whole. In this chapter the young female virgins (called "maidens" by the

Nazarites) take center stage, as they do in Mrs. Nthuli's narrative, and the larger frame of the Nazarite ritual cycle. I examine the variety of ways in which the ritual purity and power of the bodies of these maidens have been inscribed into Nazarite written texts (hymns and letters) and ritual practice, and have come to embody the spiritual power of the Shembe leaders, and indeed, of the community as a whole. As discussed in previous chapters, this has involved the skillful weaving together of a variety of cultural practices and historical moments. These include precolonial Nguni puberty rites, expressive culture, and beliefs about the power of the female body to produce progeny and to signify ritual purity; truths read in the Old and New Testaments of the mission Bible; and powers associated with Western dress and technology.

To move the African peoples of KwaZulu Natal into a selective involvement with the emergent industrial economy in the early twentieth century, Isaiah Shembe blended the archaic with the new. The bodies of these virgin girls thus became the vessels of this tricky transformation. The privilege ascribed to these maidens came at some cost. As Isaiah outlines in a letter to *ibandla lamaNazaretha* (discussed at the end of this chapter), in order to retain ritual purity each Nazarite girl and young woman would have to remain a virgin and hence closet her sexual desire. The reward, however, would be the lifetime protection of Shembe (particularly for those who live on Nazarite land) and the privilege of a continuing "special relationship" with the Nazarite prophet.

In the first section of this chapter, I examine precolonial Nguni beliefs about virgin girls and ritual power, as embodied in the cosmological relationship between the Lord of the Sky, *Nkulunkulu*, and his daughter, *Nomkubulwana*. This relationship provides a model for the earthly connection between Isaiah and his female adherents, and it is inscribed in the texts and beliefs about the composition of *izihlabelelo zamaNazaretha*, which are discussed in the second section. There is a brief analysis of the way in which these girls articulate the historical and gendered shifts in the wider society through bodily attire. The bulk of the chapter focuses on two annual rituals in which Nazarite maidens are the main actors. While these rituals have historical precedents in precolonial Nguni custom as rituals associated with a girl's coming-of-age, in *ibandla lamaNazaretha* they are overlaid with biblical narrative and local politics. They serve to remind the religious collectivity of the way in which the ritual power of virgin bodies was used by Isaiah to fight battles with the most polluting of all outside forces, the racism of the colonial state.

Gender Relations and Nazarite Poetics

Throughout colonized Africa indigenous cultural constructions have drawn on the stories and myths of the biblical Old Testament. These have provided a rich store of analogous sociocultural and political contexts for the integration of African traditional beliefs with those of Western Christianity. The religious culture of Isaiah Shembe is no exception. Isaiah combined the biblical story of Jephthah the warrior and his daughter (Judges 11) with Zulu traditional cosmological values to create the Nazarite religious epistemology pertaining to virgin girls. This cultural and religious bricolage constitutes the exegesis of one of the girls' rituals discussed later in the chapter.

The most important deity in Zulu cosmology is the figure that Berglund (1989 [1976], 64–77) translates into English as the "Lord-of-the-Sky." The Zulu version of this English phrase refers to *Nkosi yezulu* or *Nkosi yaphezulu*. In Christian terms, the Lord above is called *Nkulunkulu*, and he is believed to live in the sky. His residence is contrasted to that of the ancestors, who inhabit the space beneath the earth. The next most prominent figure in the minds of Zulu traditionalists is *Nomkhubulwana* or *Nkosazana yeZulu* (the Heavenly Princess). *Nomkhubulwana* is characterized as a virgin. As such she is associated with young girls of marriageable age and with fertility (of girls, animals, and agriculture), rain, springs, and mist. She also acts as an adviser to girls on issues of personal behavior and the selection of a marriage partner.

For many she appears with the first spring mists at the tops of hills or mountains. Normally it is only women and children who may "see" her, for she often emerges completely naked except for a string of white beads around her waist. In addition, those who spoke with Berglund assured him that *Nomkhubulwana* never came in dreams[2]—she was never seen, though she was always heard.[3]

Furthermore,

> [t]o a number of Zulu she is the daughter of the Lord-of-the-Sky. It is in this capacity that she is regarded as being everlasting in that she neither becomes older nor changes. [Ibid., 65.]

In addition to her capacity to grant fertility to girls, animals, and the land, an intimate relationship between *Nomkhubulwana* and *Nkulunkulu* is perceived in traditional cosmology. For many, *Nkulunkulu*

> is claimed to tell his daughter everything she wants to know and hence she is able to tell her earthly sisters things they wish to know.

My informants said that the Princess loved human beings very much and that this was the reason for her giving them good advice from time-to-time, introducing new customs and teaching people "the new ways of behaving in a proper way."

One of Berglund's informants told him:

To those who do not believe (i.e. pagans) she is what the angels are to me. She gives them advice as to their behavior so that they may be looked upon as good and reliable girls. . . . She tells them many things which we do not know of. . . . So the angels are my friends who helped me through everything. It is the same relationship between *Nomkhubulwana* and the pagan girls. She tells them everything so that they do not transgress the rules and cause trouble. [Ibid., 70–71.]

It is both *Nomkhubulwana's* control over fertility and the intimacy of her relationship with *Nkulunkulu* that enables her to help a community to sustain itself over time. Krige writes,

the deity *Inkosazana* who personifies vegetation and fertility is conceived of as a virgin girl and in many ceremonies associated with her the actors are virgin girls, very often naked. It is they who through right living are in the best position to protest against any evil that has befallen the community. It is said, "*Inkosazana uyajab ula uma umsebenzi wakhe usetshenzwa izintombi saka ngoba naye uyi ntombi*—Inkosazana is happy when her work is carried out by pure young girls because she[4] herself is a virgin." Failure to observe moral rules connected with sex is believed to cause evil to befall the community. [1968, 175.]

Berglund's writing on the cosmological relationship between *Nomkhubulwana* and *Nkulunkulu,* and Krige's on Zulu girls' fertility rites, parallels the relationship between Isaiah Shembe and the virgin girls in several ways. First, the Princess is a virgin, who in her capacity to bring rain and embody the fertility of people, animals, and fields symbolizes the well-being of the religious community. Second, she and *Nkulunkulu* are linked through kinship connections—he is the father, she the daughter. Nazarites call Shembe *Baba* (father). Third, she is associated with the mountain—as is the ritual power of Nazarite girls, who are metaphorized as *Intabayepheza* (the mountain of abstinence). Finally, *Nkulunkulu* is used in the Nazarite context to refer to both God and Shembe, pointing to a blurring of spatio-temporal boundaries between the earth and the cosmos and between Shembe as Prophet and God.

Clearly, the cosmological relationship between *Nkulunkulu* and *Nomkhubulwana* provided a model for the construction of the close kin relationship between Shembe and the virgin girls, and the strategic role played by these girls in the welfare of the community.[5] I shall suggest later in this chapter that the ritual principles underpinning this relationship are embodied in the two annual Nazarite fertility rites for girls. Celebrated from the early decades of *ibandla lamaNazaretha*, the Nazarite girls' rituals have never been explicitly associated with *Nomkhubulwana* and the fertility of crops. Rather, Nazarite girls are treasured for their value as spiritual vessels. There is nevertheless a remarkable coincidence in the writing of Esther Roberts (1936) concerning the dates of both the girls' festivals and those for the blessing of the crops. Roberts says,

> In the summer people must not eat green food before the 25th of September, because this is the day on which Shembe blessed the new crops. [Ibid., 91.]

She comments further:

> The celebrations held on the 25th of September are known as "The Festival of Maidens," and girls from different missions gather at Ekuphakameni to hear Shembe's preaching, to feast, and to dance. [Ibid., 107.]

At another point she writes,

> Every day during the Festival in July, services are held and towards the conclusion of the celebrations, the seeds for planting are taken to the Grove of "Paradise" and Shembe prays that they may be fruitful and blesses them. [Ibid., 106.]

While there was clearly a connection between these two rituals in the early days of *ibandla lamaNazaretha*, to my knowledge there is no longer a time set aside for the blessing of crops by Amos Shembe at *Ebuhleni*, though the girls' rites continue to hold a central place in the Nazarite ritual cycle. With this in mind, I propose that the Nazarite rituals that draw on traditional Zulu girls' fertility rites have been transformed by Shembe from celebrations of female fertility and the onset of sexual desire into religious performances that encourage the sacrifice of the self and the closeting of such desire. In *ibandla lamaNazaretha*, the relationship between the spiritual father and daughter overrides that of a young girl and her young male lover. This will be demonstrated amply in the analysis of female rituals later in the chapter.

The spiritual intimacy between Shembe and the virgin girls in *ibandla lamaNazaretha*, reinforced by the mythological characters of *Nkulunkulu* and *Nomkhubulwana*, is represented further through Nazarite expressive culture. While I primarily examine the domain of song, the importance of the young virgins to Shembe is also inscribed in the structure and attire for *ukusina* (sacred dance), and intersects with the domain of dreams and visions. Shembe's stress on expressive culture as a central medium for the articulation of religious ritual was one of his most effective means of drawing in young women. Evidence of this appeal is contained in a letter written in 1921 by the Deputy Commissioner of Police in Pietermaritzburg (KwaZulu Natal) to the Commissioner of Police in Pretoria. He suggests that the appeal of Shembe's movement for young girls lay in the uniforms and ritual performances characteristic of the religious group. It was not only in the performances of song, dance, and narrative that the young girls featured, but in the very formulation of the hymnal of *ibandla lamaNazaretha* in the early decades of this century.

Like the rest of the Nazarite members, officially, Nazarite girls do not compose new songs or create new dance forms. These girls do not tell of their dreams in public. They have nevertheless played a critical role in Isaiah's formulation of Nazarite ritual content. In chapter 4, I explained that Isaiah's hymn composition was facilitated through the female voices of heavenly messengers or angels. In light of the preceding secondary material on *Nomkhubulwana* presented by Berglund, which stresses that it was only girls and women who heard *Nomkhubulwana*, the sound of a young girl's voice in the ears of a young man was a rather extraordinary event. The fact that Isaiah heard the voice of a young girl points to the metaphorical equivalence drawn between the creative powers of young girls to enable the birth of both physical progeny and religious song.

Several important issues emerge from Sundkler's account. First, a poetic relationship between Isaiah and the cosmology—in the voice of the young girl—was created through the gift of song. Second, the cosmological/creative relationship between *Nomkhubulwana* and *Nkulunkulu* later assumed human form when Isaiah (now perceived to be the personification of the cosmology by his followers) gave the Nazarite girls hymn number 84 in the first girls' camp event, called *Ntanda*, in the early 1930s (*Ntanda* is discussed below).

Lasukake nezulu.	Then came the thunderstorm.
Laduma kakhulu impela!	It crashed loudly indeed!

Lazidla lazichita zonke.	It devastated and routed them all.
Lezo zitha zethu.	Those enemies of ours.
Amen, amen, amen.	Amen, amen, amen.
Umuhle wenangwe yethu.	How magnificent you are, our Leopard.[6]
Umuhle wena Krsetu wethu.	How magnificent you are, our Christ.
Sukuma wena, Nkosi yethu.	Stand up, our Lord.
Uchoboze izitha zethu.	And crush our enemies.
Amen, amen, amen.	Amen, amen, amen.
(Hlab. 84/5,6)	(Hymn 84/5,6)

This gift of song was given while the girls were seated on grass circles, which symbolized sexual purity and moral power. (They are discussed further in the context of the girls' rituals.) The grass rings added power to the prayers of Shembe and the young girls for victory over a white man. This victory was gained through the mustering of cosmological forces.

These cosmological powers are embedded in the text of Hymn 84 in the metaphorical devastation caused by thunder. In this regard, Berglund comments (ibid., 37) that while thunder is always attributed to *Nkulunkulu*, it may have male or female characteristics. The first type of thunder—the male thunder—simply brings rain after drought. The female thunder, however, is sudden and cracking thunder, accompanied by forked lightning and enormous destruction. Such unexpected cracks of lightning are like the "tongue of an angry woman who speaks frightful things . . . because she is angry" (ibid., 38). The violence articulated in the text of Hymn 84 clearly points to this kind of thunder—a cosmological power of the female order. Such force is believed to destroy the enemies of the Nazarite community.

There are several other hymns that point to Nazarite constructions of gender, as they pertain to young girls. Analysis of these texts provides insight into the articulation of experience, hidden forms of consciousness, and, in this instance, the substance of religious belief.[7] In this section I shall focus on five hymn texts in which the impassioned voices of Isaiah and Galilee inscribed female experience into the sacred repertory of Nazarite song. In his hymn texts, Shembe memorialized the experiences of African women and men through the metaphor of the body. He focused particularly on his female followers by manipulating the themes of defilement, loss of community, social order, and hope, and the embodiment of emotion through tears and weeping. Finally, he called on Nazarite girls to rise up to enter the spaces of sanctuary, and in so doing to retain bodily purity so that they may dance the sacred dance—the embodiment of cosmological empowerment—with hope.

The first text comes from Isaiah's Hymn 45, stanza 3, quoted at the beginning of the chapter (and cited again for clarity).

We ntombi yaseNazaretha	O Nazarite maiden
Mawu kahle umpompoze	May you weep like a waterfall
Ngehlazo elikwehleleyo	Over the shame that has befallen you
Ezweni lakini	In your own land.
Zizwe lalani uzulu ezwakale	The nations are sleeping so that the Zulus
Phambi ko Msindisi.	Can be heard before the Savior.

In this stanza Isaiah exhorts the young maidens to "weep like a waterfall" over the loss of honor that has befallen them in their own land. The image of the waterfall is highly suggestive. It portrays the embodiment of emotion in the form of a powerful, overflowing stream of sorrow. It evokes a sense of the strength of water as the agent of cleansing and purification. The juxtaposition of the two images—weeping and societal shame—reinforces the lamentations of Isaiah for the societal disorder. Finally, the waterfall and weeping are both images linked to girls and women—girls are the bearers of good rains and, by extension, powerful waterfalls, and the women are the singers of sorrow or weeping.

The demise of the sense of African community is articulated in the images of homestead destruction and the kind of women who are weeping—the widows and orphans—traditionally ascribed a marginal status. In Isaiah's spaces, however, they formed the majority. Thus Hymn 21, stanza 1, reads:

Izwe lakithi lichithekile	Our country has been laid to waste,
Nemizi yakithi	And our homesteads
Ayisahlali muntu;	Are no longer occupied by people;
Singabafelokazi nezintandane	We are widows and orphans.
We Nkosi yeSabatha	O Lord of the Sabbath
Usishiyelani?	Why do you forsake us?

While Isaiah was clearly referring to social processes in the early decades of this century, this hymn text is particularly poignant in the context of the extreme violence and violation that has torn communities apart, and that has created subsequently an exodus of people. South African journalist Rich Mkondo (1993, 47) describes the plight of such areas after the unbanning of the African National Congress in February 1990. He writes:

hostel dwellers or squatters fought running battles with residents, while police added to the death count. There were also occasional calculated attacks and counter-attacks by both residents and hostel dwellers. Soweto streets soon resembled battlefields. Within days, some areas of these townships were devastated, shacks razed to the

ground, burnt furniture strewn amidst the desolation and destruction, some scattered across the townships' open fields which had become battle zones. Horrific scenes of burning bodies became everyday occurrences. . . . Homeless refugees moved from one open
patch of veld to another.

The next hymn, number 46, laments the loss of a particular social order
in the face of colonization. It articulates an anguished plea to the African
people, urging them to rise up because they are being overtaken by other
nations. They have become doormats on which others wipe their feet. In
stanza 5, reference is made to the young women, who are metaphorized as
white milkwood trees.

Phakama Africa	Rise, Africa!
Funa uMsindisi	Seek the Savior.
Namhla siyizigqwashu	Today your white milkwood trees
Zokwesula izinyawo zezizwe.	Are the slaves of nations.

The name of the tree strongly suggests purity in its whiteness, and fertility in its association with milk (Berglund 1976, 337–38). In other words,
Shembe is addressing those young women who have been drawn into
wage labor as "slaves" or domestic servants in white households. Such labor was strongly condemned by Isaiah in the Nazarite catechism.

The funeral hymn, number 220, which was written by J. G. Shembe in
1938 for the death of Isaiah, articulates a loss of hope. It is sung annually
at the commemoration of the death of the founder, at one of the main religious sites, called *Gibisile*. Stanza 4 reads:

Izintombi nezintsizwa	Maidens and young men
Zadabuka, zikhala;	Were saddened, crying;
Abafazi, namadoda	Married women, married men
Baphelelwa yithemba.	Lost hope.
Nkulunkulu, Nkosi yethu,	God, our Lord,
Usishiyela bani.	For whom do you leave us behind?

The hymn presents the overwhelming sense of loss and destitution felt
and articulated by the members of the Nazarite community.

One of the solutions to social loss and defilement, particularly of the
young Nazarite girls, was to create sacred enclosures. Much as in the girls'
rituals discussed below, the images of fortress and blood found in this text
suggest the moral battle Shembe felt was being waged against the community, both by the state and by the European mission (see Gunner
1988). There is therefore a note of caution to the maidens in Hymn 223
(composed by Galilee in January 1938).

Yini Gebeleweni	What is the matter, *Gebeleweni* [person who tempts danger]?
Ntombi yomNazaretha	Maiden of a Nazarite.
Buya lizoshon'ilanga	Return, the sun is going to set,
Ungen'qabeni.	Enter into the fortress.
Isalakutshelwa	The one who ignores the warnings
Sibona ngo mopho	We see with blood.
Siya mkhalela	We are weeping
U Zumekile.	For *Zumekile* [the one who was caught unaware].

While the most obvious understanding of this hymn is that explained above, deeper insight into the structuring of sacred communities and the hegemony of the sacred as it is located in the female body is to be gleaned from this particular text. In this sense the deep metaphorical message is located in keywords: *danger, maiden, sunset, fortress, blood, weeping,* and *caught unaware.* Overall, there is a clear message of warfare articulated in the image of the fortress. In the first stanza, the young girl who tempts danger is the one who moves over the boundaries, out of the protection of the sacred and safe space—the fortress. In the second stanza we are told the consequences of such action—blood flows because of violence committed against the female body. The virgin's purity is defiled, her morality is destroyed, and the entire community sheds tears for the imminent threat to its collective power and identity.

Drawing on the writing of Girard (1972, 1–38), I suggest that an equation is formulated in *ibandla lamaNazaretha* between blood flow, violence, sexuality, ritual impurity, and the construction of the sacred. In this regard, where violence is unleashed, blood is everywhere; the threat of violence is the threat of ritual impurity; and finally, the flow of blood is associated with an inability to control the wiles of sexuality—epitomized in the female body. The response to such loss of order is the formulation of ritualized controls in sacred spaces. By definition, the sacred is the subduing of violence, and the repression of uncontrolled sexual desire.

Hymn 92 reiterates the central trope of Nazarite gender construction: female empowerment through ritual purity and dance performance.

Ngosina nginethemba	I will dance the sacred dance with hope—
Ngiyithombi yomNazaretha	I am a Nazarite maiden,
Angiyikwesaba lutho,	I shall fear nothing,
Ngoba mina ngiphelele.	Because I am perfect/virtuous.
Nathi siyawethemba,	We also say we have hope,
Nayizolo besikwethemba.	And yesterday we had hope,
Nanamuhla siyakwethemba.	And even tomorrow we [will] have hope.

What is remarkable about this text is its use of the first person singular. Here the voice of Isaiah is conflated with that of a young Nazarite virgin. This may reflect the visionary source of the song—the female voice— which according to Sundkler always gave melody, rhythm, and text together. The conflation of voice also suggests the absorption of the holiness and ritual power embedded in the bodies of the virgin girls,[8] into the person of Isaiah. Finally, the hope expressed in past, present, and future resonates with my suggestion in the conclusion of chapter 3 that the female body is the locus of the past, the present, and the future because of its connections with the cosmology and social reproduction.

Both Hymn 92 and the narrative cited at the beginning of the chapter convey the significance of the relationship between ritually pure Nazarite girls and religious dance. In a letter written to *ibandla lamaNazaretha* (cited at the end of the chapter), Shembe outlined a set of rules pertaining to Nazarite dance festivals (*umgidi*). Even though the letter is addressed to the congregation as a whole, it is the virgin girls who are the subject of much of the letter. In it Shembe articulates Nazarite beliefs about the nature of dance in *ibandla lamaNazaretha*. In direct contrast to mission ideology, dance is considered to be a religious rite, and not simply a leisure activity. Sacred dance is analogous to prayer. It opens with communication with the ancestors and it closes when Shembe says "amen" at the end of the festival. The aforementioned letter gives several rules to the young girls concerning their participation in dance festivals. First, a young girl may participate in the festival only if she is ritually clean (is neither menstruating nor pregnant). Second, she must pray before starting to dance (in other words, she must communicate with cosmological kin). Third, once the dancing has started, no girl may talk or fool about, because the dance is a holy act, and should be performed with reverence. Fourth, no girl who arrives after the festival has begun may join the dance. (This rule may relate to the mission insistence on punctuality as a sign of religious discipline.) For Shembe, dance is an enactment of this kind of religious belief. There is also a note of caution in which members are instructed to arrive on time to avoid missing the moment when the heavenly photograph is taken. Finally, a girl must use her own attire, for if she uses someone else's it will be as if the other person is dancing. It will not count for the girl who has actually danced. This suggests a close link between personal identity, religious accountability, and attire.

Although young Nazarite girls and boys learn to respond with their bodies to drumming and trumpet rhythms at a very early age,[8] the first official space for young girls to participate in the Nazarite dance is during the dance festivals called by Shembe. As indicated in chapter 3, these occur most frequently on a Sunday, but also during the week, often on a Tuesday or Thursday. While these festivals are not for young girls exclusively, the girls occupy the most important position in terms of the structure of the festival event, for they are the ones who are responsible for opening and closing the festival (see chap. 3). To mark their special position, Amos Shembe joins their dancing groups when the girls assemble in front of his house to signal the end of the day's dancing.[9] It is they who are blessed by him before all the others—the married women, young boys, and married men.

The second space for young girls to sing, blow the trumpets, beat the drums, and dance is during the meetings of the *ama25*. The third official space is during the two annual rituals discussed below—the girls' camp (*Ntanda*) and the week-long festival of dance held thereafter, and the girls' conference (*umgonqo*). For the remainder of this section I shall consider the ways in which Isaiah and Galilee Shembe engraved the historical experiences of the African peoples, and particularly of young women, on the bodies of these girls through dance attire.

For the young girls of the church to participate fully in the annual ritual cycle, eight different uniforms are required. The first two are the white surplices called *imiNazaretha* and *ujafeta*. The third is the Zulu traditional *ibhayi*,[10] worn to indicate one's virginity and ritual purity. The remaining five uniforms are those worn for the dance festivals. While MaSangweni, the leader (*umpathi*) of the young girls, did not seem to know the history behind these uniforms, she was certain that the uniform called *iskotch* had been introduced by Johannes Galilee. Other than that, she said, all the uniforms had been introduced by the church founder, Isaiah. I was told by two other older women that they thought Shembe had seen all the uniforms in dreams, and then had them copied for the girls.

It is in these five uniforms that the conflict over civilized and uncivilized, over Africanness and Europeanness, becomes evident, particularly in terms of the naked versus the covered female body. In this regard, Krige (1968, 174) writes,

> At a first fruits ceremony I attended in 1966 some girls wore vests to cover their breasts. This caused much unfavourable criticism and was taken to denote a loose sexual life. A virgin's body is her pride; an exposed body on [festival] occasions declares her innocence and purity. For a virgin to expose her body on these occasions is thus

not obscene behavior as a European might be inclined to assume.
It is enjoined in certain festive and ritual contexts.

Shembe was obviously aware of the difference in meaning and morality
ascribed to the covered and naked body. Four out of five types of uniforms
constructed for the girls' dance festival held in July cover the body. One
might interpret this covering in the spirit of Homi Bhabha (1993) as a
parody or mimicry of Western attire. It might also be understood to
encapsulate a historical moment, specifically, the conflict that Isaiah felt
existed between the civilized and the uncivilized. From either perspective,
each form of body symbolism was an inscription of cultural power, and ultimately a battle over the terms of morality.

The occasion for these five uniforms is the five days of dance that
feature the young girls after they have returned from the girls' camp
(*Nthanda*). I have been unable to find anyone who can provide an insider's
explanation for these outfits. Nevertheless, at a purely visual level, these
uniforms resemble attire worn by others outside of the religious community. The first uniform is a pink dress with white headband, white gloves,
and white waistband. The hair is always pulled back in a black hairnet (recall Mr. Hlatswayo's narrative in chap. 3). These resemble the uniforms
worn in South Africa by domestic workers, or housemaids.

The second uniform is *iskotch*. It consists of a tartan pleated skirt, red
blouse, and beads worn in the traditional places (on the arms, knees,
ankles). There is a history of this tartan skirt in the church—with a report
of the young boys wearing kilts as early as 1930.[11] These kilts are no longer
worn as such, though the young boys now wear red-and-white gingham
skirts for dancing. Furthermore, because of their long history in church
ritual, these uniforms seem to suggest some connection with the military
and musical forces connected with the colonial era in South Africa. The
third uniform includes a pink voile blouse with black tassels, a black skirt,
and a white headband, as worn with the first uniform. This may allude to
the red blouse and black skirt worn by Methodist prayer-women to their
Thursday *manyano*.[12] The fourth uniform suggests a connection with the
Indian population in the brightness of its colors, the gilt trimmings, and
the veil. This uniform consists of a royal blue blouse, a red skirt with black
tassels, and a lilac voile veil, with white fabric covering the face.[13] The fifth
uniform is a black skirt with white blouse, a black hairnet, and again, white
beads marking the limbs at traditional places in dance attire (the elbows,
knees, and ankles).[14] This clearly resembles the uniform of the Presbyterian prayer-women who attend the *manyano* on Thursday afternoons[15]
(though the beads would be a Nazarite addition, since dancing was

forbidden in the European-controlled church groups). Finally, on the sixth day a more traditional Zulu attire is worn. This is the uniform used for all dance festivals by the young girls. The prepubescent girls wear red skirts, and the postpubescent, black skirts. Thereafter the uniform is the same for all girls. They wear only the skirt, and are covered with extensive beadwork on the upper torso, arms, head, legs, and ankles.

Having described this set of uniforms, I suggest that they are to be "read" as inscriptions of colonial encounters. They appear to articulate the kinds of young women an uneducated Zulu "shepherd" boy[16] might have encountered in the early part of this century: the mission convert, the domestic worker, the Indian woman, the woman in the Salvation Army band, or perhaps a military man wearing a kilt, and finally, the young woman for whom Isaiah desired to create his community—the woman who knew her own cultural ways—the Nguni woman. They might also serve to encapsulate the diversity of oppressed peoples living in the Inanda District, the reserve area demarcated by colonial official Theophilus Shepstone for mission, African, and Indian people in the 1870s (see chap. 2).

In this regard Paul Connerton writes that to "read or wear clothes is in a significant respect similar to reading or composing a literary text." He adds that in "reading literature one assigns the object in question to a genre, in interpreting clothes one proceeds likewise" (1989, 11–12). In "reading" this particular set of uniforms, they are categorized likewise as historical inscription. What is most remarkable is the way in which Isaiah privileged his relationship with the young female membership once more. Yet again, we find the inscription and retelling of historical experience through ritualization—this time through the wrapping of the body in historically coded dance attire.[17]

Nazarite Virgin Girls' Ritual Events

Ritual is constituted at two levels in *ibandla lamaNazaretha*—as a series of purification rites, and as institutional life-cycle rites that celebrate and reenact significant moments in the life of the religious collectivity. In the first instance, ritual practice functions as a mechanism of purification. It is a continuous rite of transition for those coming onto Nazarite sacred spaces from the outside. Those outside members exist in a permanent state of liminality and structural ambiguity. The rites of purification, such as baptism, healing, participation in congregational worship on the sabbath, and so forth, facilitate a move from this liminal state to a new center—that constructed by Shembe. They are historically situated ritual practices in which members repeatedly participate. They have become an integral feature of the cycle of movement between the Nazarite center and the peripheries of the South African political economy. These rites are continually reenacted as a means to reordering the ongoing fragmentation of social experience that characterizes the lives of most Nazarite members living in rural or peri-urban spaces in South Africa.

The second set of ritual performances is enacted annually as part of the larger ritual cycle. These rites involve the movement between Nazarite sacred spaces at particular times. This includes the commemoration of Isaiah Shembe's death at *Gibisile* on May 2 and the celebration of the birth of *ibandla lamaNazaretha* on March 10 at *Vula Masango*. For this chapter specifically, the narration of moral victory in Isaiah Shembe's acquisition of land in the early 1930s, on the one hand, and on the other, the ritualization of the female body as the source of moral power in this victory, are celebrated over a three-month period from July 7 to September 26 each year.

In the Nazarite context these rituals cannot be explained without constant reference to their construction and articulation with the wider South African political economy, and other forms of institutionalized discrimination and marginalization by the state. Thus Kligman (ibid., 8–10) writes that while rituals do not necessarily "represent everyday interactions," they articulate the tenets of the "social contract on which everyday interactions are based." In South Africa, where many black South Africans continue to exist in a long-term (rather than transitory) state of liminality,[18] rituals of transition from one place in life to the next (the characteristic feature of life-cycle ritual) have come to mark spatial over temporal movement. Here they effect the transition of a migrant worker from the industrial center, where his or her social position is characterized by ambiguity, paradox, and the confusion of traditional categories,[19] to spaces of traditional order, such as *ibandla lamaNazaretha*. In these spaces, men and women have clearly defined and knowable social positions. Because of the continuous cycle of migration from one center to the other through the life of an individual, each person repeatedly participates in these rites of liminality,[20] of purification, and of transformation.

While Isaiah Shembe drew on the form and content of traditional Nguni puberty ceremonies and fertility rites for girls, he added to these structures biblical narrative and his own experiences with the racism and injustices meted out by the state and Europeans in South Africa. Thus, while the Nazarite rituals that feature young virgin girls as their main heroines may appear to be conservative, even reified, objects of cultural enactment, they have been overlaid with signification directly related to Isaiah's (and all his members') experiences with the wider political economy. These are traditional ritual practices that have come to embody specifically Nazarite cultural truths.

Nazarite life-cycle rites have been transformed from practices connected to individual transitions as celebrated by the community, to group rites celebrating the collective. Shembe functions as the father—*Baba*—of the religious kin group, and he presides over all ritual enactment. He is perceived to thereby facilitate the transition of the Nazarite community as a whole from liminality and structural ambiguity to a position of defined social history, collective identity, and greater empowerment. Kiernan (1992, 20) remarks on Isaiah's transformation of the girls' *umgonqo* rite of seclusion from an individual to a collective performance. He writes:

> The Nazarite church effectively wrested control of the puberty observances from the parents of the girls and stamped its own authority on them, transforming them from neighborhood celebrations into an orchestrated event with church significance [i.e., the maintenance of community well-being through sexual purity].

Adding to Kiernan's comments, I suggest that this rite has come to signify both community well-being and the commitment of young girls to a way of life for virgin girls created by the church founder, Isaiah Shembe.

The two life-cycle rituals that I shall focus on in this chapter center on what has perhaps been the most critical issue in the history of conflict in South Africa—that of access to land. In this sense, they are templates of historical consciousness and the embodiment of critical moments in the life and history of *ibandla lamaNazaretha* (Kligman 1988; Combs-Schilling 1989; Vail and White 1991). They are constructions of what the Comaroffs (1992, 174) call "the poetics of history" and the creation of the communal self through "imaginative play with the categories of culture."

In defining these performances as historical artifacts, I do not mean that they necessarily detail specific dates, times, or names of people and places, but rather that they are constructs or "maps of experience" (Vail and White 1991). Combs-Schilling (1989, 10) comments that "ritual reinserts culture's imagination into experiential history." For example, the girls' rituals discussed below memorialize the moment of the encounter between Isaiah and the state and its representatives over the issue of land purchase. They mark the mechanisms he used in order to win the moral battle against social injustice and discrimination.

Ritual performances and other kinds of cultural traditions have held an ambivalent position in relation to the powers of the state, particularly through the era of apartheid. As was the case in Kligman's material from the community in Ieud, Romania, for the Nazarites in South Africa, "traditional culture" was reified and harnessed by the state. Through this process it became emblematic of, and served to justify the existence of, the policies of "separate development" that underpinned the regime. In this context traditional culture was equated with notions of primitivism, backwardness, and the lack of "civilization" (Spiegel and Boonzaier 1988, 40–41). On the one hand, it was used to romanticize the past. On the other hand, it became an integral part of the ideology that enabled the state to exclude groups from access to the advantages attached to the modern state, such as education, land ownership, and social mobility.

Nevertheless, as Kligman (1988) and Comaroff (1985) suggest, traditional culture may also be used by members of a cultural group to resist[21] the state in a limited fashion. In this sense, Isaiah demonstrated a remarkable capacity, in the transformation of traditional rites, for keeping the semblance of Nazarite performance "traditional" to the outside world. To the keepers of state surveillance, such tradition was viewed as backward and therefore harmless. For Nazarites, these ritual practices encoded a clear message of collective power and resistance to the intrusion of the state on *ibandla lamaNazaretha*. In this manner, the so-called regressiveness of tradition served to sustain community expression and cohesion despite decades of extensive harassment and censure by various governments against the African peoples.[22] In addition to the reformulation of traditional performances for ritual enactment, Isaiah overlaid these performances with the authority of the written word of the Christian God (the Bible). In other words, he turned the Bible, the source of state sanctification of apartheid, in upon itself (DeGruchy n.d.). Using it as a building block in his argument with the state, Isaiah wove biblical narratives into his traditional rituals, thereby constructing cultural truth and power for his people.[23]

Ritualized Bodies of Virgin Girls

In *ibandla lamaNazaretha* the distinction between purity and defilement is metaphorized in the virgin and deflowered female body. As I have already discussed in chapter 3, the oppositional notions of purity and pollution manifest themselves at several levels both within the confines of the Nazarite religious spaces and in the interface between the purity inside the community and the defilement outside its limits. This configuration of purity and pollution coalesces with Bourdieu's conceptualization of what he calls the "logic of practice" (Bell 1990, 303). This model constitutes a series of fundamental oppositions—such as purity versus pollution, and linearity versus cyclicity. In this practice, one set of oppositions may become subject to several similar oppositions simultaneously, or a single opposition—purity versus pollution—may be applied to several contexts. This logic of practice is therefore the pattern or scheme by which all social and cultural situations are mastered or interpreted, and ultimately dominated.

In Shembe's community, ritual practice and power center on the female body. The sacrifice of sexual desire by the young female virgins enables the retention of ritual purity and augments the cosmological power that surrounds the religious group as a whole. The Nazarite "logic of practice" is manifest at many levels—the two most obvious being the ritualization of space and time.

> [I]t is in the dialectical relationship between the body and a space structured according to the mythico-ritual oppositions that one finds the form par excellence of the structural apprenticeship which leads to the em-bodying of the structures of the world. . . . [Bourdieu 1977, 89.]

I argued above that Nazarite female virgins are the central actors in the two rituals to be discussed below because they embody ritual purity and sanctity. In this section I demonstrate how Nazarite religious and social space has been structured to inculcate and reproduce the ideology of girls' ritual purity, which is maintained through the strict control of female fertility.

As in the larger church membership, there are two distinct groups of *amantombazane* in *ibandla lamaNazaretha*. The first group consists of those who do not reside permanently with Shembe, but who live in peri-urban townships or more rural areas and merely come to the religious sites by means of public transport or on foot. The second group consists of those maidens who live with Shembe. This group includes Shembe's own "daughters,"[24] and others who have elected to stay with Shembe. All these girls are assured a space of sanctuary, which is heavily guarded for the maintenance of their virginity. Those *amantombazane* who reside with Shembe stay inside the girls' area, which, unlike the spaces for other Nazarite members, is bounded by a fence and a gate. They live under the leadership of *umpathi* (or *Mpathi* as the term for formal address), an older maiden who was selected by her predecessor and affirmed by Shembe.[25] She is supported by several other older maidens called *abapathi*. *Mpathi* is responsible to Shembe for the safety and well-being of all the girls who live in her enclosure. She oversees the girls' rituals, collects annual payments, and ensures that those in her care are always well dressed and in the correct dance attire when necessary.

In many ways she assumes the role traditionally ascribed to biological mothers precisely because many of the girls have been orphaned. She disciplines those who disobey the rules and is required to check regularly that her girls have not engaged in sexual intercourse. Most important, she and her team coordinate the proposals of marriage for all young women and men in the religious community. In addition to the residential confinement procured through the fence and gate, there are stringent behavioral restrictions that apply specifically to the maidens. While there are rules about social interaction that pertain to the moral fiber of *hlonipha* (respect)[26] and are applicable to all church members, the code of conduct for *amantombazane* is perhaps the most strictly adhered to. This includes keeping one's head bowed and covered with a white shawl (*inansook* or *inansuka*), talking quietly, kneeling before all seniors, and serving food to brothers and fathers on a carefully arranged tray. Essentially, these rules apply to the interaction of young girls with all other church members. They also extend to behavior in the presence of God. Nazarite religious spaces are organized according to ascribed levels of ritual purity by gender and marital status. The Nazarite spatial layout embodies a movement from total ritual purity, centered spiritually and physically around Shembe and the young girls, to spaces of extreme defilement (such as waste disposal) at the boundaries. The central position held by the maidens in terms of the Nazarite articulation of space is replayed in the social demarcation of time through the two rituals in which Nazarite girls are the central actors.

In chapter 3 I discussed the central role played by young virgin girls in structuring *ukusina* (sacred dance) at *umgido*, or dance festivals. While these dance events were convened by Shembe, it was the girls who led the opening and closing of each festival. I suggested that their role in the overall framing of *ukusina* was linked to notions of time articulation in song and dance that functioned as metaphors for productive and reproductive cycles.

These young female virgins are also the actors in two annual Nazarite rituals that draw on traditional Nguni custom. They were re-created by Isaiah and his followers sometime in the late 1920s to establish the particularities of Nazarite experience. The first ritual derives from the traditional puberty rite held for an individual girl on her first menstruation. Known as the "girls' conference" or *umgonqo* (seclusion/confinement), it takes place at the church headquarters as a collective rite between July 25 and September 25. The second rite is linked to one of the first stages in a girl's sexual interactions with a boy. This is the "girls' camp" or *Ntanda* (to love/braid), held through the night of July 7 at a place called *Nkatheni* (the place of grass ropes), and continuing on into the afternoon of July 8.

Girls' Rites at *umGonqo*

In Nguni tradition the onset of menstruation for a young girl was the moment at which the girl's age-mates joined the girl for a period of seclusion from the community for between two days and two months. This was the puberty rite known as *umgonqo*. Isaiah transformed this rite from an individual to a collective process (Kiernan 1992). I suggest that this puberty ritual moved from being simply a rite of passage into full sexuality and the capacity for reproduction, to one that transferred the significance of her newly acquired fertility to the moral and spiritual domain. In other words, a girl's fertility was now harnessed by Shembe for the reproduction of the Nazarite moral and spiritual order. This moral order was based upon the relationship Shembe fostered with his young female followers.

It was also a moral order that required the total abstention from all contact with young boys and men for the entire two months of *umgonqo*. The girls thus remained inside the enclosure, forbidden to talk to anyone on the outside (unless they were going to religious services). In Zulu tradition, boys were allowed to visit the girls in the secluded area provided they gave a gift to *Mpathi*. All girls were required to remain quiet and demure for the duration of the seclusion. In this way, they would attain the apex of ritual purity. Interwoven into the Nazarite construction and exegesis of this rite is the biblical narrative of Jephthah and his daughter, which is recorded in the Old Testament book of Judges, chapter eleven (Mr. Sibisi, pers. comm., September 4, 1991; the Nazarite catechism; and Hymn 38). As the details of the Nazarite ritual will demonstrate, the experiences of Isaiah Shembe and his followers resonate strongly with those of Jephthah and the Israelites.

The story centers on Jephthah, a social misfit because he was born of a prostitute and rejected by the legitimate sons of his father. But he was also an Israelite warrior who was forced into battle with the Ammonites over the issue of land. He made an agreement with God that if the Israelites won the battle, he would sacrifice the first thing that met his eyes on his return home. To his horror, this was his only daughter. She agreed to the sacrifice on one condition, that he give her two months "to roam the hills and weep with [her] friends" because she would never marry (Judges 11:37). In response, an Israelite custom developed in which young girls entered a period of seclusion to commemorate the daughter of Jephthah.

The Nazarite girls' ritual performance is thus framed by the metaphor of warfare—though in their case it is not the literal warfare engaged in by the biblical Jephthah. With Isaiah, war is waged instead at the level of morality and spirituality. In this sense, the "daughters of Isaiah," like the "daughter of Jephthah," have an integral role to play in both the warfare and the victory over the enemy. The significance of this role will become evident in the analysis of the ritual performance.

The Nazarite *umgonqo* ideally opens on the evening before the 25th of July, and ends on the night of the 25th of September (Mr. Sibisi, pers. comm., September 1991). In this two-month period Nazarite maidens should stay in complete seclusion in the girls' section at *Ebuhleni*. In theory, a girl is allowed out of the enclosure only in order to attend church worship, or to spend the night in her mother's house, provided she return again early the following morning. The text of the account of the ritual is a multilayered discourse interweaving information on the way in which Isaiah seems to have constructed the performance, in terms of biblical literature, traditional custom, historical encounters, and his own interpretations of this material. As mentioned above, Isaiah created a cultural bricolage in the construction of these performances.[27] There is some conflict in the literature and indeed in Nazarite practice over the intended period of seclusion. Kiernan (1992, 20) writes that part of the standardization of this rite by the church was its reduction to seven days, and its shift from the month of September to July. (Roberts [1936] says the rite lasted for one week in September.) To this end, in Amos's church there is a "secondary" opening of the conference enacted by the girls in September. Even though it is the current Shembe who decides on the timing of this secondary opening, one of the older leaders told the girls at the 1991 conference that Shembe had previously urged them to meet for the entire two-month period. With the increasing emphasis on school education for young girls, however, it is almost impossible to enforce such an extended period of seclusion. It would seem, then, that the secondary opening facilitates a compromise, particularly for those girls who do not live permanently at *Ebuhleni*.

Ritual separation for the girls in this event is signaled not so much by physical removal from the religious site as by the blurring of boundaries between "heaven" and earth as separate categories. Beating the drum and blowing the trumpet create a sonic boundary for a Nazarite heaven. In this context, these two instruments symbolize the duality of religious epistemologies. The drum traditionally embodies the spirit of the ancestors, while sounding the heavenly trumpets is a well-documented biblical image, and connected to the angels.

At about ten o'clock on the night of July 24, 1991, the drums and trumpets sounded out across *Ebuhleni*, thereby officially opening the conference. The young girls were clad in their white shawls and *MNazaretha*s, under which they each wrapped a blanket to keep themselves warm. Every young girl made her way quickly toward the temple area, entered through the gate for *amantombazane*, and sat down in the area designated for the maidens. There was none of the usual policing by male leaders I had become so accustomed to when entering the temple area. There was nevertheless a small group of married women leaders—*abakhokheli* overseeing the meeting.

Since it was already quite late, the only light in the temple area was that provided by a single paraffin lamp and the few candles that some of the girls had brought with them. The meeting was relatively short. It comprised the singing of several of the more familiar hymns, and a short muffled address by MaSangweni, the leader of the maidens. Just as would happen in the service at *Intanda*, her message was heard by very few of the girls, because she spoke very softly in accordance with the requirements of *hlonipha*. After her address, we sang a little more, and were then sent off to bed.

The following morning, all the girls woke at about 6 a.m., drank tea, and then bathed themselves in preparation for the morning's events. At about seven, the drums and trumpets sounded out again, played by those young maidens who resided permanently with Shembe. These maidens were on their way down to the lower festival ground. By the time I arrived at the ground, many of the maidens were already busy braiding long pieces of grass into thin ropes. Each piece of grass was rolled and joined to another piece and then braided together to form a thicker rope. These were then tied around the shawl—*inansook*—which had been transformed into a head covering.[28]

Braiding grass is linked with the hair braids of virgin girls in Nazarite ritual practice. The word for both grass and braid (as in hair braid) is *thanda*, suggesting a connection between the notions of female and natural fertility through the single concept of *nthanda*. What is significant is

that the grass braid has moved from the waist/vagina, where it traditionally symbolized female fertility, to the head. In the Nazarite religious epistemology, the head is the site for communication with the ancestors—
through dreams (figurative eyes), song (mouth), and visions/voices (eyes
and ears). Such communication facilitates the cosmological empowerment of an individual, and provides evidence of Nazarite ritual purity.

Shifting the grass braid—during a rite that supposedly celebrates female fertility—from the waist to the head communicates a critical message. It reinforces my earlier suggestion that female fertility is transferred
from the sexual and reproductive domain in the physical sense, to that of
moral purity in the ritual and moral sense, as it is embodied in the girls' relationship with Shembe. In addition, the word *nthanda* also translates as
love. Traditionally this referred to the love between a young girl and boy.
The grass ropes on the head now indicate love for Shembe/God—the
sacrifice of sexual desire as an emblem of commitment to God.[29]

The dedication of the self to God was further suggested in the uniform
worn only during these rites. Having completed the braiding process, the
girls changed from the white prayer surplices they had worn to the festival
ground into another white prayer surplice called *ujafeta*. Named after the
biblical character Jephthah, the central character of the ritual, these *jafeta*
are similar in construction to the ordinary *MNazaretha*, though they have
additional tucks in the skirts and a high collar. These uniforms transformed the lack of voice given to young girls in ordinary ritual practice—
symbolized in the covering of the head and face with the white *inansook*—
to the voice of authority of the preacher (*umshumayeli*). Finally, the *jafeta*
was girded with a green ribbon,[30] and all the girls put a small skin shield in
the left hand, and a black umbrella in the right.

I noticed as the girls began to change their gowns that many of them
were wearing the traditional *ibhayi* underneath the gowns. These were the
garments also worn for the girls' camp to reflect virginity. A young maiden
was not supposed to wear any underwear while wearing *ibhayi*, an indica-
tion that she was not menstruating. She was therefore ritually pure and
not threatening to the moral well-being of the Nazarite community. En-
circling both the head and waist with the color green (in the grass and
ribbon respectively)—as the color of status transition—represents a divergence from tradition. Unlike the traditional rite, in which only the
waist was encircled, here the green is represented by two different materials—grass and ribbon, in two different places. This resembles two
Nazarite sets of oppositional principles—linearity/cyclicity and colo-
nizer/colonized.

The first opposition—between the linear and the cyclical—is embodied in the rope and ribbon, which are straight lines transformed into circles as they are tied around the girls' bodies. The traditional (the grass rope) is placed alongside the European (the manufactured green ribbon). The ribbon is tied where the rope used to be—around the waist—and the grass rope has moved to the head. In other words, the grass rope now signifies the part of the body where the ancestral realm is accessed, as I pointed out above. The green ribbon has come to encircle the waist, signifying the girls' dedication to Shembe in the Western sense—as nuns.

The small skin shield and black umbrella also suggest dual principles pertaining to young girls—fertility is represented by the black umbrella (which suggests rain); and female spirituality and moral power are embedded in the white shield, which protects the girl (and by extension, the community) in times of moral and spiritual warfare. Krige (1968, 182) writes that Zulu girls used to carry a small shield and spear in the early morning, during a rite called *ukukhipa izinkomo* (taking the cattle out to graze by virgin girls), which represented a reversal of the norm—girls are usually tabooed from any contact with cattle. In addition, she says that a central tenet of this ritual was to beg for rain and fertility of the cattle and crops. Shembe has replaced the spear with an umbrella because his philosophy of nonviolence prohibits the bearing of arms. The umbrella, nevertheless, can provide the same kind of stabbing gestures described by Kiernan (1992). Finally, in wearing the *ibhayi* underneath the prayer surplice, the traditional symbol of female virginity was once again juxtaposed with the European symbol of religious fervor.

Fully attired, the girls moved toward an area between a clump of trees where the service would be held. No prayer mats were allowed for the girls to sit on (in this instance the grass mat is replaced with the grass coil—explained later). At the same time, they had to keep their white uniforms spotless—quite a challenge with the ground as damp as it was. For this service the three drums were left outside the circle of girls and placed next to the fire, where they were later dried out, in order to restore the correct tautness of the hides (and thus the correct tuning of the drums). As traditional instruments believed to embody the spirits of the ancestors, the drums were forbidden in the Western-style *inkhonzo* religious worship.[31]

Unlike the male-controlled rigidity of *inkhonzo*, there was no fixed liturgical ordering of events. The main body of the service comprised the singing of a series of hymns, communal and individual prayer while kneeling, the preaching of sermons by the leaders of the maidens and the *umkhokheli* responsible for the girls, and the reading of the "letter" written by Isaiah Shembe, the Prophet for *ibandla lamaNazaretha* (discussed in the context of the second ritual). The sermon given by one of the old *aba-pathi* (leaders of the girls) explains why the girls had gathered for this meeting. She recalled:

> Girls, you are the ones who cover over *Kuphakama*, the place of God. Because you are here, you are the ones who encompass this place. I want to remind you that Shembe is the only parent to us. He is both father and mother, because where we are going there is no father or other *Mkhokheli* (female leader of married women). But only Shembe. As you are here, we have been called by one voice of Shembe.
>
> Some of us didn't have enough money to come here, but because of the love of Shembe, we got money to come here to this place. We've left our good works at home, our comfortable place and come here, where we don't even get a cent, only the Word of God. The Word of God that brings us here is such that if we have done all the good deeds here on earth, we stand a good chance of our names being written down in the Book of Life.[32]

The contents of this text seem to support both Kiernan's (1992) and my own analysis of the event in the following ways: the rite is collectively celebrated, all the girls are heroines, the young girls have a special place in the maintenance of ritual purity in *ibandla lamaNazaretha*, Shembe functions as parent in place of biological parents, and he provides the material means to gain access to the moral economy. It also conveys the immense power vested in the bodies of these virgin girls, in terms of the "covering over" or protection they provide for the community.

At the end of the service the girls were instructed to make a monetary offering of two rand (now about one dollar in purchase power). Their names were then written in a large black book.[33] The girls' service lasted about an hour, and coincided with the regular 9 A.M. *inkhonzo*, which took place in the temple area. It was only after the main *inkhonzo* was complete that the maidens formed a procession comprising six long lines with the leaders and musicians in front. The *umkhokheli* carried a long green pole with a white kerchief flying from the top as she walked forward to stand guard at the front of the procession (in a similar manner to the act of "policing" in regular religious *inkhonzo* rituals).[34]

As the maidens prepared for the procession, a large crowd of church members began to line up alongside the area through which they would walk. There was much ululating from the women, and the sporadic praises of an *imbongi* (praise poet/singer), extolling the powers of Shembe. Finally, all were ready, the drums began to beat, the bugles and long trumpets began to sound, and the lead dancing girls started a walk-hop-skip-clap sequence in front of the procession. This processional was remarkable in its "imaginary play" with the "categories of culture" (Comaroff and Comaroff 1991). It evoked once again the biblical link to the battle of Jephthah the military general. The sequence performed by the lead girls, or "captains," as Kiernan calls them, resembled the lead parts played by drum majors—as was commonly seen in South African Salvation Army Bands (see chap. 1); the umbrellas—the symbol of Western civilization—were opened and closed, and at times thrust in the traditional stabbing movement. The Nazarite play on images provided one further contrast in the unsolicited comments heard by Kiernan and myself in terms of this rite. Kiernan writes that he was told by his male companion that the girls "are like soldiers"; while I was told by my field assistant that they "are like *umshumayeli* [preachers]." When combined, these two images depict the girls as moral soldiers.

The large group of maidens—regularly opening and closing their umbrellas—moved from the lower festival ground, through the informal market area, past Isaiah's grave and statue, toward the temple area. Women and children ran into the temple space, this time through the nearest available gate. It seemed that on this occasion, correct point of entry, seating, and head coverings were not important. No men or boys, however, entered the temple area during this event. There was a fervent excitement among all who were standing by watching the procession.

The girls' procession circled around the temple area twice, an act that is believed to envelop the ancestors (Sikelela Msibi, pers. comm., October 1993). Thereafter they entered the temple through the proper entrance for maidens. The gathering inside the temple was brief, with a short hymn and talk by *umpathi*. The girls were then dismissed. Since this gathering was ostensibly held as part of the 25s meeting, it was expected that there would be the customary "closing" of the meeting through the night of the 25th (as happens with the married women's meetings, discussed in chap. 8). At about 8 P.M. all the girls in the *dokoda* in which I was staying went to sleep, to be awakened once again by the beating of the drum, which was calling all the maidens to the temple. There were, however, very few girls gathered at the temple for this part of the ritual. A few danced, and there was a short spurt of hymn-singing, after which all retired to their beds once again. While the 25s meeting was officially over, this also signaled the official commencement of the two-month period of seclusion for young virgins. Few of the girls I was with actually intended to stay for the entire two-month period.

Even though the official opening of the girls' conference is considered by most to be July 25, it was from after the "secondary" opening that the rules concerning the seclusion of the maidens were most strictly enforced. This is the period in the girls' rites that parallels the story of Jephthah. It is the moment that marks the transition from life to death. For Nazarite girls, this transition signals the movement into sexuality—a dangerous, but powerful, stage of life. The transition is therefore marked both spatially, in the complete containment of the virgins within the confines of the girls' enclosure, and behaviorally, in the requisite demure, respectful, and quiet demeanor. The total sacrifice of self—the complete sacralization of the female body—circumvents danger and defilement, and retains the wholeness of the social body.

On the morning of September 23 all the girls staying in the girls' enclosure were called by MaSangweni to an area inside the enclosure close to where marriage proposals are arranged. Everyone gathered wearing *MNazaretha* and shawls, and carrying their mats to sit on. They were all to be shown the gifts that had been bought for both Shembe and the *Mkhokheli* responsible for the young girls. These gifts had been purchased by the leaders using the money given in both July and September, when the girls' names had been recorded in the book. Shembe's gifts, all packed in a new suitcase, included all the symbols of Western civilization and modernity—a Pierre Cardin suit, a white shirt, a tie, underwear, pajamas, shoes, and a black hat. For *umkhokheli* the items signified her religious fervor: a towel, washcloth, and enamel basin for washing, laundry detergent, *MNazaretha, ifortini* (the black belt and white cloth headband), a shawl, knee rug, and *ibhayi*. As each item was lifted for the girls to see, they collectively responded with "*Ameni!*"

At about 10 P.M. on the evening of September 24 the drums sounded out, and all the girls gathered in their *MNazaretha* and shawls to dance and sing on the periphery of the temple area. This time the performers were enthusiastic. A group of about twelve girls formed a line and started to dance, moving slowly initially, and gradually speeding up. They were accompanied by the drums, trumpets, a bugle, and a whistle, which signaled changes of direction, tempo, and dance lines. Only one line of girls danced at a time. They danced through one verse of a hymn, with lines of the verse repeated several times. When they were finished the drumming slowed down again, and a new line of girls began to dance. All those who were not involved with the dancing stood behind the dancers, singing and

clapping and following the pulse of the feet movement. When the dancing was over, a prayer was said by the leader, the girls responded with
"*ameni*," and everyone went back to their *dokoda* to sleep.

Once more called by the sound of the drum, the girls walked down to
the temple area early on the morning of September 25 with the grass coils
in their hands. (These had been hidden in a secret place for the two-
month period.) They were clad in the white *MNazaretha* with the shawl
covering their heads, and each of them carried the rope of grass they had
braided on July 25. As we went through the gate of the girls' enclosure toward the temple, I noticed that a pile of grass had been placed on the
ground alongside the gate. At the entrance to the temple, the girls knelt
quickly as usual (much like genuflecting in the Catholic church),[35] and
then proceeded in to where the drummers and trumpeters were already
waiting. Though the words were quite hard to identify, the girls sang
stanza four of Hymn 173.

Wozani nazo lezozizwe	Come along with those nations,
Ziyadinga lona lizwe	They, who need the Word—
Elophezu konke	[The Word] of him who is above all.

A woman standing outside the temple called out a line of praise to
Shembe, and then ululated.

When the girls had assembled in the temple, everyone knelt and sang
through the verse of the hymn several times, as led by one of the oldest
maidens. The drummers and trumpets suddenly increased the tempo of
their playing, and the girls walked in a procession out of the temple toward
the pile of grass, which had now been lit and was being controlled by
umkhokheli.

Singing verse 3 of Hymn 173,

Livuliwe ngubani	Who opened it,
Lelisango	This gate?
We Mkhululi weziboshwa	Oh, Liberator of the prisoners!

the girls threw their grass ropes onto the fire, formed a circle, and walked
around the fire for about half an hour. The instrumentalists stood outside
the circle, in a line to the one side, playing the entire time.[36]

Once the fire burned itself out, the girls again walked in procession
(singing the same hymn) down to the lower festival ground. Here they
were met by several married women who had come armed with large
enamel washtubs, towels, soap, and containers of hot water. Krige (1988
[1950], 102) remarks that this bathing traditionally happens on the second day of a girl's seclusion—the bathing is intended to cleanse her from

the menstrual blood. For the Nazarite girls, however, it happens on the final day of seclusion, and not by the river, as reported by Kiernan. This was clearly a rite of renewal, as Kiernan suggests, and as is exemplified in the burning, the removal of old clothes, and the putting on of the white *jafeta*. The difference between July 25 and this time was the absence of the grass rope around the girls' heads. The dirty clothes were taken away by the women for washing, and the girls gathered for the service, which followed a similar order to that held on July 25.

The rite of aggregation is both about reincorporating the young virgins back into the Nazarite community, and giving thanks to the father and mother of the community—Shembe and *Mkhokheli*, the leader of the women responsible for the girls. The thanksgiving by the girls to Shembe is reminiscent of the appreciation traditionally shown by Zulu girls to their lovers in an act called *qoma*. Krige (ibid., 105) writes that a girl never *qoma*s twice, because this action signifies engagement for marriage. This gesture toward Shembe on the part of the girls once again points to the nature of the relationship between Shembe and the virgins. It is tantamount to an engagement for a spiritual (and moral) union with Shembe. It is a relationship that assures sanctuary and protection to young girls, in exchange for which they are required to disengage themselves from all sexual desire. (I shall return to the concept of spiritual union between Shembe and his female followers in chap. 7.)

A similar procedure for the service and subsequent procession of virgins was followed until all members of *ibandla lamaNazaretha* had gathered in the temple area to give thanks to Shembe and witness the gift-giving. Once inside the temple, everyone was called to kneel and sing. The girls all danced slowly while singing the verse of *Wozani, wozani* (Come everyone, come everyone) from Hymn 106. As Shembe arrived (with the girls kneeling), the drums and trumpets picked up tempo, and a series of "*ameni-oyincwele*" cries sounded out from all those around. Shembe came in dressed in his white *MNazaretha* and black hat, and sat down under the shelter built especially for him. MaSangweni then went up to where he was sitting and spoke to the girls, who responded with "*ameni.*"

Thereafter, the gifts the girls had been shown were once again displayed to everyone and "*ameni*" was called out. Shembe stood up, having removed his hat and glasses, and spoke to the girls, and they responded with the "*ameni.*" When all the gifts had been given, two of the leaders jumped up and performed a solo dance in response, and MaSangweni moved on to give *Mkhokheli* her gifts. The congregation then knelt down and sang an unaccompanied hymn while Shembe walked back to his house, and the men removed the chair, tablecloth, table, mats, pillow, and curtains brought in for him.[37] With all the sacred paraphernalia gone, the drums and trumpets started up again, and the girls began to dance.

The final part of this performance was the arrival of a healthy-looking ox that was to be given to Shembe as the last gift from the girls.[38] All special festivals such as life-cycle rites were closed with the slaughtering of an ox. This appeased both the ancestors and the community—because the meat was distributed for all to enjoy. All the maidens, led by the drummers and trumpet players, moved out of the temple and went into the garden of Shembe's house, where he came out to receive the ox. Once again, everyone cried out *"Ameni, oyincwele,"* the bugle sounded, and the girls began to sing the single verse of the unpublished hymn *"Thina siyabonga, webaba wethu"* (As for us, we thank you father). Shembe spoke once again, the girls responded with the *"Ameni! Oyincwele,"* and the ceremony was over. I was told that Shembe would have the cow slaughtered for the girls later in the day, although I did not stay to witness it.

Nthanda Ritual

The Nazarite ritual known as *Nthanda* (love/grass coils) takes place on the 7th and 8th of July each year. In many ways it resembles the traditional Zulu girls' ritual, in which young girls went to meet their lovers at a site with both a hill and a river (Krige 1988 [1950]). In *ibandla lamaNazaretha* this rite has been transformed to reflect the relationship young virgin girls have with their God, Shembe. In this regard, traditional actions have been overlaid with religious significance, and reconstituted in terms of a specific historical moment in the life of the church founder, Isaiah Shembe. The central issue in this ritualized reenactment and celebration of Nazarite history is that of land acquisition. The ritual power of Nazarite virgins was believed to effect the transfer of property from the hands of a white man into that of the black man—Isaiah.

I have not been able to ascertain the exact year when this rite was introduced by Isaiah, and even though it is not mentioned specifically in Roberts's thesis from 1936, I was told by the church archivist, Petrus Dhlomo, and his friend Mr. Sibisi that it was started in about 1930. In the church catechism (discussed in chap. 3), Isaiah explains his victory over the white people in his "Prayer at *Nthanda*." Through this we learn that Isaiah saw the events at *Nthanda* as representing God's provision to the young orphans and widows in the form of the acquisition of land. Furthermore, he remarks that the "great white rulers" who said that the "brown man would no longer be heard singing on those mountains"—a point I shall comment on below—had restored the property to the Nazarite community.

The *Nthanda* (to love) ritual takes place on a Nazarite religious site called *Nkatheni* (which means to love or braid at the place of grass coils). I shall not describe the *Nthanda* ritual event in this section. Instead, I shall discuss those elements that are exclusive to this ritual and not discussed in either the first rite or the translation of a text (discussed below) that is read at both the *umgonqo* and *Nthanda* rituals. This text claims to be a "letter written from Isaiah Shembe to the Nazarite congregation."[39] Three features of this event, not raised in the letter, stand out in terms of Nazarite myths and truths about the cosmological power embedded in Nazarite virgin bodies. The first pertains to the context of the event, which strongly resembles that described both by Krige (1988 [1950], 1968) for traditional Zulu rituals for girls, and by the dream narratives recorded about the appearances of the fertility Princess, *Nomkhubulwana,* by Berglund (discussed above). They all take place at a river, the Princess often appears on a misty hill or mountain, and there are reeds (sugar cane in this case) in the environment to hide the naked body of the Princess from any who might see her.

Second, during the sojourn at *Nthanda* the girls set off to find wood for the fire. They also select and cut a large branch of a tree. Each young girl takes back such a branch, up the hill and through the sugar cane the next day. The branch is at least twelve to fifteen feet long, and fairly strong. At *Ebuhleni* the following day the girls proceed around the temple, then enter the upper festival ground and form a circle with their sticks. They converge toward the center, condensing the size of the circle, point their sticks into the middle, and move back out again. In this manner they "build a house for Shembe." The procession then moves back to the road in the direction of the temple, and into the garden area of Shembe's house, where the long poles are placed in a large pile outside.

The mimetic performance with the poles suggests the circular construction of the traditional Zulu hut where the ancestors communicate with living people. (These are still a vital dimension of traditional Zulu homesteads.) The image constructed here is a poignant metaphor for the way in which the girls' bodies become the "walls" of the house of Shembe. Once again, there is an intimate connection constituted between the virgin body and the house of Shembe (also known as *Ekuphakameni*). They are therefore the means by which Shembe intercedes with the ancestors for the well-being of the entire community. The purity of their physical bodies facilitates the construction of both the physical and the metaphorical house, and thereby reconstitutes the sense of community at a broader level. Likewise, they sing sacred songs as a mechanism of cosmological communication.

The final component of these two rituals is the letter written by Isaiah to the Nazarites, but read only to the virgin girls. It is divided into four sections delineated by means of subheadings. The first section outlines a set of rules for the correct behavior of Nazarite girls—stressing the importance of sexual abstinence prior to marriage. The manifestation of the maintenance of sexual purity is embodied in a girl's participation in religious dance, which is likened to prayer. Exclusion from the Nazarite community—*Ekuphakameni*—is the consequence of nonadherence to these rules, and is portrayed in the second section, which is labeled as "[dream one]." The third section forms the substance of Isaiah's account of the history of *Nthanda.* This will be discussed below. The fourth section provides details of general rules applicable to all Nazarite members regarding who may enter Nazarite sacred space.

Here follows an English translation of the text. It was translated from a handwritten, unpunctuated piece of script by both Themba Mbhele and myself. It reads:

> Letter Written with the Rules of the Prophet Shembe
> for the Nazarite Congregation.

[Rules for the Girls]
[Shembe] says that a maiden whose marriage settlement has been arranged should not see her bridegroom. He says the bridegroom should not visit[40] the home of his wife-to-be's family until the marriage is solemnized according to Christian rites. Similarly, the maiden should not visit the bridegroom-to-be's family. If she does so, she has abused her status, and consequently she will not marry [accompanied by] the maidens, as is customary, but [in the company of] the married women, because she has broken the rule.

Within this strict set of rules, there is a rule which further stipulates that a maiden should not enter the camp for men, and the men should not enter the camp for maidens. He calls[41] those maidens, and said they are the maidens shaped by the principles of God, as they are morally upright and do not keep the company of boys. [He called them] *amadoniyakazi,* the mountain of God, the mountain which abstains from sexual intercourse [*intabayapheza*], which rises above making love to a boy. If a maiden spoils her body, she sits outside of [the place] where the maidens meet, because she feels guilty about her situation. She is confined and stripped of her *inansuka*.[42] She is also prevented from using the knife[43] that she used before, until such time as she has expressed penitence. She would then stand outside and ask for forgiveness.

Furthermore, no one is to lift her hand to another at *Ekuphakameni*. The one who does raise her hand to another is confined and excluded from the maidens because she has broken the rule. She is also precluded from taking part in the festival of dance, because the festival is holy. Here at *Ekuphakameni,* the homestead of God, noise is not allowed, because there are spiritual guards[44] who do not want loud noise and raucous laughter. This is what the pioneer of this path said, because these homesteads belong to God and not to the people. Do not spit inside the homestead of God.

When the maidens go to the festival of dance, they must pray first in the holy place [temple], then they go out and the gate is closed. Those who arrive late may not join in the dancing. There is no talking while dancing, for the maiden that talks while dancing contaminates the ship of God. He also said that should he meet a bad girl who acted rudely, she would be excluded from the dance. She would have to sit down so that everyone would see that she had broken the rules. Furthermore, he said that a person should not borrow dance attire from another person if she has left it at home. Even if someone lends you her uniform, it will mean that you are not partaking spiritually, for you are dancing for that person and not for yourself.

[Dream One][45]

There came maidens we did not know, who said they had been sent by the king of *Ekuphakameni* to ask how we had entered this homestead because we no longer honor the rules made for the maidens. We now desecrate your homestead, and you have excluded us from *Ekuphakameni*. The rule took effect when we made the oath to be Nazarite maidens.

[Historical Narrative of *Nthanda*]

The king of heaven [Shembe] spoke to God. He said he did not know where he could put the widows and orphans. God said "I understand, my child." Thereafter, a Frenchman arrived and offered land to Shembe. The King of *Ekuphakameni* was very happy. He said, "Indeed, my father, you always hear me." Then the Frenchman went away, having already taken half the money [from Shembe]. The white men asked [the Frenchman], "Why do you offer him land? It has been said that the land cannot be bought by a black man." They said this, not realizing that they were talking about God. Then the Frenchman went back to Shembe with the money he had received from the King of *Ekuphakameni*. He said, "The law is against me in Pietermaritzburg [where the law courts were situated]." The King of *Ekuphakameni* said, "Do not lie to me, for you will see that I am the Prophet."

[Shembe] was very sad. Then God spoke to him, saying, "Have you forgotten me? Why are you so sad?"

Shembe did not respond [to the Frenchman]. Instead he said he would send young children to remove the weeds from the fields of the Frenchman, [which he had bought]. The first maiden arrived. She twined together enough *izinkatha* (grass coils) for the maidens that were present. God said, "Give them to the maidens to sit on top of, while praying." Then the Prophet Shembe issued another word, saying that the maiden who knows she is not perfect in terms of God's principles [outlined above] should not take this *inkatha*.

Thereafter, a hymn came which was composed in accordance with these actions. The hymn is number 84. He said that these maidens should sit on *inkatha* and not on the grass mats. When they stand up, they should put their bound grass in a special place, known only to them. When they come back, they will take the grass from that special place. As he was talking, the Prophet knew that there was one maiden who should not be doing this—taking this bound grass. So when the maidens returned, there was one maiden who kept looking for her grass, not knowing where she had put it.

[It turned out that] the messengers of heaven [angels] had come, and they had taken it and thrown it away. Because when they had prayed for the girls, the one maiden was not there [in heaven]. The angels then left the maidens and went straight to the Frenchman that had sold the land to my Father. They asked him if he knew who the person was that he had gone against when he would not sell the land. As they left, the Frenchman's teeth began to chatter. The Frenchman then said, "I will return the money, I will go and fetch it." The following day, the Frenchman walked until he came to *Ekuphakameni*, to see Prophet Shembe. He said, "I lied to the Prophet about the land. I will give it to the king." Thus, the King of *Ekuphakameni* decreed to the maidens who had prayed, saying, "Jehovah has responded on your behalf. Thus, you, the young children, must give thanks to God on the 7th of July. You must thank God for this land. A maiden must then pay four rand, this is for those who will still be born, for generations to come. Only those maidens who are morally upright may go. The name of this temple is *Sensabathandwa.*"

[General Rules]
The rule[s] of the Prophet Shembe are that shoes must be removed at the gate, with the exception of Shembe, who may wear shoes. He even wrote on the three gates of *Ekuphakameni,* and pinned up the notices. These are the words that formed the oath for the homestead of God, written in the presence of the messengers of heaven who reside inside there. They carry paper and pens and erase the names of all who break the rules. I was sent by God to save [every] person on earth, and there is no sin that shall be delivered by me, because God chose me first, even before the creation of heaven and earth. All I have said shall not be in vain, the words of the Prophet Shembe stand forever.

At first glance this letter from the prophet Isaiah Shembe might seem to be no more than a confused set of messages transcribed rather poorly into written form. I suggest that it is a document that outlines a complex discourse on the [re-]creation of ritualized performance as a mechanism for the enactment and transformation of historical conditions and processes. At one level the document details a historical moment in time, a moment when Isaiah wished to purchase land for the widows and orphans, the poor, and the dispossessed. He incurred difficulty in this acquisition because the transaction was to take place in a context of social injustice and inequity founded on a religious and political ideology of racism.[46] Shembe overcame these problems by calling on his young female followers to fulfill certain actions. These actions were consistent with traditional Zulu beliefs regarding the power of young female virgins to safeguard the well-being of communities. They were, however, transferred into a new political frame.

The formulation of Nazarite power in this context was constituted from several elements—cosmological communication, the assistance of ritually pure virgin girls, the braiding of grass coils (the symbols of fertility and sexual purity), and the gift of song as the reward for self-discipline and sexual abstinence. Isaiah overcame racial discrimination and economic destitution by drawing on the substance of a moral economy whose transactions between people were articulated through the interface of the cosmology with everyday reality—which in this particular narrative took the form of song, prayer, and ritual performance.

Central to the efficacy of these transactions was not the authority of the written word or the force of the state judiciary. Instead, it was the power attributed to moral purity, embedded in the female body, and symbolized in the sexual abstinence of the young female membership (and hence the stringent code of conduct written into the letter). The goal of these transactions was not simply political point-scoring of black against white. For Isaiah Shembe and his followers, the acquisition of land through the power of female ritual purity was believed to safeguard the livelihood of the entire religious community. Because this was a community consisting of the politically disenfranchised and the economically dispossessed—the widows, the orphans, and the landless—the contest between Shembe and the state was being fought not only over land—economic empowerment—but over the very terms of moral purity and cultural empowerment.

The continuity of this power is now located in the annual reenactment of the two ritualized performances—*Nthanda* and *umgonqo*—by young Nazarite virgins, and the payment of a certain amount of money to ensure the reproduction of the community. In this regard the document demonstrates the way in which the historical moment is transformed into ritual enactment. History is re-presented, reenacted, and remembered in the ongoing Nazarite rituals for young virgins.

On the morning of July 8, the girls sang one of the oldest songs in the Nazarite community, the traditional song, *Impi* (Warrior). They sang as they ascended the hill on the way back to *Ebuhleni*.

Impi	Warrior!
Izinyane lendlovu	Baby Elephant
Samshi eHlobane	Who died at Hlobane!
Qubula Nkosi	Perform the war dance, O Chief,
Oka Mpande	Son of Mpande
Samshi eHlobane	Who died at Hlobane.

Impi was not a song arbitrarily selected by one of the Nazarite girls, but one that invoked the words of the ancestors themselves. The story behind this song is that it was an old praise to the Zulu king Cetshwayo (the son of King Mpande), who was believed to cause thunder, lightning, and rain immediately after it was sung. The voices of past chiefs and the powers of remembered warriors were thus articulated through the medium of song. It was the words of the Zulu ancestors that rang out in the voices of the girls over the hills of *Nkatheni* that morning. The singing of the song served to fulfill the desire of Isaiah—to hear the voice of the brown people singing on the mountains. The old Zulu chant/praise was also sung over and over as the girls walked toward the bus on July 8, and again when they reached *Ebuhleni*.

Like many of the traditional Zulu praises, the text uses a deep form of Zulu not really known by most of the younger generation of Zulu speakers. The translation of its text has therefore been difficult—the word *qubula*, for example, may have another meaning besides the one above. I was told, however, that "Baby Elephant" is a title that means "Chief."[47] Finally, when it was first sung, this piece was considered highly political, because it is a song addressed to the Zulu ancestors. In the context of European Christianity, which forbade any ancestral communication among its membership, the singing of *Impi* implied that the Nazarites were "digging too deeply in their tradition" (N. Mthethwa, pers. comm., January 1994). It thus constituted an affront to mission Christianity.

What emerges in this brief section on Nazarite virgins and sacred song is that it is these girls who, in the maintenance of the highest form of moral purity, hold the reins to cosmological communication. It is they who encompass the history of the community, the truly sacred—that which is deeply rooted in the past and contains the heart of traditional power. It is the young female virgins who carry the voices of the ancestors inscribed in their bodies and memories. It is they who continually reenact the past in the present through song; it is these same girls whose bodies contain the future in their capacity to bring forth the new generation. There is a certain irony that in the bodies of young girls, so silent, so demure, is embedded the quintessential articulation of Nazarite sacred time and space.

Rituals of Fertility and the Sacrifice of Desire

These two rituals, the hymn texts, and the letter from Isaiah to *ibandla lamaNazaretha* all speak to the "special" relationship virgin girls are believed to have with their spiritual leader, Shembe. While the two rituals have clearly drawn on the cultural heritage of Zulu girls' individual coming-of-age ceremonies and the celebration of female fertility (traditionally central to the reproduction of the homestead), they have been recreated by Isaiah Shembe as collective rites to honor the maintenance of female virginity (a critical element in the moral battle Isaiah engaged against the racist state).[48] Those Nazarite maidens, both young and old, who participate in these rituals and adhere to the stringent rules, are respectfully known as *izintabayepheza,* the mountains of abstinence, those who "rise above making love to a boy/man" (a citation from Shembe's letter to *ibandla lamaNazaretha*). Instead of weaving grass coils for their lovers, the virgins participate in ritualized braiding as a sign of their moral fortitude and ritual purity, and to symbolize their obedience to the prophet and the ancestors. As the *Nthanda* ritual enactments suggest, theirs are the bodies that become the metaphoric walls of the house of *Ekuphakameni.*

The personal cost, however, of maintaining this spiritual relationship with Shembe, a privileged position in Nazarite ritual, and protection in the Nazarite fortress (mentioned in Hymn 223) is measured in a currency of personal sacrifice. This is particularly true for young female followers. An early example of the cost of following Shembe is demonstrated in a story cited by Liz Gunner. It is the testimony of a woman, Kekana Mhlongo, who ran away from her home to follow Isaiah in the 1920s. Ms. Mhlongo recalled:

> My father said to tell me, "You mustn't go to that preacher." I was afraid. I didn't want to upset him. Father said, "I will hit you and stab you [if you go]." When they came in the afternoon, I heard it was church time. He [Isaiah Shembe] was with Mlangeni [Isaiah's trusted helper]. I said, "Grandmother, it's evening. Let me go and see that minister?" She said, "How can you? They'll be so angry." I answered, "They will be asleep."
>
> I went home before father awoke. . . . At eight in the morning I went to the river. Isaiah Shembe was going across to *UmZinto.* I looked back and saw a row of people going with Shembe. I heard the words, "Hey, Young Girl, follow me where I am going." I dropped the dishes and wanted to follow him again. . . .

She later meets Isaiah.

> He said, "You will have great trouble. Your father will beat you terribly. I will take your spirit and put it in a country you don't know so that the day he hits you—and he will hit you greatly—your spirit will go to where you see a beautiful new country. You will not feel the pain." [Gunner 1988.]

While sacrifice and struggle clearly operate at several levels and across the Nazarite community,[49] this chapter has foregrounded one particular form of sacrifice for young Nazarite girls, who are required to closet sexual desire specifically. The penalty for transgression of the moral code, particularly in terms of sexual intercourse, is public shame. Such shame is made visible by the removal of a maiden's personal knife and *inansook* shawl—the quintessential sign of virginity in the community—and, perhaps most devastating, she is forbidden to participate in religious dance or *umgido*. For this reason, there are numerous young girls and unmarried women who live away from *Ebuhleni*, who break the moral code, and who selectively participate in these ritual practices.

The cost of this protection, then, is total commitment to God (Shembe). As the story of Jephthah and his daughter demonstrates, for the Nazarite community to be victorious in its war against racial injustice, the girls are required to offer their virtuous bodies in obedience to the will of the prophet/God. It is in this sense then that I argue that for Nazarite maidens to retain sexual, ritual, and moral purity is to sacrifice desire. This might be likened to what Foucault (1988) defines as a "technology of the self," a construction of an individual and social self through adherence to a (Nazarite) religious truth embodied in sexual prohibition. This technology constitutes the virgin self at two levels: in the formation of an individual identity within the community (a maiden who wears the *inansook*, partakes of religious dance, and bears a knife), and in fashioning a social self in defiance of the outside other (the obedience of virgin girls facilitates Isaiah's victory over racist landowners).

To maintain ritual purity in the form of virginity is impossible, however, if a woman marries and engages in sexual intercourse, unless there is an overriding ideology of spirituality that counteracts the pollution, dirt, and danger endemic to the loss of virginity. In chapters 7 and 8 I explore the complexity of ritual purity as it pertains to physical marriage between earthly men and women, and the implications of this union for Nazarite female spirituality.

SEVEN

Nazarite Marriage and the "Brides of Christ"

Zafika izintombi	The virgins arrived
Zize emthimbeni,	At the wedding,
Zipethe izibani	They were carrying lamps
Nawo amafutha.	And oil.
	Chorus
Kunjalo namhla	That is how it is today
Ekuphakameni,	At Kuphakama,
Ufikile umyeni,	The bridegroom has arrived,
Wozani wezintombi,	Come, you virgins,
Ngenani ngamandla.	Enter with power.
(Hlab. 229/1)	(Hymn 229/1)

In previous chapters, I have argued that Nazarite ritual purity is embodied in the control of the fertility of young female virgins. In this context and in keeping with Nguni tradition, I have suggested that female moral and ritual purity is believed to underpin the maintenance of well-being for the Nazarite religious community as a whole. The application of this moral purity has, however, been transformed over time. Traditionally, the female fertility–ritual purity clause held metaphorical equivalence with the fertility of the land and agricultural production. In the early days of *ibandla lamaNazaretha,* virgin girls were constituted as moral warriors fighting battles with the larger state and its officials. More recently, female purity has been reframed in terms of the current climate of ongoing violence and violation within black communities in South Africa. It has increased its value as a mechanism for the survival of Nazarite individuals and of the community itself, both of which are under constant threat of violation. In this context, the sanctification of the female body is believed to afford protection and power to the social body.

Nevertheless, in both the traditional and contemporary contexts, the moral code of female purity as it is located in sexual abstinence is problematic if a girl decides to marry, if she engages in voluntary sexual intercourse, or if she is violated through rape. (Statistically, the incidence of marriage in black communities is fairly low, while the probability of black South African women and girls being raped is extremely high for those living outside Nazarite religious spaces.)[1] In addition, a fair proportion of unmarried Nazarite girls have already had children of their own. Each type of sexual activity is a breach in the clause of moral purity.

Even though marriage was traditionally the central mechanism for the reproduction of the Nguni social order, it is clear from narratives told about Isaiah's dreams and visions that he experienced inner conflict over this institution, particularly in terms of polygamy, and the *lobola* (bridewealth) transactions that occurred between the families of bride and bridegroom. Furthermore, rape is regarded as a social aberration, and as I discussed in chapter 2, within the context of massive social transformation and societal disruption, Isaiah was deeply troubled by the vulnerability of young girls in terms of rape and prostitution. This anxiety has been exacerbated by the AIDS epidemic in the region. How then did Shembe and his followers resolve the contradictions between the ideals of ritual purity located in sexual abstinence, and the inevitable loss of this purity to his female followers through marriage or sexual violation?

Isaiah Shembe solved this contradictory issue by reconfiguring the concept of physical marriage within the domain of the spiritual. In this capacity married women are referred to as the virgin "brides of Christ." Physical impurity caused by sexual intercourse between a man and woman is subsumed under the broader category of spiritual union between Shembe and his female followers. This union is based on an ideology of sacred work. In the Nazarite moral economy this work results in the accumulation of moral capital. Accumulation is fostered through participation in the cycle of ritual activities that includes sacred song and dance, women's all-night meetings, the pilgrimage to the holy mountain, and so forth. Each of these activities requires endurance and perseverance, and reflects a woman's complete commitment and sacrifice of self and desire to her God/Shembe.

This chapter is divided into three sections. I first briefly expand on my discussion in chapter 2 of the Nguni institution of marriage through several transformations—from its precolonial form, through the colonial period, and into its final shape in Nazarite religious practice. In these contexts marriage is considered in terms of its socioeconomic and political value. Second, I discuss Nazarite marriage specifically, as both a physical and a spiritual union. Third, I highlight the role of sacred song in effecting the physical union of a man and woman. Finally, I consider marriage as a spiritual union between Shembe and Nazarite women.

Nguni to Nazarite Marriage

Marriage in traditional or precolonial Nguni society was essentially a process for the creation of alliances between kin groups with separate *izibongo* (clan names), and the transfer of property through the male lineage. Marriage characteristically adhered to rules of virilocality and polygamy. As is commonly the case elsewhere, marriage incurred enormous anxiety and loneliness for a young woman, who would be required to leave her own family to live with a man, his family, and perhaps other wives.

The marriage process customarily involved the exchange of *lobola* or bridewealth (in the form of cattle or goats) from the groom to the bride's father. Krige (1988 [1950], 120–22) remarks that this was not a payment so much as it was a gift to the father who was about to lose his daughter to another family. (This meant more than simply losing someone he loved— it related to her value in agricultural production and social reproduction for her natal family.) In addition, good relationships between the two kin groups were facilitated by a series of gift-giving ceremonies between families, a process that continued for years after the consummation of the marriage. Finally, the transfer of cattle occurred only once the bride had produced her first child. In other words, at some level, cattle were exchanged for the products of a girl's fertility. Because a kin group relied on the fertility of its women for the reproduction of the homestead, the barrenness of a woman could provide grounds for the dissolution of the marriage. A man would be entitled to the reinstatement of his cattle in this case. The girl would return to her father's homestead and revert to her position as unmarried daughter (ibid., 157).

With the annexation of Zululand in 1887 by the British (Davenport 1988 [1977], 202) and the subsequent control the British wielded over all aspects of Zulu social life, Zulu marriage changed from being a long-term social process to a one-time legal contract (Klopper 1991, 163). Klopper quotes Clause 177 of the Natal Native Code of Law, 1891, which states, "All lobola cattle must be delivered on or before the marriage." In other words, the lifelong process of marriage transactions between two families was effectively reduced and objectified to consist of a single and final transaction between the groom and his father-in-law. The implications of this for women were enormous. As Klopper remarks (ibid.), the law emphasized the exchange of cattle for rights to a woman's labor value at a time when men were increasingly entering the migrant wage labor force, and it gave the affines full control over her reproductive powers, even before she entered their residence.

The final issue in this Native Law was the standardization of the value of *lobola*, which until that time had fluctuated according to the availability of cattle, both in terms of a man's personal wealth, and the general condition of his homestead as determined by drought, disease, and warfare. A new Native Law in 1897 required that ten head of cattle were to be exchanged in marriage transactions. This was commonly felt to be beyond what most men could afford, or had customarily been giving at the time. The result was that *lobola* transactions went beyond the reach of most men, who were simply not able to accumulate sufficient wealth to cover the exchange. Men and women therefore turned increasingly to prostitution and adultery, with devastating effects on the homestead economy.[2]

The dilemma Isaiah Shembe felt over the institution of marriage must be understood at two levels: in terms of the uncertainty embedded in the constitution of traditional marriage at the historical moment, and in terms of his own experiences. These experiences are best explained through the narratives of the series of dreams/visions he is reported to have had early in his life.

A number of Isaiah's dream narratives address marriage, and his relationships with women are the subject of some of his dreams or visions. Roberts (1936) reports four such cases. At the age of fifteen, Isaiah heard the "Voice" (which would guide him throughout his life). It told him that he should refrain from living with women, even though at the time he was not old enough to court women.[3] The second account is from when Isaiah was twenty-six years old and consists of three successive visions. I shall quote Roberts's version in full, as it raises a number of issues. She writes (ibid., 32–33):

> In his vision he found himself flying towards a group of people who were facing the east. Although Shembe was flying, and they remained stationary, he could not overtake them. Suddenly a man appeared and advanced towards him. When they met[,] a "Voice" told Shembe to look earthward. The people in the east pointed downwards and lightning issued from their fingers, and illuminated the earth. He looked down and saw himself prostrate in prayer. A "Voice" asked what his body looked like and he replied that it was revolting [covered in filth]. Thereupon the "Voice" said "Do you remember what the "Voice" told you when you prayed? Did not the "Voice" warn you against [an] unclean life? That is why you cannot

overtake us. You are still unclean." Shembe said that he would not return to his vile body but the "Voice" did not answer him.

On the same day, at four o'clock, the "Voice" came again and said, "Come away from among women. I want to speak to you. Build yourself a house outside the *kraal* [cattle byre] and stay there." Shembe asked what he should do about his wives and the "Voice" said "Let them choose their future life." He protested that he would feel jealous if his wives became the property of other men. He said, "Rather let them die, but spare the one you chose for me." The "Voice" replied "I hear you."

A year later one of Shembe's sons, and two other children belonging to inmates of his *kraal,* died. Shembe prayed and asked why the people were thus afflicted. His "Voice" replied "Don't you remember sitting on that hill above your *kraal* when I told you to give up polygamy and you said you preferred that your wives should die rather than that they should marry other men while you lived? Well, I do [*sic*] what you wished, but I killed the children instead of the mothers whom you wished to die in their sins. I did not cause their deaths." Shembe asked "Lord what shall I do today?" The "Voice" replied "Follow me. These women whom you willed to die are no more." Shembe thereupon renounced his wives and the visions concerning polygamy ceased.

These dream/visions reveal a number of issues that were to become central to the construction of the Nazarite view of marriage. Shembe received his instructions in communication with the cosmos through the medium of dreams. Dreams were therefore treated as sacred messages. Polygamy was equated with bodily defilement, the lack of access to the cosmology/heaven, as well as to the death of his children. Shembe clearly felt conflict over leaving his wives as instructed, for it would mean that they would marry other men. Nevertheless, his actions were confirmed when, after he left these women, his disturbing dreams on the matter of polygamy came to an end.

There is a second narrative told about the time when Shembe was being called by God to go to the holy mountain of *Nhlangakaze.* This time of calling coincided with his marriage to a young woman, which had been arranged by his parents. Nazarite member Cinikile Mazibuko (pers. comm., January 1992) recalls:

> When it was the wedding day he was getting married to . . . with singing nice, everything. . . . Everybody was happy. Just when, just when he was dancing with the bride, then came the Word of God.

He said, "Shembe, if you don't want to die now, you must leave this bride. You go follow me." He had to leave his bride. Everything. The bride was crying. Everybody was crying. Then he said to them, "There is nothing I can do because the Word of God is here. I must go now."

Just imagine leaving your bride, leaving everybody singing happy [*sic*]. Just left. The bride was crying. Then he went to follow the Word of God, when he said "You must go to somewhere in the velds, the open spaces." Then God said to him, "I want to speak to you. You leave your bride, you leave everything. Come follow me. I want to speak to you." Then he left everything. Just like that.

In this narrative people are happy because they are celebrating in accordance with traditional ways. The joy in the marriage contrasts with Shembe, who is threatened with death if he does not obey the call to break with these traditions. There was enormous sacrifice and pain involved in obeying the "Word of God," particularly in terms of marriage. According to this account, it was at the moment in which the marriage was to be sacralized—the dancing of the bride and groom—that the call came. Quite clearly, Isaiah Shembe sensed deep moral anguish over the conflicting pulls of traditional religious ways, and over his personal sense of spirituality versus that of Nguni custom.

After marrying four women, he resolved the conflict by keeping only one wife, and inviting the other three to stay at *Ekuphakameni* if they so wished (Roberts 1936). For many of his followers, however, the matter was not quite as straightforward. Mission rules required that if a traditional polygamist converted to Christianity, he would have to give up all but one wife. As Roberts (ibid.) comments, Shembe realized that if this happened these women would be marginalized by their communities, and have to resort to prostitution or illegal beer-brewing in order to survive. Isaiah thus allowed men and married women in polygamous arrangements to join *ibandla lamaNazaretha* (Makhosazane Nyadi, pers. comm., January 1992). In addition, Roberts was of the opinion that Shembe never forced the unmarried women to marry.

From the evidence presented in chapter 2 and these accounts, it is clear that by the time Isaiah began to preach and heal the African people of KwaZulu Natal in the early 1900s, the institution of traditional marriage had undergone significant transformation in the hands of both European missionaries and state officials. It had lost its ability to create alliances between people, and to provide for social reproduction and homestead production in the way it had previously functioned. Furthermore, as explained in chapter 2, the two issues that were vehemently contested by the missionaries were those of polygamy and the exchange of *lobola*, and they urged colonial officials to legislate against both practices, which they did, both directly (as explained above) and indirectly through taxation.

State taxation such as the hut tax militated against polygamy because each wife in a polygamous marriage lived in a separate hut. The more wives a man had, the more tax he was required to pay, and the longer he would then need to work outside of the homestead in order to earn sufficient cash to pay the tax. Furthermore, relatively high fees were required for a black South African to register his marriage. In response to these pressures, Isaiah sought to create a community in which marriage would not be the single means of survival, or the only mechanism for social reproduction over time.

He did not seek to deny marriage to those of his community who wished to be married. Instead, he reformulated both traditional marriage and the practices of Christian marriage into a purely Nazarite form and practice. It is this practice that provided the means for his construction of the "brides of Christ" through a spiritual union he would create for those who could not, or did not wish to, be married.

Nazarite marriage rules are still patrilineal and virilocal, although they no longer pertain to groups of blood kin with different *izibongo*, as in the traditional system. They currently apply to religious kinship as defined by temple. These temples are equivalent to one's extended family, with Shembe as *Baba* (Father) in the spiritual sense. (For some members, he is father in terms of the faith they place in him to provide for their material needs as well.) A Nazarite girl from one temple ideally will marry a Nazarite boy from a different temple—and Nazarite members are not supposed to marry non-Nazarites.

The question of *lobola* payments is a contested one in *ibandla lamaNazaretha*. According to Roberts (1936) and the church catechism, Isaiah did not require the exchange of cattle in order for Nazarite marriage to take place. Isaiah is reported to have said that a minimal amount of gift-giving should occur between families. He seemed to prefer that the girl marry, rather than have children out of wedlock or resort to prostitution. Nevertheless, any arrangements concerning the families were made in private. (For the most part, the parents of the girls continue to require the cattle transaction, which for many is the only means of economic security in their old age.)

To accommodate his more traditional membership, Isaiah also allowed but did not require the full range of actions that constituted the traditional marriage process.[4] The moments over which Shembe required control, however, were the "proposal" by the boy to the girl and the final marriage ceremony. At these moments Shembe wrested authority over the girls from their parents, and the marriage process became a collective rather than individual rite (as with the life-cycle rites in chap. 6). It is these two moments in the life of a Nazarite girl that I shall thus discuss in greater detail for the remainder of this section.

Krige (1988 [1950]) reports that, customarily, a boy and girl became acquainted with each other through a series of events that took place in the context of the girl's age-set. The boy then approached the girl to ask her if he could speak to her parents about marriage. He thereafter went to the older girls who had charge over the girl to ask their permission. It was only at this point that negotiation with the girl's parents was initiated. Marriage proposals in *ibandla lamaNazaretha* occur collectively on the last Sunday of the main festival months—January and July in particular—but also in March, May, October, and December. This Sunday is also the day on which baptisms, final marriage rites, and *ukusina* occur. Mthethwa (n.d.) explains this by saying that no religious rite is complete without its culmination in *ukusina*, the sacred dance by means of which the ancestors meet with living Nazarite members.

The procedure is as follows. A young man sees a young woman he would like to marry. He finds out her name and the temple she belongs to, and early on Sunday morning he proceeds to *Mpathi* in the girls' enclosure. He tells *Mpathi* his personal details and what kind of marriage payment or *lobola* he can offer her parents. *Mpathi* then sends for the girl, and in the early afternoon, she calls all these girls and their suitors to a space in the girls' enclosure. The girl is seated on a prayer mat, in the center of a group of young men and women who have come to watch the event, and to support their friends who are undergoing this process of marriage proposal.

The girl sits on the mat with her head bowed, the young man next to her, with *Mpathi* in front of them. *Mpathi* then explains to the girl what this man can offer her as a marriage partner. She talks quietly, and while she does so, the friends, particularly of the young man, chat excitedly among themselves. They call out to the girl, encouraging her to accept their friend. It is a highly public event, and the couple may not leave until a decision has been made. I was told that the girl had the option of refusing the man, although it seemed to me to be an extremely charged situation—one in which it would be difficult to say no. Certainly, I never saw a single girl refuse, even though some required considerable persuasion.[5]

The length of the negotiation varies quite considerably. Officially, the couple should not know each other, except for the man having seen the girl while dancing or at one of the festivals. Thus it may take some time before the girl agrees to the marriage. She does not speak at all during the period of proposal—and asks no questions. She signals her agreement by simply turning her hand over so the palm is facing upward. At this point the man's friends cheer and applaud, and everyone leaves to throw a party for the couple. Thereafter, the next young man and woman sit down with *Mpathi*, and she begins the process all over again. On a single Sunday, she can arrange between ten and twenty marriages.

While to the outsider this process of becoming engaged may seem to be a rather unfair one for the young woman, it seems to provide her with a degree of autonomy that may not have been given her if the negotiations had been left to her parents and those of the groom. Kligman (1988, 74) quotes a resident of Ieud, Romania, who remarked to her that "marriage is a type of negotiated exchange like that in the market; if you bargain with closed eyes, you'll pay dearly." In other words, while it may seem that a Nazarite girl has little choice, she is only required to agree to the marriage once she fully understands the terms. In that respect she seems to hold some leverage.

There is usually a period of about two years before the marriage is then solemnized back at the church. During this time the young man makes arrangements with the girl's parents about his payment of *lobola*, and the exchange of other gifts. The young woman prepares her dowry, which consists of blankets, woven mats, and embroidered pillowcases, all of which are placed in a wooden chest. A number of household items are now purchased, such as household furniture and kitchen equipment.[6]

As a rite of passage, marriage requires the girl to separate from her family, to pass through a period of liminality, and then to be reaggregated into the community of the bridal couple as adults (van Gennep 1960, 116–45). For the Nazarite girl such reaggregation involves incorporation into the lineage of her husband's father, which ultimately includes the ancestral line. The rites of separation and reaggregation are the moments that are overseen by Nazarite religious officials. They are held collectively for several couples simultaneously. The ceremonies between these are essentially left to the couple's family and friends.

All Nazarite marriage ceremonies take place on the last Sunday of a festival month, the same day as marriage proposals are made. On the day before the marriage ceremony (the Nazarite sabbath), the bride signifies the rite of separation from her family and total submission to the lineage of her father-in-law by entering the temple in a bodily position of total respect—her face is completely covered by the traditional blue shawl. This is closed with an elaborate pin at the forehead. She cannot see anything and is led around the temple by her close female friends. For the entire passage of the sabbath, the young woman keeps her head bowed down; she does not look at or speak to anybody. (In a similar rite of separation, the veiling and body posture is repeated at the funeral of a woman's husband.)

Isaiah originally based the Nazarite rite on the biblical narrative of Jacob, who married Laban's daughters, Leah and Rachel (Genesis 29–30). This was later formalized into the Nazarite marriage rite and written in the Nazarite catechism. The wedding ceremony displays a remarkable fusion of various elements emerging out of both Nguni traditional and European Christian practices, as well as Shembe's own interpretation of biblical readings, again creating a completely new cultural form. This new form is a tripartite structure in which dance and singing constitute the outer parts, with the Western emphasis on the authority of the written word in the middle. (Only the middle part is written in the catechism.)

The substance of the words spoken focuses on marital fidelity, the consequences of adultery, the central role of love in the institution of marriage, and, finally, the couple's need to publicly affirm whether they are to be married under customary or Christian rites (whether a man will take on additional wives or not). The enormous weight of these proclamations is embodied in the presence of two preachers and the laying of the hands of the bride and groom on top of the open Bible (signifying the authority of the Word of God) as they make their promises. In addition these solemn vows are made in *Paradis,* the temple area at *Ebuhleni.*

The song-dance-drumming complex that frames marriage is the medium through which Nazarites reclaim cultural truth as it pertains to the sacralization of marriage. It is this complex, rather than the written or spoken word, that sanctions the union of a man and a woman. In this regard, *ukusina* reinstates the social body, it heals the physical body, and it reaffirms the collective nature of the body politic (Roseman 1991). The body politic in *ibandla lamaNazaretha* incorporates both the living and the dead. In other words, sacred dance sets the cosmos in motion. It calls on the inhabitants of the cosmological realm to spiritually intervene in the flow of ritual time, and to watch over those uniting through marriage. In a cogent and highly dramatic manner, Nazarite *ukusina* claims the right to public assembly, for both the living and the dead (Kligman 1990).

The ceremony itself cannot happen without the beating of the double-headed bass drum, the sound of which is intended to amplify the pounding of the dancers' feet upon the earth (Mthethwa n.d.). To this end each groom is instructed to pay the leader of the maidens (who keeps the drums) R 1.50 as a fee for the drum. Thereafter the drum is beaten, calling the groom's male age-mates to join with him in the festival dance. Once they are dancing, the bride is escorted to the dance area (in front of the church office) by her father or brother, to join the groom. The first part of their union is signaled by their dancing together and singing a hymn while moving slowly with the beat of the drum. This dancing continues for about half an hour, at which point the drummers lead the brides and their grooms into the temple for the formal vows.

Once the vows are complete, the drummers move the procession of bridal couples to the upper festival ground, where further dancing takes place. But as Bongani Mthethwa (n.d.) suggests, it is not so much the speaking of vows and the laying of hands on the Bible that solemnize the marriage (as in European marriage) as it is the moment when the bride and groom dance the festival dance accompanied by the beating of the drum.[7] As with *inkhonzo* and *ukusina,* Isaiah interweaves the ways of the European and the African to create a new order—a marriage ritual that accommodates the requirements of two worlds, that of the state administration and that of so-called Nguni traditionalists.

There is a fascinating twist to Isaiah's formulation of the Nazarite marriage rite. Roberts (1936, 143) comments that Shembe was not authorized by the state to perform legal marriages, though "he re-married any converts who had been married by missionaries." It is in this comment that the twist reveals itself. Why would people want or need to be remarried if they had been married by state-approved marriage officers? Quite simply, marriage by state officials was symbolized by a lack of cultural appropriateness. We find, therefore, that Isaiah Shembe refashioned marriage after his own image, an image that reincorporated both religious dance and drumming. Both the drum and the dance are believed to embody the spirit and patterns of the ancestors. In this context the dancing and drumming constitute a musical metaphor for the unification of the ancestral lineages believed to occur in the sacralization of marriage.

With some modification, marriage attire for men and women becomes the attire for sacred dance. In this sense, unity in the sacralization of marriage is created through the rhythm of dance, drum, uniform, and ancestral presence. I suggest that through this renegotiation of earthly time and space to incorporate the temporal and spatial dimensions of the cosmology, Isaiah reclaimed for his people the evolving, recurrent, cyclical, and nonprogressive elements of space and time that had characterized marriage in precolonial African homesteads.

In addition to the transformation of marriage from an individual to a group ritual, and its inclusion of dancing and drumming, there are a number of other changes in Nazarite marriage that appear to have occurred since Esther Roberts's fieldwork in the 1930s. In her descriptions, Isaiah plays a central role in the marriage proposals as well as the ceremonies—roles played now by *Mpathi* (leader of the girls), *abavangeli* (male evangelists), and *abamshumayeli* (male ministers). The most significant change, however, reflects a transformation in Nazarite interaction with the wider political economy, from a stress on becoming "civilized"—rejecting "backward" and "uncivilized" ways—to the more recent self-conscious articulation of cultural and religious identity through these "uncivilized" cultural forms. This is particularly evident through the concept of "correct" attire to be worn at weddings. Roberts (1936, 137) writes:

> Just before the wedding, the man [i.e., groom] provides armlets for the girl and a blue veil and finger-rings. He also buys *a white dress, which is used as the wedding dress and corresponds to the isidwaba of the uncivilised Zulu. At a pagan wedding, the girl's outfit is provided by her father.* [Emphasis added.]

Later,

> On the day before the wedding, the girl pays six shillings for permission to lay aside her blue veil and to wear the white one.

I suggested in an earlier discussion of uniforms for girls' festivals of dance that Isaiah appeared to feel caught between two worlds—that of his own traditional ways, and that of the European. These two worlds were, however, not equally balanced, and from the accounts on Nazarite wedding attire, it would appear that in the 1930s the dominance of the West was winning Isaiah over. Nazarite girls thus removed the traditional fare, replacing it with the more "civilized." The traditional cowhide *isidwaba* and blue/green veil were discarded for the white gown and veil. If one reads the current marriage attire of the bride as a text that articulates Nazarite beliefs about the moral values and the construction of a married woman's identity, a narrative different from that of Roberts's 1936 encounter emerges.

The virgin girl as the bride has removed the two rushes of beadwork she wore on her head for *ukusina,* and instead dons an *inhloko*[8]—the "pillbox"-shaped hat woven from strands of her own hair and rubbed with red ocher. This is the headdress traditionally worn by married women, and is a style that can be traced back to about the 1850s (Klopper 1991). (Prior to this, women used to have their heads shaved in a way that would allow for a "topknot," a knot literally on the top of their heads.)[9] During the marriage ceremony, the bride wears the *inhloko* without the rushes of beadwork known as *umnqwazi* that are worn in front of the topknot of the married woman once the first child has been born.

In place of the beadwork, a handkerchief is folded to form two triangles on either side of the topknot. These two triangles may refer to the "diamond pattern" typical of much Zulu beadwork (Joseph Shabalala, pers. comm., August 1993), though in this context the woman has taken the diamond, cut it in half, and placed the halves alongside each other. I suggest that this pattern resembles the central icon of Nazarite spirituality. This is the holy mountain of *Nhlangakaze*—the pinnacle of moral purity. In this sense the young woman demonstrates she is still a virgin *intabayepheza,* a mountain of abstinence (and ritual purity).

Between her shoulders and lower hips she wears the layers of beadwork normally worn by the maidens. These symbolize her virginity. Over these beads the bride wears a leopard-skin cover given to her by the groom. Mthethwa (n.d.) remarks that leopard skins were used to signify the status of a chief, but that in Nazarite male dance attire, there is no such distinction. I would add that this leopard skin embodies the relationship between young girls and Shembe, in terms of the praise name for Shembe as "leopard" written into the text of Hymn 84, the hymn Isaiah gave to the girls as a reward for their obedience and moral goodness. The bride also wears the white bead armlets (which traditionally signified the presence of the ancestors) of the maidens in two lines around her arms, with one at the elbow and the other about three inches higher.

Her black cotton fringed skirt of maidenhood is now replaced with the cowhide *isidwaba* worn by married women. This skirt is believed to protect her from the wrath of the agnatic ancestors who control her fertility (Klopper 1991, 160). Klopper suggests that in Zululand the *isidwaba* skirt and its connection to fertility and ancestral wrath is used by migrant men as a mechanism of control over their wives when these men leave for the urban areas. Men feel that if their wives wear these skirts, they will be less likely to have affairs with other men, for fear of the anger of the ancestors. In contrast to Klopper's interpretation, I suggest that wearing the *isid-*

waba highlights the woman's body as the container of time: fertility (and the future generation), the ancestral line (the past), and the present (the woman wearing the skirt) all meet in the married woman's leather skirt, worn for the most holy of events—marriage and sacred dance.

In her left hand the virgin holds a white handkerchief tucked inside the palm of her hand and she carries the traditional shield of the maidens. In her right hand she clasps a large kitchen knife (and not the umbrella as used for *ukusina*). In Krige's account (1988 [1950]) of traditional Zulu marriage, a young woman used to carry a spear, though Krige also says that the umbilical cord of a woman's baby is cut with a knife. It would seem that the change to a knife here is also more consistent with the model of Victorian domesticity inculcated in young black women through early mission culture (Gaitskell 1990), and possibly signals a desire for children.

The attire worn by a young woman for Nazarite marriage may be interpreted in two ways: in terms of her physical marriage to a man, and alternatively, as a statement about her spiritual union with her God, Shembe (discussed in the next section). In the first instance, her attire reflects a state of transition from youthful virginity to the maturity she will achieve after she has given birth to her first child. The bride therefore continues to wear certain aspects of the girls' dance attire, and replaces three items with signs of her new status—the black fringed skirt with *isidwaba,* and the headband of beadwork (worn by the young girls) with *inhloko.* This beadwork will in turn replace the white handkerchiefs now covering the topknot. Finally, she carries a knife rather than the umbrella in her hand, symbolizing her move toward motherhood and domesticity, though she will take up the umbrella again in *ukusina* with the married women.

Spiritual Marriages to Shembe

While marriage may traditionally have been the social ideal, it is quite clear from Shembe's formation of *ibandla lamaNazaretha* that for many of his early membership, marriage failed to provide the necessary economic, political, and social security. In response to this, Isaiah created his religious spaces (or villages, as they were called) for the widows and orphans, those customarily marginalized by death, divorce, and marital estrangement. Likened to an Nguni homestead head, Isaiah played the role of husband for many women—he acquired land, which enabled women to create an economic base; he structured a form of social organization into which they could find a place—and he functioned as a political leader or chief in terms of the control he wielded over the space.

The minimal importance attached to the conjugal relationship as a sexual relationship in *ibandla lamaNazaretha* is manifest at the level of spatial organization. Residence on Nazarite sacred spaces prohibits any form of sexual intercourse. This applies to all people, including married couples. Residential space similarly separates members by age and gender. Women and their prepubescent children construct their shelters in one part of the community; after puberty, girls live inside the girls' enclosure; and married men and boys live together in another section of the space.

Once inside the temple—the center of the sacred space—women, girls, and men and boys are divided along the same lines. Even in casual gatherings of Nazarite members outside of religious ritual, men are seldom seen talking with women, and young girls engage in fleeting conversations with young boys. If a husband wishes to communicate with his wife, he sends a message with a child, who acts as the go-between for the duration of the visit to the sacred site.

The interaction between men and women is constrained by the social code of *hlonipha* (respect). Raum (1973) has provided remarkable details of the rules and ramifications of this body of social principles as they apply to Zulu-speaking people generally. In Shembe's community, they have been modified to suit both religious and traditional demands. Roberts (1936, 80) writes that the "law of the Nazarites is summed up in the command 'love your neighbor and love God.'" In terms of *hlonipha*, Roberts comments that Isaiah felt that all people should be imbued with reverence and humility (ibid., 94). The implications of this for married men and women are that men are not as easily able to control the movement of their wives as when they are outside of Nazarite space. Instead, the code of respect for Shembe/God required from both men and women is privileged over all other forms of interaction.

Despite these restrictions, from the earliest days of his ministry, Isaiah Shembe attracted large numbers of women who were already married. Gunner writes that these women frequently ran off for weeks at a time in order to follow Isaiah (1988, 224). This they did to the chagrin of their husbands, chiefs, and fathers. Gunner provides several pieces of archival evidence of the ire men felt over the split allegiance they perceived in their women. One man, Sotshobo Mbhele, was taken to court for beating his wife. His defense went as follows:

> I have this day [September 20, 1915] been convicted for thrashing my wife because she is continually leaving home without my permission and staying away sometimes two or three weeks. She states

that she has been away preaching on behalf of a sect called "The Nazareths" under the leadership of Isaiah Tshembe. . . . My wife and my sisters have been attending these services which are held in the forests and the hills. . . . I also understand that Tshembe gets the women to wash his feet. All Tshembe's washing and mending is done at my kraal by my wife which fact goes to show the hold this man has over the women. The women sometimes go away for two or three weeks to Ixopo or Durban to attend meetings. [Chief Native Commissioner (CNC) 96 (CNC/2155/12/30 Magistrate Port Shepstone to CNC, Natal 22.9.1915).]

This extract is revealing in terms of both the hold men customarily had over women and the opposing pull Shembe appears to have had over his female following. There was clearly a tension between a woman's loyalty to her husband and her loyalty to her God/Shembe. Both elements point to reasons why women chose to follow Isaiah. These included freedom from household chores and duties, and the power to move and preach that he appeared to instill in them. Furthermore, Isaiah obviously caused division in traditional communities by taking women away from the roles and behavior prescribed by cultural norms. He countered such opposition by drawing on the authority of God as contained in the Bible—specifically, the parable of the ten virgins contained in Matthew 25.

The religious ideology that enabled women to follow Shembe and to "wed" themselves to his religious ways was constructed on a merging of the categories of traditional Nguni mythology and history with the cultural truths contained in the biblical narrative of the bridegroom and the ten virgins. The manifestation of this relationship was located in a particular code of everyday behavior, in specific items of Nazarite women's attire, and in a hymn text framed by the biblical parable. Each of these reinforced the concept of spiritual union through the biblical metaphor of the "bride of Christ." This was interpreted in a literal manner to refer exclusively to married women rather than the church as a whole (as in the Western interpretation).

The cultural precedent for the bond between the Lord and women was based on the relationship between *Nkulunkulu* and *Nomkhubulwana,* as discussed in chapter 6. This relationship was dependent on the maintenance of physical virginity, and the acceptance of women as daughters, rather than wives, of the Lord. In order to "marry" themselves to Shembe/God, these women returned to being like daughters of their fathers (signaled by their running away from the husbands' homesteads for several weeks at a time, and washing Isaiah's clothes on their husbands' premises). Through spiritual union with Shembe, these women were transformed from ordinary women under the control of the patrilineal homestead head, to women of *indlunkhulu* (the great house) of King Shembe. They became royal women (in a spiritual sense), based on the model provided by the royal Zulu line. Their marriage arrangement was a polygamous one, and certainly endogamous, for Isaiah Shembe was the founding ancestor of the Shembe lineage. It was also endogamous in its need for women to be constantly on the move—to follow Shembe wherever he went. These women demonstrated the power invoked through such spiritual status in their ability to preach the word of God.

This cosmological relationship was not usually consummated in a physical sense.[10] For the most part, women remained spiritual virgins. Like the real, unmarried virgin girls in *ibandla lamaNazaretha*, these spiritual virgins were required to sacrifice sexual desire, retain ritual purity, and nurture the spiritual relationship by means of the accumulation of moral capital. Such accumulation was effected through engagement in "hard work"—dreams, religious dance, the pilgrimage to the holy mountain, attendance of the women's *ama14* meetings—all of which necessitated courage, determination, and self-discipline.

The signals of a woman's commitment to Shembe were not borne out so much by the production of physical progeny as by her life as an obedient member of her following. Congruent with the processual nature of precolonial or traditional Zulu marriage, the spiritual union with Shembe evolved over time. In both earthly marriage and the heavenly union, it was only with death that a woman was fully integrated into Shembe's lineage. In this regard, she was required to continually do good works to appease the ancestors, and thereby ensure her entrance into Shembe's heavenly kingdom at the time of death.

Both of the uniforms worn by married Nazarite women reflect the spiritual relationship these women also have with Shembe. This is most powerfully communicated in the multiple applications of the number fourteen to these women. In the first instance, to be *ifortini* means that you are a married woman who meets with other Nazarite women on the evening of the 13th through the morning of the 15th of every month (discussed in chap. 6). It suggests the most fertile moment in the female menstrual cycle (which is the moment Nazarite women spend with Shembe and other women, rather than at home with their husbands).

Fourteen also refers to the black belt worn around a woman's waist, on top of the white *MNazaretha* prayer gown. This covers the place that becomes the physical manifestation of fertility—the vagina, and the abdomen as the space where pregnancy is revealed. Gunner (1988, 223) writes that the black belt used to be worn by Shembe and other Nazarite men, around their tunics. With the increase in the number of women followers, it ultimately became part of the women's uniform. While Gunner provides no additional explanation for this change, I suggest it embodies the transfer of fertility to women from the ancestors—Shembe, in this case. It also sanctifies the pollution that occurs with pregnancy. The thin white cotton band that encircles the topknot and covers the rushes of beadwork is also called *ifortini*. This band marks the place where dreams and visions (the communication with the ancestors) occur—in the head.

The final signs of women's relationship to Shembe are in the photographs made into ornamental pins, which are pinned to the women's gowns at their breasts, and the traditional rushes of beadwork pinned onto the topknot. Nazarite women have transformed this area of traditional culture—one integrally associated with messages of love and desire between a young woman and a man—into a complex code for the expression of religious loyalty and, indeed, love for Shembe. Mthethwa (1988) asserts that the meaning of particular colors has been transferred from the realm of romantic love to that of religious fervor.

The third body of evidence of the Nazarite women's relationship with Shembe is the text of Hymn 229. This hymn is always sung at the start of the meetings of married women, and is accompanied by the reading of the biblical version in the New Testament gospel of Matthew, chapter twenty-five. The full text of the hymn (written by Galilee in 1945) and its translation are as follows:

Zafika izintombi	The maidens arrived
Zize emthimbeni,	At the wedding,
Zipethe izibani	They were carrying lamps
Nawo amafutha.	And oil.
	Chorus
Kunjalo namhla	That is how it is today
Ekuphakameni,	At Kuphakama,
Ufikile umyeni,	The bridegroom has arrived,
Wozani wezintombi,	Come, you maidens,
Ngenani ngamandla.	Enter with power/strength.
Umyeni walibala	The bridegroom was delayed,
Zozela izintombi.	The maidens fell asleep.
Aphela amafutha	The oil ran out,
Zacima izibani.	The lamps went out.

Umyeni usondele	The bridegroom approached.
Phumani nimlhangabeze;	Go out to meet him;
Bangena abalindile	Those who were ready entered
Endlini yomshado.	The house where the wedding was to take place.

Zakhala iziwula	The foolish ones cried out
"Sipheni amafutha,	"Give us some oil,
Zicimile izibani,	The lamps went out,
Besozela silele."	We were dozing and sleeping."

"Alingene thina sodwa,	"There is only enough for ourselves
Nani zithengeleni;	You must purchase your own;
Lelilifa alabiwa,	This legacy is not shared,
Liyadliwa ngamandla."	It is used up quickly."

"Nkosi sivulele,"	"Lord, open for us,"
Kusho iziwula.	Said the foolish ones.
Umyeni waphendula,	The bridegroom replied,
"Anginazi niphumaphi?"	"I do not know you, where do you come from?"

Lindani niqinise,	Wait patiently,
Alwaziswa usuku;	The day is not known;
Asaziwa nesikhathi	And the time is not known
Sokufika komyeni.	When the bridegroom will arrive.

The first clue to the nature of the relationship between Shembe and married women is the use of the word *izintombi*, which in the Zulu language refers to virgin girls and is used interchangeably in the Nazarite marriage order with the word *umakoti* (bride). This points to an ambiguity in the application of the biblical narrative to married women, who are usually referred to as *amankosikhazi*. There is an obvious play on words that points to a measure of conflict in the construction of the religious over the social identity for Nazarite women. In this regard, Hugh Tracey (1948, 52) remarks, "All the women of this sect are called Lasses [virgins] of Nazareth." The ambiguity of being physically married while retaining spiritual virginity was explained by Bongani Mthethwa (pers. comm., April 1992), who said that *izintombi* is used metaphorically to refer to the souls of both Jesus and the women. In this context Christian souls are joined in union with Jesus'/Shembe's soul—they are spiritually united. The difference in the Nazarite interpretation and that of Western Christianity lies in the literal ascription of the role of brides to women exclusively, rather than to the church as a whole.

The text of this hymn conveys two additional messages to Nazarite women. The first is articulated through the oil lamps, and the second through the warnings to be ready for the coming of the bridegroom. Women recognize the arrival of the groom as the coming of God to take them to heaven—the final union or marriage. In the first case, light and flames are associated with ancestral presence. In this regard, candles (rather than oil lamps) are lit at the start of the meetings of *amafortini* to acknowledge the ancestors. They are also lit when a person dies. They are kept alight until after the body has been buried and the community is assured of the safe passage of the individual to heaven. This suggests that candles, along with the singing of Hymn 229, enable the transmutation of women from the earthly into the heavenly realm characteristic of *ama14* meetings.

In the second instance, women indicate their preparedness for the coming of the groom by accumulating moral capital, or an individual "legacy." Such accumulation is interpreted quite literally by Nazarite women, whose homes are immaculately maintained, ready for the unexpected visit of the groom. Until fairly recently, Amos Shembe used to make unexpected visits to the homes of members. In the early 1990s, he was too old and sickly to do so.

An exegesis of the text was given by Cinikile Mazibuko (pers. comm., January 1992). She said:

> [T]hey must have candles. So this hymn now, this hymn 229 is talking about those ladies who didn't have, and others who had. So now when the Lord came, those who are ready—I am now ready—let us go to heaven. Those who didn't have, they had to stay away. . . . Now the verse 7 says, you must always *linani liqinise*, says you must always, always be ready because you don't know the day when God will come.

Just as the performance of sacred song effects a transformation of time and space by integrating the cosmos into the earthly domain, its enactment is transformative for married women. As the gift of song to Shembe by a young girl forged a relationship between Shembe and the cosmological virgin, and in turn between Shembe (in the cosmology) and the Nazarite virgins, the singing of Hymn 229 at each *ama14* meeting enveloped women in a cloak of spiritual virginity, and hence, ritual purity and power. In this manner, women were reconstituted as metaphysical virgins, and imbued with the same power of the physical virgins invoked in the life-cycle rites discussed in chapter 4. This was true for the duration of the monthly meetings of *amafortini*, if not for always.

Conclusion

I have examined the concept of marriage as it was constructed in the pre-colonial Zulu homestead economy, and as it was transformed and reinterpreted by Isaiah into a specifically Nazarite rite that included aspects of European Christian marriage. I have discussed how Isaiah metaphorized the concept of social marriage in structuring his religious ideology, particularly as it pertained to the married women in the church. Spiritual union reverses the pollution of women's sexuality caused by social marriage (and rape). In this way, Isaiah created a host of spiritual virgins who held a special place in the formulation of Nazarite spirituality and religious empowerment. In chapter 8 I shall examine how these married women (both socially and spiritually) construct and interpret everyday experiences through the spiritual empowerment with which Shembe imbues their lives, not only in the sacred spaces and in set religious moments, but also through the expressive web of song, dance, and dreaming that intersects in their lives at any moment or place.

EIGHT

AmaNkosikazi as Maidens of Royal Blood

Hlabelela wenanyumbakazi	Sing, O barren woman
Ongabelethiyo	Who is infertile;
Zihlakaze izihlabelelo	Page through the hymnal
Ucule ngamandla.	And sing with strength.
(Hlab. 95/1)	(Hymn 95/1)

In this chapter I examine the way in which married women construct and seek to restructure daily experiences through expressive culture in terms of their encounters with their God/Shembe. These expressive domains elaborate on the nature of social experience and constitute technologies for self-disclosure (Foucault 1988). Such technologies create strategies for "truth-claiming" based upon the common experience of pain and fragmentation on the one hand, and a testimony of healing, protection, and wholeness on the other. Truth-claiming is witnessed by the gathering of Nazarite women, and in this sense becomes a juridical discourse. It has the force of law in terms of a heavenly judgment at the time of death, and thereby facilitates the transition of a woman from the earthly into the heavenly domain by "writing her name in the Book of Life."

A common theme throughout these women's discourses is what Shembe has done for them, and, conversely, how difficult the Nazarite way is. These narrative and ritual performances render visible the nature of the relationship between Shembe and Nazarite women, as viewed from the women's vantage point—particularly in terms of the fertility–ritual purity–sacrificing desire clause discussed in chapter 6. It also reveals the substance of Nazarite experience and its accompanying emotions as "structures of feeling" (Williams in Rosaldo 1993 [1989], 106). Finally, the enactment of such structures demonstrates how expressive culture transforms self, space, and time. Through this process it protects women from violation from the outside, and guarantees reciprocal return in social relationships.

This chapter is divided into four parts. In the first section I discuss the manifestations of the relationship between Nazarite women and Shembe as they are vested in social space and organization; in the second section, I explain women's monthly meetings in terms of their structure and their relationship to other meetings for black South African women; in the third and largest section, I discuss the separate domains of song, dream, miracle, and dance narratives as they are shared with other women in the monthly meetings of *amafortini*. I conclude the chapter by drawing the three expressive domains into a single Nazarite metacommentary on women's experience and the religious imagination.

Shembe, Married Women, and Ritual Power

In chapter 6 I examined the process whereby the bodily experiences of virgin girls were integrated into the structure and content of ritual time, space, and performance. In this chapter, the locus of my analysis is the female body as it mediates all social experience and action (Comaroff 1985, 6; Bell 1990, 301), and externalizes a personalized version of these experiences through song and dream narrative. Here the female body constitutes the center around which the female self and social body are constructed. The body of the Nazarite woman does not exist separately from the protection and sanctuary afforded it by the cosmological power embedded in the person of Shembe. In this regard, I suggest that the structuring of married women's ritual times and spaces revolves around the sanctity of female fertility and the purification of female pollution. Both of these are believed to be located in the figure of Shembe, who for many women is the personification of God.

The assurance of bodily protection by Shembe/God to Nazarite women is fostered through total obedience to the Word of God. This calling of God often runs contrary to the demands of a woman's husband and family. Nevertheless, the relationship between Nazarite women and Shembe is holy, and therefore inviolable—even by a woman's husband, who traditionally wielded complete control over her activities and movements. The implications of the relationship Nazarite women have with Shembe are manifest at several levels: in the history of the formation of the church, in the way in which separation of married men and women is engraved into the demarcation of Nazarite space, and in the self-sacrifice required for female leaders. Ritual power emerges only when there is complete obedience to God.

In chapter 2 I suggested that Isaiah Shembe's religious community was structured along the principles of the Zulu Kingdom. In this sense, the power and authority vested in the Zulu kings was transferred into the Kingdom of God/Shembe. In a manner analogous to both the Zulu king and the Christian mission (Gaitskell 1990), Shembe gathered around him a large following of women. As devotees of the King of Heaven, these women (regardless of their status on earth) were transformed into maidens of the king—maidens of royal blood. In chapter 7 I explained Isaiah Shembe's attitude to the various forms of marriage in practice during his lifetime. Shembe articulated his ambivalence toward the institution in its several guises. On the one hand, he may have felt a desire to adhere to the "Word of God" as contained in the mission Bible and expounded by the mission churches. This teaching required monogamous marriages from its adherents. On the other hand, such teachings flew in the face of his commitment to marginalized women. As Roberts explains,

> On one occasion [Isaiah] said that he had great sympathy for women whose husbands became converts to Christianity and who put them away. He thought that this practice often led to immorality among women and for that reason he did not force his converts to send their wives away. He thought that God would not be pleased if he saved the soul of a man, but was the indirect cause of forcing his wives to become prostitutes. [Roberts 1936, 128.]

Isaiah's obvious empathy for married women is revealed in the following excerpts of narratives told by one of the earliest woman converts in *ibandla lamaNazaretha*. These are translations of texts transcribed by the late church archivist, Petrus Dhlomo. In the first excerpt, Linah Mtungwa recalls that on the day after Shembe acquired land for his church from a local chief,

> 14. Shembe said, let us go and cut some grass. They took some hoes and dug some holes, and that was the beginning of the houses. The first was *kwa 14,* made by Mdladla. In that time the house for Shembe was being built by the women, and it was made of reeds.
> . . .
> 15. The women went to sleep in the roughly built house together with the children. When they went to sleep they took out all the dishes and all their goods. They were so poor they did not have anything to eat. . . .[1]

This excerpt is remarkable for several reasons. First, the house for the married women was built before the others so as to provide shelter to the most destitute of women and children. Second, a house is traditionally built for a woman only by her husband—in this sense, Shembe (and his close associate Mdladla) is effectively a husband to these destitute women. Third, the women built a house of reeds for Shembe in return for his assistance. This action resembles the mimetic house-building by the virgin girls in the annual rites of *Nthanda*. Women also build the house of reeds for Shembe while he is on the mountain of *Nhlangakaze*. They thereby create a space for Shembe to pray to the ancestors. This hut thus encompasses the cosmological power of Shembe. By implication, the power of Shembe is dependent upon the labor of women. Finally, as I shall explain below, the hut constitutes a metaphor for the woman's body—specifically, for the womb. Its construction may allude therefore to the creation of a place from which children emerge, suggesting links among Shembe, the hut, female fertility, and empowerment.

While the first excerpt suggested the space of sanctuary Shembe provided for women, and possibly the symbolic transfer of procreative power, the second narrative, also by Linah Mtungwa, is far more explicit in defining the power Isaiah imparted to women—even those he did not know. She recalls that

1. In the year of 1910, Shembe came in this country of ours. He was preaching to all the sick people and healing them. Some understood his voice, and some couldn't understand him. Some were saying his preaching was magical and supernatural. One day, it was on Sunday, there came a man named Dladla, and he told of his illness. He said, "Lord, I've heard there was someone who came from Ntabazwe, and is sent by God to come and heal the sick."

2. Shembe asked him if he believed God was going to heal him. He said, "Yes, I believe my minister." . . . This was in the house of Judy Mdletshe, where Shembe was. . . . Then there was a lady of a different religion, the lady came in front of Shembe. . . .

3. And Shembe said to her she must lift up her hands. Shembe lifted up his hands and put them on top of the woman's. He said to the woman she must pray for the man who was sick, ask him where he was sick, and hold the place where he is sick.

4. He stopped the service, and asked the man who was sick if he was healed. He was healed on that day.

This narration of events demonstrates Foucault's conceptualization of power and its investment in bodily practices (Bell 1990, 306). In Mtungwa's account, the body is the locus both of aberrant forces (in the sick body of Dladla) and of the transformative wholeness imparted through the healing of God, which is in turn mediated through the body (the hand) of the nameless woman. In this sense the social body is reformulated by the ritualized reconstruction of social relationships (Foucault in Bell 1990, 306), with women as the mediators of cosmological power. In the first account this power was embodied in fertility, and in the second, in the ability to heal bodily illness.

Despite the spiritual force imparted to Nazarite women in these narratives, in *ibandla lamaNazaretha* women do not hold any significant positions of authority other than as leaders of the women in their own temples. These leaders are appointed by the titular head of the church on the advice of the senior male elders. They are known as *abakhokheli*—leaders of the *manyano* (prayer union)—and there are usually two appointed to each temple. Their responsibilities are to ensure that the women's meetings occur regularly, to collect the monthly and annual payments required of all women, to wash and dress corpses, and to keep an eye on the virginity of the young girls in their temples. They also comfort the women who grieve, and collect payments from those who have visited doctors or clinics. (Partaking in Western medicine is considered polluting until paid for with a small gift.) Finally, *abakhokheli* have a power imparted by Shembe to pray for and heal the sick. (This power is thought to be effective only among those women who are strong and have self-respect.)

While a certain prestige accrues to the position of *umkhokheli*, one woman told me that those who wish to hold this status do not realize how difficult it is. She explained that in this position you are the role model for all people, and everyone watches to see if you err in your ways. If you are chosen there is no way to refuse the honor. "You are *Mkhokheli* for life—no pension," she ruefully concluded (C. Mazibuko, pers. comm., January 1992).

An *i14* from KwaMashu expressed the role of *Mkhokheli* in this way. She said

> *Mkhokheli* is the one who should tell her children the right way to go when they come to this church. She should tell them that the way of *Ekuphakameni* is not an easy one. It's like a slippery rock. The cowards don't go on it. [KwaMashu, October 13, 1991.]

This conceptualization of the hardship, of the sacrifice, required in order to follow Shembe resonates with that discussed for young girls, and resurfaces in my analysis below.

Meetings of *Ama14*, the Married Women

Thursday is *manyano* day in Johannesburg, and on Thursdays the women and girls in domestic service are "off." . . . Gone are the caps and aprons of European servitude and, instead, there are the blousy jackets and collars and sashes and hats of "my *manyano*." . . . Amongst them are grandmothers of illegitimate babies, mothers of delinquent sons, wives of irresponsible husbands. They represent the sheer force of survival. . . . "where do you think we get our strength to persevere? It is in our *manyanos*." [Brandel-Syrier 1962, 27–28.]

Regular meetings of African women for women exclusively have a fairly long history in terms of mission churches in South Africa. Gaitskell (1990, 255) traces the first meetings held between mission wives and uneducated African women to the 1830s, to European and American missionaries who wished to teach the "uncivilized" African women how to sew in order to clothe themselves appropriately. From the 1880s women began to meet for the purposes of prayer, testimony, and the citation of Bible verses.

The particular history of women's meetings varies by larger church affiliation, though Gaitskell (1990, 264) remarks that from the early decades of this century a power struggle between white leaders and black members ensued in various quarters. Weekly meetings of "black women in search of God" (Brandel-Syrier 1962) have gradually become meetings controlled by black women, and held every Thursday.[2] These gatherings, or *manyanos*, draw married women together to sing, dance, pray, and share their burdens.

While Nazarite women may attend these weekly *manyanos*, the official time for them to gather together is through the nights of the 13th and 14th of each month. These monthly meetings are not exclusive to the married women in *ibandla lamaNazaretha* (see chap. 3), though Bongani Mthethwa told me (January 1990) that these women were the first group to be assigned a time for meeting by Shembe. In addition, he said that the meeting time—around the fourteenth day of each month—used to be when men were instructed to meet. For some reason, however, Isaiah gave the date to women. This change could have been linked to the symbolic moment in a woman's menstrual cycle—the fourteenth day of the month represents her most fertile period.

All married women members of *ibandla lamaNazaretha* are required to attend the monthly meetings held through the nights of the 13th and

14th of each month at the homes of one of the members of their local temple. These women are also expected to participate in the *ama14* meetings on the main religious spaces—such as *Vula Masango* in March, *Gibisile* in May, and *Judia* in October (see chap. 3). The purpose of these meetings is to share collective burdens, to confess sins, to pray for each other, and to sing and dance. The ultimate motivation is to meet with Shembe, to "write one's name in the Book of Life," to purchase a ticket with the cost of personal pain and sacrifice in order to enter heaven after death, but even more, to create a sense of "heaven-on-earth" for the present time.

One woman explained to me that one of the Nazarite leaders had told her that as a young boy he had seen Shembe outside his mother's home, where the *ama14* meeting was taking place. She recalled that at the time the women were dancing, the boy went outside and

> saw Shembe outside, the founder. He was standing, putting his right leg on the stone. . . . You must open up your hymn book,[3] the same Shembe was there outside, listening to what these women for [the] *14* meeting were saying. . . . That means that this Shembe, the founder was outside and coming to collect our needs. And coming to (at the very same time) coming to give us what we want, all the blessings, just like that. [C. Mazibuko, January 1992.]

When Isaiah initiated these meetings, the intention was that the women would stay secluded from the evening of the 13th day to the morning of the 15th. They would hold their meetings as described below, and then sit and wait together for the duration of the 14th, and start the service again in the evening. Since many Nazarite women are now involved in the formal and informal economy, they are required to leave for work early on the mornings of the 14th and 15th.

The reason for this seclusion lies in the selection of the number 14 for married women. Fourteen is the halfway point in a twenty-eight-day menstrual cycle, and the moment in the cycle when women are theoretically the most fertile. It may be surprising that Shembe calls married women at this symbolically critical point to gather for prayer over two consecutive days. For these wives and mothers, obedience to Shembe requires denial of both sexual desire and family needs. I suggest, however, that Shembe's sense of timing provides a masterful intervention in the lives of women precariously susceptible to sexual violation. It is at the symbolic height of their sexual capability that women are both powerful and extremely vulnerable to abuse. In this context, what is potentially the most intimate of moments between a husband and his wife may, however, just as easily become the most violent. This danger to women is channeled into a religious discourse (Behar 1987, 42–43) of fertility and the sacred, and located in the meeting together of married women and Shembe on the fourteenth of each month.

There is a high cost for attending these meetings with the *ama14*. To stay awake for two successive nights is acknowledged to require self-discipline and sacrifice. One woman closed off her preaching with the following words:

> It is not a nice thing to stay the whole night without any sleep, but if you are a *14,* and you do have *14* on your waist and on your head, you should keep the oath of the woman, that of going to *14*. We are here to teach and to remind each other of God's commands. [*Vula Masango,* March 13, 1992.]

Despite the physical discomforts that accompany attendance at the meetings, the identity of being *i14* is one believed to encompass considerable social power. Thus, at the main meeting at *Ebuhleni,* on August 13, 1991, one woman stood up and encouraged the others, saying,

> I raise up to thank God for giving us this opportunity. He has given us a great opportunity to be in *14*s. Women, you should know that you are the most powerful people on earth. If there is anything tough, people call on *14*s to come and pray.

This power is embedded quite clearly in women's ability to communicate with the ancestral domain—given human form in the figure of Shembe.

All women's meetings take place at night. There are several possible explanations for this. First, for women who work during the day, the night time affords freedom for regular participation. Second, the overall organization of the meetings bears a strong historical parallel with the secular Concert and Dance parties held in the urban areas in the earlier decades of the twentieth century. In contrast to the sacralization of female fertility, these parties were felt to "cheapen" the virtue of young women (Ballantine 1993, 82–83). Through a poetic process of reversal, Isaiah switched the ordering of events of the Concert and Dance parties in his structuring of the women's meetings. He thereby symbolically transposed the process of defilement of women endemic to the urban areas. Third, sexual intercourse between a man and a woman is believed to be blessed by the ancestors if it takes place at night, but "burnt by the sun" during the day (Berglund 1989 [1976]).

The overall form of the meetings is the same at individual homes as at the collective gatherings on Nazarite spaces. On the evening of the 13th of the month, women arrive at the house of the person hosting the meeting from about 8 P.M. They usually come in small groups, and before they approach the house, put on the white *MNazaretha* and remove their shoes, because the house is considered to be a holy space.[4] The inside of the house is cleared of furniture, and the women sit on the floor, on *amacansi* (the mats made by Nazarite women from grass or reeds).

Traditionally, the women are supposed to wait until everyone has arrived, and then all should stand up, exit the house, and proceed to the gate with candles, ready to sing the opening hymn. This certainly occurs at the large gatherings of *ama14* at sites such as *Ebuhleni* and *Vula Masango*. In the township of KwaMashu a variation has arisen in the procedure as a result of the highly volatile political situation in the area. Women in large groups attract attention to themselves, and could become a target of violent attack, particularly at night. At this temple, therefore, the women simply arrive, singing softly as they enter the house.

At both *Vula Masango* and *Ebuhleni*, however, the women took their candles after they had been blessed, and all proceeded out of the meeting place and moved toward the gate. Once everyone had assembled, at about 9 P.M., *Mkhokheli* intoned the opening line of Hymn 173, and all women responded by repeating after the leader, line by line. The hymn invited the ancestors to join the meeting. (CD track 13.)

Sidedele singene	Get out of the way, and let us in
Simkhonze uJehova	That we may worship Jehovah.
Sasi valelwe	We were prevented
Avuliwe amasango	[But now] the gates are open.
Mdedele angene	Get out of the way, and let him in.
Wo! Nanguzulu	Wo! He is of the Zulu nation,
Inzalo kaDingane	Descendant of Dingaan,
No Senzangakhona.	And of Senzangakhona.
Livuliwe ngubani	Who opened it,
Lelisango	This gate?
We Mkhululi weziboshwa.	Oh, Liberator of the prisoners!
Wozani nazo lezozizwe,	Come with those nations
Ziyadinga lona lelo lizwi	That are in need of the word
Elophezu konke.	Of him who is above all.

The drummer joined in, and the verses were repeated several times as the women proceeded back to the meeting place with their candles lit. The two *abakhokheli* were in front, with the drummer third in line, and all the other women behind them.

This hymn, which calls on the ancestors to join the gathering of women, transforms the physical contamination that accrues to life in South Africa's black townships to the holy and sanctified space of the Nazarite heaven. The presence of the ancestors, invoked through the song, blurs the boundaries between heaven and earth as separate spatio-temporal units. In the Nazarite religious imagination, a kind of heavenly space or ideal social order is formulated through the performance of the holy Words of God sung to the beat of the Nazarite drum and in the presence of the ancestors. Song performance in this gathering of women facilitates a state of alterity—another kind of time, space, and social interaction. In this altered state, Nazarite women re-create time, space, and the cosmos to temporarily remove the pain and fragmentation of everyday life, and to reconstitute the social body through the active participation of the individual body.

At KwaMashu, the women sitting inside the house talk quietly to each other until enough people have arrived, at which point *Mkhokheli* starts to sing Hymn 173, and the others join in. As more women arrive, singing as they come, the singing of both groups stops when the new group enters the house. At this point each of the new arrivals goes around to those already waiting, greeting them and shaking their hands. Once this is complete, and all are seated, the singing starts up again, until a new group comes to the house, when the greeting procedure is repeated.

At about 10 P.M. *Mkhokheli* intones the first line of Hymn 229 *Zafika izintombi*, the text of which is discussed in chapter 7. I suggest that singing this hymn creates a temporary transformation of married women, polluted by sexual intercourse, into a state of ritual and sexual purity—they become spiritual virgins through its enactment. They are in effect singing the Words of their God, Shembe.[5] Such utterance embodies a treasure of cosmological force and strength, and enables the movement from sexual impurity to bodily perfection required of all women by their God. Once they have been ritually cleansed—washed with the soap of God—they are able to stand up and perform the sacred dance—*ukusina*.

During the singing of the hymn, one woman walks toward the center of the room and starts to move according to the bodily patterns of the ancestors, the sacred dance. (This process is described and analyzed in full in chap. 4.) Just before midnight the dancing stops, and a meal is served by the woman who owns the house. Before anyone may eat, a bowl with warm, soapy water is taken around, and hands are washed. A collection plate is also passed to everyone to make a contribution for the meal. The meal itself usually consists of a curried mutton, served on a bed of rice, with a beet salad, coleslaw, and tomato and onion salad, and tea to drink.

Once everyone has finished eating, *umkhokheli* calls out "*Sontweni, sontweni, sontweni*" (church time). Heads are covered, shawls draped over shoulders, and the women prepare for the second part of the night—the singing, prayers, and sermons. *Mkhokheli* opens with a hymn, a prayer, and then an introduction telling of the significance of the evening. When she is finished, one of the women will initiate the singing of a hymn in which the others join her, and then she preaches. This is the pattern of the evening, until all have spoken or the time has run out.

In the words of a Soweto woman, Maureen Buthelezi,

> Then when we sit down, then we're going to start our *14*. Now then everybody's got something to say, and everybody's got [something] very bad, maybe in their heart. So she want[s] to tell the women, all the women there, what is going on. So, she's got a song inside her heart. She's going to stand up and sing that song. After she's finished that song, she's got power now to talk to the people. . . . Because after that song she starts telling them what's wrong, what's happening, what Shembe have done for her. . . . Each and everyone is preaching until it's four o'clock in the morning. Some are going to work. [April 1992.]

The women's ability to preach in this context is an extension of their construction as preachers in the girls' rite discussed in chapter 4, when they donned the *jafeta* prayer gowns. This time, however, the women are imbued with the power to speak—and to weave together their own versions of everyday realities and cultural truth. In this context they are transformed by the power of Shembe. This power is contained in the Word of the Nazarite God—the Nazarite hymn texts. A woman always preempts her preaching with the singing of one of the hymns. The juxtaposition of the Words of Shembe with the words of women's experience is what instills authority into a woman's preaching.

This opportunity for Nazarite women to publicly declare their experiences to both the living and the dead constitutes a source of enormous strength to those unaccustomed to public address. As Jean and John Comaroff (1992, 255) remark, "the power of speech was all of a piece with the capacity of persons to act positively upon the world." This power was not normally accorded to women, who were usually excluded from all forms of verbalized public performance. In *ibandla lamaNazaretha*, however, they are provided a space where they are required to speak with authority—to preach. The substance of their "sermons"—personal encounters with Shembe—acquired the authority of the Word of God, of cultural truth.

The force of authority embedded in the truth of an individual's sermon is further validated by the body of women who stand as "witnesses" to the accuracy of her testimony. While they may not have been physically present at the time of the experience, they know the emotions of other women, and the physical conditions within which other women operate. They too have experienced the miraculous intervention of Shembe/God in their lives. Such concurrence of the witnesses with the narration of events carries the weight of testimony as in a court of law. Personal experience is transformed from the individual, the psychological, the imagined, into a discourse of cultural truth equivalent to the value of the written word. It is in this sense that the illiterate say their testimony enables their "names to be written in the Book of Life." (See CD track 30.)

The meeting normally continues through to about 4:30 A.M., when the closing hymn—Hymn 152—is sung and the parallel Bible reading from Matthew 2 is read. *Mkhokheli* ends with prayer, and everyone huddles together to sleep until about 6 A.M., when the sun has risen and it is safe to walk the streets once more. Many of the women go to work, to return again at about 8 P.M. the following evening, where the same procedure is followed.

Nazarite Women's Narratives

The focus of this section is the narratives created by women in the meetings of *ama14*—those stories that constitute the sermons. I recorded these narratives on audiocassette as they were told both in the women's meetings and in more informal contexts where women normally shared with each other the powers of Shembe in their lives. I then transcribed and, where necessary, translated (with assistance from several people) the performances into written texts. It is the textual rather than the performative content that I examine in this chapter. (The creative and performative dimensions are the central units of analysis in chap. 4.)

These testimonies of the miracles of Shembe in the lives of ordinary women function at several levels. For Nazarite women, the narratives prove the power of Shembe. They transform their lives at the most ordinary plane of existence. By telling other members their own stories, they accumulate cultural treasure in the multiple contexts of enormous material deprivation that characterize the lives of most Nazarite women. As each one tells her own story, or that gleaned from someone else's experience, they pile proof upon proof, and thereby increase the value of Nazarite cultural treasure as it is stored in the memories of individual members, and externalized through expressive cultural forms for the consumption of the collectivity.

At the level of collective identity within the context of the wider political economy and competing religious ideologies, the treasure trove of Nazarite narratives proves epistemologically the cumulative power of this group over other groups. The narratives construct difference, particularly between the hegemony of Western Christianity and Nazarite piety. I was frequently told that people join *ibandla lamaNazaretha* because, for example, Shembe provides a belief system that emphasizes the experiential and visual rather than written evidence. There are no lies. Shembe constructs a tangible cultural truth for his people.[6] At the level of analysis, these texts prove to be "unsurpassed sources for revealing otherwise hidden forms of consciousness" (Bozzoli 1991, 7). Because of the frequent silence of women in the public domain and the intimacy of the situation in which these texts are created, the narratives become "expressions of consciousness and social identity" (ibid.) that are frequently not found in academic discourse.

Nazarite women's bodies are constructed as the storehouses of cosmological empowerment, and these narratives reveal how such power is conceptualized and manipulated in order to transform the fragmentation, the bleakness, and the horrors of life in black South African communities—particularly in terms of violation of women. The women see themselves as the keepers of Nazarite history and experience. For each one of them, history is an individually constructed experience of the passage of time and the impingement of political and economic forces beyond their immediate control. In that sense, these stories place women in the center of their narration, unraveling the details, local meanings, and events that make up the fabric of life on the margins of South African society.

More specifically, these narratives inform us about the effectiveness of expressive culture not simply to express experience, but indeed to transform it. This does not occur in a revolutionary manner—the political and material conditions of most Nazarite members do not change that much when they join *ibandla lamaNazaretha*. I suggest rather that these cultural forms enable the transformation of the individual and social selves in terms of the way in which they imagine and construct their everyday realities (Cucchiari 1988). The intervention of the cosmology through expressive culture into the grayness of daily struggles facilitates transcendence. It adds light, color, conversation, warmth, and reciprocal obligations in social relationships.

The peripheral position maintained by Shembe's female following within the South African political economy has been constructed by the forces of almost two centuries of colonial and state domination and appropriation. While many women do not know the details of the historical account as a scholarly historian would have it remembered, the past is represented in their narratives in the

> mythic images reflecting and condensing the experiential appropriation of the history of conquest, as that history is seen to form analogies and structural correspondences with the hopes and tribulations of the present. [Taussig 1987, 368.]

For Nazarite members, the truth of the distant past is contained in the mythical correspondences between the narratives and miracle accounts of the biblical New Testament. The texts of women's narratives are structured and presented similarly. This indicates a collective consciousness saturated in biblical mythology, particularly among the older generations, many of whom were taught either by Isaiah, who was an erudite biblical scholar, or by mission-based teachers (Vilakazi et al. 1986).

Finally, there is a discrepancy recognized by Nazarite members between those who were born into the church and those who converted to follow Shembe. One of the women born into the church told me that she did not have any of these special encounters with Shembe, precisely because she was already in the church. Nevertheless, she could tell many stories about the experiences of others, stories she had heard at women's meetings and during church services. On the other hand, there are others who are called by Shembe having never heard or seen the man before.

Related to these perceived discrepancies are the differences in the contexts of Shembe's intervention and assistance in the lives of his followers. For some, he responds to pleas for help through other people's actions—and the members attribute the actions to Shembe himself. For others, however, Shembe appears to them as a visual image, either in dreams or in an imaginary state somewhere between dreaming and waking realities. In the West we might classify these events as "hallucinatory," but those who experience these appearances perceive them as real encounters.

My analysis focuses on the way in which these women use narrative as a means to conveying emotions of fear, sorrow, vulnerability, and pain on the one hand, and on the other, the means by which hymn texts, songs, and dance performances are interpolated into these narratives to signal hope, self-respect, and the reconstitution of a specific type of religious and social community. The bulk of the narratives I collected initially were told to me in English, which is for many of these women the third or fourth language they understand and speak. The grammar is therefore not always "correct" by English literary standards. In addition, most older women are illiterate and largely unschooled.

For the purposes of content analysis and explication, I have reduced all verbal performances of narratives into two-dimensional written texts, even though such a transfer minimizes their performative and expressive dimensions (Patai 1988; Serematakis 1991). I have sought nevertheless to retain all the peculiarities of grammar and structure, for these elements come to bear strongly on the articulation of Nazarite poetics and aesthetics. Where ambiguity of content supersedes clarity of meaning, I have provided contextual information through limited textual explication and analysis.

The stories that I gathered in Zulu and then translated are fairly complex. They are characteristically nonlinear in narrative flow, highly redundant, filled with allusion, and frequently deeply embedded in codes and symbols of traditional culture not usually self-evident to younger generations or non-Nazarite members. In the process of translation (in which I have always been assisted by a Zulu first-language speaker), it became clear that enormous discrepancies exist in the structuring, vocabulary, and understanding of the Zulu language in practice, particularly between the older and younger generations.

This discrepancy is exacerbated by differences in regional practices. Those younger people who have lived only in the peri-urban townships have tended, especially if they have lived in Soweto, to be exposed to greater linguistic diversity, and have thus intermixed vocabulary from different languages. Those living in the more remote areas frequently use an entirely different set of words for the same repertory of cultural objects. (To this end, one can often date written scripts, at least by generation, according to the type of vocabulary employed.)

This kind of textual ambiguity is most poignantly illustrated in the hymn texts written by both Isaiah and Galilee, though it is perhaps less true of the last hymns written by the Western-educated Galilee. Isaiah's texts are filled with euphemisms, allusions, and archaisms. They present additional translation difficulties because of the references to biblical imagery and vocabulary, made more complex by the fact that the Bible was first translated by missionaries into a mix of Zulu and Xhosa, a related Bantu language. This was the linguistic mix that Isaiah became immersed in as he read the Bible.

There is often only a tenuous structural link, not just between stanzas of the hymns, but also from one line of text to the next within stanzas. Series of word images are therefore juxtaposed, creating a kind of "snapshot" effect.[8] When I asked the young girls what a particular hymn was about, they frequently would simply shrug their shoulders and say they did not know.

Parallel kinds of ambiguity in expressive tradition are discussed by Abu-Lughod (1988, 171–77) in terms of Bedouin women's poetry. She writes:

> Indeed, unless marked by particularly striking metaphors or haunting images, most poems have little impact in the abstract; context is crucial, not just for the appreciation but even for the understanding of the poem's meaning. [Ibid., 175.]

This is true to a certain extent with women's narratives, and definitely applies to meanings extracted from or attached to Nazarite hymns.

Nazarite narratives cover a diversity of life situations and types of miracles. These range from encounters with the white-controlled legal system to communication with the ancestors; from care for animals and the conception of children to the loss frequently incurred in families through migrant labor. Each of these narratives carries a special message from Shembe, either through his words directly, or through the way in which the storyteller interprets the story. In addition, each story provides commentary on emotions of disjuncture and rupture felt by Nazarite members as they experience the frequently conflicting demands of Nguni tradition, the family, the workplace, and the controls of what was formerly the apartheid state.

It is the marginalized black women, such as those who follow Shembe, who perhaps have most keenly felt the impact of the violence inherent in state structures, and the entrenchment of racism in institutions connected with education, labor, and the military. It is these women who, in the past decade in particular, have seen their children shot and killed, who have themselves been raped and violated both by men they know and men they do not know. Thus they have lived in constant fear of material and bodily theft.[9] They have been harassed by political groups, and had their meager resources destroyed through mass removals and the burning down of houses and shacks. They have lost their jobs (often the only means of support for a wide network of family obligations) through the pressures of mass action and economic downturns in the larger political economy. It is the stories of such women that I focus on in this chapter, uncomfortable as they may be for some to read or hear.

While the range of contexts for Nazarite women's experiences is extensive and diverse, there is one common thread woven through the telling of all the stories. This is the consistent blurring of temporal and spatial boundaries. The clear distinctions between sleeping and waking realities in Western thinking do not exist for Nazarite women. There is also a merging of divisions between the space occupied by earth and that occupied by heaven, as well as between temporal categories of past and present. Conceptually, there is little distinction drawn between what is rationally possible and what is "just in one's imagination." In this regard, I suggest that the imaginary is the space for the construction of a kind of otherness which is an integral part of the ordinary reality of Nazarite women.

The first set of stories serves to convey women's experiences in terms of their interaction with the South African political economy at three levels: in its broadest spectrum, at the level of macro socioeconomic exchange; at the more focused level of the community (in terms of social reproduction); and in its most intimate space—that of gender relations—between men and women over the issue of sexual and social violation. At each level one witnesses the breakdown of reciprocal exchange in social relationships, and conversely the transformative powers of social healing embodied in the figure of Shembe/God.

Macro Socioeconomic Exchange

I explained in chapter 2 that Isaiah Shembe formed his church in the wake of massive proletarianization of the African peasantry, a process induced by factors such as state imposition of taxation on rural populations, crop failure, disease, drought, and forced labor migration. The following narrative demonstrates one way in which a Nazarite woman has sought to transform her condition of economic lack into one of temporary empowerment.

> After standing up . . . she told us that one day, she had no money, no money to give her children to carry to school. Even her husband hasn't got money. She had only a ticket to go to work. Her husband used to collect her from work to home. That day, her husband came late to collect her.
>
> During the day, she [had] failed to get money, because even when she went to the bank, they didn't give her money. . . . On their way back home, they were not talking to each other, because they haven't got money. You know, she said on the highway next to Diepkloof, the traffic cop passed them. He was running at high speed. He passed them.

> Then she saw something like papers coming away from the scooter. Then this lady said, "What is this?" She tried to pick out of the . . . look at . . . what was it? What was falling out from the traffic cop? The traffic cop didn't wait. He just passed. Then she asked her husband to stop the car. The husband stopped the car, and they got out. Those that were coming out of the scooter was the money. It was in *fifties!* Fifty papers! They picked those, she didn't say how much. But, she said, it just went away from the scooter like papers. They, they picked it, the husband was picking, she also was picking.
>
> That's how Shembe helped them, because she said that if it was not because of Shembe, she was not going to get that money. But, because of Shembe. . . . She asked him, "Shembe, can you help me? Because I have got no money." Then Shembe put the money to this traffic cop, then blew it away. So they got the money. [C. Mazibuko, pers. comm., January 1992.]

There are several points to note in this excerpt. First, the main actors are silent. This is because they have no money, indicated by the absence of the requisite medium of exchange. The silence of the couple signifies the loss of social power, which I suggested above was afforded in the efficacy of verbal interchange. Second, in the interaction between the woman and her husband and those who normally give and take money—the bank and the traffic officer—the situation has been reversed. The bank is unable to provide the necessary finance, but the traffic officer makes it freely available. Third, the means by which this situation is transformed is attributed to the provisions of Shembe, who uses the error of the traffic officer traveling at high speed to give money to the woman. It is noteworthy that it is the traffic officer, an employee of a state infrastructure that has extracted taxes and denied economic access to the woman, who returns the money to her. In a quite peculiar manner, social justice is reconstituted for this woman and her husband.

Social Reproduction Infertile Women Conceive

> So there are lots of stories about this Shembe, especially people who don't get children. When they come, just the word. . . . With that word, "God bless you," the things come right. Even with the children. When you say, "Shembe, I've got no children." He says, "God bless you." You get the children. [C. Mazibuko, January 1992.]

> Women represent the violence of [social] death through their own bodies. [Seremetakis 1991, 74.]

Despite popular notions of Africa's population explosion, statistics indicate that black women in southern Africa have an extraordinarily high level of infertility.[10] Furthermore, South Africa has high levels of infant mortality. For black women married traditionally, and for whom bride payment or *lobola* has been paid, the inability to conceive children that live beyond one or two years poses enormous social and inter-kin difficulties. The incapacity to produce children provides grounds for divorce. In addition, as Gaitskell (1990, 271–72) remarks, motherhood has been a central trope in the construction and maintenance of black women's identity in precolonial Africa. This is true particularly through the processes of colonization and missionization, and persists into contemporary post-independence states. This concern with motherhood is certainly reflected throughout the narratives of Nazarite women.

It is the themes of barrenness, the desire for fertility, and the conception of children that have permeated so many of the stories I have heard in *ibandla lamaNazaretha*. The contexts of these stories are diverse. They include the theft and return of children, asking for children and the consequences of forgetting to give thanks to Shembe for them, the practice of killing babies if too many are born at one time, and the rebirth of children who die from illness or the lack of adequate nutrition after birth. The story below explains how Shembe interceded for one woman.

> My mother said when she was *umkhoti* or newlywed, she used to get children and the children used to die. Maybe when the child is six months, less than a year, the child dies. Now, here were six children dying.
>
> They came in *Nhlangakaze*, the very same *Nhlangakaze*, that it was in 1937 when my mother came here, to this *Nhlangakaze*. When [s]he came here, [s]he says there were them, as you always hear shouting. People must do this and this, you see. So [s]he said, they were here. Then somebody came and said, "Shembe says that all those who are here, who want to get children, who want children, must come up to him on the mountain."
>
> So my mother went up with the other women who didn't have children. Up to where Shembe was going to pray for them. They all went up. My mother said [that] then Shembe came and said, "People must be ready." They must pray, you see. You see, as we pray, we close our eyes. My mother says [that] as she [s]he was closing her eyes, [s]he heard Shembe was coming.
>
> In her vision, my mother [s]he saw that Shembe had a basket. In

the basket there was something like stars. [S]he said, Shembe was taking the stars like this, [and] he was throwing the stars like that. [S]he said some other stars too, were coming to my mother. [S]he said [s]he just took them out [like] this, and do like this to hold the stars. The stars were just flying too. But, the stars were jumping from [one] woman to the other women. Not everybody was getting these stars. But, to my mother those stars came.

She said she just put out the dress to hold the stars. The stars came. Then [he] was just praying for them, that "God, I am just praying for them, I am just asking that you please help this person, this poor woman to please get children." Like that [he] was praying, praying that side. "Amen." When Shembe said, "Amen," my mother was holding like this, because she saw that vision of the stars in the basket that Shembe was giving the people.

When my mother came down from the mountain, here to the *dokoda*, she was here with—she came with her mother. She said, "Mother, you know, I saw this vision up there. I saw Shembe had a basket full of stars, and he was throwing stars to everybody. The stars were jumping, going from [one] to [the] others, and the other stars came to me, and I just held them like this." Then her mother said, "My child, you are really going to get children. When Shembe has prayed for you, and you've seen that, you really are going to get children."

Then they went back to Natal. [They were already in Natal.] They were staying in Vryheid. They stayed there. My mother said it was hardly, eh that was in 1938. My mother said it was hardly three months and she conceived. She was pregnant. And she gave birth to this sister of mine.

This sister has her own description of the latter part of the story. She recalls that after coming down the mountain of *Nhlangakaze*:

When my mother is sleeping, she had a feeling at the back, a pain. She asked the other women, "Just look at the back. What's going on with my back? There is something." You know when you get burnt, maybe it was hot water—it was something like that. My mother was crying, and the other followers, women of Shembe, said, "No, you must not cry. It's the way Shembe is healing you." My mother said, "Whoo, how can that be?"

Then my mother went home. When she was at home, she got pregnant. One day she was sleeping and she heard somebody telling her, "I am Shembe. I am bringing you children. Your firstborn will be a girl. Her name will be *Makhosazane*." As I am *Makhosazane* now. [Cinikile Mazibuko and Makhosazane Nyadi, pers. comm., January 1992.]

Besides the beauty of the imagery, this story presents a rather incredible account of the initial loss of six babies and then the transformation of that situation into the conception of children. The link between fertility and ritual purity resurfaces in this narrative in its enactment on the top of the holy mountain, a space in which no sexual intercourse is permitted for the duration of one's stay. Second, a complex layering of belief systems is evident in this text. According to Berglund (1979, 253–54), in Zulu traditional thought the concept of heat is associated with sexual intercourse, the shades or ancestors, and hence the conception of children. In addition, the narration of events is similar in structure to accounts in the New Testament. One such example is found in Luke 1, in which Elizabeth and Mary become pregnant after the appearance of God/an angel in a dream/vision. In all three instances it is God's messenger Gabriel/Shembe who intervenes in what seemed to be impossible conditions—the virgin, the elderly barren woman, and the woman whose babies kept dying.

Perhaps the most significant interpretive element in this narrative is the way in which the fragmentation of the social order and subsequent loss of community has become etched upon the female body. In this regard, the inability to conceive children has become a metaphor for the inability of women (and men) to engage in social reproduction. It is possibly the most striking "witness" to the deep sense of social and personal loss reflected in the malfunctioning of the natural mechanisms that enable the continuity of social life and community. One might even interpret this inordinate occurrence of infertility among Nazarite women as a kind of resistance on the part of women to invasion from the outside—a theme pursued below.

The woman begins to conceive only after she has been given the stars—the ancestral power—by Shembe. This relates to my thesis that Shembe controls the fertility of married women by calling them to gather at what is symbolically their most fertile moment. In this way fertility is not perceived as dangerous or polluting, because it is enshrined by the sanctity of the meeting of Shembe with the women each month. In addition, the defilement traditionally associated with conception and childbirth is negated, for indeed it is Shembe/God who endows women with the gift of fertility. In this manner the ritual purity clause continues to be applied to women even after they marry and give birth to children.

Social and Sexual Violation

Ross (1993, 7) writes that despite the inordinately high occurrences of violence against women in South Africa, it is believed that in the case of rape, only one in twenty cases is ever reported. She attributes this to an unsympathetic legal structure, and to a number of myths pervasive in the fabric of South African society, most of which construct sexual violation as something a woman secretly enjoys, and later uses to incriminate a man.

In this section I present one or two examples of the way in which women have embodied these experiences of sexual and social violation in narrative. These are not explicit discourses but are veiled in metaphor and allusion. They are what Foucault (1980, 82–83) defines as "subjugated discourses," in which women construct a sense of self and society as a means to reorder the ongoing fragmentation and violation against their bodies. Their discourse is coded in the symbols and meanings of the traditional cosmology, to avoid retribution and further violence against them. They are not immediately recognized as discourses of violation (Crain 1991, 80).

Here is one such story.

> I remember one story of this woman, this *14*, this woman. When she was staying somewhere in Zululand. When it comes this day of the *14*s, then she must go to *14*s. She went to *14*, closed the house, closed her house. When she comes back from the . . . all the belongings, all her belongings were all stolen.
>
> This woman was so worried. She said to herself, "But *Baba* Shembe, how can I go to praise you, where you said we must go as women, when I come home and all my things are stolen? Now, how will I go, if you don't stay here? I say *Baba* Shembe, when I go to *14* you must please, look after my house. Where were you when the, when he just . . . ?" the woman was talking to herself like that. Worried. "But, how can he come into my house and steal things like that when I go to church, like that?"
>
> Come again the following month, the woman didn't go to *14*. The second month she went to *14*. Came back. When she came to the house, the house is closed. She's trying to push. But, now where is the lock? The lock was here on the door! Seems as if there was somebody

in the house. *Hau!* She goes there. Where's the lock? She call the neighbors.

"People! Come help me! I hear there's somebody in my house." But now, who is in the house? She called the men who were just around. They pushed the door. The door opened.

When they came inside they saw there was a man with all the things. All her things were just in parcels, in big luggage. He was trying to go out with the things. They asked the man, "How come you are stealing these things? How come you didn't go out with these things?" Then the man said to them, "When I went out, when I tried to go out this door, Shembe was standing there by the door."

Hau! Surprised! "What are you telling us?" The man was crying. He said, "I tried to go out, because I'm the one who stole these things from this woman, when the woman went to *14.* Now I knew that she was, that the woman was going to *14* again, so I came to steal again. But now, I couldn't go out the door, because Shembe was standing in this door. I tried to go out the window—Shembe was standing in the window."

You see. Now this is the answer to this woman. To the prayer of this woman. When she said, "But Shembe, where were you when he was stealing my things?" Now Shembe is coming to close the door, to close the window, till people come back to see that there is somebody stealing my things. You see, I'm telling you the stories of Shembe.

To the outsider, this story may seem to have many parallels in the experiences of women of faith all over the world—a woman living alone, feeling vulnerable, calls on her God for protection in a hostile and violent society. There is more to this story than immediately meets the eye, however, particularly as one discovers the use of metaphor in the text. The central metaphor here is that of the house, which I propose represents the female body—the womb specifically.

Berglund (1979) provides provocative field evidence for this analogy. He spoke to a Zulu tutor who was teaching a female novice how to become a diviner. According to this tutor (ibid., 168),

A hut is like a mother in that the child comes out naked from it. . . .

Berglund asked her

Is a hut like a mother, in that it gives birth?

The tutor replied

> It is like a woman in that it has little ones inside it. It is like this.
> The woman has a stomach (i.e. a womb). A home has a hut. That
> is how it is.

With this metaphor in mind, a rereading of the story suggests that it
might also be interpreted as a narrative about how Shembe protects
women, not only from material theft, but indeed within the intimate domain of their sexuality. Through his appearances Shembe protects women
who call upon him from invasion by strange men from the outside.

I end this section with the words of one woman from Soweto. She does
not hide behind the veil of allusion, but talks explicitly about sexual harassment and the violation of her body by her husband—hence the lack of
power she had over him. She said:

> When I met Shembe, I was in a terrible state. . . . I was suffering.
> . . . I'm fighting right now with my husband. I'm staying in a very
> tight situation. I can't ask my husband [for] money or something.
> He beats me. I can't hit him back because I'm scared for a man.
> [Later.]
> I went in front of Shembe. I was crying. I was crying so, telling the
> whole situation of mine with my husband. I couldn't say everything
> because I was crying. . . . You know, that man says to me, "God bless
> you." That's all. I was not satisfied. . . . I couldn't accept it, it was not
> enough for me. I was expecting something to touch me, as a healer,
> you know. To do some wonders for me.
> After a week, I came out with a dream. Even today, I am scared
> of that dream. A big dream.[11] Nobody dreamed like that. . . . Man,
> Shembe did plenty things for me. [Dube Temple, April 1992.]

There are two dimensions of this account that I explore in greater depth
in parts 2 and 3 of this chapter. These are the vehicle of dreaming and the
space it creates, and the embodiment of emotion—specifically, crying and
the shedding of tears. For those living on the peripheries of the South
African economy, power is acquired from the cosmology and facilitated
through dreams. This is true for those on the margins in South Africa and
indeed for many others living in an increasingly singular world economy,
all of whom have been denied access to institutionalized means of social
empowerment—access to the political, economic, and educational dimensions of society. In this regard, dreams are no less part of social reality
than the events of waking life for Nazarite members (Weiner 1991, 4).
Nazarite member Mrs. Manqele commented,

Everything happens in dreams. . . . Everything I'm doing. . . . It, I can't do anything, unless [the three Shembes] come, and then I do it. [Mrs. Manqele, August 1991.]

The penetration of the cosmology in dreams reconstitutes a dimension of life that is improvisatory, unpredictable, magical, and mysterious. In their extreme subjectivity, dreams reauthorize the value of individual experience, because they intrude from the outside and the unknown (Weiner 1991). Nobody is able to counter a dream narrative, because no one else has experienced it at the same moment in time. In a similar manner, Western technology has manifested itself in the Nazarite epistemology as an unquantifiable, magical entity—both powerful and dangerous. Still photography is one example of Western technology that has been incorporated into the religious imagination of Nazarite women. I believe this has occurred because it resembles the imagistic, "snapshot" effect of dream experiences (Serematakis 1991).

The terms of both dreaming and photography have been renegotiated in the process. In *ibandla lamaNazaretha*, photography has become a vital medium for the validation of cosmological intervention in the lives of Nazarite women. A photograph produces the evidence of the miraculous powers of Shembe to heal women on Nazarite space. One example of this is a series of photographs sold by Nazarite members in which women who have been healed by Shembe are depicted before (in a wheelchair, for example) and after (as they are seen walking) the healing. Photographs are also used as proof of the existence of heaven, and of Isaiah Shembe's residence in this space. This is demonstrated in the photographs sold by Nazarite members that simulate icons of Jesus the Shepherd with those of Isaiah Shembe. In one of these pictures, Jesus stands in a cloudy blue sky holding a sheep and a shepherd's crook, and Isaiah is seen kneeling before Jesus. In this manner, Shembe and Jesus coexist in the same space.

The juxtaposition of disjunct domains—heaven and earth—in photography resembles the way in which dreams conflate disparate images and situations. In addition, these photographs are frequently hidden (and seldom shown to others) in the hymnals of older Nazarite women. This constitutes an enclosure of the objective evidence—a picture—of the subjectivity of a personal—dream—experience. The enclosure surrounds the photograph with the written Word of God contained in the hymn texts, and infuses a sacred authority to the physical evidence of the photograph. The process of authorizing personal experience with the Word of God is linked to the way in which a woman's sermon—the narration of subjective experience—is combined with the singing of a hymn, the text of which embodies the word of the Nazarite God.

This integration of the magic of technology and dream experiences is illustrated in the next narrative in the metaphorical equivalence created between dreaming and Nazarite photographs. This is the "big dream" mentioned in the women's narrative above.

> I dreamt about the sky, you know. It was blue like this. There cries something, I don't know—like a bomb. When I looked up the sky was opening like this . . . in between. They came. You know those photos of Jesus Christ? There came Jesus with a white dress, with long hair—just like yours. This man look at me and I look at her [*sic*], and I could feel that my eyes were full of tears. But I'm trying to swallow those tears. . . . Jesus Christ said to me, with a broad smile. . . . There's a sound of a man telling me who this is. . . . [V. Shabalala, pers. comm., April 1992.]

These dream experiences are objectified as evidence in the discourses of cultural truth and power among Nazarite women. As the boundaries between the earth and cosmology are blurred, so too is the distinction between the objective (photograph) and the subjective (dream) realms of experience.

There is one further instance of the Nazarite women's mediation of experience and technology. On the second day of the pilgrimage to the holy mountain in January 1992, we had stopped for lunch at one of the Nazarite temples along the way. The sun was beating down; there was little shade, and no fresh water on the site. Suddenly, a crowd of people began to gather around one of the trees, and others ran toward the crowd from all around the temple. The crowd started to move, and I could see a woman in front, with several men chasing her from behind. I was told a little later that the woman had been sitting when she noticed that the photograph of Shembe (I am not sure which one) she had pinned to the bodice of her prayer gown had suddenly started to change. She witnessed a flipping of images—from the founder (Isaiah), to the successor (Galilee), to then leader (Amos)—"like a T.V.," I was told. Everyone began to chase after her in the hopes of capturing the power of the transforming image. One man eventually took the photograph from the woman, but it had stopped moving by that time.

In a most remarkable manner the cosmological power of iconic transformation—in the movement of images of the three Shembes—was both structured and interpreted in terms of the outside power of Western technology. Both signaled the commodification of extraordinary power, the reduction of people into two-dimensional space and time through the medium of television, and the animation of two-dimensional forms like photographs to create the sense of life and movement. Like still photography and dream experiences, television defines an additional space of alterity. All three media are simultaneously real and unreal experiences.

In the Nazarite religious imagination the clear distinctions of traditional Zulu cosmology between the realm of *Nkulunkulu* (the Lord of the Sky) and that of the ancestors (beneath the earth) have become less obvious with the superimposition of Protestant Christianity. The confusion is located in the person of Isaiah Shembe, who by some is believed to be God, and hence inhabits the sky, and for others is an ancestor, who inhabits the area beneath the feet. From most dream accounts, however, the majority consensus is that Shembe exists in the area above the earth—along with *Nkulunkulu*, and for some, *Nomkhubulwana*. To substantiate this claim, there have been a number of dreams reported in which Shembe was seen holding the "keys to the gate of heaven." One woman told the *ama14* that she had even seen Shembe replacing Jesus on the cross. In her experience, Shembe had usurped the position of Jesus as "Savior." It was in the woman's body—in her dreams—that the contest over the hegemony of symbols and meaning was located.

Dreams become the space for cosmological communication and authorizing the regime of Nazarite cultural truth. Dreaming facilitates communication between what Berglund (1979, 98) terms "the survivors and the shades" (the ancestors), and this communication always happens at night. Furthermore, Berglund reports (ibid., 97) that Zulu traditionalists believe that "[w]ithout dreams true and uninterrupted living is not possible. There is cause for anxiety when people do not dream." Certainly, dreams play an integral role in narratives about Isaiah Shembe's sense of religious calling, and in the creation and continual renegotiation of Nazarite religious culture. Nevertheless, not all Nazarite people dream, and among those who do, not all dream all of the time.

Having stated that dreams mediate between the spatial domains of the Nazarite heaven and earth, I suggest that they also bring heaven onto the physical space of the earth. The cosmological space-time is domesticated as it is transferred into daily space and time. The meetings of married women capture the cosmological realm and juxtapose it with the dirt of its surrounding area. This sense of heavenly space was poignantly illustrated by the meeting of *ama14* in December 1991 in KwaMashu, Durban. The meeting was believed to have been called by a dead woman through a dream, which meant that attendance at the meeting put the living women directly in the presence of those who had died and passed safely into heaven. (Letters of encouragement to the women in KwaMashu were read on behalf of those who had already died.) Furthermore, in the words of one Nazarite member, *Ekuphakameni* (the original site of Shembe's church) is heaven, or what heaven will be like. According to the letter written by Shembe (discussed in chap. 4), an angel stands at the gate of *Ekuphakameni*, checking to see who adheres to the church rules and who does not. These angels are in constant communication with God/ Shembe in heaven.

The identity of the angels is not restricted to those who have died or to other cosmological beings, but may also extend to the living. Thus a woman faith healer from KwaMashu told me (KwaMashu, February 1993) that she was called *isithunywa* (messenger or angel). In other words, her special powers set her apart from most members. A second woman told me how she had become an angel for Shembe because of the power of her dreams (pers. comm., Dube, Soweto, April 1992). A third woman claimed to be an angel because she had almost died in a minibus taxi accident—but had been saved by Shembe (*Vula Masango*, March 1992).

I am not suggesting that Nazarite women cannot distinguish between physical reality and the cosmological realm. When relating a story to me of what Shembe had done for women members of the church, the narrator would frequently end her story by remarking that I probably would not believe these stories, because they were miracles. Certainly, the aura of the extraordinary pervaded the telling and retelling of stories—and for Nazarite women, this served to establish the fine line between self and other, and indeed, constituted an important element of cultural identity and empowerment.

Conversely, in the narrating of stories, explicit distinctions between what I perceive as different realities are seldom drawn.[12] Spatial boundaries are extremely fluid. Earthly and heavenly events appear to exist in a single plane of experience. Just as one can see, feel, hear, and smell earthly objects, so is heaven real and tangible. Berglund (1979, 98) comments that in traditional thought patterns, dreams are not limited to the "seen and heard," but extend to the realm of physical experience—particularly in terms of bodily pain, such as that experienced by many Nazarite women.

What then is the content of these dreams? Indeed, what is the Nazarite heaven like?

In the year of 1986, in my dream, I was sleeping at night. I was with my family then, at the bottom of the hill. I saw the sun, the moon. The light of the moon was lighting straight to me, and after that I saw Shembe, Galilee. And I ran to that light. We are going down to the moon, and *Baba* was flying after me. [It was] a long distance to this place. . . . *Paradis*, to the temple of *Paradis*. I was halfway, standing there, not down, and the angel from the office came down to me on his knees, and with her [*sic*] knees, and she said to me, "God bless you." And after that another angel wearing white dresses down to their feet said, "God bless you, and you mustn't move from the lights of the moon."

And on the end, Father Galilee turned like this, and I go back to the lights. I was praying, crying tears, lots of tears, and my daughter came from her bedroom. [On] that night, it was about 12 o'clock at the time, and she asked me, "What happened, Ma?" And I said to her, "Shembe is here with me, I'm from the *Paradis* at Inanda. He said to me, "Please, you mustn't move from the light of the moon." From that day, I follow him. [Mrs. Manqele, pers. comm., August 13, 1991.]

This is the story from Mrs. Manqele partially quoted in chapter 1. It is a dream narrative in which earthly space is sacralized to create a sense of heaven through the medium of dreams. It took place one night while Mrs. Manqele was asleep, and is a critical text in linking the domains of women's meetings, the control of female fertility by Shembe, and the creation of heavenly spaces on earth.

The text is filled with Nazarite imagery and metaphor. Mrs. Manqele maps out the topography of the Nazarite sense of heaven. This combines elements from both the spaces on earth, and that imagined to be heaven. There are several significant landmarks: the hill, the sun, moon, light, *Baba, Paradis* (at Inanda), and the office, all of which represent the ancestral realm. The hill/mountain represents the ritual and bodily purity of the holy mountain of *Nhlangakaze;*[13] the moon is the metaphor for Amos Khula Shembe, and the sun refers to Amos's brother Galilee. The moon is also associated with female fertility. The light of the sun and moon (and the related concept of heat) are metaphors for ancestral power and fertility. *Baba* literally means "father" and in all Nazarite accounts refers to Shembe (Isaiah, Galilee, or Amos). *Paradis* is the name for the open-air temple space encircled with white stones at *Ebuhleni*, and finally, the office is a real office, located next to *Paradis*. This is the administrative center, the place where one registers for baptism and marriage, and where one purchases Nazarite paraphernalia such as the hymnal, bumper stickers, and so forth.

This set of images is separated from ordinary waking experience by several reversals of normal behavior and interaction. Mrs. Manqele is able to fly, and she is followed by Galilee in the flight from the hill to the *Paradis*. She communicates directly with the angels from the office—who in real life are men. Ordinarily, rules of *hlonipha* (respect) require that a woman always bend down when she talks to a man; in her dream it is the angel bending before her. Finally, these angels tell her to stay close to the light of the moon. In the Nazarite context, this is an instruction to remain in the warmth and protection of Amos Shembe, which implicitly reorders the conjugal relationship (as explained earlier in the chapter).

Mrs. Manqele's response to Shembe's calling that night after the dream issued from the boundaries of her body in three expressive modes. The first was prayer—the facilitation of earthly communication with the cosmology; the second, crying—the shedding of tears and weeping; and the third, the telling of the experience to female kin—her daughter. The emotive content of this narrative identifies the expressive modes available to Nazarite women for the structuring and sharing of emotion and experience.

> That's why I get the power [to] fly. After that I cry, pray and fly. . . . That time I didn't know nothing about Shembe. I never heard about [him]. I never heard about this church. Nothing. I never even. . . . And I was worried about these children, because they weren't . . . I was carrying them at my back. School. Food. Everything. No one. . . . I was alone with them.

In her exegesis of the dream event, dreaming invoked cosmological communication, transformation, and empowerment. Flying now enables her to make the transition from earthly to heavenly space and time. Crying and the profusion of tears validated her extraordinary experience (Christian 1987, 144). Telling her daughter increased the power, and family treasure accrued through the cosmological event.

There is one additional issue in this dream. It pertains to women, Shembe, and female fertility—and the angel's instructions to stay close to the light of the moon. Since the lunar cycles are traditionally linked to menstrual cycles, the protection of Shembe (the moon) is once again tied to the fertility cycles of Nazarite women. Mrs. Manqele recounted later that Shembe had also instructed her to leave her husband, who was not treating her well. I suggest that the dream alludes to the paternal protection afforded Mrs. Manqele, particularly in terms of the sanctity of her body/fertility, because she was alone.[14]

The second story is that quoted earlier, in which Mrs. Mazibuko's mother conceived children. In many ways this narrative parallels the previous one in its sacralization of natural forms to create metaphors of spiritual/cosmological power and connection. The mother climbs the holy mountain—a journey of spiritual upliftment and purification. Besides Shembe, she is accompanied by women only. As with dreaming, it is only when she closes her eyes to pray that she hears Shembe coming. He holds an item of women's traditional culture—a woven basket[15] from which he throws out stars—light (cosmological power).

The mother returns to the *dokoda*, the name of which signals once again the heavenly realm on earthly space. *Dokoda* refers to the makeshift dwellings constructed on Nazarite religious spaces. It also has a biblical connotation in its other meaning—tabernacle. This was the portable shrine carried by the Israelites while they were "wandering in the wilderness." The metaphorical wandering is imagery used by Isaiah in many of the hymns. One of these is the first hymn in the hymnal, and will be discussed below.

On returning to her *dokoda*, the mother tells her female kin of her experience with Shembe. In the sister's version of the story, it was sometime later that the mother was asleep again, and this time woke up to feel intense heat—which Berglund (1979) says represents the healing power of the ancestors—and started to cry. In both narratives, crying occurred because the women felt sorrow and pain over loss. In this story, the mother was told not to cry because the pain she felt would be transformed into procreative power. The healing of infertility was a cosmologically empowered gift bestowed by Shembe himself. Bodily healing was physically felt in the form of bodily heat. The bodily heat became the proof of ancestral/cosmological power, mediated through the person of Shembe.

I stated earlier that prayer, weeping, and dreaming were all integrally linked in the interpolation of the cosmology into everyday experiences of Nazarite women. In this section I suggest that hymn-singing and *ukusina* (sacred dance) equally facilitate this transformation, albeit through different means. Hence I shall examine first how hymn-singing intersects in the lives of Nazarite women, and then I shall consider the role of *ukusina* in this process. As I discussed in chapter 4, Nazarite women do not compose their own hymns. Instead, they are required to sing the hymns created by Isaiah and Galilee Shembe, so I consider how women interweave personal experiences and emotions into the fixed texts of the Nazarite repertory. I suggest ways in which these women create webs of meaning through these texts, both individually and within the context of collective performance. This analysis focuses on hymn texts specifically. Nazarite women sing hymns in order to communicate using the exact Words of God. As a woman articulates the words, her voice effectively merges with that of Shembe. In this conflation of voices lies the power of sacred song. This is also what lends authority to the personal narratives that make up the sermon preached by a woman in the meetings of *ama14*. The woman will therefore preface her preaching with a hymn text that refers directly to her sermon. It may also be a song she always sings. She thereby uses song to establish a personal identity—a "signature" tune. As one woman said to me, "The songs, they mean something, they talk you see. Like other songs—also like songs for thanking God, songs of being worried." She added later, "Like you, maybe you got something worrying you, maybe you pick up your song that goes with you, you see. *Ja*, it's just like that." In this way a woman may be identified by the community of women.

Conversely, the intimacy of a woman's relationship with Shembe is articulated in the way in which his texts memorialize his own experiences and in turn become metaphors for the experiences of these women themselves. The narration of the subjectivity of personal experience, juxtaposed with the authority of the Word of God in the singing of a hymn, enables women to construct a personal space in the broader history of the community. By the association of a single hymn with the experiences of a woman known to the community, the experience of that woman is memorialized, and both the hymn and her experience are relocated in the present. In this regard, Shembe's hymns may be classified as "historicizing discourses" (Seremetakis 1991; Abu-Lughod and Lutz 1990) and maps of collective experience (Vail and White 1991, 40).

One woman illustrated this in a narrative she told me when I asked her which of the hymns was her favorite. She replied,

> It's not to say that we favor them or we like them. These *hlabelela*, they talk. Like the first *hlabelela*, number one. It tells, you see, *Nkosi Sikele uBaba*. That means, "God please help *Baba*." Save our *Baba* . . . Save him because he was going in, sleeping in the *veld*, like this. When he [had] nobody to help him, [he was] just going up and down. He had no place to sleep. So he was sleeping in the forest sometimes. In the *veld*, in the rain. [At] that time he was sent by God to preach. . . .

So that's why I say these *hlabelela* they talk. Even today still the same founder who is still here, today people who were laughing at him, chasing him away. . . . They thought maybe by chasing—as he was called by God, you see—to come to this mountain—the people of this place. They even used to say, they called the *induna*s to say, the person who is staying here, that person is stealing our goats, is stealing our cattle. Then they all came here to find and kill him. . . . He used to hide there [in a cave on the mountain] from people who wanted to kill him, because they said he was here to pinch, to take their sheep and goats away like that. Then he used to hide in the mountains. So this *hlabelela* number one is talking about that life, that even he used to hide from people who wanted to kill him.

The text provides a poignant statement on the way in which the experiences of the founder interweave with and confirm the experiences of women—particularly those whose daily experience is one of incessant fear pertaining to violence, theft, and harassment.

A second song interpreted by the woman parallels her own anxiety. Hymn 145 is explained in this way:

Shembe was so worried when he composed this hymn. It's talking about that everyday my heart . . . I'm always worried. But, I know you Jehovah, you are the only one who came [to] help me. [At] that time I think he even says, yesterday, today . . . my heart was so worried. I was thinking of my children. I don't know where I left my children, because the voice of God, the Word of God was there saying "You must follow me."[16] He says, "You Jehovah, I know you are with me. I ask you to be there with my children at home." . . . You know it means when you look at this hymn, he was worried when he composed this song.

It is as structures of feeling, as the embodiment of emotion in a highly charged daily context, that these songs continue to resonate with the experiences of Nazarite women. It is through a shared moral inference, a common experience and emotional communication over time, that Nazarite women are connected with their founder in the words of sacred song.

Nazarite hymns are also used to honor the memory of the dead and to mark relationships between the living and the deceased. Through the singing and re-singing of a hymn while she is alive, a mother shares emotions with her daughter and the women she knows. When she has gone, these emotions are inscribed in kin history each time the hymn is sung. Each reenactment of the song serves to reinforce cosmological relationships. In this way the woman cited above always thinks of her mother when she sings Hymn 227. She recalls:

> My mother says, 227, *Kepha wena ufihliwe*. That, my mother used to say. This. "O God, O *Baba* Shembe, I love you so much, but you are hidden to me. I don't, even if I want to follow you, there are some things that comes, eh, makes me not to follow you." You see.
>
> It even says, "I wonder, where will I get that river? Where will I just wash myself? That I can be nice and clean, and follow you. Sometimes I even ask, where will I get those *MNazarethas?* Where will I put on those *MNazarethas* and look so nice? When you remember me." That was when my mother was, when her children were dying. She told us she used to sing this song.
>
> "I wonder," it says in verse 5 "*Iminyaka eminingi/ Bengihlezi emnyameni . . .*" "For so many years I was in darkness . . . but you God, you *Baba* Shembe, loved me so much that the light came to me." That was when she saw that she was now pregnant. "I wonder what will I do to you? I'm just asking you to please be with me. Even if I die, I'm asking you to die where you are—to follow you till I die."[17]

In the previous section on dreams, I drew a connection between closing one's eyes in sleep or prayer, and opening a window into the cosmology. Roseman (1991, 181) defines this as "setting the cosmos in motion." Singing Nazarite hymns effects a similar process of spatio-temporal transformation. Herndon (1986) writes in this regard that "[songs] are the means by which a transformation . . . of circumstance is attempted . . . [they create a] bridge between sacred and secular, sleep and wakefulness." To illustrate this transformative power, Cinikile Mazibuko told me a story about a time when she was encountering difficulties with municipal authorities in acquiring a house. In desperation, praying and crying to Shembe, she finally fell asleep. During the night she had a dream in which her late father appeared to her. She asked him, since he was in heaven with Shembe, to please request Shembe's help in finding her a house. The result was that the next day, a home was provided. Through the dual means of prayer and dreaming, Cinikile invoked the cosmos.

She also recalled one day that just thinking about her late father caused her to sing the song that she remembered he had always sung when he was alive, thus invoking his presence through the medium of song. She said:

> I was just thinking of my father. Then I thought of this song: *Nku-lunkulu Nkosi/Ungishiyela bani.* It says "Oh God, why do you leave me? If you leave me like that, my enemies laugh at me. They say, 'Where is your God? You always tell us about your Shembe.'" You see, that's the song.
>
> I mean if you're worried, there's something worrying you, you think ooooh. Let me rather sing this song. *You see if I sing this song, I'm praying at the same time.* Like that [Hymn] 104. My father used to sing that song when he was worried. So, I was not worried, *but I was thinking of my father, and I just sing the songs he likes,* you know. Let me sing this song today. [Emphasis mine.]

In addition to invoking cosmological relationships, this narrative embeds several historical layers of experience. Isaiah felt anxious and wrote a text, which Cinikile's father then sang, identifying with Isaiah's anxiety, and in turn, Cinikile sings the song as a reminder of her father.

A second story of quite a different nature was told by a woman at the *ama14* meeting held in March 1992 at *Vula Masango,* on the south coast of KwaZulu Natal. This is an area that continues to be plagued by killings, house burnings, and refugee resettlement. Those who live there do so in constant fear of attack, and have been rendered powerless by indiscriminate and unabated political and interclan warfare. This woman recalled:

> There has been violence in Umkomazi.[18] That's where I live. No one was able to stop that violence. Only Shembe could, because he wanted to show that he is great. But, even then people didn't recognize him. Shembe the prophet [i.e., Isaiah] appeared to a certain woman of Umkomazi. And when he appeared to her, she wasn't sleeping. It was four o'clock in the morning. That was the time that this woman would wake up to do her morning prayers. She had just woken up. She saw Shembe singing the song she had just sung, song number 129.
>
> Do not delay me
> You who are my enemy;
> When Jehovah calls me
> I must move and follow him.
>
> Thunderstorms come out of season
> In the heart that is guilty;
> Hope has been dispelled.
> Only anxiety remains.

It is not of their will
That they do not come to the Lord;
They have lost hope,
And their love has vanished.

Whose [child] am I?
Today Lord
The conscience of my heart
Has denounced me before you.

She continued:

> The prophet sang this song. And when he was in the middle of this song, the woman saw him changing as if he were the present Shembe [i.e., Amos]. When he had just finished the song, he said, "Today I have come to put an end to this violence in this area." Good people, in the same week, delegates from Ulundi[19] came to settle the dispute in our area. Because violence was too high, we couldn't stay in our homes. We had moved from our homes. But, when Shembe came, and the delegates came, we went back to our homes after many years of not staying in our homes. I don't know how we can thank Shembe for what he does, because there are so many great things that he does. [Translation assistance from Khethiwe Mthethwa.]

This is a remarkable account on several levels. First, we are told that the woman was in the midst of performing the morning prayer, which might involve a reading through of the liturgy for the morning service, prayer, and the singing of a hymn—implying that all four expressive domains are integrated into this narrative. In this case, it was immediately after the singing that Shembe appeared. The incorporation of the power of the cosmology into everyday life was effected through the woman's singing the Words of God. This is a similar process to that discussed at the beginning of the chapter, where I suggested that women's bodies become the medium for the flow of the power of Isaiah into earth. Second, song performance embodies the social principle of reciprocity—the woman gives the gift of song and Shembe replies in the same song—returning its cosmological force to her. His words became her words, which then became his words again. The final outcome is the ending of violence in the area—a feat no one else had been able to achieve. Third, the transformation of imagery—from Isaiah to Amos—links with my earlier discussion on the flipping of images in visionary experience, which I likened to the moving imagery of television. There is a remarkable shifting in cosmological actors—from Isaiah the prophet to Amos the present leader. I have argued here that Nazarite hymn texts fuse the nature of experience and the structuring of emotion between Isaiah and the present membership—many of whom are too young to have known the founder. The transformation of images from Isaiah to Amos in the above account is best explained by an earlier statement about the importance of being able to see miracles and not only to read about them. In this regard, Amos is the one who effects transformation in the political context, because he is the present embodiment of the Shembe lineage and the one in personal contact with the Ulundi officials.

In contrast to the daily and sabbath congregational worship, which are largely defined by the printed liturgies contained in the front of the hymnal, *ama14* meetings are structured around the singing of particular hymns. In this sense, I suggest that singing hymns is believed to effect the transformation of the meeting of women into a temporary "heaven-on-earth." I have already discussed the first two hymns that are always sung to open these meetings. The meeting closes with Hymn 152—*Jerusalema Betlehema*—a hymn chronicling the birth of Jesus and the arrival of the wise men at the palace of Herod, where they ask where the King of the Jews was born. The hymn emphasizes the anger of Herod, his desire to kill the baby, and the need for the parents to hide the child away. In the *14*s meeting this hymn accompanies the giving of small monetary gifts—of fifty or seventy cents—to *Mkhokheli*, who collects the money together and takes it to Shembe twice a year.[20] This song is accompanied by the reading from the Bible of the parallel story in Matthew 2.

The specific order of the three hymns, as well as those individually selected by women for preaching, facilitates a movement into the Nazarite cosmology. The meeting starts with an invitation to the ancestors (including Shembe), who embody the cosmology. Once into this imaginary space, women are transformed into spiritual virgins—they become ritually pure by singing Hymn 225. Thereafter, the performance of a personally selected hymn enables each woman to individually inscribe her name and self into the historical archives of the cosmology. The final form of heavenly accountability—the giving of monetary gifts—is what accompanies the singing of the closing hymn. In this manner the hymn-singing (re)creates the structures of the cosmology on earth.

Nazarite Women and Religious Dance

About four months into my research, I had my car parked at a local supermarket when two women, selling grass mats and baskets, came toward the vehicle. They had seen the sticker "Shembe Is the Way" on the car, and had obviously come to investigate. I told them that I was visiting *Ebuhleni* to study the songs and dances of Shembe. Immediately these women began to dance the Nazarite style of dance in the parking lot. They vocalized among themselves the rhythmic pattern of the large trumpets, and moved with it. The exuberance and enthusiasm in their movements signaled to me the treasure these women felt they possessed in being able to dance the dances of Shembe.

The sacred dance *ukusina* or *umgido* (which means festival and is the word used by the women when referring to this dance) was first introduced into Nazarite religious worship in the late 1920s (Mthethwa 1989, 245–55).[21] It derived from the traditional practice of walking in procession to the sound of a drum around the temple area to invoke the presence of the ancestors. This practice was combined with another tradition, that of ritual dance, to create what is now Nazarite *ukusina*. The performance includes dance movements derived from the traditional *isigekle*[22] dance style, specific dance attire for each group, and the singing of hymns accompanied by the drum, trumpets, and handclapping.

While *ukusina* is never performed in the context of *inkhonzo*, the congregational church service, this dance plays an integral role in the totality of Nazarite religious worship. Cinikile Mazibuko (pers. comm., January 1992) explained:

> You know when you dance you enjoy your dancing. But the main thing is the part of praying. Because it is written in the Bible that we must praise him with the drums. You must praise him with the dancing.

Dancing, like hymn-singing and dreaming, is a form of prayer, a communication with the ancestors. Dance festivals conclude with the words "Amen. Amen." In this vein Mthethwa (1989, 245) remarked that *ukusina* "is the dance performed by the living and the dead." Thus dance is a nurturing of and interaction with the ancestors, believed to be present at all dance festivals.

Linked to this, and mentioned in chapter 4, is that dance ensures the "writing of one's name in the Book of Life,"[23] an action performed by the ancestors. Dance performance acquires a ticket of entry into heaven. It is an integral element of the re-creation of a moral and precapitalist economy, based on principles of reciprocity and respect. For the Nazarites, *ukusina* is defined as "work," as hard work for the accumulation of symbolic capital. This stands in stark contrast to the reduced concept of "work" as wage labor associated with capitalist modes of production.[24] The presence of the ancestors in dance is reinforced in Nazarite belief by the actual dance movements, which for the women means a fairly slow and controlled, nonspectacular series of body movements. There is no official sanction for any kind of innovation in these movements, because they are believed to be the exact patterns that were performed from the inception of the dance at the "beginning of time." Dancers have an obligation to continue these patterns in order to make the ancestors feel comfortable while they dance with the living.

Nazarite Hymn 112 is suggestive in its articulation of the power associated with sacred dance.

Thina Nkosi	We, O Lord
Sisinela Wena;	Dance for you;
Ngalawo mandla	For that power
Obukhosi bakho.	Of your kingdom.
Aziqiniswe	May they be strengthened,
Izinyawo zethu,	Our feet,
Sisinele wena	So that we may dance for you
Simakade.	Eternal One.
(Hlab. 112/2,3)	(Hymn 112/2,3)

I was told on several occasions that learning the dance is an arduous task—dance is hard work, and can take women many years to master. (There were parallel statements made to me about hymn-singing.) I propose that the ability to dance is not limited to fitting into the patterns of bodily movement—for when I tried to dance, these did not seem to be that difficult. The difficulty lies instead in the ability to endure and sustain the mind and body over extended periods of time, both physically and spiritually. Because of the connection with the ancestors, I suggest that *ukusina* reflects the attainment of a high level of spiritual maturity that incorporates not only dance, but the ability to both preach and speak in public.

A dream recounted by the husband of a woman hosting a *14*s meeting exemplifies this relationship. The man dreamed about the moment when Amos assumed leadership of the church. He recalled that Amos had been very young and shy, and not well versed in the ways of the church. He said:

After some time I saw him really dancing. He could dance like *Bombela* [train] and he fitted anywhere he went to. . . . After that event he came to sit with his people. He was not shy now. He just sat there and looked at his people. He was grown up now. He had learnt to dance and even talk to people during church services and to preach.

This excerpt suggests, then, that spiritual maturity is reflected not only in Amos's ability to preach, but also in his knowledge of *ukusina*.

A second dimension of *ukusina* participation is the sheer physical stamina required in order to dance continuously for about five hours, with just a single break in the middle of this time. (For married women, the uniforms introduce an additional weight, being multilayered and extremely heavy. In the winter this might keep women warm, but in the summer heat, this attire can only feel burdensome.) In several of the women's narratives, the capacity to speak, sing, and dance symbolized the healing of the physical body. In one case a woman was unable to conceive, but having been blessed by Shembe, she gave birth to a son sixteen years after her first son was born. In the words of the grandmother's sister, "he's so clever. He's four years. He's very—if you could see him dancing! . . . Whooh, if I can tell you these stories!" Such performance reverses the fragmentation of the individual and social selves discussed particularly in the first section above, in the narratives about the body, infertility, and rape. If the physical body is deformed, there can be no dance, and thus no reformulation of the social body through its enactment. As Roseman (1991, 180) states for the Temiar, "[they] recognize that body, social order, and cosmological order are interwoven like a cloth." When the physical body is synchronized with the cosmology, the social body is reconstituted.

Ukusina is important not only within religious relationships in *ibandla lamaNazaretha* and its cosmology, but also as a marker of identity in the patchwork of religious beliefs in South Africa. One woman explained that while her mother had been a member of the Methodist church in her lifetime, it was the sacred dance that had attracted her to Shembe's following. She recalls:

> My mother liked *Ekuphakameni*. Sometimes she would imitate the dance of the maidens. She would imitate them in such a way that you would see that she really likes the things of *Ekuphakameni*. In my view, I think that when my mother died, in heaven she found that the Nazareths were the dominating people. At the gates she found *Baba*. [*Ama14*, October 13, 1991.]

Conclusion

In this chapter I have considered the way in which Isaiah Shembe created mechanisms to protect and imbue with holiness the fertility of the bodies of married Nazarite women. He facilitated a process whereby the pollution of sexual intercourse and defilement was purified. He did this by creating a spatio-temporal domain—the monthly meetings called *amafor-tini*—or a "heaven-on-earth." In this space women effected the transition from ritual impurity to ritual purity through the expressive modes of song, dance, prayer, and preaching. In the Nazarite religious imagination, each individual woman is required to "write her name in the Book of Life" by actively accumulating moral capital through hard work. In the Nazarite community this involves attendance at gatherings of *ama14*, sacred dance, preaching, and singing. Each of these actions will ultimately generate a woman's passage to heaven after death, where the final judgment will be held. At that moment the heavenly beings will check the Book of Life for the name of each woman. It is in this context that Nazarite women engage in technologies of self-disclosure to create discourses that will provide sufficient evidence of their good works on earth.

A Last Word

Ekuphakameni, the headquarters of the Nazareth Baptist Church, is a shining example of how different political persuasions can live together in peace. There, refugees from the so-called strongholds of both the African National Congress (ANC) and the Inkatha Freedom Party (IFP) have found shelter. *Ekuphakameni* has become a shelter for many who have been uprooted by violence in their homes.

Let us cherish our unity. Enemies of peace and humanity never ceased their efforts to undo our noble achievements. The Nazareth Baptist Church has achieved its successes because it has a leadership that has always acted in a united, collective way. It would be tragic if enemies of peace were to take advantage of this time of stress and sorrow to drive wedges within your leadership. As we join the Nazareth Baptist Church in mourning the departure of this outstanding leader, let us join hands and deny any opportunity to those who set us against one another. We are one people. [Speech by Nelson Mandela in English and Zulu, October 1995.]

With these words State President Nelson Mandela concluded his speech to *ibandla lamaNazaretha* at the funeral of Amos Shembe in October 1995. Mandela had skillfully used the funeral site as a space in which to articulate a particular vision of nationhood and political unity, so critical to the strife-torn province of KwaZulu Natal. Many attributed the turmoil to the conflict between the political allegiances to the two dominant parties, the ANC and the IFP. The bulk of Mandela's words had sought to unite the interests of the ANC and *ibandla lamaNazaretha* (frequently called the Nazareth Baptist Church) by retelling the history of KwaZulu Natal, and the Inanda Valley in particular. He positioned Isaiah Shembe alongside the likes of some of the great men from the Inanda Valley, including John Langalibalele Dube and Mahatma Gandhi.

About a week later, during the monthly meeting of married women at *Ebuhleni,* one woman stood up to preach to the other Nazarite women gathered together that night. Like State President Mandela, she also invested Shembe with a particular kind of power and position, though from quite a different perspective.

> O Nazarites, so beautiful in the eyes of the Lord, the news is great. The news is great from *Ekuphakameni,* my relatives in the Lord. . . . I saw a miracle, beautiful Nazarites in the Lord, I saw God, dearly beloved, coming in through the gates of heaven, dearly beloved, praise the Lord, Amen. I saw the opening of heaven, dearly beloved, and when the thunder spoke, the Lord himself was silent and a great thunderstorm ensued. When it spoke, dear faithful—first on this side and then on the other side, then it cut a white shaft in the middle, similar to the dresses that you see us wearing now—you could see with the naked eye, our king entering heaven, the moon [Amos] of heaven entering paradise.
>
> The spectacle was big, dear Nazarites. Let us be one, like the clay of cement, because it was said that if we are one like the clay of cement, everything will be put right. The moon of heaven strode in, dearly beloved, I've never seen anything like it with my naked eyes. We are really grown up to have seen that miracle. It is said we should be one like clay because the Nazaritehood is great. This Nazaritehood assembles from all corners of the globe. It assembles the black nation. Today it has gathered the white nation.
>
> If [Isaiah] Shembe had lived in our times he would have been honored with degrees. It is said that he would have been long dressed with degrees. The word [of Mandela] said that it is "Doctor" Shembe. When Shembe was revealed, his work was tread upon by time so that his fame did not spread, and few realized how important [big in godliness] he is. Today, Shembe stands revealed because he speaks on the radio, on the TV, and so even those who did not want to hear Shembe's word, today realize how big he is, children of *Ekuphakameni.* [Translation assistance from Sazi Dlamini.]

While not a historical account per se, this book spans two distinctive moments in the history of twentieth-century South Africa from the perspective of a large group of women in KwaZulu Natal. Both excerpts cited above speak to these two moments: the early part of the century, a period of massive transformation for African peoples instigated by environmental disaster, the Christian mission, and modern capitalism; and contemporary South Africa, a country seeking to create a national and democratic identity in a late-twentieth-century global economy.

If one considers the two moments purely from the vantage point of political economy, there are significant parallels between them: in both, the people of South Africa face the challenge of massive sociopolitical and, indeed, technological transformation, of how to reconfigure their relationships to each other and the world at large. My project in this book has not, however, been a conventional analysis of political economy. Instead, it has been to engage in a more gendered understanding of the period from the perspective of one South African community.

Mandela, the Nazarite *ifortini*, and I have each suggested that the first moment, the period of South Africa's emergence as an industrial economy, was one in which things associated with women, expressive culture, and Africanness were castrated or denigrated by the political center. In a word, they were feminized. Disturbed by these processes, Isaiah Shembe created a space of sanctuary for women and girls, and reinvested African expressive forms with an aura of the sacred. But it was not only African women who were disempowered by the force of economic transformation. Although not central to my story (but certainly featured by other writers), many African men who migrated to urban centers through the course of the twentieth century have been similarly stripped of traditional signs of gendered power. As the genre of *isicathamiya* has revealed, nineteenth-century "Zulu warrior" masculinity was changed into a twentieth-century "tiptoe guy" migrant identity. And so Isaiah Shembe's previously women-dominated sanctuary now demonstrates in its public spectacle a more equal representation of, and power attributed to, women and men.

At Amos Shembe's funeral, President Mandela reminded the Nazarites that in contemporary South Africa, signs of "Africanness" were returning to the political center. The shift is also voiced by the Nazarite woman. She comments that while Isaiah's power (in the feminized margins) was dismissed and "trodden" on, he is now recognized because he appears on national television and radio. There is an additional move. This *ifortini* recognizes that in the late twentieth century, Nazaritehood, a local manifestation of "Africanness," is integrally entwined with modernity: radio, television, Ph.D.s, and the world at large.

For this book at least two questions remain: what about women in contemporary South Africa, and Shembe in the twenty-first century? It is too early to know for sure, though I shall speculate by analyzing two brief scenarios. The first is Mbongeni Ngema's late-1980s production of *Sara-*

fina! and the second is President Nelson Mandela's recent marriage to Mozambican Graca Machel. I am interested in these two stories for the ways in which they point to gender dynamics in a "new" South Africa.

Briefly, we are told that South African protest-theater playwright Mbongeni Ngema was inspired to develop the *Sarafina!* production after a conversation with then "mother of the nation" Winnie Mandela. She encouraged him to create a performance about the children of Soweto, which he proceeded to do. The intriguing part of the performance is Sarafina herself, a *female* protagonist, an atypical characterization in the otherwise male-dominated protest-theater milieu. Surprisingly, toward the end of the piece, in a dreamlike manner, Sarafina is transformed from an outspoken, politically astute female student in Soweto to the person of (then imprisoned) Nelson Mandela. At the time, this gendered conversion was believable precisely because, other than the security guards at the prison, nobody knew what Mandela really looked like. Photographic images of the man were banned in South Africa in the 1980s.

Certainly, if we read the conversion at a more symbolic level, it proves to have been prophetic: in real life, the castrated Mandela was represented in Soweto (and Ngema's production) in the public figure of an outspoken, politically canny female figure, Mandela's second wife, Winnie. The problem was that once Mandela was free to appear in public again, the female protagonist had to be eliminated. And so

> [o]n April 13, 1992 at a press conference in Johannesburg, flanked by my two oldest friends and comrades, Walter [Sisulu] and Oliver [Tambo], I announced my separation from my wife. The situation had grown so difficult that I felt that it was in the best interests of all concerned—the ANC, the family, and Winnie—that we part. . . . I shall personally never regret the life Comrade Nomzamo and I tried to share together. Circumstances beyond our control however dictated it should be otherwise. [Mandela 1995 (1994), 718–19.]

This leads into the second short story. Encouraged by Archbishop Desmond Tutu to set an example to South Africa's youth, State President Mandela married the wife of the late Mozambican president and liberation leader, Samora Machel, on July 18, 1998 (*Raleigh News and Observer,* July 19, 1998, 2A). Legally joined in a Christian ceremony by Methodist Bishop Mvuve Dandala, the "father of the nation" nonetheless conveyed qualities of the contemporary "Africanness" he spoke of at Amos Shembe's funeral. In contrast to the tarnished public image of the fallen "mother of the nation," Winnie Mandela, who stood accused of killing children, the new Mrs. Mandela was reported to be a woman who had gained respect from the world for her commitment to children. In a spirit of true Africanness, Nelson Mandela sent *lobolo* cattle to his new wife's family. Straddling Westernness and Africanness, Nelson Mandela embodied further Africanist dreams of polygamous marriage, only, like so many others', his is a form of serial monogamy rather than polygamy. Graca Machel is Nelson Mandela's third wife.

There are many ways of reading and understanding what these two stories might mean for South Africa in the future, and, by extension, for Shembe, *ibandla lamaNazaretha,* and the female members. The first narrative speaks of the reinstatement of more traditional gender roles in a post-apartheid, Mandela-ruled society: the feminized man regains his public place as a man in political life. The second story reconstitutes marriage as a central sociopolitical and economic arrangement for the moral and physical reproduction of society. Public credence is accorded to African women, not just as mothers, but as wives as well. From the outside, these two gestures may seem to be extremely conservative, far removed from the kinds of freedoms women are claiming elsewhere in the world. Certainly, it is hard to say just how South African women will find the "new" South Africa. How they do is likely to inform the relationship Nazarite women currently foster with Shembe through sacred song, dance, prayer, dreaming, and miracles. For the present time, there seems to be an uncanny similarity between African women, the mission of Isaiah Shembe, and the contemporary politics of nation-building.

Glossary

Abavangeli	Evangelists.
Amabutho	Regiments of young men and women.
Amacansi	Mats made of reeds.
AmaKhanda	Secluded areas for the wives or young women, given as tribute to a Zulu king.
Apartheid	The name given to the Afrikaner government's policy of separate development for all race groups between 1948 and 1990, in South Africa.
Baba	Father; term used to address Shembe.
Dokoda	Tabernacle; temporary shelter.
Dompas	Stupid Pass. The notorious passbook that controlled all movement of black South Africans for several decades.
Ebuhleni	The place of splendor; the new Nazarite headquarters in Ndwedwe, KwaZulu Natal, under the leadership of Amos Shembe.
Ekuphakameni	The elevated place; heaven; the first Nazarite settlement in Inanda, KwaZulu Natal.
Elinda	To wait; the name of a Nazarite sacred space in northern KwaZulu Natal, near Nongoma.
Gibisile	To conquer misfortune; the name of a Nazarite sacred space in KwaZulu Natal, close to Richards Bay.
Hlabelela	To sing.
Hlonipha	Respect; a set of bodily postures and social behaviors varying according to age, gender, and marital status, which have been the moral force in traditional Zulu society. They were modified by Isaiah Shembe for his community.
Ibandla lamaNazaretha	Nazarite congregation.
Ibayi (Ibhayi)	A long cape worn to cover the shoulders of married women, or a piece of fabric wrapped around the body of a virgin girl, tied over one shoulder, to signify virginity and ritual purity.
Ifortini	A married Nazarite woman who attends the all-night monthly meetings; a white cotton band worn around *inhloko;* a wide black belt worn around the waist by married Nazarite women.
Ilanga	Sun; the name for Galilee Shembe.
Imbongi	Praise poet/singer who may both praise and criticize an individual.
Imijondolo	Temporary shelters for squatters.
Inhloko	Women's topknot.
Inkhonzo	Congregational worship.
Inkosazana	Princess.
Inkosazana yase Zulweni	Princess of the Heaven; daughter of the Lord of the Sky in the Zulu cosmology.
Indlunkulu	The Zulu king's great house.
Intabayepheza	Mountain of abstinence; the title given to the Nazarite female virgins.
Indlela yegama	The path of the words; the melody.

Inthanda (Ntanda)	July ritual for Nazarite virgin girls, modeled after the traditional Zulu girls' puberty rite.
Isangoma	Traditional healer.
Isibongo	Praise poem (pl.: *Izibongo*).
Isidwaba	Skirt of cowhide worn by Nazarite women for sacred dance, and by traditional Zulu women who are married.
Isigekle	Wedding songs from which Nazarite hymn-singing and dancing derive.
Isihlabelelo	Hymn (pl.: *Izihlabelelo*).
ISkotch	Pleated tartan skirts worn by prepubescent boys and virgin girls for Nazarite sacred dance.
Izigodlo	The upper part of the Zulu king's homestead, in which his wives and their children reside.
IziHlabelelo zamaNazaretha	Nazarite hymns; title of the Nazarite hymnal.
Izimbomvu	Nazarite indigenous trumpets, like alpine horns, used to accompany sacred dance.
Judia	Named after the biblical town, it is a Nazarite space in KwaZulu Natal, close to Gingindhlovu.
Kholwa	Believer; Christian convert.
Kombi	Minibus taxi.
Kraal	Zulu homestead.
KwaMashu	A peri-urban black township on the outskirts of the Durban functional region. It is named after a military general called Marshall.
Lobola/o	Bridewealth.
Manyano	Prayer union for women held on Thursday afternoons.
Maskanda	Neotraditional Zulu migrant musician, usually a guitarist or accordion player.
Mfecane	Large-scale migration of black people in southern Africa in the nineteenth century, often caused by warfare and raids.
Mfundisi	Teacher; minister of religion.
Mkhokheli	The one who pays; Nazarite leader of married women.
MNazaretha	The white prayer surplice worn by all Nazarite members.
Mshumayeli	Preacher; form of address/title for a male Nazarite leader
Mvangeli	Evangelist; form of address/title for a male Nazarite leader.
Mvelinqangi	Name for the Creator, the Supreme Being.
Nansook (inansuka)	Long white shawl worn by virgin girls to cover the heads, faces, and shoulders in congregational worship.
Ncome	Blood. There was a historic battle fought between *trekkers* and Zulus at the Blood or *Ncome* River in 1838.
Nguni	This is the collective term for the southern Bantu-speaking people. The group includes those who speak Ndebele, Swazi, Xhosa, Zulu, and Tswana.
Nhlangakaze (Nhlangakazi)	The big reed; the name of the Nazarite holy mountain.
Nkhosikazi	Married woman.
Nkosi yezulu	Lord of the Skies/God in Zulu cosmology.
Nkulunkulu	Lord of the Heavens/God in Zulu cosmology.
Nomkhubulwana	Princess of the Sky; the daughter of *Nkulunkulu;* associated with fertility of crops and young girls.
Ntanda	Ritual for Nazarite girls held on July 7 and 8 each year.
Paradis	The name of the open-air temple at *Ebuhleni.*
Sabatha	Sabbath, which is a Saturday in *ibandla lamaNazaretha.*
Sontweni	To be at church.

Thanda (*ukuthanda*)	To weave or braid; to love.
Ughubu	Large indigenized bass drum modeled after those of the Salvation Army marching bands; used for Nazarite sacred dance.
Ujafeta	Prayer surplice worn by female virgins, resembling the attire of preachers. The name connects with the biblical account of the warrior Jephthah.
Ukubuyisa	The ceremony performed one year after the death of an individual to facilitate the individual's spirit's entry into the ancestral domain.
Ukuhlobonga	A premarital practice of unconsummated sex in Zulu traditional custom.
Ukusina	Sacred dance.
Umndlunkulu	Maidens of royal blood; the name given to married Nazarite women.
Umqwazi	Rushes of beadwork worn on a woman's topknot.
Umgonqo	Nazarite rite of seclusion for virgin girls, starting on July 25 and ending on September 25. It is also derived from Zulu traditional puberty rites for girls
Umuthsha	Loincloths made of animal skin or fiber.
Umgidi/o	Festival, ceremony.
Umputhi (*Mputhi*)	One in charge; leader of the virgin girls.
Vula Masango	Open the Gate. The name of one of the Nazarite sacred spaces on the southern coastal area of KwaZulu Natal.
Washiwa	"You are being left out." The call of the dance leader to encourage those dancing to keep going.

Notes

Chapter One

1. All texts cited at the beginnings of chapters are taken from *The Hymns of the Nazaretha (Composed by Isaiah and Galilee Shembe),* as edited by Galilee. They were translated by the late Bongani Mthethwa with assistance from Themba Mbhele and Sazi Dlamini, and edited, introduced, and annotated by myself. These will be published in 1999 by the University of Natal Press.

2. All italicized words used more than once in the text are defined or explained in the glossary.

3. KwaZulu Natal is the name of one of the nine provinces of the post-1994 revised borders of the South African Republic. The region is referred to in several ways in the literature. In nineteenth-century literature, the area south of the Tugela river and north of the Umzimkulu river in the south was known as Natal. The area north of the Tugela river and up to the border with Mozambique was known as Zululand. This was essentially the division (though it became more complicated under the apartheid governments) in the region until 1994, when the area came under a single provincial control.

4. The words *Zulu* and *African* are frequently used by black South Africans in ambiguous ways. For some, *Zulu* equals only those who speak the Zulu language. For others, *Zulu* and *African* are used interchangeably, and refer to black South Africans generally (Sikelela Msibi, pers. comm.). The use of the word *African* is ambiguous, and frequently contentious. On the one hand, there are many black South Africans who now prefer to be called black, rather than African. On the other hand, the term *African* historically refers to the collective identity of all (black) South Africans, in opposition to the domination and discrimination typical of (white) European people. More recently, many white South Africans who have ancestry that can be traced back as far as the eighteenth and nineteenth centuries have also come to see themselves as "African"—as opposed to "European." Clearly these terms are polysemic, and often problematic. (To make matters more complex, there are now many white politicians who have joined the Zulu nationalist Inkatha Freedom Party, under the leadership of Chief Mangosutho Buthelezi. How do we define them—as white non-Zulu-speaking Zulus?) I tend to use *African* in the context of the historical past, and *black* for the more immediate context, though they are used in ambiguous ways in South Africa.

5. See Mthembeni Mpanza (1993) for discussion of the multivalence of the name *Shembe* and discussion on the concept of the Holy Spirit in the Nazarite context.

6. The reasons for this violence are extremely complex, though the Truth and Reconciliation Commission and related court cases in 1995 and 1996 began to unpack the extent of "Third Force" activities. These were vicious attacks on frequently innocent victims, by an unofficial and apparently nonexistent security force of white and black South Africans. They were often armed by the South African security forces or allied groups (such as the now defunct KwaZulu Police).

7. I was invited by Professor Pippin Oosthuizen, then head of the Unit for the Study of New Religious Movements and Indigenous Religion, under the auspices of the Centre for Science Development, and housed at the University of Zululand. Oosthuizen has visited the Nazarites quite regularly and written extensively about Shembe and his following. His book (1967) on the theology of Isaiah as articulated in the hymn texts is one of the most frequently discussed in the secondary literature.

8. See *Drum* magazine, March 1980.

9. See Muller 1997a for discussion of the significance of the path and the mountain in Nazarite epistemology.

10. The stress on religious song, accompanied by the organ (the church instrument) on the top of the mountain and in the center of the plateau, is extremely important symbolically. As I explain in chapter 4, the birth of the Nazarite church and the sense of Nazarite song style (as created by Isaiah Shembe) occurred on the plateau of this same mountain early in the twentieth century. Isaiah's vision of this repertory was, however, as unaccompanied song, while Amos's (in the mid-1980s) included the organ. It clearly suggests a shift in traditional consciousness between father and son.

11. Bongani Mthethwa was tragically murdered on June 2, 1992, after leaving the University of Natal. He was attacked by unknown assailants who shot him in the head and heart, threw his body out of his motor vehicle, and then burned the vehicle. As of this writing there have been no conclusive findings as to the motive for his murder.

12. *Natal Witness*, Echo Section, January 13, 1994.

13. See, for example, papers by Ted Swedenburg, Orin Starn, and Enrique Mayer in Marcus (1992) and Feldman (1991).

14. "One settler, one bullet" was the highly controversial slogan used in the liberation struggle that was also apparently called out as Biehl's killers attacked her and her friends.

15. This statement must be qualified by saying that this audio technology did immediately create a distance between myself and the Nazarites, because of the economic resources required to purchase even my rather humble equipment. I was not, however, the only person among the Nazarites with access to the equipment, but we constituted an extremely small minority.

16. This is what Guy (1991) refers to as the advantages of secondary orality, or orality encoded using sound-recording technology, which is, relatively speaking, a far more accessible technological medium than that of learning to write and read.

17. Feld (1982, 11) comments on the way in which he used a fictive kinship with Bambi and Buck Shieffelin to enter the Kaluli community. The Nazarites created their own fictive relationship between Bongani and me as a means of allowing me to enter their community.

18. The phrases are taken from Comaroff and Comaroff (1992, 155–80). In the Nazarite context, I use it to articulate the means by which Amos Shembe reconstituted the politics of race and empire while I was on his territory.

19. The hymn refers to Zulu and other African peoples as brown rather than black. According to Bongani Mthethwa (pers. comm., January 1990), *black* is considered derogatory to the African people as a consequence of the influence of the black consciousness movement in South Africa in the 1960s, as led (in South Africa) by Steve Biko. Mthethwa's opinion is certainly not held by all people of African descent in South Africa, though it may explain why the word *brown* rather than *black* has been used in this context.

20. This openness to all races, particularly to white people, has not always been part of Nazarite religious epistemology. Kiernan (1992) remarks, for example, on Londa Shembe's desire to shelter his community from outside intrusion by white people, and in fact, of the ire of one of the women members when she saw Kiernan with Londa Shembe. The popularity of particular Nazarite hymns has changed with political transformations. Hugh Tracey (1948), for example, tells of the wide popularity of the hymns of Shembe, particularly with the radio audiences of the late 1940s (see chap. 4).

21. Serematakis (1991) discusses how she began to have dreams of warning and death similar to those of the women she was working with. Taussig (1987 [1986]) attempted a similar kind of understanding by physically consuming the narcotics of the shamans he was working with in Colombia.

22. *Temple* here may refer to the specific site where religious worship takes place, a site on which members may be living permanently, or come to visit for short periods of time. It also refers to the congregation of people.

23. See Jacklyn Cock (1991) for a comprehensive account of the construction of the military embodied in the South African Defense Force.

24. Daphne Patai (1991) raises a number of important issues in terms of the imbalances in the re-

lationship between First and Third World women, particularly in the assumption of sisterhood between all women; especially in terms of whether First World women should attempt to raise the consciousness of Third World women into "liberation," or whether they should simply respect the ways of these women. Patai makes the point that frequently the inherent differences between First and Third World women in terms of education, access to material wealth, and so on serve to raise hopes and increase dependency on the part of the Third World women.

25. This relationship is well documented by Jacklyn Cock (1980).

26. Discussed further in chapter 8.

27. This tradition of the victim is discussed by Brian Winston (1988). While it applies to documentary filmmaking, it is useful for the discussion on representation generally, as it suggests that such representation frequently evokes empathy, but little social action.

28. I am grateful to my student Anastasia van Schalkwyk for pointing this out to me in the course of her work on women's political performance, particularly in the Toyi Toyi (see van Schalkwyk 1993).

29. I have expanded this idea in the context of the Images and Empire conference held at Yale University (February 1997). This paper examines the creation of a visual imagery in the constitution of the Shembe empire.

Chapter Two

1. Mandela's reference to the "children of Dinizulu" is an extremely important political signifier in contemporary South Africa. While the Inkatha Freedom party (along with Hollywood films) has quite consistently claimed "King" Shaka as the hero of "Zulu" resistance to colonialism in the region, the African National Congress has decided instead to use Dinizulu, the last of the Zulu chiefs to resist European domination. He was sent into exile after the Bambatha rebellion. On several occasions, when unity is called for in KwaZulu Natal, I have heard the historical figure of Dinizulu, rather than Shaka, used to signify black African resistance. This was poignantly demonstrated in Mandela's speech at the Sonke Festival, October 24, 1993, in Durban.

2. See Vilakazi et al. (1986), Sundkler (1961 [1948]), and Roberts (1936) for further explanation of Shembe's calling and visions.

3. The term *Ekuphakameni* is used in several contexts to refer to the original settlement, to heaven, and to the current church headquarters, also known as *Ebuhleni*. (See chap. 3.)

4. The Inanda Reserve is a property consisting of about 11,500 acres in an area situated about forty miles northwest of the city of Durban (Hughes 1990, 200–201).

5. I am using the idea of religious empire here as it is explained by Jean and John Comaroff (1991, chap. 7) for the civilizing mission in South Africa. Such an empire is likened to the Christian idea of the "kingdom of God." This differs from a more conventional Western separation of religion and politics. It certainly digresses from the idea of empire as a political entity constituted by aggressive military force. My use of the term *empire* is rather in keeping with the nineteenth-century South African Christian mission's "insistence that they sought only to rebuild the lost *Empire of God*" (Comaroff and Comaroff 1991, 255, my emphasis). As the Comaroffs comment, although the mission intended to keep ideas of church and state separate, in practice and in conversation it frequently blurred the boundaries. In contrast, historically Tswana and Nguni people have considered the political and the religious (and, I would add for Shembe, the economic) as part of a single set of practices.

It is in this sense that I refer to the Nazarite religious collectivity as a kind of "empire." I am suggesting, therefore, that while the Shembe "empire" was not engineered through military aggression (as was the "Zulu kingdom" discussed by Guy [1994], Colenbrander [1989], and others), it has, nonetheless, come to have grand ideas about the spiritual powers of the Shembe leaders (the founder, Isaiah, in particular) as well as about regional and global conversion and connection, what Said calls "ideas of overseas rule" (1993, xxiii). From the earliest days, followers of Isaiah Shembe are reported to have called him *Nkulunkulu* (the Zulu equivalent of "God"), while others likened his powers to those of Jesus Christ (Roberts 1936, 39).

These imagined global and heavenly connections are also evident in the freedom with which

Isaiah Shembe interpolated his own ideas in mission hymn and religious texts, as well as in numerous narratives told by Nazarite members. One such narrative is found at the beginning of chapter 5, in which the storyteller concludes "the nations of the world have been waiting for the Lord. Now they have heard that he is at *Ekuphakameni.*" Similarly, in the narrative at the beginning of chapter 3, Mr. Hlatswayo's dream reconstitutes the kingdom of heaven into one inhabited by Isaiah Shembe himself, a radical departure from the "heaven" of the Euro-American civilizing mission in southern Africa. More recently, ideas about the global possibilities for Nazarite religious practices have been demonstrated in the purchase of top-of-the-line motor vehicles for the leaders by their followers, and now, there are plans for Shembe to visit the superpower of the late twentieth century, the United States of America.

Imaginings of spiritual empire by the Nazarite community are for the most part just that, fictional constructions and connections. But I think my use of the term to discuss the Nazarite religious collectivity raises several questions about the ways in which "empire" has been privileged and critiqued in Western discourse. It also feeds into ideas of power and resistance. So, I wonder, do we imagine empire as an exclusively "Western" occupation, and resisting empire, a Third World prerogative? Can "resistance" ever be redefined for these "other" communities as an articulation of its own kind of power, that perhaps the "West" has to resist? This is certainly a question pertinent to contemporary South Africa, where "Western" culture and religions have in the past simultaneously been dominant yet minority forces. This is no longer the case. Further discussion of these issues will be fleshed out in a later publication.

6. I use the words *community* and *empire* when referring to the Nazarite religious collectivity, to articulate two different positions. *Community* will be used when I discuss the internal workings of the church, and *empire* will refer more to the relationship of *ibandla lamaNazaretha* to the larger regional, national, and global political economies.

7. Stuart and Malcolm (1986 [1951]), Preston-Whyte (1974), and Krige (1988 [1950]).

8. While Shembe functioned as a chief in the 1920s and 1930s, his position differed remarkably from that of other chiefs because he owned title deeds to the land he dispensed.

9. British sterling remained the monetary currency in South Africa until 1961, when South Africa became a republic separate from the British Commonwealth countries.

10. Witnesses before the 1930–32 Commission of Inquiry into the Social and Economic Conditions of Natives in South Africa (in the State Archives, Pretoria, K26/13,14,16) suggest repeatedly that "European" diseases, like syphilis, were contributing to the marked increase in infertility and stillbirths among African women.

11. *Mfecane* is the term given to this period of interclan warfare in southern Africa in the early nineteenth century, with Shaka as the most feared and vicious of all leaders. More recently the apartheid regime has used this period as its historical validation for "black on black violence" in the 1980s. See Comaroff and Comaroff (1991, 167–69); Wright and Hamilton (1989, 68–69).

12. Walker (1990, 177) remarks that a century later, women in the Native Reserves found themselves in a similar position, with the men away as migrant workers. She writes, "Already by 1920 the reserves were producing less than 50 per cent of the subsistence needs of their populations. . . . The onerous responsibility for food production under increasingly adverse circumstances fell more and more heavily on women."

13. It is not clear when or why polygamy became a traditional practice in southern Africa. It may have been practiced by the wealthy prior to King Shaka. With Shaka it seems to have become the ideal to which all should aspire.

14. See chapter 5 for a reference to Shembe in the song *"Oyinkosi amakhosi"* (He is the king of kings). This is a new text sung by the Nazarite youth choirs, to the tune of the Christmas carol "Joy to the World."

15. Krige (1988 [1950]) and Henry Fynn in his diary (Stuart and Malcolm 1986 [1951]) comment on the practice of *ukuhlobonga* (sexual activity not including penetration), which was permitted in Shaka's regiments, and among Zulu traditionalists, as a means of avoiding the loss of virginity in young girls.

16. Shaka, Dingane, and Mpande were all descendants of Senzangakhona, and are mentioned in Isaiah's liturgy, hymns, and catechism. Their historical errors are believed to be the sins for which subsequent generations have been cursed and are suffering.

17. *Nguni* is the collective term for the southern Bantu-speaking peoples, including the Ndebele, Swazi, Xhosa, Zulu, and Tswana (Branford 1991, 217).

18. Each homestead consisted of a main hut for the male head of the homestead, and several other huts, most of which contained one wife/concubine. In Henry Fynn's drawing of his homesteads (between pp. 110 and 111 of his published diary), there are at least ten huts per homestead. Of course, it is not known if these were accurate drawings in terms of the number of huts, but it still suggests an enormous entourage of women for Fynn!

19. Both of these are reproduced in Duminy and Guest (1989).

20. The reason for this strict control is explained by Stoler as reflecting the desire on the part of colonial governments to help the male settlers to acclimate to the new country quickly, through the help of native women. In addition, men were encouraged to find these women quickly, because it was believed that sustained abstention from sexual activity would result in poor health. The advantage to the colonizing governments in having men without families was that they could keep salaries low, and the men would work harder, undisturbed by the demands of European family lifestyles. Stoler goes so far as to say that European governments and businesses restricted the emigration of European women to the colonies, and refused to hire married men.

21. Katie Makanya (McCord 1995) recalled how her family had despised the Zulu clan in the latter part of the nineteenth century, and sought to avoid Zulus at all costs.

22. See Stuart and Malcolm (1986 [1951], 225), in which Fynn explains why the refugees turned on their own people. He writes:

> To account for this strange conduct on the part of the inhabitants of Natal, it must be remarked that the natives who are living under the protection of the traders are persons who have been dispossessed of their property and driven from their country by the Zulu chief, and who have the most inveterate hatred for him and the people under his subjection.

23. Etherington (1989a, 172) comments that under the "Shepstone system," colonial officials in control of the native reserves were supposed to make legal decisions for the African people according to "Native Law." "The customary practices of Natal's indigenous population were assumed to be the basis of Native Law but no one systematically studied them or wrote them down. Consequently, Native Law was what its interpreters said it was." This obviously created enormous tensions between the African people and the keepers of the law.

24. The discovery of gold (first in the 1870s, with the most important discovery being in 1886) and diamonds (also in the 1870s) signaled the birth of industrial capitalism in South Africa, and the subsequent need for cheap labor. (See Davenport 1987 [1977], 92, 102.)

25. The 1913 Land Act effectively pushed 87 percent of the entire South African population onto 13 percent of the land. There was also legislation such as the 1937 Native Laws Amendment Act, which sought to control black influx into the urban areas by removing "surplus" blacks from the region (Davenport 1987 [1977], 315).

26. See Marks (1970), Lambert (1989), Bosman (1907), and Stuart (1913).

27. The advantages of education for Africans were still contested by the African population. See Etherington (1989) and Marks (1989) on education in the Eastern Cape.

28. See Hughes (1990, 197–220).

29. Gaitskell (1990) writes that it is no coincidence that these skills acquired at the mission also trained young women for domestic service in European households.

30. Chatterjee (1989) discusses similar issues in the civilizing discourse of the British in terms of Indian women, and traditional ways in nineteenth-century India.

31. I suggest that in the centralized political economy of the royal homesteads of Shaka and Dingane, the control of marriage by the state was critical to the survival of the kingdom. Such control kept

the king's men as warriors and not as husbands. Henry Fynn's Diary (Stuart and Malcolm 1986 [1951]) suggests that the only men under Shaka's kingship allowed to marry were the very senior men—those who were too old to be good warriors.

32. *Kraal* has several meanings. It refers to (1) an enclosure for animals, (2) a village or settlement of an indigenous tribe, (3) a cluster of huts occupied by a clan group, or (4) the seat of the chief. It is derived from the Dutch word *kraal* (Branford and Branford 1991, 164–65).

33. Bongani Mthethwa and I did the translation from the Zulu in 1992. The Zulu, taken from pp. 4–6 in the hymnal, is as follows:

19.

Usinike ukukhuthala Nkosi Jehova emisebenzini yokusiphilisa ubuthongo bokuvilapha bungasembathi. Nkosi Jehova usinike umoya wokukhuthala silime sih-lakule silinde esilulimileyo nesikuhlakulileyo.

20.

Uyibusise Nkosi Jehvoa imisebenzi yezandla zethu. Siyakuncenga ukwamkele ukuncenga kwethu kungabi ngokusho kwethu kube ngokusho kwakho Nkosi yethu Thixo wethu.

21.

Ningavilaphi yisono ukuvilapha. Umuntu ovilaphayo ufana nenja ehlala ngokucela ukudla kubantu. Ekupheleni kwalomthandazo thabatha igeja ulime uzophila ngakho ungahambi ucela ukudla kubantu.

24.

Noma libalele lima, ngokuba awusazi isikhtathi uNkuluknulu azonisa izulu ngaso. Noma liyana lima, uhlakule, ulinde; kungonakali okulimileyo nokuhlakulileyo. Oboba uyezwake: ungabi yisedeleli sala mazwi.—Duteronomi 17:12.

33.

Ngokuba kwathiwa umuntu uyokudla umvuzo wezithukuthuku zeza ndla zakhe, washo uThixo ka Adam.

34. Durban is a coastal resort and its beachfront is lined with hotels. These women sit outside the hotels, selling beadwork, basketry, and an assortment of cheaply imported goods. For many of these women, this constitutes the sole means of survival for them and their children.

35. This information is contained in the Nazarite catechism, a document discussed further in chapter 3.

36. I was told this by a church member whose name I do not recall, but who attended the March gathering at *Vula Masango* (Open the Gate) on the KwaZulu Natal south coast, in 1992.

37. One example of this kind of discourse is to be found in a letter dated May 30, 1944, from the office of the Chief Native Commissioner of Natal, in Pietermaritzburg. It was written by the acting Chief Native Commissioner, who said the following about Galilee's desire to purchase land:

> I am unable to recommend that application as it is considered that the presence of a large community of the Shembe Sect in Clermont [just outside of Durban] would constitute an embarrassment in the maintenance of public health and aggravate the control over such diseases as smallpox in as much as members of this Sect object to vaccination and other protective measures. [Natal Archives, Pietermaritzburg NTS Vol. 3331 Ref. 1968/307.]

38. This document, however, reflects an apparent change of heart on the part of Dube toward Isaiah in its questioning of Isaiah's leadership. While I have not seen the document myself, I was told by Bongani Mthethwa that in this document Dube seems to be set on discrediting Isaiah. I suggest that this may reflect the conflict in African society in the first decades of this century. This conflict was felt between those educated Africans who sought respectability and incorporation into the larger South African political economy through education, Christianization, and the rejection of African tradition (viewed as backward and primitive), and Isaiah's insistence on the value of traditional cultural ways. See Coplan (1985) and Marks (1989) on the issue of respectability.

39. Bean (1989, 369) writes that Gandhi sought the revival of artisanship among his people.

> From the establishment of the Phoenix farm in 1904, Gandhi had committed himself to the simple life of labor. Machines were labor-saving devices that put thousands of laborers out of work, unthinkable in India where the masses were underemployed. Factory production facilitated the concentration of wealth in the hands of a few big capitalists, and transformed workers into "utter slaves."

40. The education of young girls in South Africa by missionaries in the nineteenth century is a relatively unexplored domain. Nevertheless, the work of Hughes (1990) and, more recently, of Dana Robert (1993) on Dutch Reformed work among rural Afrikaans-speaking girls suggests that American women missionaries played a crucial role in this process.

41. See Middleton-Kern (1978, 191–205) for a discussion of the training of the traditional healer (*isangoma*).

42. In chapter 3 there is some discussion of the distinction made between the concepts of illness and disease as discussed in Roseman (1991), Comaroff (1985), and Schofeleers (1991).

43. Serematakis (1991, 217) writes that

> [m]odernization has brought a paradigmatic shift in the social construction of reciprocity. The archeology of emotions has been marginalized and displaced by the literal economies of exchange. . . . It is the reduction of feeling to a psychological condition.

Chapter Three

1. *Bomhela isitimela samaMpondo* (the train from Pondoland) was one of the ways in which Isaiah Shembe was known by his followers. His movement as healer and preacher between Pondoland (south of KwaZulu Natal) and Zululand (north of the Tugela River) was likened to that of a train.

2. Nazarites would know the image from photographs of Isaiah on a horse. These reproductions are sold by church members in their local church markets.

3. We have translated the Zulu word *umoya* here as "wind," though it also refers to spirit. In this instance, the wind might be equated with the power of the "holy spirit," which in Nazarite epistemology is the way in which ancestral powers of Isaiah, Galilee, and Amos are spoken about.

4. The mist is usually a sign indicating the presence of female characters in the Nazarite cosmos. *Nomkhubulwana*, for example, appears to young girls when there is mist around (see chaps. 2 and 6).

5. Lighting a candle is not just about providing light. In *ibandla lamaNazaretha*, candles embody ancestral force for members. Married women, for example, make a monthly payment to cover the cost of candles, and candles are lit immediately after a member dies. They are kept alight until the body is buried.

6. The ambiguity is expressed in my juxtaposition of God/Shembe.

7. See Keirn (1978, 194) for a fuller explanation of ancestors in the traditional life of Zulu people; see Turner (1967, 9–16) for a similar process among the Ndembu of northwestern Zambia.

8. James Kiernan (pers. comm., 1993) says that in the early exchanges of missions with the African population, money became the symbol used in the measure of religious accountability (through the payment of membership fees, which were recorded in writing).

Serematakis (1991, 63) writes, "In a fully commodified society . . . the circulating currency is accepted as a permanent substitute of material objects and their value. In contrast, in economies that are not fully commodified, money has a limited autonomy in reference to other economic media . . . the token is directly connected to its material reference, author or site of origin."

9. Similarly, I explain in chapter 4 how song performance diverges from the printed hymn text.

10. Shembe requires that members stand up and share their experiences with others. This is explained further in chapter 8.

11. As explained in chapter 2, after the Bambatha Rebellion was so ruthlessly crushed it was an-

other fifty years before any African people considered the option of armed resistance. See Rich Mkhondo (1993, 179).

12. Ong (1988, 32) writes that spirit possession by young women in Malaysian factories protests against the transgression of moral boundaries; and Roseman (1991) writes for the Temiar (also of Malaysia) that where the balance between tradition and innovation is lost, illness occurs.

13. There are several Nazarite narratives that I have gathered in which these experiences have been talked about. Consistently, the restitution of community has been sought through the traditional Nguni modes of cleansing and sacrifice—such as the slaughtering of a goat to appease the ancestors. This frequently results in the return of living family members, or the appearance of those who have died, in the dream of an individual.

14. De Pina-Cabral (1987, 721) writes that the ordering of time and space both is created by and creates social order. In other words, a sense of community is evoked through the structuring of time. Discussing a rural community in Portugal, he remarks:

> On the one hand, community is essentially defined spatially, in socio-geographic terms; on the other hand, it depends for its reproduction on the preservation of social order. This, in turn, is achieved by manipulating temporality through a set of rituals which rely on repetitive time. . . . Thus, the destruction of community autarky is in-terpreted in terms of irreversible (linear) time, whilst its maintenance is dependent upon repetitive (cyclical) time.

15. Armstrong (in Keil 1979, 197) defines a trope as a space-time metaphor. This concept is linked to the notion of "affecting presence"—embodied in various expressive domains—and articulates a particular cultural value, feeling, or emotion (ibid., 194).

16. Roberts (1936) says that Isaiah owned about twenty pieces of land at the time of his death.

17. I am using the term *resistance* to refer to a process of boundary definition between groups, and cultural (re)construction within a group, which, in the South African context of conquest and domi-nation, has assumed a highly politicized face, and in that sense constitutes actions of resistance. The notion of "resistance" has been discussed extensively by Jean Comaroff (1985) and defined in terms of the Tshidi case, not as an assertion of "the viability of Tshidi resistance," but as a demonstration of "the cogent, if implicit, logic of their opposition to neocolonialism." She adds that this form of resistance is "frequently part and parcel of practices of subjective and collective construction" (ibid., 195).

18. Angela Davis (1998) discusses a parallel desire for freedom of movement in African-American communities in the Southern part of the United States in the 1920s.

19. Influx control legislation controlled the movement of black people between the white-controlled industrial centers and the bantustans—homelands. These laws required "non-European" people to carry passbooks (*dompas*) at all times. Comaroff (1985, 164) writes, "The usurpation of the freedom of movement and the setting up of barriers and boundaries seemingly capricious as they were insurmountable was a basic fact of Tshidi reality. . . . It was this regimentation of space, time, and passage that Tshidi rites of resistance sought to redefine."

20. Archival evidence suggests that Isaiah had enormous problems in purchasing land, with a number of court cases held by the state against him. He was frequently labeled a "cult" or "sect" leader, and various moral accusations were laid against him. Equally, in Clermont, KwaZulu Natal, the state rescinded a decision enabling Galilee to purchase land after he had paid for it.

The concern over the freedom of movement is manifest in South African black performance modes through the prevalence of the travel motif. See Gunner (1991) and Coplan (1987) for further discussion.

21. The sanctity of the circular shape resembles the form of the cattle byre, which, in traditional Nguni custom, is considered the most holy of spaces—the place inhabited by the ancestors. Unlike the temple, however, the cattle byre could not be approached by young virgins, who were not permit-ted to pass too close to cattle. Furthermore, historically, Zulu king Dingane's royal homestead was also circular in shape (see Stuart and Malcolm 1986 [1951], 325)—Shembe's temples resemble the arrangement of this homestead, though with far less social hierarchy demarcated.

22. I certainly have not visited all of these sites. Limited by time, I visited only those places where the main gatherings of Nazarite members are held.

23. When these notions are applied to the young female virgins, as discussed in chapter 6, they constitute not only the difference between self and other, but also cultural power.

24. Sundkler (1976, 197) writes that there are as many as fifty hymns in the hymnal that focus on *Ekuphakameni*.

25. See Roberts (1936) for more discussion of Nazarite *hlonipha*.

26. For more information on these rites see Vilakazi (1954, 98–101).

27. In this regard, Hymn 11, stanza 4, reads, "So that they rejoice with those/ who came from the clouds/ Whose robes are cleansed/ And made pure white."

28. Edwards (1991, 19) writes that in early Christian groups there was also a predominance of women, but that by the end of the second century men within Christianity "recognized the challenge to gender roles [posed] by women and gave religious authority to men. The growing institutionalization of Christianity, which might have given women a greater voice in an important cultural sphere, instead restricted women's religious activities. The establishment of Christianity as a state religion brought more extensive participation and control by men." She continues, saying that women's participation in musical performance paralleled their wider church involvement: thus initially both men and women sang in church worship. By the fourth century, however, women's voices had been silenced completely. There was also a general complaint with mission churches in South Africa in the nineteenth century that they gave little space to black male authority, and there was a desire to accommodate traditional chiefly authority. This may account for the traditional forms of institutional authority in the church that have increasingly silenced the voices of women in terms of public preaching, though not in song.

There was a need for a religious leader to embody political leadership, because of the lack of representation of African people in the state. See Combs-Schilling (1989, 292) for a discussion of a similar situation with Moroccan Muhammad V.

29. Turner (1967, 100) says "Authority of the elders is absolute, because it represents the absolute, the axiomatic values of society in which are expressed the 'common good' and the common interest." Turner remarks however, that the authority of the leaders extends only insofar as they represent the common good of society.

30. Bongani Mthethwa suggested that the women were required to observe certain traditions of respect toward the men, which, in the eyes of Galilee, took too long. While I do not know what those gestures of respect included, Vilakazi (1954) writes that in Zulu traditional belief a woman may not speak in public when men are present. This is corroborated by Comaroff and Comaroff (1992, 255), who say that the

> power of speech was all of a piece with the capacity of persons to act positively upon the world—most cogently in the form of curses, spells, praise poetry, and oratory, the "great words"... that men might use as weapons.... That is why women, as beings of limited social competence, were excluded from such... "words" as public debate, poetic recital, or ritual incantation.

31. The 9 A.M. services are not usually held in homes where men and women work, and children attend school.

32. It may also be that these "holy months," six months apart, reflect the breaks in six-month-long mining contracts for migrant laborers. As I suggest below, the return to the sabbath on a Saturday facilitates the rite of transition and purification between the defilement of the workplace and the purity of the traditional performance.

33. The "gate" is a metaphor that appears frequently in the texts of the hymnal, and, I suggest, refers to the opening of the gate that is at the entrance to the way of Shembe. See van Gennep (1960) on the sacralization of openings to facilitate territorial passage.

34. The commemoration of the chiefs, particularly in December, probably had a dual purpose—first, to retain chiefly support. Isaiah frequently raised the ire of chiefs for drawing young women, in

particular, away from their families, the hold of patriarchy and by extension chiefly control (see chap. 4). Second, December is an important month in the history of the struggle of black South Africans in KwaZulu Natal against European imperialism, for it was in December 1838 that the Afrikaner *trekkers,* under the leadership of Andries Pretorius, dealt a crushing defeat to Zulu forces, under Dingane. This took place at the *Ncome* River, and is remembered as the "Battle of Blood River."

As Colenbrander (in Duminy 1989, 91) remarks, this battle, in which three thousand Zulus lost their lives and an enormous amount of land to the Boers, has come "to serve as a potent symbol in Afrikaner folk consciousness." But it is also most poignantly written about in the catechism from the Zulu perspective. In Nazarite eschatology, this battle, and the subsequent battle for power between chiefs Dingane and Mpande, and the flight of Mpande to the side of the Boers, spelled the demise of the Zulu nation. Colenbrander cites Zulu oral tradition, which expresses these moments in Zulu history, in the year of 1838, as "the breaking of the rope that held the nation together"—the death of the nation. Shembe's liturgy refers to these actions as the sins of the forefathers, for which subsequent generations are suffering—living in a post–death-of-the-nation situation. The only remedy perceived is the confession of "sin." See also Rich Mkhondo (1993, 62–63) on current Shaka Day celebrations in KwaZulu Natal under Chief Minister Buthelezi and King Zwelethini.

35. There is a remarkable resonance here with the biblical account of the birth of Jesus in the New Testament, which then becomes blurred with the Old Testament story of Moses, the children of Israel, and the provision of manna from heaven.

36. I have interviewed a woman faith healer in *ibandla lamaNazaretha* (February 1993) who tells a similar story about her own birth, only she explains the reason for her being a woman, rather than a man, is that her grandfather did not obey the commands of Shembe. As punishment to him for his disobedience the child born with special powers was a girl, rather than a boy (see Muller 1993).

37. Cucchiari (1988) defines conversion as a mechanism for new ideological affiliations of group formation. In other words, she does not see conversion as a purely inner transformation, but one that transforms the self toward more integrative systems of meaning, personal autonomy, and moral responsibility. Conversion is an individual affair, which involves one in a lifelong struggle that is communally oriented.

38. Comaroff (1985, 207) says that the Tshidi Zionists distinguish between "praying with words" and "praising with the feet."

39. Isaiah changed to Saturdays rather than Sundays in the 1920s after a dream—see Vilakazi et al. (1986).

40. Roberts (1936, 96) writes that services were held "along the lines" of the Wesleyan structure. They are now more clearly defined, and embody the historical images more consistent with Nguni understanding.

41. Nazarite members are all expected to own watches so that they will know when to hold their services when they are not with other members, and to arrive on time for those held communally.

42. The catechism warns people who do not arrive on time: "Do not be late for the service or you might not appear in the heavenly picture of the people present when the photo was taken."

43. The story associated with the bell is outlined at the beginning of chapter 6.

44. These sermons usually embody personal experiences of healing or miracles in the lives of members. In this regard, Crain's (1991) discussion of Ecuadorean narratives is pertinent. She says that the use of dream imagery and similar encounters in the narratives is informed by local knowledge in order to construct a political discourse from the margins. In this context, these stories attempt to reshape society increasingly controlled by external forces. "The stories are filled with public meaning and they speak of the collective troubles facing the community" (ibid., 86). (These will be discussed in greater detail in chap. 8.)

45. See Comaroff (1985, 236) for a similar situation with the Zionists in South Africa.

46. Vidal (1989, 111) defines a festival as "an annual event or anniversary in remembrance or commemoration of a god, spirit, ancestor, king, or historical occurrence." Quoting Ogunba, he says that the festival "is a great artistic tradition in Africa . . . with deep spiritual values." In the Nazarite community, festivals of dance occur whenever they are called for by Shembe, but they also commemorate the ancestors.

47. See earlier discussion of money in Nazarite ritual.

48. Sundkler (1960) writes that this pilgrimage used to be called the Feast of the Tabernacles after the Jewish festival of the Old Testament. The kinds of huts built now are temporary shelters, which in the black townships are called *imijondolo*. In the Nazarite context, however, they have a double meaning—the first is tabernacle, in line with the festival. The second translation of the term *idokodo* is a temporary shelter constructed from grass and branches in times of war (Doke et al. 1990, 165). In chapter 6, I suggest that the young virgins function as spiritual warriors in Shembe's war against moral degradation and the destruction of community. The *dokodo* then picks up an additional nuance on the mountain—as the site of total moral purity.

49. Dube (1992, 76) quotes a portion from a Nazarite sermon that stressed both *(a)* the importance of freedom of movement for Nazarite worship and *(b)* that those who worship should not involve themselves in politics, because political activity was life-threatening.

50. The pass laws were perhaps the most hated of all apartheid legislation, for they effectively monitored all movement of black South Africans in and out of the urban areas—which was always considered by the state as only a temporary place of residence for black South Africans (even if a person had lived and worked there all his or her life). The laws were administered by requiring all those who were not white to carry passbooks, more commonly known among those who carried them as the *dompas* (the stupid pass).

51. Rörich (1989, 81) quotes an unnamed South African singer who told her, "You whites see psychiatrists; we blacks sing. It's our therapy, our way of expressing our experience."

52. The symbolism of the bird is not really clear—Berglund (1989, 38–40; 57) mentions two birds, one a sign of good fortune, the other of bad; but it seems to be linked with lightning anyway. Hymn 101/1 includes the eagle, which may be what Mrs. Manqele is referring to. It reads: Mighty winged eagle, raise your wing/ that we may get inside/ and hide in you, Rock of Ages/ Good hen, love and protect us.)

Kombi is a means of public transport, particularly for black commuters. There have been numerous attacks on innocent victims using taxis. The process of getting out of a taxi and kneeling down may be an imitation of what has actually happened to her or her friends while in a taxi. There is a small body of literature on the taxi industry in South Africa. See, for example, Leslie Bank, 1991, "A Culture of Violence: The Migrant Taxi Trade in QwaQwa, 1980–90," in Preston-Whyte and Rogerson (eds.), 124–42.

53. The last fifteen years have seen the ethnographic analysis of dreams and dreaming given a new lease on life in, among other literature, three collections that have focused specifically on dreaming: the volume of *Ethos* dedicated to dreams (1981), Barbara Tedlock (1987), and Shaw and Jedrej (1992).

54. They are never used as a means of seeking out the individual who has brought misfortune, but rather, of discovering how the recipient of misfortune has sinned—which is more in line with the confessional mode of Christianity as explained by Foucault (1988).

55. These terms are defined in the glossary and explained in more detail in chapter 8.

Chapter Four

1. Rycroft (1971, 219) writes that the Zulu style of song and dance performance called *isigekle*, a style Joseph Shabalala says is used for contemporary traditional marriages, is a style "without fixed notes," i.e., does not use fixed pitch or melodies. *Isigekle* is more improvisational in character. It is not clear just what Cinikile Mazibuko meant in this context, though, as the discussion on women's performance practice demonstrates, she could as easily be referring to any or all of these interpretations.

2. In Appendix H of Williams (1983) there are translations of a selection of hymns that were composed by Tiyo Soga and published in Xhosa by the Lovedale press in 1864.

3. A rather unusual collection of traditional texts set in four-part harmony by Dube has been transcribed by David Rycroft and published by Natal University Press.

Yvonne Huskisson compiled a list of other black choral composers when she worked at the South African Broadcast Corporation. In addition, there is some discussion of mission-influenced composition by black South Africans in Malan (1979, 1:85–107), under "Bantu Composers of South Africa."

4. There were three broad religious responses among African people in South Africa to the impact of the European and American mission: they converted and joined the established denominations; they created their own religious groups, drawing on the forms and practices of the mission church, but with their own leaders (Zionists); or they, with a philosophy of "Africa for Africans," created religious groups that used the Bible (and the Old Testament specifically) as their guide (Ethiopianists). (See Sundkler on this subject.) *Ibandla lamaNazaretha* is best categorized as Ethiopianist.

5. There are also accounts of this process, in terms of other repertories, by Ballantine (1993), Cockrell (1987), and L. Meintjes (1990).

6. An analysis of this process of the transformation of certain parts of the Wesleyan and Baptist hymn repertory into a specifically Nazarite mode of performance and style was done by the late Bongani Mthethwa in his incomplete doctoral thesis. While Mthethwa provides an important discussion on the way in which Isaiah transformed the mission repertory to suit his own traditional cultural ways, he does not analyze the origins of the mission hymns in terms of possible African-American connections. Nevertheless, he does say that the melody of one of Isaiah's hymns is strongly suggestive of the American "Battle Hymn of the Republic." This might provide evidence of possible links between Isaiah's hymns and the African-American influence.

There are two further intriguing, albeit unexplored, links between Isaiah's repertory and the Baptist spirituals sung by white Southerners in the United States. The recording by Lomax (1977) provides remarkable parallels in terms of performance practice, soundscape, and theology between the spirituals and Isaiah's own hymns. Isaiah's song style is commonly acknowledged to be quite different from other traditional and neotraditional Nguni songs, although they draw on traditional principles such as call-and-response (and other aspects I discuss in chaps. 3 and 4). The texts of the spirituals and those of Nazarite women's narratives have several religious metaphors in common. For example, both use the ticket as the means to entering heaven (see Lomax 1977, B/8, which reads, "Get your ticket for the airplane ride, for Jesus the Savior is coming again"); and religious accountability is articulated in terms of recordkeeping (ibid., B/9). In Nazarite narratives this is expressed in terms of "writing one's name in the Book of Life."

Finally, while the connection between white spirituals and Isaiah Shembe may seem tenuous at best, I should point out that Isaiah was himself a member of the African Baptist church before forming his own religious group. Obviously, extensive historical research would be required to substantiate these musings on specific transatlantic connections.

7. Oosthuizen is criticized by several scholars from a number of angles. The most powerful criticism, however, has been that his intellectual framework lacked an understanding of the ethnographic context. In other words, while the idea of examining indigenous texts in order to construct indigenous theology is academically sound, his lack of understanding of the media and style of inscription has led him to perhaps draw incorrect conclusions about the religious group.

8. The metaphor of the path in musical performance is not unique to Nazarite performance. For example, see also Bruce Chatwin (1988 [1987]) for a discussion of Australian aboriginal musical beliefs, and Marina Roseman (1991) on the Temiar of Malaysia.

9. The reference to "hymn-carpentry" alludes to the problem in mission churches in Africa in which European hymns were frequently translated into indigenous languages with total disregard for the rules intrinsic to tonal languages such as Zulu. Mthethwa (n.d.) discusses this matter, focusing on the fact that a single word in Zulu can have several meanings depending on the tonal contours of its articulation. Quite often missionaries were not aware of the variations in meaning, and many a Christian hymn became a site of obscenity for those who truly knew and understood the language.

10. Before Isaiah's followers began to sing his compositions exclusively, he had drawn on the hymn translations of the Wesleyan mission. Blacking (1980) and Kiernan (1990) discuss the parallel practice of using mission repertories in Zionist communities in South Africa.

11. This reference to the heavenly messenger as masculine seems to contradict what Sundkler writes about the female messenger giving the hymns. This may be explained by the fact that Sundkler

spoke directly with Galilee, while Vilakazi et al. (1986) were (possibly) given this information by church members. It may also be an arbitrary assigning of gender, as the Zulu language does not distinguish between male and female indefinite articles. See, for example, my transcriptions of narratives in which English versions often refer to Shembe as she, and not he. I have indicated this by changing the she to [he].

12. Comaroff and Comaroff (1991) remark on the importance of newspapers in educating and civilizing the black South African elite.

13. Similarly, William Taylor (1987) writes about the keeping of miracle events in books at certain Mexican shrines.

14. Nazarite member Mvangeli Mthembeni Mpanza told me in July 1997 that a new version of the hymnal has been published, although I have not seen it yet. The format of this version is intended to more accurately reflect the syntax and poetics of traditional Nguni poetry than the 1940 version of the hymnal does.

15. See Okphewo (1992, chap. 4).

16. This is an interesting slip, because in traditional Zulu thought, the snake represents the ancestors (Berglund 1989 [1976], 94), and the skin of the snake is traditionally used to cure a woman having difficulty in giving birth (ibid., 96).

17. Roseman (1991, 59) discusses a similar process with the Temiar in Malaysia; as does Feld (1982) for the Kaluli in Papua New Guinea, who connect personal history and the landscape as a means of evoking collective emotions of sorrow and nostalgia.

18. The sacralization of the natural environment, and the rural areas in particular, was not unique to Isaiah Shembe. Sundkler (1960 [1948], 93) remarks that "[w]hereas the City is the breeding ground of sects, the Reserve is the hatching-ground, and as such it is indispensable to the City Church." He continues by saying that to the Zionist groups (I have classified Isaiah as Ethiopianist rather than Zionist; see n. 4 above), "the Reserve is the Canaan with Bethesdas and Jordans, the pools and rivers where the sick are healed, and Hills of Zion, the holy hilltops where prayers and sacrifices are presented to Jehovah."

19. Rycroft (1971, 214–15) is of the opinion that other than the friction drum used in female initiation songs, most of the drums now used in South Africa have been borrowed from non-Nguni neighbors. He writes that there "is no evidence that elaborate drums and percussion ensembles like those found elsewhere in Africa have ever held a place in [Nguni] communal dance music."

Nevertheless, the drum remains a contested symbol in indigenous religious groups. It is used extensively by the Zionist movement. Jean Comaroff (1985, 230) endorses Rycroft's theory of the absence of drum ensembles for precolonial Tswana, though she says that Tswana Zionists are adamant that the drum has always been part of their dance tradition. Contrary to Rycroft, Comaroff cites Harriet Ngubane (*Body and Mind in Zulu Medicine* [Cambridge: Cambridge University Press, 1977]), who says that the drum "was part of the *ngoma* cult of possession, divination, and healing" among the Zulu.

20. Dargie (1987) writes that for the Xhosa Zionists, the drum they use is called *igubu,* and "is patterned on the European brass-band bass drum, and is usually made by stretching cow-hide over both ends of a section cut from a 44-gallon drum." The impact of the Salvation Army on black performance culture—not only in South Africa, but certainly in those areas in Africa that were colonized by the British and Americans—has not yet been analyzed. Ranger (1975) and Coplan (1985) both make passing references to the Salvation Army in their research. Certainly, in my own research in KwaZulu Natal, I am finding increasing numbers of black musicians who have in one way or another been provided instruments and/or training by the Salvation Army.

21. I was given this information by Rob Allingham (August 1993), archivist at Gallo Records in Johannesburg, South Africa, who also provided me with a copy of the recording. See chapter 5 for further discussion of these recordings.

22. Where permission has been obtained, all songs discussed in this book have been included on the accompanying compact disc.

23. Kirby provides no evidence for the historical "authenticity" of the sound, and I suggest, based

on the work of Bongani Mthethwa, that Kirby's statement is incorrect. In this regard, Mthethwa strongly contends that Shembe's repertory is a cultural accommodation and synthesis of two different musical styles—that of Euro-American hymnody (i.e., distilled in the Baroque period of European music history) and that of Zulu tradition.

24. Rycroft (1971, 216) debunks the assumption that all Nguni music is pentatonic, saying only that "[e]arlier claims by some writers that Nguni music was pentatonic were no doubt based upon limited experience, perhaps of only one type of Nguni music. . . ." He also remarks that "even within a single tribe or family, a variety of 'scales' may be found" (ibid.).

25. Vilakazi et al. (1986) suggest that hymns 1–157 are all in either the Western or Shembe style. Hymn 158 is the first in the indigenous style, and is meant for religious dance. This is the style into which the Nazarite women's performance fits. (They remark that the hymns in "Shembe's style" have also increasingly been used for religious dance.)

26. Comaroff and Comaroff (1991, 250) write that for Protestants "it was the Word, the literal message of God, that, more than anything else, bore the divine light into the dark recesses of heathen hearts and minds." They continue (ibid., 251) that this Word "was, of course, the written word; its faith, the faith of the book."

27. The organization of sacred time in the Western Christian church is, to some extent, cyclical. This is borne out by the repetition of specific rituals at particular moments in the twelve-month period of a single year—Easter, Christmas, and so forth. There is, however, a marked distinction in the way in which this time is objectified, measured, and spent in the Western sense, and the stress upon taking time in *ibandla lamaNazaretha*. I am suggesting in this chapter that the differences in approach are well illustrated in the different approaches to time in the Western style of Nazarite worship, and that of sacred dance.

28. Graeme Ewens (1991, 188) quotes South African musician and filmmaker Molephe Pheto, who recalled,

> Religion, remember, was a very strong influence on us, and the guitar was the instrument of Satan. The religious attitude was that if you played guitar you were going to Hell, whereas if you played the trumpet you were going to Heaven. Well, it's in the Bible somewhere that trumpets shall sound.

29. Since my research has been with the female membership of *ibandla lamaNazaretha*, and I have been unable (because I am a woman) to attend men's meetings, I have recorded only women's singing, youth choirs, and congregational worship. Based on these recordings, my conclusion is that there does seem to be a range of song performance styles in this religious group, both diachronically and synchronically. I have focused largely on women's religious dance, and in chapter 5, discuss the youth choir and cassette repertories.

30. For discussion of *maskanda* performance see Muller (forthcoming, 1999a).

31. For further discussion of the study of tonal shifts in language and melodic contours in South Africa, see Blacking (1995, chap. 2).

32. Msomi (1975, 31) describes this drum as follows:

> [a] wooden drum—It is sometimes used nowadays and appears to be borrowed, and the term is used chiefly as the modern word for European drum, because of its real meaning of anything hollow like a calabash emptied of its pulp. It has a wooden resonator (made from a tree trunk), two skin heads laced in position by thongs, and two padded beaters. The method of performance is identical with that of the European. It is nowadays played by the religious sects called "Zionists" in South Africa and the witch doctors, as well as Shembe's religious sect, the Church of Nazareth.

33. I was told that the women who sing above the others in a performance, and also those who start the singing, are the ones who are considered to be the most powerful in the spiritual sense (N. Mthethwa, pers. comm., August 1993). Similarly, Bongani Mthethwa told me that in Zulu tradition, the political power of a leader should always be reinforced by his musical leadership.

Chapter Five

1. The words were written by Eric Nthuli, Assistant Secretary General of the Nazareth Baptist Youth for Shembe. The song was the set piece for the first youth choir competition in *ibandla lamaNazaretha* (1991), and was sung to the music of the popular Christmas carol "Joy to the World."

2. Even though many of its song texts have a religious focus, *isicathamiya* is positioned quite differently from the Nazarite hymn repertory, because it includes both religious and secular texts. Its context of performance is also typically a competition, rather than ritual performance, and while Shabalala is clearly the best-known exponent of the genre and has shaped its recent stylistic sensibility, the history of the genre precedes Shabalala (see Erlmann 1995) and is not tied to a religious group in the way Shembe's song repertory is.

3. I am indebted to Kay Shelemay, who pointed out this relationship to me in her urban ethnomusicology seminar at New York University in 1987.

4. All information on Radio Zulu (or Ukhozi Radio, as it is now called) comes from an interview conducted with Rev. Prince Zulu at Natal Radio, July 11, 1997.

5. *Makwaya* refers to black South African choral performance whose historical roots go back to nineteenth-century Western popular song and classical choral repertory written in solfege, with Handel's *Messiah* as the most frequently sung. See Erlmann (1991) and Coplan (1985) for further discussion of this style.

6. Pewa lists Sam Shabalala's program *Umculo waMakwaya* (*Ukhozi* Radio, Sundays at 1 p.m.) and the televised programs directed by Thulasizwe Nkabinde, initially called *uNqambothi* and later changed to *Mathe-Melodi*, also broadcast on Sundays (Pewa 1995, 6).

7. The binary between "African" and "Western" is typically a crude reduction of historically variable and politically contested meanings and attributions that cannot be explored here. See chap. 1, n. 3, for some discussion of the "African" label.

8. Chicco's claims have been refuted by various people, who suggest that his involvement in drug trading has earned him more money than his music business. All the same, Chicco clearly managed to tap into a fairly large market. Sales figures in the music industry, at whatever level, are generally hard to come by.

9. See Comaroff (1985) and Kiernan (1990) for discussion of Zionists in South Africa.

10. See, for example, Erlmann (1993), Feld (1988), Garafalo (1993), Hernandez (1993), Lipsitz (1993), L. Meintjes (1990), and Taylor (1997).

11. I would like to thank Duke University graduate student Georgiary McElveen, who brought this controversy to the attention of a seminar I ran on African and African-American Music at the University of North Carolina, Chapel Hill, in 1997. The controversy generated considerable debate in mainstream news media, like the *Village Voice* and *Newsweek* magazine.

12. Unfortunately, these kinds of cassettes are highly sought after by many, though few have the money to buy them. I cannot comment on the contents because the copy I purchased disappeared from my research collection while I was living in South Africa.

13. Though there may have been other cassettes that generated controversy in *ibandla lamaNazaretha*, I have focused here on Mbatha's cassette for very pragmatic reasons—I have a copy of it and was able to interview him, and all the people I spoke to about the cassette knew exactly what I was referring to, suggesting that there was fairly widespread discussion about it in the religious community.

14. The idea of the "self-made" person is fairly common among other musicians in KwaZulu Natal. For example, the Zulu guitarists in the genre called *maskanda* typically claim that no one taught them how to play guitar. What they learned from others they learned by watching and listening, by imitation, but not through formal instruction. Individual musicians pride themselves on the peculiarity and individuality of their compositional and stylistic achievements (see Davies 1994 and Muller 1996a).

15. R 1500 would translate directly to about $350 in international exchange rate terms. It is per-

haps more informative to say that for many migrant workers in South Africa, R 1500 would be a good monthly salary.

16. This use of the word *father* in reference to church leader Vimbeni Shembe is to be understood on many levels. First, each Shembe is respectfully called *Baba,* a Zulu word meaning "father." On the one hand, then, Mbatha adheres to a Nazarite convention. On the other hand, the appellation of *father* for Shembe the religious leader takes on an extraordinary political significance in the region, because President Mandela is now viewed by millions as the "father" of the nation. Years of political turbulence and the migration of young males (young fathers) from rural to urban areas have contributed to the significant breakdown of both extended and nuclear family units among black South Africans. In the families of the majority of ordinary black South Africans, very few of the present young generation have any direct contact with their fathers. So political and religious figures take on the symbolic roles of fathering, in particular.

This trend is powerfully exemplified in two recent political contexts: the numerical predominance of mothers telling the stories about sons, fathers, and husbands, and Mbongeni Ngema's *Sarafina!* production, whose central protagonist was a woman. In a provocative discussion with students in my seminar on South African performance at New York University (spring 1997), which grew out of a paper written by Stephanie Haber-Hirsch, we unpacked one reading of the female protagonist (in a male-dominated protest-theater tradition) as Sarafina symbolizing the castrated Nelson Mandela. In this sense, through the apartheid years, the political scene might be characterized as a feminized one, i.e., dominated by incarcerated (and symbolically castrated) male leaders, led by the powerful presence of the "mother of the nation" (Nelson's wife Winnie; Sarafina in the stage production) who will never really lead, because she only stands in for Nelson Mandela while he is imprisoned. When Nelson is released, Winnie is castrated; (female) Sarafina becomes the (male) person of Nelson.

17. In South Africa, religious repertories are treated differently from other popular performances in terms of royalty collection. While the individual composer may copyright his or her compositions, royalties are not collected for church performances. However, if an individual, like Mbatha, makes an arrangement of these tunes, that arrangement is governed by the regular rules of copyright (pers. comm., South African Music Rights Organization/SAMRO representative, May 1998).

Chapter Six

1. Mr. Dhlomo kindly gave me copies of many of the stories told to him by women members. He had typed these on long rolls of paper, making them look like biblical images of scrolls. This abbreviated story was translated by Sazi Dlamini, a graduate student at the University of Natal, Durban.

2. Traditional Nguni cosmology distinguishes between dreams—which happen while a person is asleep—and visions, which happen while one is awake. Dreams are the medium for communication with the ancestral domain, and occur quite frequently for most people. Visions are thought to constitute a trance, and are associated with spiritual empowerment. Visions come to those called to be spiritual leaders, such as *izangoma* (traditional healers) and religious prophets (such as Isaiah Shembe) (Themba Mbhele, pers. comm., June 4, 1993).

3. This distinction seems to suggest that the appearance of *Nomkhubulwana* was considered a rare and extremely special event in the life of an individual.

4. The relationship between the female figure of *Nkosazana yezulu* and virgin girls shifts in *ibandla lamaNazaretha,* where the special spiritual connection is now between Shembe (the man) and the virgins. The gendered reversal is tantalizing to say the least, and resurfaces in my later discussion of the hymn texts, in which Isaiah takes the voice of a woman in one of these hymns.

5. I must point out that theologically and epistemologically, drawing the relationship between the Lord and the virgin figure into the earthly realm is a highly contested matter, both within the church membership and among other scholars of religion. This is not so much about the relationship between the Lord and the virgin as it is about whether Shembe is the black Christ, whether the followers of Shembe are Christian or not, whether Shembe is an ancestor only, or if he is in fact God incarnate.

6. Krige (1988 [1950] 233) says that "Leopard" was a title frequently used in praise of a chief, whose name was considered sacred, and thus unutterable.

7. See Bozzoli (1991), Coplan (1988), and Erlmann (1991) for the analysis of texts as a means of understanding consciousness; and Oosthuizen's (1969) contested analysis of Nazarite hymn texts as a means of extracting the "theology" of Isaiah Shembe. The central issue in the contest is whether one can infer from the hymn texts if the followers of Shembe are Christian or not.

8. Those children living on Nazarite religious spaces learn the rhythms of Nazarite singing and dancing from a very early age. I found several children vocalizing rhythmic patterns and stressing the beats with their feet on several occasions. In September 1991, one of the grandchildren of Shembe, a little boy who was only just old enough to walk, danced for me while the girls' procession was moving around the temple. He responded to the drum rhythms he heard by lifting and stamping his feet, articulating the rhythms and melodic shape through the raising and lowering of his legs.

9. Chernoff (1979) writes that a chief's moral integrity is represented by his participation in dance festivals.

10. Doke et al. (1990) define *ibayi* as a "piece of cloth worn by Native girls, generally tied over one shoulder (for purposes of modesty); shawl." Klopper (1991, 148) writes that the *ibayi* was formerly short and made of leather. It was replaced by a blanket wrapped around the body, and cotton clothes as early as 1850.

11. In the *Illustrated London News*, February 8, 1930, p. 203, there is a photograph of the boys dancing in uniform. This is an important historical detail. The dance style and indigenized uniform of the older men strongly resembles English/Scottish fife and pipe band parade uniforms.

Roberts (1936, 92) also comments on the kilts. She says that the tartan ones are worn with white tunics, rugby socks, and heavy black boots, with bead circlets around the head. The black pleated skirts are worn with pith helmets.

12. See Brandel-Syrier (1962) and Gaitskell (1981).

13. Indian here refers to immigrants from India who came initially as indentured laborers to work in the sugar fields in Natal and Zululand (now the province of KwaZulu Natal) between 1860 and 1911. Maureen Swan (1985, 1) explains, "Natal offered its Indian workers a five-year term of indenture which began on the day of arrival in the colony. A free return passage was available after five years indentured plus five years free labor. Until 1890, an ex-indentured worker had the choice of exchanging his return passage for a plot of land." She goes on to say that 52 percent of migrants stayed on. In addition, in 1875, the first Indian merchants, who paid their own way to South Africa, began to arrive in Natal.

There are a number of Nazarite stories that include Indian and European people who came to Shembe for healing.

14. A South African Press Association article reported in the *Natal Witness* (November 30, 1992, 5), entitled "I feel so strong wearing my beads," quotes historian Andre Procter as saying that beads are not valued so much for their aesthetic beauty as for their communicative ability in the domains of religion, politics, social order, and gender. Of the white beads worn by a traditional healer, he remarks, "They are not just decorations or insignia. They are an absolutely intrinsic part of the process of communicating with the spirit world."

15. The term *manyano* refers to the prayer unions of black South African women. These are discussed further in chapter 8, and by Brandel-Syrier (1962).

16. *Illustrated London News* (February 8, 1930, 203).

17. Khaba Mkhize, *Natal Witness* (September 30, 1993), in an article entitled "Clothing that Talks," writes on the array of traditional attire worn with great pride, particularly by women, at political rallies in South Africa. He discusses the meanings encoded in each item of clothing. This marks a significant transformation of attitudes toward African traditions, which for decades have been devalued and labeled "uncivilized," "primitive," and resistant to progress.

Similarly, Powell (in Maurer 1979) writes about a parallel mode of historical inscription by Native Americans. He says:

> Being preliterate societies, these [people] . . . relied on the spoken word and image to convey the essence of both myth and history. Just as a warrior would recount his successful adventures in great detail through oration and song, so would his clothing, its decoration, and his personal adornment proclaim these valorous actions.

18. This was effected for migrant workers through legislation such as the Natives Registration and Protection Bill (1923), Native Trust and Land Act (1936), and the Influx Control Act (1937), all of which considered all workers as temporary sojourners in urban areas.

19. Turner (1967, 97–98) describes this condition as one in which there is a physical, but not a social, reality.

20. See Schechner's discussion (1991 [1990], Introduction) on liminality and ritual performance.

21. The notion of resistance has been hotly debated in recent literature—Abu-Lughod (1990), Comaroff (1985), Serematakis (1991), and Foucault (1980), to name a few. My suggestion that it is a limited form of resistance draws on Bell's discussion of ritual and power (1990), in which she writes:

> Ritualization may be a particularly effective strategy for the social construction of a *limited form of empowerment when explicit discourse is impossible or counterproductive.* [Bell 1990, 311, emphasis my own.]

This is the light in which resistance must be viewed in the analysis of *ibandla lamaNazaretha,* for there is a strong sense of defiance against the state, particularly in the earlier decades of the movement—which was, however, veiled in religious discourse.

22. See Kunene (1981) for one example of state censure of the arts, and of literature in particular.

23. While this will be discussed in detail below, see Warner (1983 [1976], 7) for a discussion of the way in which Gospel writer Luke similarly interweaves Old Testament images to create a powerful narrative on the coming of the Christ; and Guevin (1989) for discussion of the use of parables to shape the moral development of a community.

See also Hebdige's (1979) discussion of Rastafarianism and the use of the Bible as a mechanism of cultural empowerment and resistance.

24. While Amos had only one wife, he is believed to have more than a hundred children. These children were either given as gifts or procreated through concubinage.

25. MaSangweni is the leader of the maidens at present. She has been with Shembe since 1945, when she was given to Galilee Shembe.

26. See Roberts (1936, 94) and Raum (1973) for further discussion of this notion in the Zulu cultural context.

27. The account and analysis of the *umgonqo* ritual draws on two main sources: my own fieldnotes, which consist of my own observations and those of church members, and the secondary literature by Krige (1968), Kiernan (1992), and Klopper (1991). As will become evident, these sources often present conflicting explanations and details about the ritual. In addition, Roberts (1936, 120–23) provides a much earlier account of puberty rites held for the girls living with *umpathi.* This description bears a remarkable resemblance to Krige's later (1988 [1950]) observations. They are however, now quite different, insofar as they form part of the larger ritual cycle.

28. There is some conflict in the secondary literature on the wearing of grass ropes around the waist in terms of it being a specifically Nazarite (Kiernan 1992) or a more general Zulu traditional custom (Krige 1988 [1950], 101).

29. In chapter 7 I discuss the placement of the beads (instead of the grass braids) on the topknots of married women to signify a similar union of Shembe with married women.

30. The green ribbon tied around the waist is explained by Kiernan (1992, 24) as being

> the color of early growth, of grass, shrubs, trees and especially of crops; more correctly, perhaps, it stands for growth and accretion. Analogously to growth in the natural environment, the use of green in this ritual is a symbolic statement of the social growth of girls and of their passage to the new status of marriageable young women. Here, green is the color symbol of status transition.

31. The placement of the drums alongside the heat of the fire in order to be correctly tuned is paralleled by the belief about the fine tuning of Nazarites by the ancestors, symbolized by the heat of the fire (Berglund 1989 [1976]). The trumpets, on the other hand, were placed against a tree, on the inside of the circle of maidens. Krige (1968) says that the leaves of the *umsenge* tree embody fertility. In

addition, in Hymn 46, discussed above, the virgin girls are metaphorized as "white milkwood trees." Both examples suggest there is a link between female fertility, virginity, and trees, though the specific tree may no longer matter.

32. I recorded the Zulu version of the sermon on September 25, 1991, at *Ebuhleni*, and the translation was done by Khethiwe Mthethwa, a member of *ibandla lamaNazaretha*.

33. The prevalence of this kind of religious accountability—in terms of gift-giving, hard work, and good deeds being written down—is pervasive in *ibandla lamaNazaretha* and other religious groups, particularly those imbued with the Protestant work ethic. Thus, recordings of Negro spirituals from the early twentieth century in the United States reflect titles such as "My Lord Keeps a Record," and "Jim and Me," a song about hard work. In this regard, Erlmann (1991) and Cockrell (1987) analyze the transplantation of American Negro spirituals to South Africa in the latter part of the nineteenth century.

34. There is a juxtaposition of white and green color symbolism again. See also Kiernan (1992, 24) and Berglund (1989 [1976]) on the significance of the reed (the long pole) as the central metaphor of creation. This perhaps links to the idea of the important role played by young girls in the reconstitution of the Nazarite community.

35. See Van Gennep (1960, 16–17) on the entrance as marking the sanctity of a territory for its owners and inhabitants.

36. Krige (1988 [1950], 103) comments on the burning of the grass ropes in traditional puberty ceremonies as happening after the girl has come out from her seclusion. If the ropes crackle while on the fire, it signals that the girls have not properly adhered to the rules for the period of seclusion. As far as I know there was no such omen for Nazarite girls.

37. Krige remarks that the pillow and mat are given by a woman married in polygamous marriage to her husband when he comes to visit her in her hut. In the Nazarite context, the pillow and grass mat represent the altar—*ilayiti*.

38. Krige (1988 [1950], 102) mentions in her account that traditionally, the father of the girl in seclusion offers an ox on the day of her coming out. There has obviously been some kind of reversal in terms of the giver and receiver of the ox in the case of Shembe. Kiernan (1992, 22) remarks that in Londa's rite, the ox slaughter had been completely forgotten, though Londa assured him he would reinsert the tradition the following year.

39. The handwritten text lent to me by MaSangweni was probably a copy of an original. It was an extremely complex text, which seemed to have been copied by someone not schooled in Western literacy. In this translation we (Themba Mbhele and I) have tried to convey the essential meaning over the exact translation of the text. This is particularly so in terms of tense usage and punctuation, but I inserted the subtitles so as to frame the text for the reader.

40. In this letter "to visit" implies having sexual intercourse.

41. We have left this in the present tense because (Isaiah) Shembe may call through dreams, or it may refer to the Shembe lineage, as explained in chapter 1.

42. The *inansook* encloses a young girl's virginity—it covers the head, shoulders, eyes, and mouth.

43. This may refer to the knife used by the midwife to cut the umbilical cord of a baby. When a woman marries she carries a knife with her. It does suggest a link between the knife and social reproduction.

44. These "spiritual guards" fulfill an equivalent function to police in everyday life, and are personified in the form of male *phoyisa* who control movement in Nazarite religious space.

45. I have labeled this as a dream because in one of the women's meetings I attended, the husband of the home told a story of how young women had entered *Ekuphakameni* dressed like virgins, but were actually ritually unclean. They were eventually driven out by other Nazarite girls with sticks and whips. It is not clear from that narrative if this really happened or was something he dreamed. Many of his previous stories had been told as dream narratives rather than actual events.

46. See DeGruchy (n.d.) for the theological bases underpinning apartheid.

47. Krige (1988 [1950], 233) writes that "noble elephant" was commonly used to praise a chief, whose name was considered too sacred to be uttered.

48. The significance of female virginity was underscored for me when I was invited to attend the twenty-first-birthday celebration of one of the Nazarite members in 1991. Her parents and several guests told me how proud they were of the young woman because she had remained a virgin. They suggested that this was extremely rare in their community in KwaMashu. It seems that those who live away from Nazarite sacred sites are now celebrating the purity and marriageability of their daughters with the English-derived tradition of twenty-first-birthday parties. These may include the slaughter of goats and sheep to honor the ancestors.

49. This idea of struggle and sacrifice is deeply embedded in Nazarite epistemology. In chapter 4, for example, in my discussion of sacred dance, I discussed how married women consider this dance to be hard work; similarly, staying up all night long, two nights in a row once a month, and then going off to work in between, also requires an element of sacrifice of desire—though in this case it would be the desire for sleep and comfort. Sacrificing desire occurs each Friday evening when women prepare meals for the sabbath—all food is cold and no fires are lit on the sabbath. In this case, the desire is for warm food, but it is simply not permitted until sundown on a Saturday.

Chapter Seven

1. Statistics given at the Ninth International AIDS Conference held in Berlin in 1993 indicated that a quarter of all South African women will be raped, that one women is raped every 83 seconds in South Africa, and that 95 percent of the women raped are black. These were figures reported by a representative from the Johannesburg City Health Department. (South African Broadcasting Corporation, English Radio 6 O'Clock News, June 8, 1993.)

2. John Lambert (1989, 386) cites figures for the drop in traditional marriages. He links these to the effects of both the *lobola* legislation and the rinderpest epidemic. In 1896, 5,087 marriages were recorded, and by 1899, there were a mere 2,678.

3. A similar account of this experience is provided by Vilakazi et al. (1986, 24).

4. See Krige (1988 [1950]) for full details of this process.
A traditional ceremony is held. It lasts between one and three days and is held at the homestead of the young woman's parents before the couple returns to the church for the final solemnization of the marriage.

5. I was told that the *Mpathi* who was doing the negotiation in July 1991 was particularly good at getting couples to agree to marriage.

6. The catechism forbids the purchase of expensive "Western" items such as wardrobes and household furniture. However, I attended the traditional marriage of Amos's only daughter from his official wife. (Amos is reported to have over one hundred children born from a number of women.) He told the congregation the previous day that this daughter's dowry cost R 15,000 (about $10,000 in purchase power), and it included all the furniture necessary to fill the house that had been built for the newly married couple. This was paid for with the offerings church members had given to Shembe.

I was not told what happened if a young woman changed her mind in this two-year period, though Krige mentions that if a girl has been promised in marriage to a man she does not wish to marry or if there is a man she wishes to marry that her father does not want her to marry, she may *balekela* (run away to the young man she wishes to marry, to force the parents to begin negotiations). In addition, should a girl break the engagement, she could be captured by the boy and his friends and carried off secretly (Krige 1988 [1950], 124–25).

7. This is not unique to *ibandla lamaNazaretha*. See Lange (1975, 92), who writes that dance may have "the meaning of a legal act and [be] the equivalent of a formal ceremony."

8. The topknot is equivalent to the wedding ring in Western marriage.

9. Virginia-Lee Webb's article (1992) has a photograph that illustrates this practice—taken in the 1870s. The photograph (ibid., 59) itself is housed in the Metropolitan Museum of Art, New York City.

10. There were clearly some exceptions to this, because Amos Shembe, who had only one official wife, is reported to have fathered over a hundred children. I was told this by one of his sons, who was waiting to see his father at Gibisile in May 1991.

Chapter Eight

1. Both excerpts are taken from the typewritten manuscripts transcribed by the late Mr. Petrus Dhlomo, church archivist. He joined Isaiah Shembe sometime in the 1920s and remained loyal to all three Shembes until his death in August 1993. His main occupation was to record the witnesses who attested to the miraculous deeds of Shembe. This text was translated by Richard Zondi.

Dhlomo numbered sections of the written transcriptions of Nazarite testimonies much as Bible verses are numbered. They do not necessarily reflect meaningful linguistic units. These numbers are, nevertheless, important signifiers of the cultural models on which Dhlomo modeled his texts.

2. Bongani Mthethwa explained to me (January 1990) that women meet on Thursday afternoons because when Jesus was crucified (on Friday), it was only the women who were with him, and not the men. Gaitskell (1990, 257) suggests that the reason for Thursday as the time for meeting may have been linked to the fact that many of the women who joined the prayer unions or *manyanos* were washerwomen. The cycle of the washing week went as follows: washing was collected on Monday, washed on Tuesday, and ironed on Wednesday. This left women free to attend the meetings on Thursday.

3. The photograph of Isaiah Shembe referred to here was taken by Esther Roberts in 1935 and appears at the beginning of the hymnal. The blurring of boundaries between dream and photographic realities is an important subtext in this chapter, and will be discussed in the section on dreams.

4. This holiness is ritualized by the local temple members when they come to the home to bless it and place white stones around the boundaries of the property.

5. While I have stated that the women are singing the words of their God, Shembe, it should be understood that Shembe is variously interpreted as the ancestor of the spiritual lineage given human form in the Nazarite religious group, and as God. I suggested earlier that there was a blurring of boundaries between the domain of the ancestors (believed to exist under the ground) and that of the Lord of the Sky. This blurring is evidence of the impact of mission Christianity, which demarcated the territory of God as above the earth, and that of the devil, below the earth. This difference between the two belief systems hinges on the way in which the ancestors are portrayed. In mission Christianity the worship of the ancestors was equated with demons, while in Nazarite belief, it is a constituent element of personal and social life and identity.

6. Reporter Vusi Ngema (*New African*, August 8, 1991, 4) quotes a follower of Shembe, who told him,

> What is particularly appealing to most people about our gospel is that we are talking about someone we have seen and whose spirit lives through his various descendants, not someone we read about in a book, who lived miles away from Africans.

7. This connection is taken quite seriously by one of the more educated members of the church, Mr. Mpanza, who is a qualified legal practitioner. In this regard, he presented to me (pers. comm., December 1991) a carefully considered case for the addition of these transcribed stories of Shembe as the third testament of the Bible. He suggested the Nazarite testament should be placed after the existing Old and New Testaments.

8. Seremetakis (1991) describes a similar process in Greek women's laments.

9. I cited some statistics of this violence against women in chapter 7. Ross (1993) provides additional information, suggesting that about 300,000 women are raped in South Africa annually (although the statistics given in chap. 3 suggest the figure should be doubled). Ross's calculation is equivalent to a woman being raped every three minutes, while that given in chapter 5 suggests one is raped every eighty-three seconds. See also Cock (1991) for information on violence against women perpetrated by the South African Defence Force in the 1980s.

10. Turner (1967) attributes this to dietary deficiencies, which may also be the case for many Nazarite women who live well below acceptable living standards. I suggest that infertility may also relate to the high level of violation against women's bodies, and Shembe's intervention in this process, in order to protect women.

11. This dream is discussed in the section on dreams.

12. See Basso in Tedlock (1987, 91–92) for elaboration on this matter.

13. See Berglund (1989 [1976], 42) for a discussion of the hills and mountains in the province of KwaZulu Natal to which people retreat in times of crisis. They plead and pray to the ancestors on the mountain plateau.

14. This instruction to stay by the light of the moon may also relate to Shembe's prohibition of the use of contraceptive pills, though I have no further evidence of this at this stage.

15. Mrs. Manqele explained to me that the Zulu dish, *qoma,* a large woven grass basket, is a "thing for heaven."

16. This account relates to the story about Shembe's calling (i.e., he had to renounce his wives and children). See chapter 7.

17. This is the same woman as the one about whom the story was told in the section on infertility and conception.

18. Umkomazi is an area on the coast of the province of KwaZulu Natal that has been racked by violence since the early 1980s. While I do not have figures for that area specifically, in the province as a whole, there were, for example, four hundred deaths due to political violence in March 1994. These were recorded by the Human Rights Commission, and reported on the radio programming of the South African Broadcast Corporation, April 3, 1994.

19. Ulundi was the KwaZulu seat of government under the leadership of Chief Mongasutho Buthelezi until the provinces were reorganized in 1994.

20. There is a wonderful narrative told of a woman who took some of this money for herself—and was subsequently haunted by an enormous coin that kept following her around!

21. Becken (in Tshabalala 1983, 15) suggests 1925 as the specific date.

22. The word *isigekle* refers to a style of traditional Zulu dance performed at weddings. Bongani Mthethwa translates its meaning into English as "ordinary," while Joseph Shabalala told me it meant "daylight." I suggest that Shabalala's translation is the more appropriate if dance is in fact a kind of prayer—a heavenly discourse, as suggested below. In this regard, Hymn 89/2 characterizes heaven as the place where the sun never sets—where there is constant daylight (and continual dancing).

23. Hymn 70 articulates the importance of this inscription. For example, the fourth stanza (translated) reads: "All the great and small will be apportioned according to the writing in their books."

24. See Comaroff and Comaroff (1992, 155–80) for further discussion of the two meanings of work with the Tshidi.

References

Published Sources

Abu-Lughod, Lila. 1990. The Romance of Resistance: Tracing Transformations of Power through Bedouin Women. In Sanday and Goodenough 1990, 313–37.

———. 1986. *Veiled Sentiments: Honor and Poetry in a Bedouin Society*. Los Angeles: University of California Press.

Abu-Lughod, Lila, and Catherine Lutz, eds. 1990. *Language and the Politics of Emotion*. New York: Cambridge University Press, 1–23.

Agu, Daniel C. 1992. Youth Songs: A Type of Igbo Choral Music in Igbo Christian Worship. *African Music* 7/2, 13–22.

Appadurai, Arjun, ed. 1997 [1996]. *Modernity at Large: Cultural Dimensions of Globalization*. Minneapolis: University of Minnesota Press.

———. 1986. *The Social Life of Things: Commodities in Cultural Perspective*. New York: Cambridge University Press, Introduction.

Armstrong, Robert P. 1977. The Affecting Presence in the Time-Space Ambient. Pp. 73–82 in C. Seeger, ed., *Essays for a Humanist: An Offering to Klaus Wachsmann*. New York: Town House Press.

———. 1971. *The Affecting Presence*. Urbana: University of Illinois Press.

Atkinson, Paul. 1990. *The Ethnographic Imagination: Textual Constructions of Reality*. London: Routledge.

Axelson, Olof. 1981. The Development of African Church Music in Zimbabwe. *Papers Presented at the Symposium on Ethnomusicology. Rhodes University, Grahamstown, 24–26 September 1981*, 2–7.

Baker, Paul. 1979. *Contemporary Christian Music*. Westchester, Ill.: Crossway Books.

Balia, Daryl. 1991. *Black Methodists and White Supremacy in South Africa*. Durban: Madiba Publications (University of Natal).

Ballantine, Christopher. 1993. *Marabi Nights: Early South African Jazz and Vaudeville*. Johannesburg: Ravan Press.

Ballard, Charles. 1989. Traders, Trekkers and Colonists. In Duminy and Guest 1989, 116–45.

Barthes, Roland. 1981 [1980]. *Camera Lucida: Reflections on Photography*. Richard Howard, trans. New York: Hill & Wang.

Baumann, Richard. 1984 [1977]. *Verbal Art as Performance*. Prospect Heights, Ill.: Waveland Press.

Baynes, John. 1992 [1906]. *Letters Addressed to His Excellency the Governor of Natal, and His Majesty's Secretary of State for the Colonies Regarding the Absence of Consideration in Our Form of Government for Our Coloured Population*. With Introduction by John Lambert. Pietermaritzburg: University of Natal Press.

Bean, Susan. 1989. Ghandi and *Khadi*, the Fabric of Indian Independence. In Weiner and Schneider 1989, 356–76.

Becken, Hans. 1990. "I Love to Tell the Story": Oral History in the Nazaretha Church. Unpublished paper presented at the NERMIC Symposium, University of the Witwatersrand, Johannesburg, July 1990.

————. 1989. African Independent Churches as Healing Communities. Pp. 227–40 in G. Oost-huizen, ed., *Afro-Christian Religion and Healing in Southern Africa*. Lewiston: Edwin Mellen Press.

Becker, J., and A. Becker. 1981. A Musical Icon: Power and Meaning in Javanese Gamelan Music. Pp. 203–15 in Wendy Steiner, ed., *The Sign in Music and Literature*. Austin: University of Texas Press.

Behar, Ruth. 1987. Sex and Sin, Witchcraft and the Devil in Late-Colonial Mexico. *American Ethnologist* 14/1, 35–54.

Bell, Catherine. 1990. The Ritual Body and the Dynamics of Ritual Power. *Ritual Studies* 4/2, 299–314.

Berglund, Axel-Ivar. 1989 [1976]. *Zulu Thought-Patterns and Symbolism*. Bloomington: Indiana University Press.

Blacking, John. 1995. *Music, Culture, and Experience. Selected Papers of John Blacking*. Edited and with an Introduction by Reginald Byron. Chicago: University of Chicago Press.

————. 1985. The Context of Venda Possession Music: Reflections on the Effectiveness of Symbols. *Yearbook for Traditional Music* 17, 64–87.

————. 1982. The Structure of Musical Discourse: The Problem of the Song Text. *Yearbook for Traditional Music* 14, 15–22.

————. 1980. Political and Musical Freedom in the Music of Some Black South African Churches. Pp. 35–62 in Ladislav Holy et al. (eds.), *The Structure of Folk Models*. ASA Monograph 20. London: Academic Press.

————. 1977. Some Problems of Theory and Method in the Study of Musical Change. *Yearbook of the International Folk Music Council* 9, 1–26.

Blacking, John, and Joann Keali'inhomoku, eds. 1979. *The Performing Arts: Music and Dance*. The Hague: Mouton.

Bloch, Maurice. 1989. *Ritual, History and Power: Selected Papers in Anthropology*. London: Athlone Press, chap. 2.

Boonzaier, Emile, and John Sharp, eds. 1988. *South African Keywords: The Uses and Abuses of Political Concepts*. Cape Town: David Philip.

Borker, Ruth. 1978. To Honor Her Head: Hats as Symbols of Women's Position in Three Evangelical Churches in Edinburgh, Scotland. In Hoch-Smith and Spring 1978, 55–74.

Bourdieu, Pierre. 1989 [1977]. *Outline of a Theory of Practice*. Trans. R. Nice. Cambridge: Cambridge University Press.

Bozzoli, Belinda, with Mmantho Nkotsoe. 1991. *Women of Phokeng: Consciousness, Life Strategy, and Migrancy in South Africa, 1900–1983*. Johannesburg: Ravan.

————. 1983. Marxism, Feminism and South African Studies. *Journal of Southern African Studies* 9/2, 139–71.

Brady, Margaret. 1987. Transformations of Power: Mormon Women's Visionary Narratives. *Journal of American Folklore* 100/398, 461–68.

Brandel-Syrier, Mia. 1962. *Black Women in Search of God*. London: Lutterworth Press.

Branford, Jean, and William Branford. 1991. *A Dictionary of South African English*. Fourth Edition. Cape Town: Oxford University Press.

Bregman, Lucy. 1987. Baptism as Death and Birth: A Psychological Interpretation of Its Imagery. *Journal of Ritual Studies* 1/2, 27–42.

Brown, Duncan. 1995. Orality and Christianity: The Hymns of Isaiah Shembe and the Church of the Nazarites. *Current Writing* 7/2, 69–96.

Buchanan, Donna A. 1991. The Bulgarian Folk Orchestra: Cultural Performance, Symbol, and the Construction of National Identity in Socialist Bulgaria. Unpublished Ph.D. diss., University of Texas at Austin.

Budlender, Debbie. 1991. Women and the Economy. CASE Publication. Cape Town: University of the Western Cape.

Burnim, Mellonee. 1980. The Black Gospel Music Tradition: Symbol of Ethnicity. Unpublished Ph.D. diss., Indiana University. Ann Arbor: UMI, # 8105956.

Butler, Judith. 1990. *Gender Trouble: Feminism and the Subversion of Identity*. New York: Routledge.

Callaway, Henry. 1991 [1970]. The Initiation of a Zulu Diviner. Pp. 27–35 in Philip M. Peek, ed., *African Divination Systems: Ways of Knowing*. Bloomington: Indiana University Press.

Caraveli, Anna. 1986. The Bitter Wounding: The Lament as Social Protest in Rural Greece. Pp. 169–94 in Jill Dubish, ed., *Gender and Power in Rural Greece*. Princeton: Princeton University Press.

————. 1982. The Song beyond the Song: Aesthetics and Social Interaction in Greek Folksong. *Journal of American Folklore* 95/376, 129–58.

Caraveli-Chaves, Anna. 1980. Bridge between Worlds: The Greek Women's Lament as Communicative Event. *Journal of American Folklore* 94, 129–57.

Carby, Hazel. 1988. It Jus Be's Dat Way Sometime: The Sexual Politics of Women's Blues. Pp. 227–42 in Alexandra Todd and Sue Fisher, eds., *Gender and Discourse: The Power of Talk*. Vol. 3, *Advances in Discourse Processes*, ed. Roy Freedle. Norwood, New Jersey: Ablex Publishing.

Charman, Andrew, Cobus De Swardt, and Mary Simons. 1991. The Politics of Gender: Discussion of the Malibongwe Papers and Other Current Papers within the African National Congress. Paper presented at the Conference on Women and Gender in Southern Africa, University of Natal, Durban, January 30–February 2, 1991.

Chatterjee, Partha. 1989. Colonialism, Nationalism, and Colonized Women: The Contest in India. *American Ethnologist* 16/4, 622–33.

Chatwin, Bruce. 1988 [1987]. *The Songlines*. London: Picador.

Chernoff, John. 1979. *African Rhythm and African Sensibility: Aesthetics and Social Action in African Musical Idioms*. Chicago: University of Chicago Press.

Chirenje, J. Mutero. 1987. *Ethiopianism and Afro-Americans in Southern Africa, 1883–1916*. Baton Rouge: Lousiana State University Press, introduction and chaps. 1–3.

Christian, William, Jr. 1987. Tapping and Defining New Power: The First Month of Visions at Ezquioga, July 1931. *American Ethnologist* 14/1, 140–66.

Clifford, James. 1990. Notes on (Field)notes. In Sanjek 1990, 47–70.

————. 1988. *The Predicament of Culture: Twentieth Century Ethnography, Literature, and Art*. Cambridge, Mass.: Harvard University Press.

Clingman, Stephen, ed. 1991. *Regions and Repertoires: Topics in South African Politics and Culture*. Johannesburg: Ravan.

Cobb, Charles, and James Nachtwey. 1993. The Twilight of Apartheid: Life in Black South Africa. *National Geographic* 183/2, 66–93.

Cock, Jacklyn. 1991. *Colonels and Cadres: War and Gender in South Africa*. Cape Town: Oxford University Press.

————. 1980. *Maids and Madams: A Study in the Politics of Exploitation*. Johannesburg: Ravan.

Cockrell, Dale. 1987. Of Gospel Hymns, Minstrel Shows, and Jubilee Singers: Towards Some Black South African Musics. *American Music* 5/4, 417–32.

Colenbrander, Peter. 1989. The Zulu Kingdom, 1828–79. In Duminy and Guest 1989, 83–115.

Comaroff, Jean. 1991. Missionaries and Mechanical Clocks. *Journal of Religion* 71/1, 1–21.

————. 1985. *Body of Power, Spirit of Resistance: The Culture and History of a South African People*. Chicago: University of Chicago Press.

Comaroff, Jean, and John Comaroff. 1992. *Ethnography and the Historical Imagination*. Boulder: Westview Press, chaps. 1, 3, 5, and 9.

————. 1991. *Of Revelation and Revolution: Christianity, Colonialism, and Consciousness in South Africa*. Vol. 1. Chicago: University of Chicago Press.

————. 1989. The Colonization of Consciousness in South Africa. *Economy and Society* 18/3, 267–96.

Combs-Schilling, M. E. 1989. *Sacred Performances: Islam, Sexuality, and Sacrifice*. New York: Columbia University Press.

Connerton, Paul. 1989. *How Societies Remember*. New York: Cambridge University Press.

Coplan, David. 1988. Musical Understanding: The Ethnoaesthetics of Migrant Workers' Poetic Song in Lesotho. *Ethnomusicology* 32/3, 337–68.

————. 1987. Eloquent Knowledge: Lesotho Migrants' Songs and the Anthropology of Experience. *American Ethnologist* 14/3, 413–43.

————. 1985. *In Township Tonight! Music of South Africa's Black City Music and Theatre.* Johannesburg: Ravan Press.

Cordwell, Justine, and Ronald Schwarz, eds. 1979. *The Fabrics of Culture.* New York: Mouton.

Cowie, A. P., ed. 1992. *Oxford Advanced Learners' Dictionary of Current English.* Oxford: Oxford University Press.

Crain, Mary. 1991. Poetics and Politics in the Ecuadorean Andes: Women's Narratives of Death and Devil Possession. *American Ethnologist* 18/1, 67–89.

Cucchiari, Salvatore. 1988. "Adapted for Heaven": Conversion and Culture in Western Sicily. *American Ethnologist* 15/3, 417–40.

Dargie, David. 1988. *Xhosa Music: Its Techniques and Instruments with a Collection of Songs.* Cape Town: David Philip.

————. 1987. Xhosa Zionist Church Music. Report for the Research Unit for the Study of New Religious Movements and Indigenous Churches in Southern Africa (NERMIC), University of Zululand.

————. 1982. The Music of Ntsikana. *South African Journal of Musicology* 2, 7–28.

Davenport, T. R. H. 1988 [1977]. *South Africa: A History.* Cape Town: Southern Book Publishers.

Davies, Nollene. 1994. The Guitar in Zulu *maskanda* Tradition. *World of Music* 36/2, 138–47.

Davis, Angela. 1998. *Blues Legacies and Black Feminisms.* New York: Pantheon.

Davis, J., ed. 1982. *Religious Organization and Religious Experience.* London: Academic Press.

De Gruchy, John. n.d. The Making of South African Theology: From Colonial Theology to the Kairos Document. Hoff Lecture Series. n.p.

De Pina-Cabral, Joao. 1987. Paved Roads and Enchanted Mooresses: The Perception of the Past among the Peasant Population of the Alto Minho. *Man* (N.S.) 22/4, 715–35.

De Vale, Sue Carole. 1984. Prologemena to a Study of Harp Sounds in Uganda: A Graphic System for the Notation of Texture. *Selected Reports in Ethnomusicology Volume V: Studies in African Music.* Los Angeles: University of California Press, 285–318.

Dilley, Roy. 1992. Dreams, Interpretation and Craftwork among Tukulor Weavers. In Jedrej and Shaw 1992, 71–85.

Doke, C. M., et al. 1990. *English-Zulu, Zulu-English Dictionary.* Johannesburg: Witwatersrand University Press.

Domowitz, Susan. 1992. Wearing Proverbs: Anyi Names for Printed Factory Cloth. *African Arts* 25/3, 82–87.

Doubleday, Veronica. 1988. *Three Women of Herat.* London: Jonathan Cape.

Douglas, Mary. 1966. *Purity and Danger: An Analysis of Concepts of Pollution and Taboo.* London: Routledge & Kegan Paul.

Dube, Sydney W. 1992. Text and Context: The Ministry of the Word in Selected African Indigenous Churches. Unpublished M.A. thesis, University of Natal, Durban.

Duminy, Andrew, and Bill Guest, eds. 1989. *Natal and Zululand from Early Times to 1910: A New History.* Pietermaritzburg: University of Natal Press and Shuter & Shooter.

Eades, J. 1982. Dimensions of Meaning: Western Music and the Anthropological Study of Symbolism. In J. Davis 1982, 195–207.

Edwards, J. Michele. 1991. Women in Music to ca. 1450. In Pendle 1991, 8–30.

Ehlers, Tracey B. 1991. Debunking Marianismo: Economic Vulnerability and Survival Strategies among Guatemalan Wives. *Ethnology* 30/1, 1–16.

Erlmann, Veit. 1993. The Politics and Aesthetics of Transnational Musics. *World of Music* 35, 3–15.

————. 1991a. Tradition, Popular Culture and Social Transformation. Pp. 121–35 in *Music in the Dialogue of Cultures: Traditional Music and Cultural Policy,* ed. Max P. Baumann. Wilhelmshaven: Florian Noetzel Verlag.

————. 1991b. *African Stars: Studies in Black South African Performance.* Chicago: University of Chicago Press, chaps. 2 and 6.

Etherington, Norman. 1989a. The "Shepstone System" in the Colony of Natal and beyond the Borders. In Duminy and Guest 1989, 170–92.

———. 1989b. Christianity and African Society in Nineteenth Century Natal. In Duminy and Guest 1989, 275–301.

Ewens, Graeme. 1990. *Africa Oye! A Celebration of African Music.* Introduction by Manu Dibango. London: Palladium.

Fabian, Johannes. 1990. *Power and Performance: Ethnographic Explorations through Proverbial Wisdom and Theater in Shaba, Zaire.* Madison: University of Wisconsin Press, chap. 1.

Fanon, 1986. *Black Skin, White Masks.* Charles Lam Markamm, trans. London: Pluto Press.

Favret-Saada, Jeanne. 1989. Unbewitching as Therapy. *American Ethnologist* 16/1, 40–56.

Feld, Steven. 1988. Notes on "World Beat." *Public Culture* 1/1, 31–37.

———. 1986. Sound as a Symbolic System: The Kaluli Drum. In Frisbie 1986, 147–58.

———. 1984. Communication, Music, and Speech about Music. *Yearbook for Traditional Music* 16, 1–18.

———. 1982. *Sound and Sentiment: Birds, Weeping, Poetics, and Song in Kaluli Expression.* Philadelphia: University of Pennsylvania Press.

———. 1981. "Flow Like a Waterfall": The Metaphors of Kaluli Music Theory. *Yearbook for Traditional Music* 13, 22–47.

Feldman, Allen. 1991. *Formations of Violence: The Narrative of the Body and Political Terror in Northern Ireland.* Chicago: University of Chicago Press.

Finnegan, Ruth. 1991. Problems in the Processing of "Oral Texts": Some Reflections on the Researcher's Role in Innovation and Consolidation. In Sienart et al. 1991, 1–23.

———. 1989. *The Hidden Musicians: Music-Making in an English Town.* Cambridge: Cambridge University Press.

Foucault, Michel. 1990 [1988]. *Politics, Philosophy, Culture: Interviews and Other Writings, 1977–1984.* Lawrence Kritzman, ed., and Alan Sheridan et al., trans. New York: Routledge.

———. 1988. *Technologies of the Self: A Seminar with Michel Foucault.* Luther Martin, Huck Gutman, and Patrick Hutton, eds. Amherst: University of Massachusetts Press.

———. 1980 [1972]. *Power/Knowledge: Selected Interviews and Other Writings, 1972–1977.* Colin Gordon, ed., and Colin Gordon, Leo Marshall, John Mepham, and Kate Soper, trans. New York: Pantheon Books.

Fox, Richard, ed. 1991. *Recapturing Anthropology: Working in the Present.* Santa Fe: School of American Research.

Franco, Jean. 1985. Killing Priests, Nuns, Women, and Children. Pp. 414–20 in Marshall Blonsky, ed., *On Signs.* Baltimore: Johns Hopkins University Press.

Frisbie, Charlotte, ed. 1986. *Explorations in Ethnomusicology: Essays in Honor of David P. McAllester.* Detroit Monographs in Musicology, Number 9. Detroit: Information Coordinators.

Frith, Simon. 1989. Why Do Songs Have Words? *Contemporary Music Review* 5, 77–96.

Fynn, Henry Francis. 1986 [1951]. *The Diary of Henry Francis Fynn.* James Stuart and D. McK. Malcolm, eds. Pietermaritzburg: Shuter & Shooter.

Gaitskell, Deborah. 1990. Devout Domesticity? A Century of African Women's Christianity in South Africa. In Walker 1990, 251–72.

Gandelman, Claude. 1991. *Reading Pictures: Viewing Texts.* Bloomington: Indiana University.

Garafalo, Rebee. 1993. Whose World, What Beat: The Transnational Music Industry, Identity, and Cultural Imperialism. *World of Music* 35, 16–32.

Gates, Henry Louis, Jr. 1988. *The Signifying Monkey: A Theory of African-American Literary Criticism.* London: Oxford University Press.

Giddens, Anthony. 1990. *The Consequences of Modernity.* Cambridge: Polity Press.

Gill, Lesley. 1990. Like a Veil to Cover Them: Women and the Pentecostal Movement in La Paz. *American Ethnologist* 17/4, 708–21.

Ginsburg, Faye. 1992. Indigenous Media: Faustian Contract or Global Media? In Marcus 1992, 356–76.

————. 1989. Dissonance and Harmony: The Symbolic Function of Abortion in Activists' Life Stories. In Personal Narratives Group 1989, 59–84.

Girard, Rene. 1972. *Violence and the Sacred.* Patrick Gregory, trans. Baltimore: Johns Hopkins University Press, chap. 1.

Gluck, Sherna B., and Daphne Patai, eds. 1991. *Women's Words: The Feminist Practice of Oral History.* New York: Routledge.

Guevin, Benedict. 1989. The Moral Imagination and the Shaping Power of the Parables. *Journal of Religious Ethics* 17/1, 63–80.

Gunner, Elizabeth. 1988. Power House, Prison House—An Oral Genre and Its Use in Isaiah Shembe's Nazaretha Baptist Church. *Journal of Southern African Studies* 14/3, 204–27.

————. 1979. Songs of Innocence and Experience: Women as Composers and Performers of *Izibongo,* Zulu Praise Poetry. *Research in African Literatures* 10/2, 239–67.

Guy, Jeff. 1991. Literacy and Literature. In Sienart et al. 1991, 395–413.

————. 1990. Gender Oppression in Southern Africa's Precapitalist Societies. In Walker 1990, 33–47.

Hamilton, C. A. 1985. Ideology, Oral Traditions and the Struggle for Power in the Early Zulu Kingdom. Unpublished M.A. thesis, University of the Witwatersrand, Johannesburg.

Hamm, Charles. 1991. "The Constant Companion of Man": Separate Development, Radio Bantu and Music. *Popular Music* 10/2, 147–73.

————. 1988. *Afro-American Music, South Africa and Apartheid.* Institute for Studies in American Music Monographs, number 28. Brooklyn, New York: Conservatory of Music, Brooklyn College, City University of New York.

Hanna, Judith. 1977. African Dance and the Warrior Tradition. Pp. 11–33 in A. Mazrui, ed., *The Warrior Tradition in Modern Africa.* Leiden: Brill.

Harris, Olivia. 1991. Time and Difference in Anthropological Writing. In Nencel and Pels 1991, 145–61.

Havel, Vaclav. 1990. *Disturbing the Peace.* Paul Wilson. trans. New York: Alfred Knopf.

Hebdige, Dick. 1979. *Subculture: The Meaning of Style.* London: Methuen.

Hernandez, Deborah. 1993. A View from the South: Spanish Caribbean Perspectives on Worldbeat. *World of Music* 35, 48–69.

Hoch-Smith, J., and Anita Spring, eds. 1978. *Women in Ritual and Symbolic Roles.* New York: Plenum Press, chap. 1.

Homiak, John. 1987. The Mystic Revelation of Rasta Far-Eye: Visionary Communication in a Prophetic Movement. In B. Tedlock 1987, 220–45.

Howe, James, and Lawrence Hirschfeld. 1981. The Star Girls' Descent: A Myth about Men, Women, Matrilocality, and Singing. *Journal of the American Folklore Society* 94/373, 292–322.

Hughes, Heather. 1990. "A Lighthouse for African Womanhood": Inanda Seminary, 1869–1945. In Walker 1990, 197–220.

Hunt, Lynn, ed. 1989. *The New Cultural History.* Berkeley: University of California Press, introduction.

Jackson, Irene, ed. 1985. *More than Drumming: Essays on Afro-American Music and Musicians.* Westport: Greenwood Press.

Jackson, Michael. n.s. Knowledge of the Body. *Man* 18, 327–45.

Jane-Berman, John. 1993. *Political Violence in South Africa.* Johannesburg: South African Institute of Race Relations.

Jedrej, M., and Rosalind Shaw, eds. 1992. *Dreaming, Religion and Society in Africa.* New York: E. J. Brill.

Johnson, Mark. 1987. *The Body and Mind: The Bodily Basis of Reason and Imagination.* Chicago: University of Chicago Press.

Joseph, Rosemary. 1987. Zulu Women's Bow Songs: Ruminations of Love. *Bulletin of the School of Oriental and African Studies, University of London* 50/1, 90–116.

Kauffman, Robert. 1979. Tactility as an Aesthetic Consideration in African Music. In Blacking and Keali'inhomoku 1979, 251–54.

Keil, Charles. 1987. Participatory Discrepancies and the Power of Music. *Cultural Anthropology* 2/3, 275–83.

———. 1979. *Tiv Song: The Sociology of Art in a Classless Society.* Chicago: University of Chicago Press.

Kiernan, J. 1992. The Ritual Looking-Glass: An Analysis of the Girls' Puberty Ceremony in the Nazareth Church of Isaiah Shembe. *Journal of the Study of Religion* 5/1, 17–30.

———. 1990. The Canticles of Zion: Song as Word and Action in Zulu Zionist Discourse. *Journal of Religion in Africa* 20/2, 188–204.

———. 1982. Authority and Enthusiasm: The Organization of Religious Experience in Zulu Zionist Churches. In J. Davis 1982, 169–79.

Kirby, Percival. 1971. The Changing Face of South African Music South of the Zambezi. In Wachsmann 1971, 243–56.

Kirschner, Suzanne. 1986. "Then What Have I to Do with Thee?": On Identity, Fieldwork, and Ethnographic Knowledge. *Cultural Anthropology* 1/4, 211–34.

Kivnick, Helen. 1990. *Where Is the Way: Song and Struggle in South Africa.* New York: Viking Penguin.

Kligman, Gail. 1990. Reclaiming the Public: A Reflection on Creating Civil Society in Romania. *East European Politics and Societies* 4/3, 393–437.

———. 1988. *The Wedding of the Dead: Ritual, Poetics, and Popular Culture in Transylvania.* Los Angeles: University of California Press.

Klopper, Sandra. 1991. You Need Only One Bull to Cover Fifty Flies: Zulu Women and "Traditional" Dress. In Clingman 1991, 147–76.

Koskoff, Ellen, ed. 1989 [1987]. *Women and Music in Cross-Cultural Perspective.* Urbana: University of Illinois Press.

Krige, E. 1988 [1950]. *The Social System of the Zulus.* Pietermaritzburg: Shuter & Shooter.

———. 1968. Girls' Puberty Songs and Their Relation to Fertility, Health, Morality and Religion among the Zulu. *Africa* 38/2, 173–85.

Kubik, Gerhard. 1987. African Space/Time Concepts and the *Tusona* Ideographs in Luchazi Culture, with a Discussion of Possible Cross Parallels in Music. *African Music* 6/4, 53–89.

———. 1979. Pattern Perception and Recognition in African Music. In Blacking and Keali'inhomoku 1979, 221–50.

Kunene, Daniel. 1981. Ideas under Arrest: Censorship in South Africa. *Research in African Literatures* 12/4, 421–39.

Laband, John, and Paul Thompson. 1989. The Reduction of Zululand, 1878–1904. In Duminy and Guest 1989, 193–232.

Lambert, John. 1989. From Independence to Rebellion: African Society in Crisis, ca. 1880–1910. In Duminy and Guest 1989, 373–401.

Lange, Roderyk. 1975. *The Nature of Dance: An Anthropological Perspective.* London: MacDonald & Evans.

Lawson, E. Thomas, and Robert N. McCauley. 1990. *Rethinking Religion: Connecting Cognition and Culture.* Cambridge: Cambridge University Press.

Leppert, Richard, and Susan McClary, eds. 1992 [1987]. *Music and Society: The Politics of Composition, Performance and Reception.* Cambridge: Cambridge University Press.

Levinsohn, Rhoda. 1984. *Treasures in Transition: Art and Craft of Southern Africa.* Barbara LaVine, ed. Johannesburg: Delta Books.

Lipsitz, George. 1993. *Dangerous Crossroads: Popular Music, Post-Modernism, and the Poetics of Place.* London: Verso.

Malimela, Perfect. 1997. *The Nazarite Church Newsletter.* Durban: Malimela & Associates.

Maltz, Daniel. 1978. The Bride of Christ Is Filled with His Spirit. In Hoch-Smith and Spring 1978, 27–44.

Mandela, Nelson. 1995 [1994]. *Long Walk to Freedom: The Autobiography of Nelson Mandela.* London: Abacus.

Manuel, Peter. 1993. *Cassette Culture: Popular Music and Technology in North India.* Chicago: University of Chicago Press.

Marcus, George, ed. 1992. *Rereading Cultural Anthropology*. Durham: Duke University Press.

Marcus, George, and Michael Fischer. 1986. *Anthropology as Cultural Critique: An Experimental Moment in the Human Sciences*. Chicago: University of Chicago Press, chaps. 3 and 4.

Marks, Shula. 1989. The Context of Personal Narrative: Reflections on "Not Either an Experimental Doll"—The Separate Worlds of Three South African Women. In Personal Narratives Group 1989, 39–58.

Marwick, J. S. 1993 [1918, 1917]. *A Lecture on the Natives in the Larger Town. 7th August, 1918. and S. G. Rich. Notes on Natal. 1917*. Pietermaritzburg: University of Natal Press.

Maurer, Evan. 1979. Symbol and Identification in North American Indian Clothing. In Cordwell and Schwarz 1979, 119–42.

McCord, Margaret. 1995. *The Calling of Katie Makanya*. Cape Town: David Philip.

Meintjes, Louise. 1990. Paul Simon's *Graceland*, South Africa, and the Mediation of Musical Meaning. *Ethnomusicology* 34/1, 37–74.

Meintjes, Sheila. 1990. Family and Gender in the Christian Community at Edendale, Natal, in Colonial Times. In Walker 1990, 125–45.

Merriam, Alan. 1981. African Musical Rhythm and Concepts of Time-Reckoning. Pp. 123–42 in Thomas Noblitt, ed., *Music East and West: Essays in Honor of Walter Kaufmann*. New York: Pendragon Press.

Middleton-Keirn, Susan M. 1978. Convivial Sisterhood: Spirit Mediumship and Client-Core Networks among Black South African Women. In Hoch-Smith and Spring 1978, 191–205.

Mkhize, Hlengiwe. 1991. Towards the Emancipation of Women in a Post-Apartheid South Africa: A Case of a Prayer Woman. Unpublished paper presented at the NERMIC conference, University of the Witwatersrand, Johannesburg, July 3–5, 1991.

Mkhize, Khaba. 1993. Clothing that Talks. *Natal Witness*, Thursday, September 30, 1993, 13.

Mkondo, Rich. 1993. *Reporting South Africa*. London: Heinemann.

Mohr, M. 1992. The Burden of Neutrality: Zulu Zionists in Times of Political Unrest and Instability. Paper presented at the meeting of the South African Anthropological Association, September 1992.

Moller, Valerie. 1991. *Lost Generation Found: Black Youth at Leisure*. University of Natal, Durban: Indicator Project.

Mpanza, Mthembeni. 1993. The Concept "Holy Spirit" in the *Ibandla lamaNazaretha*. In Gabriele Lademann-Premier, ed., *Traditional Religion and Christian Faith: Cultural Clash and Cultural Change. Festschrift für Hans-Jürgen Becken*. Hamburg: Lottbek Jensen, 229–40.

Msomi, J. E. B. 1975. Ethnomusicology and the Different Types of Zulu Music. Unpublished M.Sc. thesis, Syracuse University, New York.

Mthethwa, Bongani. n.d. The Hymns of Isaiah Shembe, IziHlabelelo zamaNazaretha: An Ethnomusicological Study in Zulu Musical Change. Unfinished Ph.D. diss., University of Natal, Durban.

———. 1989a. Shembe's Hymnody: Its Influence on the Ethnical Standards and Worldview of the AmaNazaretha. Paper presented at the NERMIC Symposium, University of South Africa, Pretoria, June 28–29, 1989.

———. 1989b. Music and Dance as Therapy in African Traditional Societies with Special Reference to the iBandla lamaNazaretha (the Church of the Nazarites). In G. Oosthuizen, ed., *Afro-Christian Religion and Healing in Southern Africa*. Lewiston: Edwin Mellen Press, 241–56.

———. 1988. Decoding Zulu Beadwork. In Edgard Sienart and Nigel Bell, eds., *Catching Winged Words: Oral Tradition and Education*. Durban: Natal University Oral Documentation and Research Centre.

———. 1983. Western Elements in Shembe's Religious Dances. Papers presented at the Third and Fourth Symposia on Ethnomusicology, Rhodes University, Grahamstown, September 16–19, 1982, and October 7–8, 1983, 34–37.

Muller, Carol. 1999a (forthcoming). *Chakide*—The Teller of Secrets: Space, Song, and Story in Zulu *Maskanda* Performance. In Duncan Brown, ed., *Oral Literature and Performance in Southern Africa*. London: James Currey; Pietermaritzburg: University of Natal Press.

————, ed. 1999b (forthcoming). *The Hymns of the Nazaretha, Composed by Isaiah and Galilee Shembe.* Translated by Bongani Mthethwa with Themba Mbhele and Sazi Dlamini. Pietermaritzburg: University of Natal Press.

————. 1997. "Written" into the Book of Life: Nazarite Women's Performance Inscribed as Physical Text in *Ibandla lamaNazaretha. Research in African Literatures* 27/1, 3–14.

————. 1995. Zulu Women, Ritual Performance, and the Construction of Cultural Truth and Power. In Margaret Daymond, ed., *Feminists Reading South Africa, 1990–1994: Writing, Theory and Criticism.* New York: Garland.

————. 1993. Life Story of a Nazarite Woman Healer: Religious Patriarchy Redefined? In Gabriele Lademann-Premier, ed., *Traditional Religion and Christian Faith: Cultural Clash and Cultural Change. Festschrift für Hans-Jürgen Becken.* Hamburg: Lottbeck Jensen.

Nencel, L., and P. Pels, eds. 1991. *Constructing Knowledge: Authority and Critique in Social Science.* London: Sage Publications.

Ngema, Vusi. 1991. Trains of Gospel. *The New African.* August 8, 4.

Okpewho, Isidore. 1983. *Myth in Africa: A Study of Its Aesthetic and Cultural Relevance.* Cambridge: Cambridge University Press, chap. 1.

Ong, Aihwa. 1988. The Production of Possession: Spirits and the Multinational Corporation in Malaysia. *American Ethnologist* 15/1, 30–42.

————. 1987. *Spirits of Resistance and Capitalist Discipline: Factory Women in Malaysia.* Albany: State University of New York Press.

Oosthuizen, Gerhardus C. E. 1987. The Birth of Christian Zionism in South Africa. Published under the auspices of NERMIC, University of Zululand.

————. 1976. Black Theology in the History of Africa. *Journal of the University of Durban-Westville* 2/4, n.p.

————. 1967. *The Theology of a South African Messiah.* Leiden: E. J. Brill.

Owens, Craig. 1983. The Discourse of Others: Feminists and Postmodernism. Pp. 57–82 in Hal Foster, ed., *The Anti-Aesthetic: Essays on Post-Modern Culture.* Port Townsend, Wash.: Bay Press.

Patai, Daphne. 1991. U.S. Academics and Third World Women: Is Ethical Research Possible? In Gluck and Patai 1991, 137–54.

————. 1988. Constructing a Self: A Brazilian Life Story. *Feminist Studies* 14/1, 143–66.

Peacock, James. 1991 [1990]. Ethnographic Notes on Sacred and Profane Performance. In Schechner and Appel 1991 [1990], 194–207.

Pendle, Karin, ed. 1991. *Women and Music: A History.* Bloomington: Indiana University Press.

Personal Narratives Group, eds. 1989. *Interpreting Women's Lives: Feminist Theory and Personal Narratives.* Bloomington: Indiana University Press.

Pewa, Elliot. 1995. *Zulu Music Competitions: The Continuity of Zulu Traditional Aesthetics.* Unpublished M.A. thesis, University of Natal, Durban.

Preston-Whyte, Eleanor. 1974. Kinship and Marriage. In W. Hammond-Tooke, ed., *The Bantu-Speaking Peoples of Southern Africa.* London: Routledge & Kegan Paul.

Preston-Whyte, Eleanor, and Christian Rogerson, eds. 1991. *South Africa's Informal Economy.* Cape Town: Oxford University Press.

Ranger, Terence. 1975. *Dance and Society in Eastern Africa 1890–1970: The Beni Ngoma.* London: Heinemann.

Rasmussen, Susan. 1991. Veiled Self, Transparent Meanings: Tuareg Headdress as Social Expression. *Ethnology* 30/2, 101–17.

Raum, O. F. 1973. *The Social Functions of Avoidances and Taboos among the Zulu.* New York: Walter De Gruyter.

Ray, Keith. 1992. Dreams of Grandeur: The Call to the Office in Northcentral Igbo Religious Leadership. In Jedrej and Shaw 1992, 55–70.

Reynolds, Pamela. 1992. Dreams and the Constitution of Self among the Zezuru. In Jedrej and Shaw 1992, 21–35.

Rice, Timothy. 1980. Aspects of Bulgarian Musical Thought. *Yearbook for Traditional Music* 12, 43–66.

Robert, Dana. 1993. Mount Holyoke Women and the Dutch Reformed Missionary Movement, 1874–1904. *Missionalia* 21/2, 103–23.

Roberts, Esther. 1936. Shembe: The Man and His Work. Unpublished M.A. thesis. University of the Witwatersrand, Johannesburg.

Robertson-De Carbo, Carol. 1976. *Tayil* as Category and Communication among the Argentine Mapuche: A Methodological Suggestion. *Yearbook of the International Folk Music Council* 8, 35–52.

Robertson, Carol. 1979. "Pulling the Ancestors": Performance Practice and Praxis in Mapuche Ordering. *Ethnomusicology* 23/3, 395–416.

Rörich, Mary. 1989. Shebeens, Slumyards and Sophiatown: Black Women, Music and Cultural Change in Urban South Africa. *World of Music* 31/1, 78–101.

Rosaldo, Michelle. 1984. Toward an Anthropology of Self and Feeling. Pp. 136–57 in Richard Schweder and Robert LeVine, eds., *Culture Theory: Essays on Mind, Self, and Emotion*. London: Cambridge University Press.

Rosaldo, Renato. 1993 [1989]. *Culture and Truth: The Remaking of Social Analysis (with a New Introduction)*. Boston: Beacon Press.

Roseman, Marina. 1991. *Healing Sounds from the Malaysian Rainforest: Temiar Music and Medicine.* Berkeley: University of California Press.

———. 1988. The Pragmatics of Aesthetics: The Performance of Healing among the Senoi Temiar. *Social Science Medicine* 27/8, 811–18.

Ross, Kathryn. 1993. Women, Rape and Violence in South Africa: Two Preliminary Papers. University of the Western Cape: Community Law Centre.

Rycroft, David. 1976. The Zulu Bow Songs of Princess Magogo. *African Music* 5/4, 41–97.

———. 1971. Stylistic Evidence in Nguni Song. In Wachsmann 1971, 213–42.

Said, Edward. 1993. *Culture and Imperialism.* New York: Vintage Books.

———. 1989. Representing the Colonized: Anthropology's Interlocutors. *Critical Inquiry* 15, 205–25.

Sanday, Peggy, and Ruth Goodenough, eds. 1990. *Beyond the Second Sex: New Directions in the Anthropology of Gender.* Philadelphia: University of Pennsylvania Press.

Sanjek, Roger, ed. 1990. *Fieldnotes: The Makings of Anthropology.* Ithaca: Cornell University Press.

Schechner, Richard, and Willa Appel, eds. 1991 [1990]. *By Means of Performance: Intercultural Studies of Theatre and Ritual.* New York: Cambridge University Press.

Schoeman, H. 1968a and b. A Preliminary Report on Traditional Beadwork in the Mkhwanazi Area of the Mntunzini District, Zululand. Part One and Part Two. *African Studies* 27/2– 3, 57–81; 107–33.

Schoffeleers, Matthew. 1991. Ritual Healing and Political Acquiescence: The Case of the Zionist Churches in Southern Africa. *Africa* 61/1, 1–25.

Seeger, Anthony. 1987. *Why Suya Sing: A Musical Anthropology of an Amazonian People.* New York: Cambridge University Press.

———. 1979. What Can We Learn When They Sing? Vocal Genres of the Suya Indians of Central Brazil. *Ethnomusicology* 23/3, 373–94.

Serematakis, Nadia. 1991. *The Last Word: Women, Death and Divination in Inner Mani.* Chicago: University of Chicago Press.

———. 1990. The Ethics of Antiphony: The Social Construction of Pain, Gender and Power in the Southern Peleponnese. *Ethos* 18/4, 481–509.

Shaw, Rosalind. 1992. Dreaming as Accomplishment: Power, the Individual and Temne Divination. In Jedrej and Shaw 1992, 36–54.

Shelemay, Kay. 1991. *A Song of Longing: An Ethiopian Journey.* Urbana: University of Illinois.

Shembe, Galilee, ed. 1940. *Izihlabelelo ZamaNazaretha.* Durban.

Shembe, Isaiah. 1993. *Nazareth Baptist Church Umngcwabo.* (n.p.) Hans Becken, trans. Lewiston, New York: Mellen Press.

Shepherd, John. 1992 [1987]. Music and Male Hegemony. In Leppert and McClary 1992 [1987], 151–72.

———. 1991. *Music as Social Text*. Cambridge: Polity Press.

Sherzer, Joel, and Sammie Ann Wicks. 1982. The Intersection of Music and Language in Kuna Discourse. *Latin American Music Review* 3/2, 147–64.

Sienart, Edgard, et al., eds. 1991. *Oral Tradition and Innovation: New Wine in Old Bottles?* University of Natal Oral Documentation and Research Centre.

Slobin, Mark. 1993. *Subcultural Sounds: Micromusics of the West*. London: Wesleyan University Press.

Spiegel, Andrew, and Emile Boonzaier. 1988. Promoting Tradition: Images of the South African Past. In Boonzaier and Sharp 1988, 40–57.

Stoler, Ann. 1989. Making Empire Respectable: The Politics of Race and Sexual Morality in 20th Century Colonial Cultures. *American Ethnologist* 16/4, 634–60.

Sugarman, Jane. 1989. The Nightingale and the Partridge: Singing and Gender among Prespa Albanians. *Ethnomusicology* 33/2, 191–215.

———. 1988. Making *Muabet:* The Social Basis of Singing among Prespa Albanian Men. *Selected Reports in Ethnomusicology* 7, 1–42.

Sundkler, Bengt. 1976. *Zulu Zion and Some Swazi Zionists*. Cape Town: Oxford University Press.

———. 1961 [1948]. *Bantu Prophets in South Africa*. London: Oxford University Press.

Swan, Maureen. 1985. *Gandhi: The South African Experience*. Johannesburg: Ravan Press.

Swedenburg, Ted. 1992. Occupational Hazards: Palestine Ethnography. In Marcus 1992, 69–76.

Taussig, Michael. 1991 [1987]. *Shamanism, Colonialism, and the Wild Man: A Study in Terror and Healing*. Chicago: University of Chicago Press.

———. 1980. *The Devil and Commodity Fetishism in South America*. Chapel Hill: University of North Carolina Press.

Taylor, Timothy. 1997. *Global Pop: World Music, World Markets*. New York: Routledge.

Taylor, William. 1987. The Virgin of Guadalupe in New Spain: An Inquiry into the Social History of Marian Devotion. *American Ethnologist* 14/1, 9–33.

Tedlock, Barbara. 1986. Crossing the Sensory Domains in Native American Aesthetics. In Frisbie 1986, 187–99.

———, ed. 1987. *Dreaming: Anthropological and Psychological Interpretations*. Santa Fe: School of American Research Press.

Tedlock, Dennis. 1972. On the Translation of Style in Oral Narrative. Pp. 114–33 in A. Paredes and R. Bauman, eds., *Toward New Perspectives in Folklore*. Austin: University of Texas Press.

Thompson, E. P. 1967. Time, Work-Discipline, and Industrial Capitalism. *Past and Present* 38, 56–97.

Thompson, Robert. 1974. *African Art in Motion*. Los Angeles: Unversity of California Press, chaps. 1 and 2.

Toren, Christina. 1988. Making the Present, Revealing the Past: The Mutability and Continuity of Tradition as Process. *Man* 23/4, 696–717.

Tracey, Hugh. 1948. *Lalela Zulu: 100 Zulu Lyrics*. Johannesburg: African Music Society.

Trawick, Margaret. 1990. Untouchability and the Fear of Death in a Tamil Song. In Abu-Lughod and Lutz 1990, 186–206.

———. 1988. Spirits and Voices in Tamil Songs. *American Ethnologist* 15/2, 193–215.

Treitler, Leo. 1989. *Music and the Historical Imagination*. Cambridge, Mass.: Harvard University Press, Introduction.

Tshabalala, Mbuyisazwe Z. H. 1983. Shembe's Hymn Book Reconsidered: Its Sources and Significance. Unpublished M.Theol. thesis, University of Aberdeen.

Turino, Thomas. 1993. *Moving Away from Silence: Music of the Peruvian Altiplano and the Experience of Urban Migration*. Chicago: University of Chicago Press.

———. 1990. Structure, Criteria, and Strategy in Musical Ethnography. *Ethnomusicology* 34/3, 399–412.

Turnbull, Colin. 1991 [1990]. Liminality: A Synthesis of Subjective and Objective Experience. In Schechner and Appel 1991 [1990], 50–81.

Turner, Victor. 1991 [1990]. Are There Universals of Performance in Myth, Ritual, and Drama? In Schechner and Appel 1991 [1990], 8–18.

————. 1967. *The Forest of Symbols: Aspects of Ndembu Ritual.* Ithaca: Cornell University Press.

Vail, Leroy, and Landeg White. 1991. *Power and the Praise Poem: Southern African Voices in History.* Charlottesville: University Press of Virginia.

————. 1983. Forms of Resistance: Songs and Perceptions of Power in Colonial Mozambique. *American Historical Review* 88/4, 883–919.

Van Gennep, Arnold. 1960. *The Rites of Passage.* Trans. Monika B. Vizedom and Gabrielle E. Caffee. Chicago: University of Chicago Press.

Van Schalkwyk, Anastasia. *The Voice of Protest: Urban Black Women, Song, and Resistance in the 1980s.* Unpublished M.Mus. thesis, University of Natal, Durban.

Vidal, Tunji. 1989. The Role and Function of Music at Yoruba Festivals. Pp. 111–28 in Jacqueline Djedje et al., eds., *African Musicology: Current Trends.* Los Angeles: University of California Press.

Vilakazi, A. 1954. *Isonto LamaNazaretha.* The Church of the Nazarites. Unpublished M.A. thesis, Hartford Seminary, Connecticut.

Vilakazi, A., B. Mthethwa, and M. Mpanza. 1986. *Shembe: The Revitalization of African Society.* Johannesburg: Skottaville.

Wachsmann, Klaus, ed. 1971. *Essays on Music and History in Africa.* Evanston: Northwestern University Press.

Walker, Cherryl, ed. 1990. *Women and Gender in Southern Africa until 1945.* Cape Town: David Philip, 1–32; 168–96.

Warner, Marina. 1983 [1976]. *Alone of All Her Sex: The Myth and Cult of the Virgin Mary.* New York: Random House.

Waterman, Christopher. 1991. *Juju* History: Toward a Theory of Sociomusical Practice. Pp. 49–67 in Stephen Blum, P. Bohlman, and D. Neuman, eds., *Ethnomusicology and Modern Music History.* Urbana: University of Illinois Press.

————. 1990. *Juju: A Social History and Ethnography of an African Popular Music.* Chicago: University of Chicago Press.

Webb, Virginia-Lee. 1992. Fact and Fiction: Nineteenth Century Photographs of the Zulu. *African Arts* 25/2, 50–59, 98–99.

Weiner, Annette. 1992. *Inalienable Possessions: The Paradox of Keeping-While-Giving.* Berkeley: University of California Press.

————. 1989. Why Cloth? Wealth, Gender, and Power in Oceania. In Weiner and Schneider 1989, 37–74.

Weiner, Annette, and Jane Schneider, eds. 1989. *Cloth and Human Experience.* Washington: Smithsonian Institution, Introduction.

White, Landeg. 1982. Power and the Praise Poem. *Journal of Southern African Studies* 9/1, 8–32.

Williams, Donovan, ed. 1983. *The Journal and Selected Writings of the Reverend Tiyo Soga.* Cape Town: A. A. Balkema.

Winston, Brian. 1988. The Tradition of the Victim in Griersonian Documentary. Pp. 269–87 in Alan Rosenthal, ed., *New Challenges for Documentary.* Berkeley: University of California Press.

Interviews

Rob Allingham, July 1997
Petrus Dhlomo, September 1991
Mrs. Manqele, August 1991
Cinikile Mazibuko, January 1992
Ndodo Mkhwanazi, June 1992
Nathoya Mbatha, July 1997
Mthembeni Mpanza, November 1991, July 1997
Bongani Mthethwa, June 1991
Patrick Ngubane, July 1997
Eric Nthuli, October 1991

Princess Makhosazane Nyadi, January 1992
Joseph Shabalala, August 1993
Mr. Sibisi, September 1991
Nazareth Baptist Youth for Shembe—Kwa Mashu Temple, June 1991
Faith Healer—Njengobani Manqele, February 1993
Various Soweto Women—Dube Temple, April 1992
Rev. Prince Zulu, July 1997

Informal Conversations

Sazi Dlamini
Mrs. Dube
Khethiwe Mthethwa
Ntombemhlope Mthethwa
Samu Nthini, and all her friends from Kwa Mashu
Mr. and Mrs. Nthini
Themba Mbhele
Sikelela Msibi

Recordings

GENERAL

Lomax, Alan. 1977. *The Gospel Ship: Hymns and White Spirituals from the Southern Moutains.* Recorded Anthology of American Music. New York: New World Records.
The Spirit of African Gospel. 1996. West Sussex: Arc Music International.
Tracey, Hugh. ca. 1948. Shembe Singers (996T). Johannesburg: Gallo Records Archive.
———. n.d. *Sound of Africa* series. Record 9: A/1–6: Six Hymns from the Church of Nazareth (Shembe); B/1–2: Two Hymns from the Church of Nazareth. Roodepoort, South Africa: International Library of African Music.

NAZARITE CASSETTE AND COMPACT DISC PRODUCTIONS

Ama-Nazaretha, Ngiyalithanda Ngokulizwa. 1995. Johannesburg: Gallo.
Nathoya Mbatha: Ngivuse Nkosi. n.d. Empangeni: Revolver Records.
Nazareth Baptist Church, Bishop A. K. Shembe ubu Nazaretha. 1993. N.p.: Paradise Music (BMG distribution)
Nceku Yenkosi: AmaNazaretha (Amos Shembe). 1993. Johannesburg: Mbali Music Publishers.
Shembe: Abadumisi Base-Ekuphakameni Ibandla lamaNazaretha. 1995. Johannesburg: Soul Brothers (Tusk Music).

Index

abakhokheli, 224, 228
accountability, 289n. 33, 292n. 23
African, defined, 271n. 4
African Americans, 90
African Baptists, 89, 282n. 6
African National Congress, xiii, 4, 23, 261,
    273n. 1
Africanness, 263–65
Afrikaner trekkers, 36–37
agriculture, xv, 28–29, 40–41, 45–46, 199
Allingham, Rob, 283n. 21
ama14, amafortini, 21
    experience of as structures of feeling, 220,
        252
    expressive culture
        dance in, 229, 250, 256–59 (see also
            ukusina; umgido)
        dreams and photography, 244–50
        as metacommentary, 259–60
        preaching in, 230–50
        song in, 229–31, 250–56
        transformative power of, 229, 231, 253–55
    meetings of, 218, 225–31
        and the Book of Life, 220, 226, 260
        candles, 228, 277n. 5
        "14," significance of, 226–27
        Hymn 152, 231
        Hymn 229, 229
        Matthew 2, 231
        structure of, 228–31
    relationship to Shembe, as "maidens of
        royal blood," 220–24, 229
    ritual power of, 221
    sacrifice of desire, 226
    technologies of self-disclosure of, 220
ama23, amatwentythree, 284n. 29
ama25, amatwentyfive, meetings of, 171
amabutho, 31–33
amankhosikazi. See *ama14*
amantombazane. See girls

ancestors, 57, 195–96
angels, xiii–xvi, 66–67
Anglo-Zulu War (1879), 33, 39
apartheid, xiv, 1
    legislation, 2
    political geography of, 5
    regime, 3
attire, Nazarite ritual. *See* ritual attire
authority, religious, 57

Baba, 10, 17, 286n. 16
Bambatha Rebellion, 19, 25, 39
baptism, 82–84, 206
Battle of Blood River, 37, 279n. 34
beadwork, 5, 287n. 14
belief systems, religious, xv
bell, 160, 280n. 43
Bible, mission, xv
Biehl, Amy, 8
bird, symbol of, 281n. 52
black South Africans, xiii–xvi, 10, 272n. 19
    men, xv
    women, xv, 14–15, 18
BMG Records, 148–49
Bokwe, John Knox, 89–90
Bombela, 51, 277n. 1
body, 11
    female, xiv–xv, 1, 18, 20
        mediates social experience, 221
        protection of, 221
        and ritual purity, 176–98
        and sanctuary in Hymn 223, 168
        and social transformation, 161
    performance, 20
    and ritual attire, 85–87
    social, 20
Book of Life, xvi, 119, 184
Botha, Lieutenant Colonel, xiii–xvi
Brides of Christ, 200, 214–17
Buthelezi, Maureen, 230

cassette
    commercial, 121, 146–49
    pirated, 120–21
cassette culture, 21
catechism (*umngcwabo*), 5, 97
Cetshwayo, 195
Chicco, 285n. 8
choir. *See* youth choirs
Christianity, mission, xv, 55
Church of the Nazarites. See *ibandla
    lamaNazaretha*
commodification, xvii, 123–24
    of hymns, 96–99, 154–56 (*see also* hymnal;
        Mbatha, Nathoya)
    as a cottage industry, 121, 130
    radio, 124–28
    tensions over, 123, 157–58
    by Tracey, 124–26
    transcriptions, 128–29
    for transmission, 157
commodities
    global circulation of, 10
    Nazarite, 5
community, 3, 20–21, 274n. 6
    demise of, 167
    Nazarite, 8–12
    religious, xiv–xv, 6, 19
    sense of, 87
Concert and Dance, 227
congregational worship. See *inkhonzo*
conversion, 26, 82
cosmology, xv–xvi
    lineage, 2
cultural history, 17
    insiders, 17
    power, 21
    treasure, 20
    truth, 18, 20
cycles, menstrual, 21
cyclicity, xv, 64
    musical, 17
    reproductive, 17
    See also time

dance, xvi, 1
    attire, 5
    festival, 11
    as sacred, 56
    See also *ukusina; umgido*
Daniel 6:9, 71
death, fear of, 83

democracy, xvii, 3
Deuteronomy, 62
Dhlomo, Petrus, 222, 286n. 1, 291n. 1
Dingane, 36, 275n. 16
Dingane's Day, 70
Dinizulu, children of, 23, 273n. 1
discourse
    of personal experience, 60
    as truth claims, 60
disease, 277n. 42
    European, 274n. 10
dokoda, 7, 79, 281n. 48
dreams, xvi, 1, 56
    and ancestors, 56
    and Nazarite history, 85
    and visions, xvi, 2, 17, 52, 56–57, 61, 84–85,
        88, 92–95, 200, 286n. 2
drum, 283n. 19, 284n. 32, 287n. 31
Dube, John Langalibalele, 23, 49, 90, 261,
        276n. 38
Durban, 276n. 34

Ebuhleni, 2–3, 6, 11–12, 69
economy
    captured/enclave market, 145
    free market, 145
    global, xvii
    homestead, xv, 25–30
    industrial, xv
    market, xv, 22
    mission, 39–43
    moral, 22, 60, 62
    Nazarite
        agricultural production, 45–46
        Protestant work ethic, 45
        women's production, 43–47
    political, xvi, 2, 11
    spiritual, 160
Ekuphakameni, 2, 12, 23, 26, 30, 66, 261
    location of, 49
    purchase of, 64–65
elections, democratic, 7
Elinda (Elinde), 70
emotion, artifacts of, 58–63
empire
    builder, 16
    religious, xiv–xvii, 19, 26, 273nn. 5, 6
ethnography
    authority, 18
    ethnographic present, 3
    female perspective, 17

representation in, 18
research site, 4
in South Africa, 16–17
ethnomusicology, 9, 16–17
evangelist. See *mvangeli*
exchange
 market, xvii
 reciprocal, 47, 53
 ritual, 20, 58–63
 theory, 60–61
experience, xiv, 2, 17, 19–20
 mediated through the body, 64
 ritualized, 64
 and technology, 57
 and writing, 57
expressive culture, xvi, 1, 3
 and the Bible, 89
 commodified, 20
 as inalienable, 55
 permanent codification of, 61
 and Protestant hymns, 89
 and ritual exchange, 59
 as sacred, 55, 57
 and spiritual alliances, 61–62

faith healer, 280n. 36
Farewell, Francis, 33–36
feet, 12, 79
 image of mountain on, 80
feminization, xiv–xv, xvii, 154–57, 263
fertility, 28–30, 163–65, 179–89, 196–99, 221,
 237–41
 rituals of, 1, 20, 161, 174–76, 178–98, 215–18
festival, 280n. 46. See also *umgido*
field, 12–13
field assistant, 11, 120
fieldwork, 8–9, 12–13
 acceptance of, 11, 13
 and apartheid, 13–15
 ethics, 14–15
 experience, 13
 permission for, 10–11
 and personal history, 16
 and power, 15
 and technology, 9, 272n. 15
 and violence, 8, 13
First Fruits Ceremony, 28
flag, 161
flight
 Mrs. Manqele in, 243
 Shembe in, 202

followers. *See* members, female
Fort Hare College, 93
Fynn, Henry, 33–36

Gaba, Ntsikana, 89
Gallo Records, 125
Gandhi, Mahatma, 49–50, 261
Gardiner, Allen, 39
gender, 68–69
 and cosmos, 162–73
 of thunder, 166
Gibisila (Gibisile), 70
girls
 hlonipha (respect), 178, 181
 leaders of, 177–79
 relationship with Shembe, 161–70
  in hymn texts, 165–70
  likened to *Nkulunkulu* and
   Nomkhubulwana, 161–65
  through hymn composition, 165
 residential patterns of, 177–78
 ritual attire, 171–73
 umgido, 74
 virgin, xv, 1, 17, 20
  bodies as spiritual vessels, 164
  ritual power of, 161–98
 See also hymns, composition of
girls' camp (*Nthanda*), 69, 171
 girls' bodies as metaphorical walls, 190–91,
  196–97
 grass coils, 193–94
 history of *Nthanda*, 189–90, 192–94
 and land acquisition, 195
 ritual of fertility, 197
 site for orphans and widows, 189
 ties to traditional rite, 189–90
 See also Letter from Shembe to *iBandla
  lamaNazaretha*
girls' conference (*umgonqo*), 69–70, 171
 ama25 (July and September) incorporated
  into, 181, 185–87
 drums and trumpets in, 181, 183, 185
 fire, 187–88
 fertility, 181–82
 gifts to Shembe, 186, 188–89
 girls as preachers, 182, 185
 grass braids/ropes (*nthanda*), 181, 187
 green, color of fertility, 182
 Judges 11, 179, 185
 moral warfare, 180, 183
 procession during, 184–85, 187–88

girls' conference (*continued*)
   puberty rites, 179–89
   seclusion of, 180–88
   sermon in, 184
   service in, 183–85
   shield and umbrella, 183, 185
   singing and dancing, 186, 188
   spiritual union with Shembe, 188
   uniforms for, 182–83, 187
   See also Letter from Shembe to *iBandla*
      lamaNazaretha
God, 3, 21, 43, 55–57, 88–89, 96–97, 100, 102,
      107, 160, 163, 176, 178–79, 182, 184,
      189, 191–94, 198, 213–15, 218, 221–22,
      229–31, 240, 246, 251–52
   Word of, 48, 60, 95, 184, 203–4, 221–22, 251
gospel music, in South Africa, 136–37
Gqoba, 90
graveyard, Nazarite, 69
green, symbolism of, 164, 182–83, 287n. 30

healer. *See* Shembe, as healer
healing, xv, 26, 74
   illness and, 81
   rites, 80
   ritual of affliction, 81
   spiritual, 24
   Vaseline for, 74
heavenly messenger, masculine attributes of,
      282n. 11
Hlatswayo, 54–55
homestead
   African, 4
   Euro-African, 33–39
      concubinage, 35
      division of labor, 36
   Nguni, 27–30
huts, traditional, 7. See also *dokoda*
hymnal (*iziHlabelelo zamaNazaretha*), 5, 7
   creation and printing of, 96–99
   use of, 96
   as word of God, 97–98
Hymns
   1, 251
   11, 279n. 27
   15, 104
   21, 167
   22, 104
   34, 88
   45, 159, 167
   46, 23, 168, 289n. 31
   61, 144
   63, 120, 144
   67, 62–63
   70, 292n. 23
   84, 165–66
   88, 144
   89, 292n. 22
   92, 169
   95, 23, 220
   101, 52
   103, 94
   104, 254
   106, 144, 188
   112, 258
   114, 144
   124, 108, 114
   126, 125
   129, 254
   142, 144
   145, 252
   151, 144
   152, 158, 231, 256
   153, 1, 11
   160, 144
   173, 79, 125, 187, 228
      explanation of, 229
   179, 144
   183 (Lalela Zulu), 105, 125
   210, 125
   220, 168
   223 (226), 125, 168
   224, 54
   225, 256
   227, 253
   229, 199, 216–18, 229
   233, 144
   242, 130–31, 150–53
   243, 94
hymns, xvi, 284n. 25
   authentic style, 149–50
   composition of, 1, 92–96
   as connection to cosmology, 92–93
   and dance performance, 107 (see also
      ukusina)
   indigenizing Christian hymns, 88–18
   mission translation of, 106–7, 282n. 9
   Nazarite history of, 88–89, 92–99
   Nazarite style, 106–7
   performance practice, 72, 88–89, 98–99
      early recording of, 104–6
      embroidery of voices, 105

harmony, 106
  linearity and cyclicity in, 107
  "main melody," 105
  reconstitutes community, 101–18
  rhythm in, 109
popularity of, 272n. 20
popularization of, 1, 120–58 (see also
    Mbatha, Nathoya; commodification;
    cassette)
  Africanness/Zuluness in, 96, 105, 122,
    146, 149–50
  BMG Records, 121, 140, 143, 145,
    148–49
  Bongani Mthethwa and the, 130
  recording of, 124–28, 139–53, 155
  rhythm of, 93, 95
  sacralization of, 95
  as "singing book," 118–19
  as songs, 100–101
  standardization of, 96–99
  as structures of feeling, 103–4
  transcription of, 98–99
  transmission of, 95
  Wesleyan influence on, 91
    resistance to, 95
hymn texts
  body metaphors memorialized in, 166
  as gendered consciousness, 166
  models of, 99–100
  poetics of, 99–104
    bodily disorder in, 103–4
    license in, 101
    Nazarite imagination in, 102–4
    sanctified natural environment, 102–3,
      283n. 18
    about sacred song-dance, 108–9
    in Xhosa and Zulu, 94, 100

ibandla lamaNazaretha (Nazareth Baptist
    Church), xiv–xvii, 1, 3, 12, 26
  birth of, 70–71
  headquarters of, 13
  history of, 77–78, 86
ibhayi, ihayi, 171, 287n. 10
ifortini, 70, 262–63, 215–16
iJudia. See Judia
imbongi, Nazarite, 6
imiNazaretha, 5, 6, 11
"Impi," 195–96
Inanda Native Reserve, 2, 273n. 4
Inanda Seminary, 50

Inanda Valley, 3, 23–24
inansuka, inansook, 178, 181–82, 192, 289n. 42
Indians in narratives, 287n. 13
indigenizing Christianity, 89–91, 282n. 4
influx control, 65, 278n. 19
inhloko, 87
Inkatha Freedom Party (IFP), 261, 273n. 1
inkhonzo, 20, 72–74
Inkosazana yase zulweni (Princess of the Sky),
    28. See also Nomkhubulwana
instrumental accompaniment
  inkhonzo, 128–31
  ukusina, 75
Intabayepheza. See girls
isicathamiya, 122, 285n. 2
isigcklo, 281n. 1, 292n. 22
iskvtch, 172
izihlabelelo. See hymns
iziHlabelelo zamaNazaretha. See hymnal

jufetu, ujufetu, 172, 182, 188
Jephthah, 162, 179–80, 198
Jesus, 2, 51
Jordan River, 138–39
Judia, 8, 70

keyboard, 128–31, 136–37, 146, 152
kholwa, 40
kinship, spiritual, 72
Kirby, Percival, 105
knife, 192, 289n. 43
kraal, 276n. 32
KwaMashu, 13
KwaZulu Natal, xiv–xvii, 2, 4, 271n. 3
  political history of, 23–24

Land Act (1913), 275n. 25
land division, in nineteenth-century Natal,
    37
  land purchase, 19, 64–65
  Nazarite, 12, 26
law courts, xvi
leadership, authorized, 26
Letter from Shembe to iBandla lamaNazaretha,
    161, 170
  history of Nthanda, 192–94
  power of ritually pure body, 191, 194–95
  religious accountability, 194
  rules for dance, 170, 192
  rules for Ekuphakameni, 194
  rules for virgin girls, 170, 191–92

linearity and cyclicity, 67–68, 183
literacy, 9, 18
liturgy, 21, 72–73
lobola, lobolo, 27

Machel, Graca, 264–65
Makanya, Katie, 275n. 21
makwaya, 133, 135–36, 285n. 5
Mandela, Nelson, 1, 4, 7, 23–24, 261–65,
    286n. 16
  song about, 122
Mandela, Winnie, 264–65
Manqele, Mrs., 17, 82–83, 243–44, 248–50,
    292n. 15
market
  captured or enclave, 47, 145
  global, 145
  See also economy
marriage
  Africanness in, 264–65
  of Amos Shembe's daughter, 290n. 7
  Isaiah Shembe's ambivalence toward, 200,
    202–6
marriage, Nazarite
  as physical union
    attire for, 209–12
    authority to perform, 209
    ceremony, 206–8
    hlonipha in, 213
    lobola and, 200, 205, 207
    polygamy in, 204
    proposals and negotiation of, 206–7
    song and dance for, 207–9
    temple kinship and, 205
  as spiritual union, 43, 214–18
    bridegroom in, 216
    "Brides of Christ" (maidens), 215
    candles for, 218
    cost to girls of, 213–14
    Hymn 229 about, 216–18
    Nkulunkulu and *Nomkhubulwana,* 214
    Shembe as husband in, 212
marriage, Nguni, 42–43
  legislation pertaining to, 201–2, 205
  lobola for, 201, 205
  and political alliances, 31
  polygamy, xv, 27, 201, 205, 274n. 13
  precolonial form, 27, 41–43, 201–2, 206
  social reproduction, 27–28, 31, 200
  state control of, 275n. 31
  taxation and, 205

  and violence against women, 200
  women and, 27–28, 201–5
Masinga (at SABC), 125
mat, prayer, 183
Matthew 2, 256
Matthew 25, 214, 216, 231
Mazibuko, Cinikile, 88–89, 102, 203–4, 218,
    223–24, 226, 236–39, 250–54
Mbatha, Nathoya
  arrangements of hymns, 123
  authorization, 140, 142–43, 145
  and Bongani Mthethwa's model, 146–47
  and BMG Records, 143, 145
  cassette cover, 143–45
  cassette piracy problem, 120, 145
  cassette production, 146–47
  and C&G Records, 143
  comparison with version of Hymn 142,
    150–53
  compositional process, 153–55
  controversy over, 145–46, 155–58
  conversion, 142
  forest vs. stage, 154–55
  gospel style, 143, 147, 153
  popularizing the repertory, 141–42
  and Revolver Records, 143, 145
  training, 142
McAdoo, Orpheus, 90
Mdladla, Mr., 223
Mdletshe, Judy, 223
meetings, monthly, 16, 72. See also *ama14,
    ama23, ama25*
members, Nazarite, xiv, xvi, 1, 2, 3, 11, 13, 18,
    23
metaphor, xvi, 17
  of the body, 104, 241–43
  of the gate, 279n. 33
  of the path, 282n. 8
  of the rock, 18
  way of Shembe as slippery rock, 224
migrant labor, 263, 279n. 31, 287n. 18
miracles, xvii, 2, 52, 55–57, 156
  and technology, 56
  of healing, 3
mission, xiv
  Christianity, 39–43
  education
    black elite, 90
    for girls, 50
  traditional marriage, impact on, 41–42
mkhokheli, 68–69

money, as ritualized exchange, 59–60
moon. *See* Shembe, Amos, as moon
mountain. *See Nhlangakaze*
Mpande, 195, 275n. 16
Mpanza, Mthembeni, 148–49
Mthethwa, Bongani, 128–33, 146–47, 272n. 11
    as organist, 6, 10
Mthethwa, Mvangeli, 133
Mtungwa, Linah, 222–23
music, African, 17, 100–101, 105, 114, 135
mvangeli, 6, 68

Namba, Mthunzi, 148
narrative, 1, 278n. 13
    about Amos Shembe's entrance into heaven, 262
    about Amos Shembe learning to dance, 258
    biblical and experience, 21
    about bird song and pregnancy, 102
    dream, 2, 17, 55, 82–84, 289n. 45
    about dream of heaven, 245, 248–49
    about expectation of Shembe as healer, 243
    about fifty papers, 236–37
    about first Nazarite house for *kwa14*, 222
    about healing of white girl from England, 159–60
    and heaven, 5
    about hymns and life experience, 251–56
    about Isaiah Shembe's arrival in KwaZulu Natal (1910), 223
    about Isaiah Shembe's calling, 88–89
    about Isaiah Shembe's photo in hymnal, 226
    miracle, 1, 2
    about miraculous birth, 238–40
    about mother dancing in the style of *Ekuphakameni*, 259
    Old Testament, 71
    about protection from violence, 86–87
    and ritual exchange, 57
    about sexual violation, 241–42
    and technology, 54
    treasure, 17
    about violence in Umkomaas, 254–56
nation-building, 15, 265
Native Law, 42–43
Native Reserves, 37, 64
Natives Land Act (1913), 26
Nazareth Baptist Church, 26
Nazareth Baptist Youth for Shembe, 131–39
Nazarite provider, xvii
Ndima, Robert, 140

New Testament, 4, 6
Ngema, Mbongeni, 263–64, 286n. 16
Nguni, 275n. 17
    cosmology, xiv
    homestead, xv
    music, 284n. 24
    precolonial cultural forms, 20
    ritual-fertility, 1
    tradition, xiv, xv, 18
    traditionalist, 25
Nhlangakaze, 4–7, 69
    Amos Shembe on, 7
    organ on, 6–7
    path up, 5
Nkatheni, 190
Nkulunkulu, 162–65, 246
Nomkhubulwana, 28, 162–65, 246
    associated with mountain, 163
    similar relationship between girls and Shembe, 163
    virgin daughter of *Nkulunkulu*, 163
Nthanda. *See* girls' conference; girls' camp
Nthini, Samukelisiwe ("Samu"), 11, 120
Nthuli, Eric, 133, 285n. 1
Nthuli, Mrs., 159–61
Nyadi, Makhosazane (Princess), 239–40

Ohlange (high school), 23
Old Testament, xv, 4, 162
    poverty in, 62
Oosthuizen, Pippin, 271n. 7
oral history, Nazarite, 26, 71
orality
    orality-literacy debate, 96–97
    secondary, 19, 272n. 16
organ, 6, 128–31, 152
"Oyinkosi amakhosi," "Uyinkosi amakhosi," 120, 274n. 14

pain, bodily, xvi
    suffered by women, 12
Paradis, 17, 208, 248
pass laws, 80, 281n. 50
photographs, 5, 8, 50–52
    of Isaiah Shembe, 291n. 3
pilgrimage, 11–12, 69, 78–80
police. *See* South African Police; white policeman
pollution, 64, 82
Port Natal (nineteenth century), 33–36
    African refugees, 33–34

possessions, inalienable (inalienable treasure), 20, 53, 58–63, 99
power, 2, 20
  of the cosmology, 20
    feminized, 166
  economic, xvi, 3
  gendered, 18, 21
  resistance, 65, 278n. 17
  ritual, xv
  spiritual, xvii
prayer gown. See *imiNazaretha*
prophet, Isaiah Shembe as, xiv, 3
Protestant tradition, 6
puberty rites, as Nazarite rites, 20
purity, female, 199
  and pollution, 65–67
  ritual and spiritual, 12, 198

racism, triumph over, 20
Radio, Bantu, 126
Radio Zulu (Ukhozi Radio), 126–28, 140, 153
refugees, 33–34, 275n. 22
religion, indigenous, 1, 25–26
research. *See* ethnography; fieldwork
resistance, 65, 278n. 17
rhythm, counterpoint, 76. *See also* hymns; *ukusina; umgido*
right to public assembly, 66
ritual, xiv, xvi, 1, 19, 57
  attire, 6, 68–69, 75, 85–88, 171–73
  cycle, 69–85
  exchange, 53, 58–63
  for girls, 164–66, 176–98
  leadership, 68–69, 76–77
  Nazarite, 173–76
  order, and memorializing African experience, 63–69
  practice, xiv, 58
  purity, 21, 29, 67, 107
  spaces, 64–69
  for women, 225–31
  as work, 290n. 49
river, in song texts, 138–39. *See also* girls' camp; girls' conference; *inkhonzo; ukusina; umgido*

sabbath, 4, 6, 13, 71–72
sacralization of female body, 21
sacred, xiv, 21–22, 56–58, 60, 93, 95, 99, 102, 113, 123, 133, 145–47, 155–58, 169–70, 196, 209, 227

sacrifice, xv, 1, 29, 157–58, 164, 177, 196–98, 220–21
  of desire, 1, 21, 196–98
sale of religious goods, 5
Salvation Army, 26, 283n. 20
sanctuary, xv, 12, 19, 67
Sarafina!, 263–64
sermons, xvi, 55, 280n. 44
  about dreams and visions, 84
Shabalala, Vielwa, 245
Shaka, 21, 275n. 16
Shembe, xvii, 2, 3, 13, 17
  and ancestors, 59, 291n. 5
  authorizing leadership, 47–52
    bureaucracy, 47
    knowledge of Bible, 48
    land purchase, 47, 278n. 20
    miracles, 48
    written word, 48
  as healer, 2, 52
  houses of, 67
  and motor vehicles, 50
Shembe, Amos, 2
  funeral of, 23–24, 261–63
  as moon (*iNyanga*), 17, 248–49
Shembe, Galilee (Johannes), 2, 3, 17
Shembe, Isaiah, xiv–xvii, 2, 3, 11, 19, 23–26
  calling of, 88–89
  as chief, 29
  death of, 70
  dreams, 88–89, 203
  female voice of, in Hymn 92, 169–70
  as healer, 160
  polygamy and, 203
  as prophet, xiv, 3, 159–60
  visions of, 24, 202–3
  "Voice," 202–3
  and Wesleyans, 91
  wives of, 204
  and Zulu poetry, 91
  See also Letter from Shembe to *iBandla lamaNazaretha*
Shembe, Mayekisa, 25
Shembe, Vimbeni, 2
"Shembe is the Way" sticker, protection of, 5, 84
Shembe's Church Choir, 126
Shepstone, Theophilus, 37–38
  system, 275n. 23
shoes, removal of, 194
Soga, Tiyo, 89–90

song, xvi
  congregational, 56
  gift of, 166, 194
  religious
    and market value, 155–56
    on mountain, 272n. 10
Sound of Africa, 125–26
South Africa, "new" 1, 11
South African Broadcast Corporation,
    124–26
South African Communist Party, xiii, 4
South African Defence Force, xvi
South African Police, xiii, xvi
space
  feminized, xvi
  Nazarite, 11
  sacred (religious), xiv, 6, 10, 20, 68
spirituals, 282n. 6
St. James Church, xiii
St. James Massacre, xiii–xiv
stones, painted white, 67, 72
structures of feeling, hymns as, 99–104
sun, 17. See also Shembe, Galilee

tax
  hut and poll, 39
technology, 9, 50–52
  recording, 8
  of the self, 198
temple, 12, 65–66, 71–72, 272n. 22
  noise in, 74
tent, 5, 9–10
"There Are Many Rivers to Cross," 138
"There's a River Flowing Down There,"
    138
"Thina Siyabonga, weBaba Wethu," 189
Thulisa Brothers, 122–23
ticket to heaven, 282n. 6
Tile, Nehemiah, 89
time, 18, 280nn. 41, 42
  cyclical, 18
  inkhonzo, 73
  reckoning, 75–77
  sacred, 284n. 27
  ukusina, 74
townships, 13
Tracey, Hugh, 105, 124–26
treasure
  cultural, 57
  on earth, 2
trumpet. See ukusina

Truth and Reconciliation Commission,
    xiii–xvi, 271n. 6
truth claiming, 84

Ukhozi Radio. See Radio Zulu
ukusina
  accompaniment of, 104, 112–15
  aesthetics of, 109–18
  as juridical discourse, 113
  and women's bodies, 108
  women's performance of
    call and response in, 109–17
    drums and, 109–14
    melody in, 112, 116
    rhythm in, 110–18
    spiritual and musical leadership, 117–18
    trumpets and, 109, 114–15
    "the word" and, 109
umgido, umgidi, 72, 74–77
  rules of, 191–92
  See also ukusina
umgonqo. See girls' conference
Umkomazi, 292n. 18
umpathi, mpathi, abapathi, 10, 206–7
Union of South Africa, 19, 24

violence, xiii, 3, 7, 12, 167, 271n. 6
  black on black, 274n. 11
  in KwaZulu Natal, 7–8, 261–62
  and the sacred, 169
  sexual (rape), 200, 291n. 9
    narratives about, 241–43
virginity, female, 1
  avoiding loss of, 274n. 15
  and control of fertility, 21
  and twenty-first birthday, 290n. 48
  and white milkwood trees, 289n. 32
Vula Masango, history of, 70–71

warfare, moral/spiritual, xv
warriors, 21
  spiritual xv, 21, 199, 281n. 48
water for healing, cleansing, as tears and rain,
    167
wealth, 31
Wesleyan, 89
white policeman
  letter (1921) of estimating Isaiah Shembe's
    following, 2
  vision of, xvi
white South Africans, xiii–xvi, 4, 10, 14

women, xiv–xv, 14–15
women, African, 14–15, 40–46
  conversion to Christianity, 41–43
  labor power, 27–28, 42, 45–47
  married, 1, 17
  meetings of, 225
  in Native Reserves, 274n. 12
  production and reproduction, 27–31
  rape and violence against, 199–200, 241–43, 290n. 1
  refugees, 36
  status in nineteenth century, 31–32
  widows and orphans, 5, 12, 19, 30

youth choirs
  in *ibandla lamaNazaretha*, 131–39, 150–52
  in schools, 133, 134–37

Zionists, 60, 81, 114, 121, 148, 157, 282n. 4, 283nn. 18, 20
Zulu, Rev. Prince, 127–28
Zulu, defined, 271n. 4
  kingdom, 33, 222
  nation, in nineteenth century, 30–43
Zululand, annexation by British (1889), 33, 201
Zuluness, 87, 122
Zulu traditionalists, 89